P9-DHT-483

Prince Charles

Anthony Holden

PRINCE CHARLES

NEW YORK *Atheneum* 1983

Excerpts from *King Edward the Seventh* by Philip Magnus, appearing on pages 41 and 42, are © 1964 and reprinted by permission of John Murray (Publishers) Ltd.

Excerpts from *Prince Charles* by Helen Cathcart (Taplinger, 1977), appearing on page 60, are © 1976 by Helen Cathcart and reprinted by permission.

Excerpts from *Prince Philip: An Informal Biography* by Basil Boothroyd, appearing on pages 108 to 110, are © 1971 and reprinted by permission of Curtis Brown Ltd.

The material on the investiture of the future Edward VIII as Prince of Wales, quoted on pages 175 and 176, is from *A King's Story* by the Duke of Windsor (G. P. Putnam's Sons) © 1947, 1950, 1951 by H. R. H. Edward Duke of Windsor.

C. Day Lewis's poem, appearing on page 190, is reprinted by permission of A. D. Peters & Co. Ltd.

"I've Danced with a Man . . ." (lyric appearing on page 220), a popular song by Herbert Farjeon and Harold Scott (1928), is reproduced by kind permission of Ascherberg, Hopwood and Crew Ltd.; Chappell Music Ltd.

Excerpts from *King George III* by John Brooke, appearing on pages 245 to 247, are © 1972 and reprinted by permission of the McGraw-Hill Book Company.

The excerpt from Prince Charles's review in *Books and Bookmen,* appearing on page 248, is reproduced by kind permission of The Prince of Wales from *Books and Bookmen,* November 1976.

Library of Congress Cataloging in Publication Data

Holden, Anthony, 1947–
   Prince Charles.

   Bibliography: p.
   Includes index.
   1. Charles, Prince of Wales, 1948– 2. Great
Britain—Princes and princesses—Biography. I. Title.
DA591.A33H6   1979   941.085′092′4   [B]   79-52176
ISBN 0-689-70638-3

Copyright © 1979, 1983 by Anthony Holden
All rights reserved
Manufactured by American Book–Stratford Press, Saddle Brook, New Jersey
Illustrations printed by Philips Offset Company, Inc., Mamaroneck, New York
First Atheneum Paperback Edition

For Sam, Joe, *and* Ben

Introduction to the Paperback Edition

> *"A princely marriage is the bril-*
> *liant edition of a universal fact,*
> *and as such it rivets mankind."*
>
> WALTER BAGEHOT,
> *The English Constitution*

IN THE THREE YEARS since this book was first published in the United States, one aspect of Prince Charles's life has changed dramatically. As all the world knows, he has at last found the bride for whom he searched so long; she has become a gracious international superstar in her own right, and has swiftly and efficiently presented him with a son and heir, Prince William of Wales, born on June 21, 1982.

More than five hundred million people all over the world had watched the wedding of Charles, Prince of Wales to Lady Diana Spencer in St. Paul's Cathedral, London, eleven months before. It was, quite simply, the largest audience ever to watch any single event in history. On that day Diana, within a month of her twenty-first birthday, became the ninth Princess of Wales in British history, and the first future queen of England to have once worked for her living. Britain's July showers disappeared, and an unseasonably warm sun shone on the climax of their twentieth century fairy-tale romance. Endearingly enough, the new princess managed to get the groom's unwieldy name wrong as she said "I do," and he in turn managed to endow her with all her own worldly goods instead of his. Such moments only made an intensely human day even more so. When, at his bride's suggestion, the prince kissed her on the balcony of Buckingham Palace, it seemed that the joy of an otherwise austerity-ridden Britain knew no bounds. The Iron Maiden in Downing Street having uncharacteristically given everyone the day off, fireworks lit the sky as the nation danced all night.

It was a remarkable illustration of the monarchy's continuing power to lighten what have been a dark few years for its country. Diana's frequent public appearances in dashing new designer clothes gave a much-needed boost to the rag trade; hairdressers all over the country were being asked to provide the "Lady Di look" to countless teenagers. A new generation of the royal family was emerging in full panoply as its parents embarked on their late middle age and, perhaps, a quieter life. When, a year later, Charles's younger brother Andrew returned from active service in the Falklands War, the rejuvenation of the British throne was gloriously complete.

In his choice of bride, Prince Charles added yet another item to his long list of royal "firsts": he became the first Prince of Wales in British history not to be married by political arrangement. His son Prince William, moreover, is the first future monarch ever to have been descended from all the British kings and queens who had issue. For Diana brought Stuart blood to the royal line, the only blood it lacked, as well as links on the family tree with Charlemagne and Bonnie Prince Charlie, Humphrey Bogart and Rudolf Valentino. Her father, the eighth Earl Spencer, whose own ancestors include prime ministers and dashing sea lords, felt moved to call his daughter "a superb physical specimen" when reassuring press and public that she was a girl without "a past." There was not a dissenting voice to be heard.

Prince Charles's bride was, quite literally, the girl next door. Diana was born on the royal estate at Sandringham, in a cottage rented from the queen by her father before he inherited his earldom. As a child, she played with Charles's younger brothers, who were more her age than the heir to the throne (the Spencer family had a swimming pool, a luxury their royal neighbors had decided they could not afford). Her parents divorced when she was six, a traumatic experience which seems to have matured the young Diana beyond her years. Her public conduct has always belied the twelve-year age gap between her and her husband, who once escorted her elder sister, while she herself was always thought of by both families as Prince Andrew's belle.

Diana's mixed educational record—she went to the normal run of smart upper-class girls' schools before a spell at a Swiss finishing school, cut short by homesickness—did not exactly mark her out as an academic prodigy. Nor is that exactly what either Prince Charles or his future subjects were looking for. She was, above all, an English rose, the daughter of one of the country's most distinguished families. (The house in which she grew up, Althorp, in Northamptonshire, is bigger than any of the royal residences outside London.) In the months before the engagement was announced, she proved both her staying power and her capacity for discretion during a long ordeal of pursuit by pressmen. Once the betrothal was public knowledge, she turned overnight into a seasoned princess, practicing the royal wave with aplomb and metamorphosing with remarkable speed from coy young girl to elegant symbol of teenage aspirations the world over.

As well as being naturally beautiful, Diana is remarkably photogenic—a prerequisite, these days, of membership of the royal family. It quickly became clear, however, that she also had a strong and independent mind of her own; contrary to the expectations of a few dissenting voices, she was not going to submerge her identity in that of her distinguished husband. The princess-to-be's strength of character was on very public display in her first outing with her fiancé, when she emerged from the royal Rolls-Royce in that now famous low-cut black evening gown. If a few eyebrows were raised in royal circles, it confirmed Diana in her new-found role as the nation's sweetheart.

Since her marriage, moreover, she has continued to demonstrate that she intends to be royal in her own original way. She has been seen around the gusty corridors of sundry palaces with a Sony Walkman clamped to her ears, rock music shutting out the demands of the busy world outside. She has equally shown a capacity for imposing her colorful personality on the more staid side of her husband's. The cut of Prince Charles's suits, of which I complain with such feeling in chapter four, have grown more sharp and dashing of late; his once unadventurous hair style has undergone a remarkable transformation by blow-dryer; he has been seen less on the polo field, and not at all in steeplechases. The only member of the royal family to bear a positive aversion to horses, having fallen off one when she was a child, Diana has reined in her husband's more daredevil ways with them; where his mother occasionally failed to sway him, his wife can obviously succeed. She has also made clear her disapproval not merely of some of his former friends, but of those of his activities which exclude his wife and child.

For the prince, his marriage brought other unexpected novelties. He was unaccustomed, for instance, to second billing on his public appearances; now he found himself left alone at the back of huge crowds fighting for a glimpse of his princess. During her pregnancy, when she occasionally had to drop out of joint outings, his hosts were often embarrassingly unable to conceal their disappointment. Whenever she did "go walkabout," as the royal family like to call their newly informal mingling with crowds, her natural charms carried the day. On a post-wedding tour of her new principality, she won all hearts by tripping gaily through a few words of Welsh when receiving the freedom of the capital city, Cardiff. In Scotland she set new royal trends by doing her own shopping in the village stores near Balmoral.

The couple have set up home in a Georgian country house in the Cotswolds, Highgrove House, purchased for them by the Duchy of Cornwall from Maurice Macmillan, M.P., son of the former prime minister. A London apartment has been refurbished for them in Kensington Palace, where they have hired a new butler by the name of Fisher, who used to tend to the domestic needs of a rather less regal figure, the late Bing Crosby. Characteristically, the princess was not going to settle for the traditional royal nurse, all starch and military discipline, to look after her son; she employed a young blue-jeaned nanny to share the duties with her. To the nation's delight, it was made public that she was breast-feeding her child, and that even in infancy he was setting a proper example to his future subjects by being inoculated against whooping cough.

The birth of his son, in short, gave the Prince of Wales a greater chance for privacy and tranquillity than he had known in his adult life. At Highgrove as in London, the latest Laura Ashley designs provided the backdrop to a brave new world of royal domestic bliss.

So the interim assessment of Prince Charles in this book still stands, except in so far as he is no longer the solitary figure of his prolonged bachelorhood, having found a partner as forceful as she is *sympathique*. The queen was so delighted by the qualities Diana brought to court that she quickly gave her public endorsement in the form of important personal assignments: the task, for

instance, of representing Her Majesty at the funeral of Princess
Grace of Monaco. To his parents as much as himself, Prince
Charles's choice of a bride provided not merely relief at the end
of his long and painful years of indecision; Diana brought a new
gaiety and joie-de-vivre as much to the public as to the private
face of the royal family. From the serene smile on her face at their
wedding, and in many public appearances since, Elizabeth II has
consciously made it public that it is not just her son in whom she
is well pleased, but her radiant new daughter-in-law too. Thanks
to Diana, the omens for Prince Charles's eventual inheritance of
his birthright, his mother's throne, are more propitious than ever.

ANTHONY HOLDEN
London
October 1982

Foreword

THIS IS NOT an official or authorized biography, despite assorted newspaper reports to that effect while I was writing it. It would be most unusual for such a book to be commissioned about an heir to the throne, and prospective king of England, in his own lifetime. Such books, moreover, tend to be written by historians rather than journalists.

There are those at Buckingham Palace who would have preferred this book to have been written by a historian. "You have deliberately adopted an unhistorical, journalist's approach," I was told by one member of the Prince of Wales's staff who had—at my request—read some of the manuscript. I decided to take the remark as a compliment.

Journalists are, in their modest way, contemporary historians, even if on occasions such as this they decide to dispense with the academic impedimenta of footnotes and source references. Half of this book is an account of the Prince of Wales's life so far, to a point just beyond his thirtieth birthday; the other half is an analysis of his life, work, and personality today, with a brief glance toward the future. That seemed to me the correct balance in a book about a man whose career has only just begun in earnest, but who has been a focus of the world's attention since the moment it was announced that his mother was pregnant.

If this approach involves comparing the present Prince of Wales with his recent predecessors, and making some general observations about their office, the author nevertheless lays no claim to being a professional historian. The only claim I would make, as a professional journalist, is that I have aspired to factual accuracy in a field where it is extremely difficult to achieve. When you write about the royal family, most journalistic rules are inverted. The more sources you have for a story, the less likely it is to be true. The more conscientiously you allow your subject to comment on the factual matter of your work, the more obfuscated those facts become. The irony is that there is no subject in the world who would be less likely to answer back were you just to sit down and make the whole thing up.

As this last is a process not unknown in the chronicling of the British royal family, I have attempted to pursue the most rigorous journalistic practices in the gathering and checking of material. I have spent a good deal of time amid the prince's entourage and enjoyed many a casual (and off-the-record) chat with him. I have talked to most of the senior—and some junior—members of his staff, to his friends and acquaintances, to people who have passed through his life or played some role in it. Many of them, for fear of endangering their relationship with the royal family, requested that their contributions be off the record, so the acknowledgments that follow simply list some of the names of those to whom I have reason to be grateful, without detailing the nature of their assistance. Many requested complete anonymity, so their names do not appear at all.

The Prince of Wales's staff assisted me patiently while I was researching and writing the book in 1978–79, though—again because of newspaper comment—they have since asked me to say here that "the facilities were the same that would be given to any serious writer." A number of people inside the palace read a draft manuscript comprising three-quarters of the book as it now stands, and gave me their comments on it, in whole or in part. They did so at my request, as the only method of sorting fact from fiction in those areas where no other source or sources could be relied upon. Nothing they have done, however, should be taken to imply acceptance or approval by Buckingham Palace, or any of its occupants, of the book's contents. There were disagreements of fact and emphasis between us, some resolved, some not. No editorial control was ever given to anyone at the palace, or indeed sought by anyone there. The responsibility for the finished product remains entirely mine.

As the book has no direct source attributions, for reasons I have explained, I should also like to record here that a number of individual chapters have been read for factual accuracy by other interested parties. Chapter 7, for instance, was read by Colonel

Henry Townend, headmaster of Hill House School; Chapter 9 by Peter Beck, headmaster of Cheam School during Prince Charles's time there; Chapters 10 and 11 by Robert Waddell, the only Gordonstoun master still at the school who was there throughout Prince Charles's time; Chapter 12 by Dr. Denis Marrian, senior tutor of Trinity College, Cambridge, while the prince was an undergraduate there, by Lord Butler, then Master of Trinity, and by Edward Millward, the prince's tutor in Welsh language and literature at the University College of Wales, Aberystwyth. Other chapters have been read by other protagonists, who made specific requests for anonymity.

In alphabetical order, therefore, for assistance great or small, I would like to express my thanks to Ronald Allison, Robin Baring, Dr. Tony Barker, Julian Barnes, Beth Barrington-Haynes, Sir Cecil Beaton, Peter Beck, Basil Boothroyd, Humphrey Burton, Lord Butler, Helen Cathcart, Geoffrey Chandler, David Checketts, Jane Cousins, George Darby, Frances (Lady) Donaldson, Sally Emerson, Oliver Everett, David Frost, Sir Ian Gourlay, John Grigg, Harold Hayward, Sally Head, John Heilpern, Derek Homer, Anwar Hussein, Susan Jeffreys, Hywel Jones, Sir Emmanuel Kaye, John Kempe, Mary Kenny, Robert Lacey, Serge Lemoine, Magnus Linklater, Sir Tom McCaffrey, John Maclean, Sir Philip Magnus, Jack de Manio, Dr. Denis Marrian, Helen Martin, Dickie Miller, Edward Millward, Sir Iain Moncreiffe of that Ilk, Cliff Morgan, David Niven, Richard Nixon, Paul Officer, Lord Olivier, George Pratt, Dr. Anil Seal, Lord Snowdon, Nicholas Soames, Norman Stone, David Taylor, George Thomas, Colonel Henry Townend, Hugo Vickers, Robert Waddell, Sir Brian Warren, Michael Wheeler, James Whitaker, Alastair Wilson, Sir Harold Wilson; the Right Reverend Robert Woods, bishop of Worcester; Hugo Young.

I would also like to thank the master and fellows of Trinity College, Cambridge (one of the perks of my researches was an invitation to their Candlemas Feast); British Rail; the staff of Caernarvon Castle; Lewisham Police; the Welsh Office; the staffs of the Prince's Trust, the Prince of Wales's Committee, the Royal Jubilee Trusts, the United World Colleges; the Queen's Flight; the librarians of Islington public library, the *Guardian*, the *Times* and especially of the *Sunday Times*; and, for their hospitality, Her Majesty's ambassadors to Brazil, Venezuela, and

Foreword

Yugoslavia. Lynda Poley carried out the picture research and Jackie Pyle typed the manuscript.

For their friendship, encouragement, and professional advice, and for between them having had the idea that I should write this book, I thank John Curtis, Hilary Rubinstein, and Godfrey Smith. Pat Knopf and Barbara Anderman of Atheneum have been both kind and helpful, as has Perry Knowlton of Curtis Brown. The editors of the London *Sunday Times* and the London *Observer*, Harold Evans and Donald Trelford, were most understanding about my requests to be freed from newspaper duties at the beginning and end, respectively, of my work on the book. Nor could it ever have been written without the help and support of my wife, Amanda, not least in her heroic efforts to keep its dedicatees out of the way.

Above all I am deeply indebted to John Dauth, assistant press secretary to the queen, and his secretary, Sarah Brennan, for time, effort, and Buckingham Palace notepaper expended far beyond the call of duty; and to the Prince of Wales himself for authorizing his staff to assist me, giving certain of his friends clearance to talk to me, and for tolerating my shadow around the world for some eighteen months. Any criticisms contained in the resulting work he knows to be leveled with the best intentions, by one his own age who does not envy him his job.

Not that he envies me mine. He once said to me: "It must be such hell writing a book. They're so *long*, aren't they?" I couldn't agree more.

Cast of Characters

ADEANE, *Edward* (b. 1940): Private secretary to the Prince of Wales, 1979–. Formerly libel barrister.

ADEANE, *Sir Michael* (*now Lord*) (b. 1910): Private secretary to Queen Elizabeth II, 1953–72. Father of Edward Adeane.

ALBERT, *Prince Consort* (1819–61): Husband of Queen Victoria; father of King Edward VII and great-great-great-grandfather of Prince Charles.

ALBERT, *Prince, Duke of York:* see *George VI*.

ALEXANDRA, *Princess* (b. 1936): Cousin of Elizabeth II; daughter of Prince George, Duke of Kent.

ALEXANDRA, *Queen* (1844–1925): Wife of King Edward VII.

ANDREW, *Prince* (b. 1960): Second son of Queen Elizabeth II; next to Prince Charles in line of succession to the throne.

ANNE, *Princess* (b. 1950): Only daughter of Queen Elizabeth II; sister of Prince Charles. Married Captain Mark Phillips, 1973; one son (b. 1977).

ARMSTRONG-JONES: see *Snowdon*.

BATTENBERG: see *Mountbatten*.

BERTIE: see *Edward VII* and *George VI*.

BOWES-LYON: Family name of Queen Elizabeth, the Queen Mother.

BUTLER, *Lord* (b. 1902): Former Conservative cabinet minister; master of Trinity College, Cambridge, during Prince Charles's time there.

CHARLES, *Prince* (b. November 14, 1948): Prince of Wales; eldest son of Queen Elizabeth II and Prince Philip, Duke of Edinburgh. See Appendices A and B.

CHARTERIS, *Sir Martin* (b. 1913): Private secretary to Queen Elizabeth II, 1972–77; formerly private secretary to Princess Elizabeth (1950–52) and assistant private secretary to Elizabeth II (1952–72).

CHECKETTS, *Squadron-Leader David* (b. 1930): Private secretary to the Prince of Wales, 1970–79; formerly equerry to the Prince of Wales (1967–70) and to the Duke of Edinburgh (1961–66).

CLARENCE, *Prince Albert Victor, Duke of* (1864–92): Elder son of King Edward VII; elder brother of King George V. Known to his family as Eddy.

COLVILLE, *Sir John* (*"Jock"*) (b. 1915): Private secretary to Prime Ministers Neville Chamberlain, Winston Churchill, Clement Attlee and to Princess Elizabeth (1947–49).

COLVILLE, *Commander Sir Richard* (1907–75): Press secretary to King George VI (1947–52) and to Queen Elizabeth II (1952–68). Cousin of Sir John Colville.

CORNWALL, *Duke of:* Title held by Prince Charles as heir apparent.

DAVID: see *Edward VIII.*

DICKIE: see *Mountbatten, Lord Louis.*

EDDY: see *Clarence, Duke of.*

EDINBURGH, *Duke of:* see *Prince Philip.*

EDWARD, *Prince* (b. 1964): Third son of Queen Elizabeth II; third in line of succession to the throne.

EDWARD VII, *King* (1841–1910, reigned 1901–10): Eldest son of Queen Victoria; great-great-grandfather of Prince Charles. Prince of Wales 1841–1901. Known to his family as Bertie.

EDWARD VIII, *King* (1894–1972, reigned January 20–December 11, 1936): Eldest son of King George V; great-uncle of Prince Charles. Prince of Wales 1910–36; abdicated December 1936, becoming His Royal Highness the Duke of Windsor. Known to his family as David.

ELIZABETH, *the Queen Mother* (b. 1900): Née Lady Elizabeth Bowes-Lyon, daughter of the fourteenth Earl of Strathmore. Married Prince Albert, Duke of York (later King George VI), 1923; mother of Queen Elizabeth II; grandmother of Prince Charles. Queen consort 1936–52; Queen Mother since 1952. Formally known as Queen Elizabeth (Elizabeth II is referred to as the Queen).

ELIZABETH II, *Queen* (b. 1926): Elder daughter of King George VI; mother of Prince Charles. Married Lieutenant Philip Mountbatten (subsequently known as Prince Philip, Duke of Edinburgh) 1947. Acceded to the throne February 6, 1952; coronation, June 2, 1953.

GEORGE V, *King* (1865–1936, reigned 1910–36): Second son of King Edward VII; great-grandfather of Prince Charles. Became heir to the throne on the death of his elder brother, Prince Albert Victor (Eddy), Duke of Clarence, and married Eddy's fiancée, Princess May of Teck (Queen Mary). Duke of York until his father's accession in 1901; Prince of Wales 1901–1910.

GEORGE VI, *King* (1895–1952, reigned 1936–52): Second son of King George V; father of Queen Elizabeth II; grandfather of Prince Charles. Duke of York 1920–36. Known to his family as Bertie.

GLOUCESTER, *Richard, Duke of* (b. 1944): Second son of Prince Henry, Duke of Gloucester (1900–74), younger brother of Edward VIII and George VI. His elder brother, Prince William, was killed in a plane crash in 1972. Known as Prince Richard of Gloucester before succeeding his father. Married with two children. Cousin of Prince Charles.

KENT, *Edward, Duke of* (b. 1935): Elder son of Prince George, Duke of Kent (1902–42), and Princess Marina. Became Duke of Kent when seven years old on his father's death in a wartime air crash. Married with three children. Cousin of Prince Charles.

KENT, *Prince Michael of* (b. 1942): Younger brother of the Duke of Kent and Princess Alexandra. Married (1978) Baroness Marie-Christine von Reibnitz, renouncing his right of succession to throne to marry a Catholic divorcée. One son.

LASCELLES, *Sir Alan* (b. 1887): Assistant private secretary to Edward, Prince of Wales (1920–29), to King George V (1935–36), to King Edward VIII (1936), and to King George VI (1936–43); principal private secretary to King George VI (1943–52) and to Queen Elizabeth II (1952–53). Known as Tommy.

MARGARET, *Princess, Countess of Snowdon* (b. 1930): Younger daughter of King George VI; sister of Queen Elizabeth II; aunt of Prince Charles. Married Antony Armstrong-Jones, 1960; divorced 1978. Two children: David, Viscount Linley (b. 1961); Lady Sarah Armstrong-Jones (b. 1964).

MARY, *Queen* (1867–1953): Daughter of Francis, Duke of Teck; previously known as Princess May of Teck. Engaged to Prince Albert Victor (Eddy), Duke of Clarence, and after his death married his brother George, Duke of York, later King George V. Princess of Wales 1901–10. Great-grandmother to Prince Charles.

MOUNTBATTEN: The name adopted by the Battenberg family in 1917 and by Prince Philip of Greece in 1947.

MOUNTBATTEN, *Lord Louis* (b. 1900): Earl Mountbatten of Burma, uncle of Prince Philip, great-uncle of Prince Charles.

MOUNTBATTEN-WINDSOR: *Prince Charles's "hidden" surname.* See Appendix D.

PHILIP, *Prince* (b. 1921): Husband of Queen Elizabeth II, father of Prince Charles. Born Prince Philip of Greece; naturalized British citizen 1947 as Lieutenant Philip Mountbatten; on his marriage that year to Princess Elizabeth, created Baron Greenwich, Earl of Merioneth, and Duke of Edinburgh. Granted the style and title of Prince of the United Kingdom by his wife in 1957.

PHILLIPS, *Peter Mark Andrew* (b. 1977): Son of Princess Anne and Captain Mark Phillips; fifth in line of succession to the throne.

SIMPSON, *Wallis:* see *Windsor, Duchess of.*

SNOWDON, *Earl of* (b. 1930): Antony Armstrong-Jones, photographer and designer. Married Princess Margaret 1960; created Earl of Snowdon 1961; divorced Princess Margaret 1978; married Lucy Lindsay-Hogg 1978. As constable of Caernarvon Castle, was responsible for design of Prince Charles's investiture as Prince of Wales in 1969.

VICTORIA, *Queen* (1819–1901, reigned 1837–1901): Britain's longest-ruling sovereign; mother of King Edward VII (Bertie, Prince of Wales) and great-great-great-grandmother of Prince Charles.

WALES, *Prince of:* see *Charles, Prince; Edward VIII; George V; Edward VII.*

WINDSOR, *Duke of:* see *Edward VIII.*

WINDSOR, *Duchess of* (b. 1896): Née Wallis Warfield. Married Earl Winfield Spencer, Jr., 1916; Ernest Simpson 1928; HRH the Duke of Windsor (formerly King Edward VIII) 1937.

WOODS, *Right Reverend Robert* (b. 1914): Bishop of Worcester since 1970. Formerly Dean of Windsor and domestic chaplain to Queen Elizabeth II (1962–70). Conducted confirmation service of Prince Charles and was closely involved in decisions on his education.

The Order of Succession to the Throne

Prince Charles; Prince Andrew; Prince Edward; Princess Anne; her son Peter Phillips; Princess Margaret; her son, Viscount Linley; her daughter, Lady Sarah Armstrong-Jones; the Queen's cousin, the Duke of Gloucester; his son, the Earl of Ulster; the Queen's cousin, the Duke of Kent; his elder son, the Earl of St Andrews; his younger son, Lord Nicholas Windsor; his daughter, Lady Helen Windsor; the infant son of Prince Michael of Kent (who renounced his own right of succession on his marriage in 1978); Prince Michael's sister, Princess Alexandra; her son, James Ogilvy; her daughter, Marina Ogilvy.

Contents

Contents

PART IV: I'VE DANCED WITH A MAN WHO'S DANCED WITH A GIRL WHO'S DANCED WITH THE PRINCE OF WALES

PART V: KING CHARLES III

Illustrations

Illustrations

The Queen with Princess Marie-Astrid of Luxembourg (Photographers
    International)
A plug too far: in a promotional T-shirt (Photographers International
    —Jayne Fincher)

*All the world and the glory of it,
whatever is most attractive, whatever is most seductive, has always
been offered to the Prince of Wales
of the day, and always will be. It is
not rational to expect the best virtue
where temptation is applied in the
most trying form at the frailest time
of human life.*

WALTER BAGEHOT,
The English Constitution

Prologue

W E ARE ALL the victims of our parents' genes, but none
more so than Charles Philip Arthur George Mountbatten-Windsor, heir to the loftiest position on earth still determined solely by
heredity. The odds against being born to his fate are incalculable.
He was the first child to be born in direct line of succession to
the British throne since his great-uncle, the future King Edward
VIII and Duke of Windsor, fifty-four years earlier. Princess Elizabeth was only the fourth heiress presumptive in British history to
give birth to a male child—and only one of those children, Henry
II, subsequently became king. Queen Elizabeth II has herself
talked of "the uncertainty of human life"; but should her son in
due time become King Charles III, Britain will have to go back
seven hundred years to the Plantagenets to find six successive
generations of unbroken descent down a family tree.

He is the twenty-first English Prince of Wales, but the first in
direct descent from both the great Welsh princes, Owen Glendower and Llewelyn-ap-Gruffydd, the last native prince of all
Wales. He is descended from all the British monarchs save his
namesake Charles I and his sons, and from every royal house of
Europe. His ancestors include Charlemagne and Genghis Khan,
El Cid and George Washington, Shakespeare and Count Dracula.
He is the thirty-ninth in descent from King Alfred the Great,
thirty-second from William the Conqueror, fifth from Queen Victoria, and eighth from a London plumber named John Walsh.

He is the first Prince of Wales in British history to have gone
to school, the first to have won a university degree; the first to
have captained his own ship and led a national sports team; the

first to fly helicopters and supersonic jets, the first to train as a
frogman and a commando, the first to make a parachute jump. He
and the Duke of Windsor are the only two Princes of Wales in
history to have been invested at Caernarvon Castle, symbol of the
English usurpation of Welsh sovereignty, and the only two since
James Stuart, the Old Pretender, to have reached the age of thirty
unmarried.

He is Earl of Chester, Duke of Cornwall, Duke of Rothesay,
Earl of Carrick and Baron of Renfrew, Lord of the Isles and Great
Steward of Scotland, Knight of the Most Noble Order of the Gar-
ter, Knight of the Most Ancient and Most Noble Order of the
Thistle, Great Master and Principal Knight Grand Cross of the
Most Honorable Order of the Bath. He is personal aide-de-camp to
Queen Elizabeth II; commander, Royal Navy; wing commander,
Royal Air Force; colonel-in-chief of ten regiments; member of a
dozen international orders of chivalry; president, patron, or mem-
ber of some two hundred clubs, charities, committees, and learned
organizations.

A thousand years of history merge in this diffident, self-
conscious, deeply vulnerable, desperately well-meaning man, a
bachelor in his thirties still living with his parents, embarrassed
about his jug ears and weak chin, vain enough to try to hide an
incipient bald patch. He enjoys his ex-officio sex appeal, and is
jealous of his younger brother's better looks. He hates, yet shares,
the obsession of the British press and people about whom he will
marry; he talks to friends these days of little else. He has a quick
wit, a talent for mimicry, a sharp tongue, and a good seat on a
horse. He paints watercolors, plays polo, listens to opera, hunts
foxes, shoots pheasants, loves babies, dances with as much rhythm
as abandon, skis with more recklessness than skill. He is a countryman at heart, but would rather like to have been an actor. He is
proud, ambitious, romantic, and anxious to carve himself a place
in history.

Unless you're a member of his family, you call him "sir."
"Your Royal Highness" is equally correct, but a bit of a mouthful; if you follow it with "I humbly crave to submit . . ." he
will soon be stifling a yawn. If you call him "Your Majesty," he
will giggle and correct you. If you call him "Wales" to his face,
he will probably never speak to you again. He is not a pompous
man, but it is tempting at times to say he gets ideas above his

station. He expects the deference due to his office, takes its pomp and circumstance very seriously, enjoys the archaic rituals of royal ceremonial. He is more intelligent than most of his predecessors, which only makes him more confused about his destiny. He is often bored and more often lonely. He has few friends and can arrive nowhere unannounced. He has spent most of his life in a world of older people.

He usually breakfasts alone and has seven homes in which to do it. His birthright provides incomparable material comfort and international respect, adulation, even awe. Government departments look after various aspects of his business and pay people to tidy up after him. On his birthday flags fly, guns sound, and judges don their scarlet robes; when he becomes king, he will have *two* birthdays, one an official one whose date he can choose himself. All red lights turn green for him. He will never have to stand in line, do his own dishes, service his own car, muck out his own polo ponies, worry about losing his job, change his children's diapers, or fret about their education. He does not handle money or, with an unearned income of some $250,000 a year after tax, much have to worry about it. He is landlord of a 130,000-acre property company, and heir to one of the greatest private fortunes in the world.

He carries out about a thousand public engagements a year—planting trees, unveiling plaques, inspecting soldiers, launching ships, making after-dinner speeches, receiving honorary honors, distributing political honors, declaring things open, declaring things closed. Every word he speaks is remembered or written down. His presence unnerves people: they snigger, they lose the power of speech, they are astonished to find that he is human, they fight to touch him as if he were divine.

He cannot walk down a street without several months of preparation by a large number of people. This is not a fate he has sought, or earned, or to which he has fought for election. He was born to it; it has been, for him, ever thus. Yet he enjoys his privilege and is rarely resentful of all it denies him. It is a comfortable form of inherited imprisonment.

THE ROYAL HOUSE
OF WINDSOR

VICTORIA = Albert
(b. 1819) of Saxe-Coburg-Gotha
1837-1901 Prince Consort 1819-61

xandra = **EDWARD VII (2)** | Alfred | Helena | Louise | Arthur | Leopold | Beatrice
Denmark | (b. 1841) | Duke of | Princess | Duchess | Duke of | Duke of | Princess
4-1925 | 1901-1910 | Edinburgh | Christian | of Argyll | Connaught | Albany | Henry
| | 1844-1900 | of Schleswig- | 1848-1939 | 1850-1942 | 1853-84 | of Battenberg
| | | Holstein | | | | 1858-96
| | | 1846-1923

rt Victor | **GEORGE V** = Mary | Louise | = Alexander Duff | Victoria | Maud = Haakon VII
e of Clarence | (b. 1865) of Teck | Princess Royal | Duke of Fife | 1868-1935 | 1869- of Norway
-92 | 1910-1936 1867-1953 | 1867-1931 | 1849-1912 | | 1938 1872-1957

RGE VI = Elizabeth | Mary | = Henry | Henry = Alice Montagu- | George = Marina | John
95) Bowes-Lyon | Princess Royal | Viscount Lascelles | Duke of Douglas-Scott | Duke of Kent Princess of | 1905-19
-52 1900- | 1897-1965 | 6th Earl of Harewood | Gloucester 1901- | 1902-42 Greece
| | | 1882-1947 | 1900-1974 | 1906-68

ld = Angela | William | Richard = Birgitte | Edward = Katharine | Alexandra = Angus Ogilvy | Michael = Marie-Christine
elles | Dowding | 1941-72 | Duke of van Deurs | Duke of Worsley | 1936- 1928- | 1942- von Reibnitz
- | 1919- | | Gloucester 1946- | Kent 1933- | | | 1945-
| | | 1944- | 1935-

k | Henry | Alexander | Davina | George | Helen | Nicholas | James | Marina
- | 1953- | Earl of Ulster | 1977- | Earl of St Andrews | 1964- | 1970- | 1964- | 1966-
| | 1974- | | 1962-

Frederick
1979-

Part I: *H R H*

I

The People's Prince

*"Were it not for my ability to see the
funny side of my life, I would have
been committed to an institution
long ago."*

IT IS AN ICY, blizzardy Friday in February, and we are
a thousand feet above snow-clad Hampshire in a tiny twin-engined de Havilland Otter, the Prince of Wales at the controls. For
thirty minutes our fragile aircraft has been buffeted by strong
winds, rendering the prince's assistant private secretary a color
similar to that of the landscape beneath. In the cockpit our pilot's
headphones sit incongruously above his pin-striped city suit; he
resembles nothing so much as a hardened, if harassed, international businessman—which, in a way, is precisely what he is. This
is the only time he has sat down all day. Behind him lies a fact-
finding tour of a light industry plant, followed by a stand-up
lunch with fawning executives; ahead lies another welcoming
committee and another speech.

Every so often the gold, three-feathered signet ring on his
left little finger catches the light as he reaches for the flap controls. It reminds his handful of passengers in whose hands they
have placed their lives. The prince's private secretary, his detective, and his R.A.F. escort officer have seen it all before, but the
clutch of local worthies giggle nervously. Every dip of the wings,
every change in the engine note will be something to tell their
grandchildren. Beneath us, the royal Rolls cruises along the M3
highway to meet our descent. Ahead, the runway lights of Farn-
borough beckon.

We are losing height. In the foothills just outside the air-

3

field's perimeter we pass over a squad of army personnel on tank exercises. They are also on discreet guard duty, we can tell, as they snap to a salute in our direction. Two minor bumps, and the Otter is down. The passengers gird their loins for the ceremonies ahead, but suddenly the engine note rises again. There is just time for a quick glance to the cockpit, where our pilot is pulling back hard on the throttle, before we are airborne again. The Prince of Wales is enjoying himself.

His private secretary is not. There is a low moan from his direction as we bank steeply to circle the Royal Aircraft Establishment. On the ground, outside hangar P72, the expectant crowd radiates astonishment. The prince looks down with a grin, then chats cheerfully with his copilot. A look at his watch tells him he is still five minutes ahead of his scheduled arrival time. He's going to do it again.

Back over the startled military detachment, who snap to attention again; down, this time rather more bumpily; and up again, even more sharply.

Before we took off, the prince had been warned of icy runways at both ends of his journey. The deputy Captain of the Queen's Flight, Group Captain Derek Homer, had suggested, tentatively, that His Royal Highness might be content to take the copilot's seat, and leave the takeoff and landing to the Otter's regular pilot. There was a curl of the royal lip, rather like that of the spoiled child deprived of a cherished toy. There was a look of mingled frustration and annoyance, then a few sharp words too staccato to overhear. Wing commander the Prince of Wales had pulled rank. After he had climbed aboard, his head briefly reappeared through the hatch to assure his private secretary of the abundance of air-sickness bags. Now he is extracting his revenge on protocol for attempting to cheat him of his day's best moment. He is taking six icy risks for the price of two.

For the third time we are saluted, and for the third time we are down—this time, it seems, to stay. The prince taxis slowly—it is still one minute to three—toward the arrival area, where we jolt gently to a halt twenty yards from the assembled dignitaries and journalists. They peer curiously through our windows. Instinctively, they are smiling.

In the tiny, cramped fuselage we sit tight. Protocol decrees that the Prince of Wales must be first out of the aircraft, and there is room for only one stooped figure in the aisle. An appreciative pat of the dashboard and the stooped prince joins us, now the airline captain asking if we've enjoyed the flight. He braces himself to remember where we are: at an exhibition of the British Transglobe Expedition, of which he has graciously consented to be patron. It's now exactly 3:00 P.M. "How long are we here?" he asks his private secretary, who stoically conceals his continuing discomfort. "Until four twenty-five, sir."

"*That* long?" There is a sudden cold draft behind us, and the sound of cheering.

1500:   His Royal Highness alights from the aircraft and is met by Group Captain G. W. F. Charles, commanding officer, Experimental Flying, Royal Aircraft Establishment, representing the director of the Royal Aircraft Establishment, who welcomes HRH to RAE. Sir Ranulph Fiennes, leader of the Transglobe Expedition, will then introduce to His Royal Highness the following:
The Right Honorable the Lord Hayter
Sir Vivian Fuchs
Brigadier Wingate Gray

1510:   Captain Giles Kershaw, expedition pilot, and Sir Edmund Irving, chairman of the executive committee, remain with His Royal Highness for two to three minutes for press photographs. Sir Edmund will then invite His Royal Highness to enter the hangar, where Sir Ranulph will introduce to the patron certain expedition committee members.

1515–1545:   His Royal Highness inspects the exhibitions.

1545:   The training film will be shown.

1615:   Presentation to His Royal Highness by Sir Edmund Irving on behalf of the expedition of a commemorative crystal chalice.

1620:   His Royal Highness speaks about the expedition.

1625:   His Royal Highness the Prince of Wales departs.

All standing up. In the space of seventy-five minutes, the Prince of Wales shakes some three hundred hands and talks to perhaps half their owners. The expedition, at least, is something which gets his adrenaline going again. It is the kind of thing he would like to do himself if he were not a prince. He examines the tents, the water shoes, the prefabricated Tri-Wall huts, the skis, the snow cats, the canoes, the maps, and the tins of baked beans as closely as if he *were* himself going on the expedition.

When the time comes for the formalities, he inspects the commemorative crystal chalice minutely, then passes it deftly backward, where it disappears with an aide. He is supporting the expedition, he says, "because it is a mad and splendidly British enterprise." He will hope, he goes on in a fit of enthusiasm, to drop in on it "somewhere in the world in the next three years—if it can be arranged." His staff shoot each other morose glances.

The exhibitors applaud—and the journalists drink—as the prince conscientiously lists those trade names generously giving financial assistance.

1625 (precisely): The Prince of Wales departs. 1630 (or thereabouts): The vast hangar is suddenly deserted.

It is his complexion that first strikes you: the ruddy, weathered face of the countryman, its rosy cheeks offset by tired and deeply bagged blue eyes. You can see that he once broke his nose playing rugby. He lets his sideburns advance, wedge shaped, across his cheeks. When talking to him, it is hard to take your eyes off them.

In private, the automatic public gestures remain. The wringing of the hands, for want of being able to put them in his pockets (offstage, when he suddenly realizes he is no longer on display, he will sink his hands deep into his trouser pockets); the nervous smile, the apprehensive frown whenever the conversation takes an unexpected and possibly undesired direction. He inclines his head, like a child, and looks at you through his eyebrows, wondering what you're after. His guard is never down.

Onstage or off, he lives on his nerves. He grinds his signet ring around his little finger, he licks his lips, he strokes the contours of his nose. His mouth has an involuntary tic, which drags its corner down toward his chin, unhappily giving an impression of disapproval. He can get so wrapped in his own thoughts, remembering what he must do next, guarding against the unexpected, that he can appear unduly solemn: he forgets to laugh at people's jokes, lets glowing compliments pass by without his practiced, graceful smile.

His voice has the unmistakable huskiness of his father's, but his vowel sounds remain his mother's. Whatever he is saying, however ponderous or flippant, those vowel sounds remain in danger of undermining it. They are not of the real world. They pigeonhole his every pronouncement in some remote eyrie of inherited privilege. It is as well people read, rather than hear, most of what he says.

And yet it is not: he has an excellent line in repartee, which falls limp on the printed page. His comic eye is for the absurd, and he is both quick and remorseless with puns. Meanwhile, he has his own ways of amusing himself. The tiniest detail, he knows, can create an enormous effect. He will occasionally substitute "My mother . . ." for the more correct "The Queen . . ." to insert a calculated frisson into the conversation. It helps him take control.

At five feet ten he is slightly shorter than you expect; his 154-pound frame wears its fitness and strength lightly, its slight shoulders and trunk settled on generous hips. His waist, thanks to constant exercise, remains a trim thirty-one inches, but his chest a rather disappointing thirty-seven. His movements are sudden and awkward—he has a tendency to knock things over—but furiously ever onward. Wherever he is in the world, he is the focal point of an ebb tide flowing this way and that on the tightest of schedules. The pace in his company is exhausting. When he stops for a conversation his eyes keep moving, working out where to go next, unable to ignore the frantic activity around him.

It is all the more of a shock, in quieter moments, to be fixed by his eye and held by it while you talk. You have to spend some time in his company, sort out the face in front of you from the icon, before you can concentrate on what he is saying. You can be talking to him on the terrace of Buckingham Palace, on a bright, clear summer's day, watching a gleaming red helicopter cross the sun. Gradually you realize it is heading toward you, and you watch with awe as it lands noisily, gigantically, fifty yards away on the lawn.

"Who's that for?" you ask with wide eyes.

"Well," he says with some diffidence, "me, actually," and starts toward it. "I've got to go to Wales and open a hospital they've named after me."

Will it ever be possible, you wonder, to talk straight to this man? As you watch him fly himself off over London, you go over the conversation you've just been having: it was relaxed, insubstantial, quite amusing, nothing special. Yet you can't stop remembering that once, the previous year, in a remote corner of western Africa, more than a million people traveled hundreds of miles to fight for a glimpse of him.

2

---◆---

The Private Prince

"The children soon discover that it's much safer to unburden yourself to a member of the family than just to a friend. . . . You see, you're never quite sure . . . the pressures are a bit . . . a small indiscretion can lead to all sorts of difficulties. . . ." PRINCE PHILIP

I F INVITED to visit the Prince of Wales at home, you present yourself at the South Center Gate of Buckingham Palace, where the policeman on duty will be expecting you. He will point you to the Privy Purse Entrance, some fifty yards ahead, toward which you scrunch across the gravel of the palace forecourt. The eyes of a thousand tourists bore into your back, wondering who you are. Sentries will snap to attention, march across your path, even present arms; they are most unlikely, alas, to be doing it for you.

The first red carpet you meet is somewhat weatherbeaten, for it extends down the Privy Purse steps into the forecourt itself. The heavy mahogany door opens as if by its own accord; the policeman has telephoned news of your approach, and your identity, to the footman on duty. He is an unctuous, red-waistcoated, brass-buttoned figure who will take your coat, fold it immaculately on a table, and buzz for the secretary to the Prince of Wales's Office to have someone come and collect you. (If you are a journalist, it will be the press secretary; if you are a general or a portrait painter, you are treated to the equerry.) You wait in a small but grand anteroom, garlanded by paintings from the Queen's collection; on the table lie the *Times* (or, during its non-appearance, the *Daily Telegraph*) and the *Daily Express*, ironically enough the prince's least favorite newspaper.

Your escort will take you deeper into the palace, past a huge portrait in oils of Elizabeth II's coronation, into a scarlet corridor filled with the busts of Victoria, Albert, Edward VII, and their contemporaries. From here you take a sharp left through the luggage door, out into the inner courtyard, across which you are conducted to the Prince of Wales's door. Through this into the secretary's office, where he will check by telephone that the prince is ready for you. And so into the elevator.

On the second floor you take a sharp left past a lady-in-waiting's room, down another red-carpeted corridor, this one with green walls and illuminated display cases. The rooms now on your right are the Prince of Wales's suite, overlooking the Mall and St. James's Park. The first door you pass is the prince's luggage room. The second is his study.

It is a brown, rather somber room which Prince Charles regards as his most private. Its centerpiece is a large desk, at which he sits with his back to the windows, complaining about the traffic noise (loud enough to render radio and TV interviews impossible). Two walls are book-lined; against the third is a large, glass-fronted display cabinet in which he keeps his prized collection of glass, gold and silverware, much of it modern, most purchased rather than given him; in the evenings, the cabinet is rather dramatically illuminated from inside.

You can't sit opposite the prince's desk. A long sofa is ranged against its front, making with three comfortable chairs a conversation area to which he will motion you. If it's that time of day you'll be offered a drink, though your host will be unlikely to join you. At the end of a long day he can make short work of a stiff gin and tonic; with his family, he is happy to share a pre-prandial martini. Otherwise, he is most likely to drink water. He is particularly averse to red wine.

Past the sofa and the desk, by the windows, is the connecting door to the prince's sitting room, about half again as large, blue, and densely cluttered with what his staff call, slightly satirically, "the boss's *objets*." The prince is something of a hoarder. He is presented, of course, with a great many things, of which he must

express polite admiration in public. Those that subsequently receive the accolade of a place on display in his sittting room, lost
in a jungle of treasures from all over the world, are a constant
source of surprise to his friends.

There are two more large bookcases; beside his window is a
table piled high with yet more books, mostly new ones, a large
and ever changing collection. He will turn first to historical biographies and anything by Alexander Solzhenitsyn; anthropology
remains an abiding interest, and E. F. Schumacher's *Small Is
Beautiful* something of a bible, but he will fall asleep over a
novel. In the far corner is his television set and video cassette re-
corder, alongside the best stereo system that money can buy. In
the center of the room is another suite of sofa and chairs, ranged
around a glass-topped coffee table—one of the few expressions of
individual taste amid the prince's furnishings. Most of his suite,
originally decorated for him by Lord Mountbatten's son-in-law,
David Hicks, is standard Buckingham Palace baroque.

His bedroom, also blue, is dominated by a great four-poster,
beside which is a button to be pressed for all requirements or in
any emergency. There is a bathroom, hung with his favorite royal
cartoons, and that is that. The prince's London home is much like
any other spacious Mayfair or Belgravia flat, with the richly comfortable, rather dated look so characteristic of inherited wealth.
The only difference is that one floor down, 150 yards along a corridor, at the other end of an internal telephone, lives the Queen.

Prince Charles begins and ends most of his days here in his
London home. One of his two valets, the only people allowed to
see the prince of Wales in bed, enters the bedroom each morning
at 7:30 A.M.—as often as not, to find him already up. He takes a
cold shower first thing every day; at Buckingham Palace he will
have a swim in the pool before breakfast, at Windsor he will jog
round the castle estate. He returns to find clothes laid out for him,
fresh from the pressing room across the corridor. Only rarely will
the prince reject the valet's choice. His taste in clothes is too conservative to inspire Bertie Wooster–type disagreements.

His valets, Stephen Barry and Ian Armstrong, are men of the
prince's own age who have graduated from being junior footmen.
They do all the prince's shopping for him, though he himself exercises the final choice over his clothes. His sartorial taste is much
less daring than that of other Princes of Wales of recent memory.

If, however, you have in your time been named as the World's Worst-Dressed Man one year and the World's Best-Dressed Man the next, there is little incentive to do more than opt for comfort.

Turnbull and Asser, the upper-crust shirtmakers of Jermyn Street, regularly send a selection of shirts and ties to the palace for the prince's perusal. He dislikes man-made fibers, preferring silk or cotton next to his skin, and is far too hardy to bother with undershirts. His suits—three or four new ones a year—and most of his uniforms are made by Hawes and Curtis of Dover Street, whose master tailor, Edward Watson, applauds the prince's conservatism: "He likes to dress in the classic style in which we have been making our suits for the past thirty years. He tells me exactly what he wants, the only stipulation being that nothing should be too way out." At some £300 each, his suits come with vests, which he never wears. They are designed to be worn with suspenders, which he also refuses to wear; thus, to Mr. Watson's chagrin, the prince's trousers often hang baggily around his ankles.

Charles owns a pair of jeans, though they have never been seen in public, and a pair of Gucci boots for evening wear. At Balmoral he favors kilts, of which he owns a large variety, all specially tailored to prevent high winds causing royal embarrassment. His hair is cut once every two weeks at the palace, by a barber from Truefitt and Hill of Bond Street.

Here, in his Buckingham Palace sitting room, the Prince of Wales breakfasts alone, with his personal mail and the morning newspapers. If the day ahead is a public one, he will take the elevator down to the Prince of Wales's Office to go over the arrangements with his staff. If not, he will spend most of the day in these rooms, his inner sanctum, writing speeches, going through state papers, reading, listening to music, watching video tapes of TV programs he has missed. In the autumn of 1978, for instance, public engagements kept him busy for every Wednesday evening on which British TV was showing a series about his great-uncle's abdication, *Edward and Mrs. Simpson;* Prince Charles got the company to send him a set of tapes, which he watched more than once. As a child, his mother complained, the prince watched too much television, which is why he came late to books. As an adult, he still watches his fair share, preferring absurdist comedies (such as *Monty Python's Flying Circus*) and heavyweight documentary series. Often the television is his only evening companion. In his sitting room he will dine alone, off a tray brought up in the elevator, with a glass of milk or water. It can be a very solitary life.

These are some of the few rooms in Buckingham Palace not frequented by corgis. The prince prefers Labradors. If a posse of corgis does lumber over the threshold, it heralds the arrival a few seconds later of the Queen, who is not likely to drop in without telephoning first. The prince is very close to his parents, and deeply reliant on them, but it is only at their country homes that they can enjoy anything approaching a normal family life. In London, in the palace, the Prince of Wales must often make an appointment to see his mother. There is a constant flow of guests, dignitaries, members of staff seeking decisions, which can lead to embarrassing interruptions. Only by looking at each other's daily printed schedules do the members of the family keep track of each other's whereabouts. They are rarely all at home at once; family dinners have to be arranged as much as a week or two in advance.

On the other hand, impromptu moments can become memorable occasions. In February 1979 Prince Charles and the Queen were preparing for a two-month separation; she was to return from a three-week tour of the Persian Gulf states on the same day he flew out on a six-week swing through the Far East, Australia, and Canada. The Friday before she left, the phone in his study interrupted a solitary morning's work. Would he like to come and have lunch? When he arrived downstairs, he found the Queen alone with the prime minister, James Callaghan. The three enjoyed a quiet meal together—unusually, no other staff or advisers were present—and the Prince of Wales reckoned he got the better of the PM in one or two exchanges on the small print of recent Cabinet memoranda.

It was the kind of occasion of which posterity might be expected to know more—from the royal diaries made available, posthumously, to an official biographer. But Prince Charles, in a rare break with royal tradition, does not keep a diary. He hates paperwork, of which his job already generates considerable amounts. And he is not the kind of man to clear half an hour for diary writing before retiring at night, like most of his immediate forebears. Apart from anything else, he gets too tired. The prince has an unfortunate tendency to drop off during the daytime: in the middle of a portrait sitting, a car journey between engagements, even a committee meeting. His first words to many of the people who visit him at the palace are: "Now *do* wake me if I doze off." An unnerving introduction to the royal presence.

He likes to be in bed by midnight, and to rise later than usual when on vacation. At Buckingham Palace the working day starts soon after 8 A.M.; at Sandringham and Balmoral breakfast is at nine. By a tradition no one quite understands, the Prince of Wales eats alone in London, but joins his staff at the royal country residences. His taste in food is unpredictable, and subject to passing crazes, often inspired by his foreign travels; at one time his staff had to go to great lengths to serve ugli fruit for breakfast every day. He does not ordinarily drink tea or coffee. Buckingham Palace relays this useful information in advance to prospective hosts, who are advised to provide a wide choice of fruit juices; the prince is capable of then embarrassing everyone by calling for a cuppa. His perennially favorite dish, which he can eat at any time of day or night, is smoked salmon with scrambled eggs. If it is followed by peach Melba smothered in whipped cream, the Prince of Wales will be in Elysium.

Spending as much time as he does with his staff, the prince has come to rely on them for their friendship as much as anything else. The requirements of public office dominate and restrict his private social life. He rarely makes excursions to London clubs or restaurants. He has been known to go dancing at Annabel's and dining at Boulestin or Rules, but only in large parties and after much persuasion. The fuss involved embarrasses him, the gaze of fellow revelers destroys more than his appetite. He prefers to entertain in the palace, where the Chinese dining room or the India room can stage elegant, formal dinner parties. Very few friends are close enough to share the evening tray in his suite.

And he frequents only a handful of private dining tables around London, on the strict condition that he knows in advance who the other guests will be. One such belongs to Princess Elizabeth of Yugoslavia. Prince Charles's second cousin, Elizabeth has been married twice; in the 1970s she enjoyed a much publicized romance with Richard Burton when he was between marriages. Twelve years older than Charles, she is one of several married or once-married women on whose friendship the prince places a special value. Like his great-uncle when young, the Prince of Wales enjoys the "safeness" of female friends unlikely to provoke marriage rumors; before he met Wallis Simpson, Prince Edward liked to surround himself with surrogate families.

At Princess Elizabeth's Chelsea home early in 1979, Charles listened as a fellow dinner guest, the financier Sir James Goldsmith, waxed lyrical about the delights of being a newspaper proprietor. Already owner of *l'Express*, the French news magazine, he was in the throes of setting up a right-wing English weekly, *Now*; to the other guests it seemed Goldsmith saw himself as a second Beaverbrook, undisguisedly owning newspapers for propaganda purposes. To the other guests it also seemed that the Prince of Wales was jealous. Here was a man with power, and a naked enjoyment of it—the kind of power a Prince of Wales tastes and sees in action, but can never exercise.

Charles can talk candidly on such occasions, because his friends protect him with a Berlin Wall of secrecy. They never talk to the press about him and will rarely gossip elsewhere. The penalty for so doing, they know, is instant excommunication. "I trust my friends implicitly," he says. "And they know it. The more discreet, the more trustworthy they are, the better. Those people who do get drawn into conversation and do natter about me find they get into the papers. But I hear they don't get paid much. . . ."

Thus he has very few friends, and those from a very narrow slice of life. Most are polo players or aristocrats. Others are much older, trusted confidants, friends of his parents, churchmen, specialists in his own areas of interest. There are few to help his view of the world, from behind the lace curtains of his palace windows, become much more realistic.

They even come and go less than most other people's friends. No friend of Prince Charles will see him much more than once every few months; but if you become a friend, you are likely to remain one. The accolade is to become a fixed point on his annual routine—like Charles and Patti Palmer-Tomkinson, who host his annual skiing trip to Klosters; Lady Jane Wellesley, the most enduring of his girl friends, whose father, the Duke of Wellington, is (for public purposes) the prince's host on his regular shooting trips to the family estate in Spain; Guy Wildenstein, to play on whose polo team, Les Diables Bleus, Prince Charles makes his

August visit to Deauville; and the Tryons, whose fishing lodge on the River Hofsa in northeast Iceland is the setting for an annual late-summer house party.

Lord and Lady Tryon, Tony and Dale, are among the few friends on whom Charles may drop in unheralded. He has been known to turn up unannounced in the middle of a dinner party, refuse all invitations to stay, and slink off home in embarrassment. Lord Tryon, thirty-eight-year-old son of the Queen's late treasurer, is a director of the merchant bankers Lazard Brothers, and chairman of the finance firm English and Scottish Investors, Ltd. His financial advice has often proved useful to Charles. Dale, Australian born, is ten years younger than her husband, and another of the married women to whom the prince is particularly close. She is a vivacious, extroverted woman, in striking contrast to her more somber and forbidding husband. When she married Tony Tryon in 1973, she gave up her own two passions, riding and skiing, for his, shooting and salmon fishing. Prince Charles occasionally joins them for a pheasant shoot on their seven-hundred-acre estate in Wiltshire, but all three prefer the solitude of their summer fishing in Iceland.

The Tryons' lodge is near Egilsstadir, a remote and rugged spot where there is no danger of being disturbed. There are no ghillies, as at Balmoral, to help you find the fish; each member of the party goes a separate way and swaps the day's yarns over dinner that evening. It is de rigueur not to boast about, even mention, numbers of fish caught, but everyone is expected to have some heroic saga of the one that may or may not have got away.

Guy Wildenstein, a year older than the prince, is the son of a Parisian art dealer and editor of his own art magazine, *Le Gazette de Beaux Arts*. Rich, well-born, physically diminutive and politically ambitious, he had played polo against Prince Charles often before, in the late 1970s, he became his friend. There was many a palace hoop to jump through before he could achieve his ambition of persuading the heir to the British throne to join his French polo team. They share three passions: polo, art, and beautiful women. In the summer of 1978 Guy flew one of the prince's old flames, Laura Jo Watkins, over to Deauville from her California home—a surprise that was not altogether appreciated. The Deauville weekend is always one of high living: all-night parties, visits to nightclubs, a chance for the prince to indulge his passion for dancing. But Charles rarely socializes before or after other polo matches. He will arrive with just enough time to change—at Windsor he will come already kitted out—and drive home immediately afterward. Very occasionally, after much persuasion, he will have a quick drink in the clubhouse before leaving. Not all polo players are trusted friends.

There are many who are: notably Mark Vestey, who married the prince's former girl friend Rosie Clifton; his brother, Lord (Sam) Vestey, head of the family meat firm; and the prince's polo coach, Sinclair Hill, an Australian millionaire who spends only his summers in England. Polo is a brusque, hard-fought business which gives the public one of its few chances to hear royal four-letter words, and Sinclair Hill talks to Prince Charles more directly than most. He can get away with swearing at him—just —so long as he adds the afterthought of "sir." Hill is a stocky and somewhat boorish character. "It's unlikely," says another polo friend, "that they spend much time discussing opera."

Even most of these rather depressingly one-dimensional friends are now drifting off to get married and make their own lives. "Whenever I give a dinner party these days," Charles recently confided to one of them, "more and more of the guests seem to be married." As he has lost special girl friends, such as Lady Cecil Kerr, to other suitors, so he is losing trusted male confidants. One bachelor chum who remains devoutly loyal is Nicholas Soames, son of Lord Soames (formerly British ambassador to Paris and the EEC) and grandson of Winston Churchill. In the early 1970s Soames was constantly at Charles's side as his equerry; now that he has taken himself off into into the world of finance they see rather less of each other. But he is a survivor from a group of early friends Charles has now outgrown, those of the caste satirized by television's Monty Python team as "Upper-Class Twits of the Year," who preserve undergraduate life in aspic. The prince these days favors more substantial figures, such as his barrister friend Richard Beckett, who serves on the committee of one of his trusts, and Hywel Jones, a socialist economist who shared his staircase at Cambridge.

Other married friends include the van Cutsems and the Tollemaches, who, like the Tryons, have provided the Prince with godchildren. (The van Cutsems and the Tryons named their sons after him.) The van Cutsems dine with Charles in London, but more often entertain him on their Newmarket estate, with its excellent shooting. Lord and Lady Tollemache—Timothy and Alexandra—introduced Charles to his new passion of cross-country riding, and have pleasant house parties at Helmingham Hall, their stately home in Suffolk. Though heir to the Tollemache Cobbold brewery fortune, the fifth baron has recently felt obliged to open Helmingham's gardens to the public.

This safe, small, well-born group provides the Prince of Wales with an occasional escape hatch; they constitute the only life he has forged himself outside his family's. They are a means to weekend sport and relaxation. But for intellectual companionship he invariably turns to people of his parents' generation or older. He has remained close to Lord Butler, the former Conservative politician, who was master of his Cambridge college; he enjoys the company of Sir John Miller, the sixty-year-old crown equerry, who first encouraged him to hunt despite the controversy it was bound to cause. His interest in anthropology has led to a friendship with Laurens van der Post, the South African–born writer now living in London, who has helped develop his strong views on racial prejudice. His religious convictions were first encouraged by the Right Reverend Robert Woods, when Dean of Windsor and chaplain to the Queen; now bishop of Worcester, Woods is gratified to find the prince unassailed by doubts. Charles is a regular communicant and in his speeches even something of an evangelist. As the future head of the Anglican Church, he is anxious to use his position to encourage rapprochement with Rome. Ecumenism, he feels, is one of the few delicate contemporary issues on which he can speak his mind. In the process he has developed a friendship he especially prizes with Cardinal Basil Hume, archbishop of Westminster.

The prince's closest friendships, however, remain within his family, by reason of his position and his own nature. His mother is the mainstay of his life. Both have inherited the fundamental diffidence of King George VI; with a conscious effort of will, both have fought to overcome it. Neither wholly enjoys excursions into the outside world—the polite conversations, the strain of eternally correct and decorous behavior. Both like to slump in a chair afterward, kick off their shoes, and swap stories about the absurdities of their day, the arch and often ludicrous behavior of those delegated to escort their respective royal personages. There is a bond between them unlike that between any other members of the family. They have, after all, a unique fate in common.

Prince Charles calls the Queen "Mother" and Prince Philip "Papa." He began life hero-worshiping his father. Throughout his childhood and schooldays, much of Charles's time seemed to be spent emulating the energetic young Prince Philip's achievements. It was always something of an ordeal to follow so closely in his father's footsteps. Charles is a very different type of man: circumspect, gentle, and kindhearted, where his father is often brash, outspoken, and occasionally severe. Even now Philip can lose his temper with his eldest son, chide him for "monkeying about" in public, for an incautious speech, an ill-guarded aside. The Prince of Wales's respect for his father is almost unbounded, so he tends to lose the arguments. His face will pucker up in surrender, and he will concede the point. Off duty, however, on vacation at Sandringham and Balmoral, the two are constant and warm companions in the outdoor life. Philip is pleased that his son has taken up the polo mallet he himself had to lay down in middle age, but disappointed that Charles does not share his love of sailing. He introduced Charles to the contemplative pleasures of watercolor painting, but does not otherwise share his son's love of the arts. He would like Charles to have shown more interest in science and technology, but is happy to see him joining with increasing vigor in his own familiar broadsides against British industry, and his campaigns for the conservation of the environment.

In his childhood, Prince Charles was probably closer to his father than his mother; in his adulthood, their roles have been reversed. The one constant has been his special affection for his grandmother, the Queen Mother, perhaps his closest confidante. Queen Elizabeth is said to see more of her late husband, King George VI, in Prince Charles than in any of her other grandchildren. She was a pillar of his childhood, almost a mother-confessor when the requirements his parents made of him seemed too great to sustain. At Balmoral she taught him fly-fishing, at which she was long the family expert. In his parents' lengthy and frequent absences, she nourished in him the gentleness and concern which she now cites as his outstanding qualities. She and his great-uncle, Lord Mountbatten, share the secrets he won't always confide in his parents, notably about affairs of the heart.

Throughout his life he has always revered his "Uncle Dickie"—Earl Mountbatten, elder statesman of the royal family. The two have become something of a mutual admiration society, who go to great lengths to be sure of seeing each other at least once a month. Mountbatten's daughter and son-in-law, Lord and Lady Brabourne, longstanding friends of the Queen and Prince Philip, have now become as close to Charles. He holidays frequently at their home on the Caribbean island of Eleuthera, where their svelte young daughters, the Knatchbull girls, play hostess. Their son, Norton Knatchbull, was at Gordonstoun with the prince and remains a regular companion. He works in the motion picture industry, as does his father (among whose latest productions are two Agatha Christie films, *Murder on the Orient Express* and *Death on the Nile*.) Occasionally he has even persuaded Charles to don the promotional T-shirts of films he has worked on, such as *A Bridge Too Far*. In royal circles, the prince's appearance in the shirt at a Windsor polo match was thought a plug too far.

Of the other members of the royal family, Charles has remained an apologist for his aunt and godmother, Princess Margaret, through her long years of unpopularity around the nation and occasionally within the family. His own emergence as a fully-fledged public figure, during the Queen's Silver Jubilee Year in 1977, coincided with the height of the Queen's displeasure with her sister, then separated from her husband, Lord Snowdon, and providing the popular press with its most salacious story for years: her romance, conducted largely on the private Caribbean island of Mustique, with Roddy Llewellyn, a hippie-turned-pop-singer fifteen years her junior. Publicly, Charles's seizure of the popular imagination helped deflect a few of Margaret's less savory headlines; privately, he remained sympathetic and supportive. When finally the marriage ended in divorce, Charles also went out of his way to maintain his friendship with Tony Snowdon, who soon remarried. Snowdon's unorthodox, somewhat Bohemian presence in the royal circle had added a colorful dimension to Charles's teens and twenties; as constable of Caernarvon Castle he had also been the mastermind behind the prince's investiture in 1969, the most traumatic ordeal of his life so far.

Throughout their childhood together, Prince Charles's relationship with his sister, Princess Anne, was always somewhat combustible. Anne was his complete opposite, as much like their father as Charles was like their mother. She was stubborn and strong willed where Charles was meek and defensive, petulant and haughty where he was bashful and withdrawn. She has remained so, to the public dismay; several times in the 1970s she was voted the royal family's least popular member, less popular even than her wayward aunt. In their teens, she and her brother grew apart; they had different interests, different friends, different attitudes to their curious destinies. They pursued largely separate lives. Charles would often despair of Anne's public outbursts, the rage toward press photographers which was always so counterproductive.

Once when he was abroad, news of the latest incident between Anne and her public was relayed to him. She had come up against a group of anti-blood-sports protesters when about to go hunting. An exchange of abuse climaxed with the princess saying: "Who's paying you to do this?" Charles groaned when he heard it. He knew exactly what was coming next: "Well, *we're* paying *you* to do that," from angry taxpayers. It is a cardinal royal sin to fall into such traps; avoiding them requires a cautious and prescient way with words, which the prince has long since perfected.

When Anne married Mark Phillips in 1973, on Prince Charles's twenty-fifth birthday, brother and sister grew even further apart. The prince found little in common with his new brother-in-law, whose brainpower does not always match his horsemanship. But the arrival of Charles's first nephew—and seventeenth godchild—four years later brought a renaissance. He dotes on young Peter Phillips, and now visits the family at their Gloucestershire home much more often than before. As he approached his thirties he was, like his great-uncle before him, feeling the need for some surrogate children.

To his younger brothers, Andrew and Edward, he is a playful, if occasionally patronizing, companion. As Charles approached thirty, Andrew was growing to manhood. He was twelve years younger and free from the restraints of heirdom. His dashing good looks began to steal some of Charles's thunder, wounding his vanity and causing a few acid remarks. "Ah, the one with the Robert Redford looks?" he would say when asked about Andrew's progress. In 1978 they teamed up for parachute training after

Charles had become colonel-in-chief of the parachute regiment; when Andrew teased him gently about his age—"You're getting on a bit for this sort of thing, aren't you?"—Charles would lose his temper and slap him down for familiarity in front of outsiders. Prince Edward, sixteen years his junior, is still as yet a wide-eyed younger brother, in whose company Charles delights. Fortunate enough to have a few more years of protection from the public gaze, Edward is reputed to be the most contemplative and artistic of the royal children.

It is a family large enough to provide a close circle of friends, with a special understanding of his problems, for a man who cannot afford intimates outside it. Few people beyond the royal entourage can grasp the complexities of Prince Charles's life, or appreciate the self-doubt and heart searching they cause. He is a piece of public property who must fight for a strangely impersonal form of privacy. He must develop informed views on the ways of the world but never express them in public. He is privy to all state secrets—even his father does not receive "the boxes"—but cannot discuss them with anyone but his mother and the prime minister. In public he must contain most of his thoughts; in private he must be careful to whom he expresses them. He must maintain a facade of suave self-confidence while inwardly riddled with uncertainty and apprehension. He must insist on the deference due to his office while regretting the limitations this naturally places on all friendships.

The result is that he takes the safest option: the company of his own kind—either sporting or born to inherited privilege. There is no one in his life to challenge him, to question his received attitudes, to offset the benign but deeply conservative influence of his parents. Many who meet him, especially among those of his own age, come away itching to fill this role. They find him impressionable, receptive, even gullible; his quick-wittedness surprises them, entrenched as it is in so deep and unquestioning a belief in the status quo.

On further acquaintance they find him defensive, vulnerable, and thus the more appealing. But it is precisely for this reason that they cannot become his friends. The prince has had to struggle to master himself, to understand, accept, and believe in the role to which he was born. He is well aware of its irrationalities and keenly feels its frustrations. To have them too intelligently challenged would be too great a psychological strain. It would undermine him.

Thus he courts physical rather than intellectual danger. The price of such thrills and spills is a deep monotony elsewhere in his life. He must be his own best friend and guard the while against becoming his own worst enemy.

3

Prince Charles Ltd.

QUESTION TO THE PRIME MINISTER:
*"Will the royal family be subject to
the government's pay policy?"*
ANSWER: *"No."*

T HE PRINCE OF WALES once gave an old joke new life by
calling the monarchy "the oldest profession in the world." His
grandfather, King George VI, used to refer to the royal family as
"the firm," and his father, Prince Philip, has talked about living
"over the shop." Prince Charles's own corner of this capital-inten-
sive spider's web is a network of businesses and charitable trusts
managed by a disparate array of hardheaded businessmen and
enlightened amateurs. Each is answerable to a chairman who
likes to play a very active role. For all his other preoccupations,
Charles is not the delegating type.

Headquarters is undoubtedly the Prince of Wales's Office, a
corridor of large, universitylike rooms straddling the eastern
corner of the ground floor of Buckingham Palace. If the Prince is
chairman of the parent company, which we might call Prince
Charles Ltd., the managing director is his private secretary,
backed up by an assistant private secretary. The company secretary, responsible for financial and other administrative matters,
is the secretary to the Prince of Wales's Office. There is a public
relations officer in the shape of his press secretary, and a succession of equerries to act as personal assistant to the chairman.

This is the group responsible for the day-to-day running of
the prince's affairs. As members of the royal household, they
lead a pleasant life. They can legitimately complain of being

24

overworked and underpaid, but they have chosen their jobs for other reasons. Lunch is a pleasant affair; a different sumptuous royal heirloom, complete with a card detailing its history and provenance, adorns the dining table each day. Tea—an elegant mélange of silver teapots, dainty sandwiches, and bone china monogrammed cups—is taken in the equerries' room. The prince's staff inhabits splendid offices, with double doors, huge desks, sofas, cooking facilities, and large wardrobes (to accommodate the many changes of formal clothes required in this line of business). On the press secretary's wall hang a Van Dyck and a Frans Hals; the private secretary's French windows open onto the palace forecourt, where a military band serenades him through the day.

This is the prince's inner cabinet. Every six months he chairs a major planning meeting, to chart his diary in outline for a year and more ahead and in detail for the immediate half-year. In the private secretary's office is a large map of Britain with several overlays of transparent plastic; this records the prince's recent movements, in different colors for different years, to show which areas of the country he has lately been neglecting. He prefers to know personally of every invitation sent him—up to a hundred a week—and likes to make his own choice, often against his staff's advice. Once the public schedule is agreed on, the prince will fit in his private engagements around it. A trip to his principality in Wales, for instance, will often enable him to stay en route at his sister's manor farm in Gloucestershire. Weekends, whenever possible, are sacrosanct, and his whereabouts rarely made public.

Every letter written to the prince—several hundred in an average week, into four figures after a speech or a press speculation—will be answered by a member of his staff. Charles himself signs only official documents and personal letters to family or friends. The schedule must allow time for the enormous amount of paperwork his job generates—the aspect of it all he likes least. His staff cite as his most irritating habit the late return of documents given him for perusal and signature, the last-minute delivery of speeches, statements, letters for typing. (He writes all his own speeches, though since 1978 a journalist, Byron Rogers, has helped with research.)

Also on the force are his two valets, two (female) grooms, and six secretaries, or clerks, all of whom are paid out of the prince's own pocket. Even less orthodox in a company structure are his two armed detectives, assigned from Scotland Yard's Special Branch. Detective Chief Inspectors John Maclean and Paul Officer have both been with the prince for more than ten years. Only when he is safely at home do they leave his side; the rules insist on the presence of one of them everywhere else— even, for instance, hunched in the back of his sports car when he takes a girl friend out for the evening. Both extremely genial men, capable nonetheless of turning ugly when circumstances require it, they have developed a satisfactory agreement about the regular overseas perks of their job: Maclean's annual treat is the skiing, Officer's the Caribbean. As the two human beings who have spent more time with Prince Charles than anyone else in his adult life, they are certainly—especially the more bluff and ex- troverted Maclean—to be numbered among the closest of his friends.

It was the aptly named Officer who perhaps saved the Prince of Wales's life in the one serious and violent attempt so far made upon it. There are regular "incidents"—in 1978 a man was jailed for hitting the prince with a bottle thrown through his car window—but nothing to compare with the events of one dramatic night in April 1974. The prince, a lieutenant aboard the frigate HMS *Jupiter*, was taking a shore course on underwater warfare at Portland, in Dorset, and had been installed in regular quar- ters in the RN barracks. Just after 2 A.M. he was awakened by a noise in his sitting room. He got up, opened the connecting door, and was pounced on by an armed assailant. Officer was asleep next door, but the sound of the ensuing struggle awoke him. He ran in to find the prince floored in the darkness, and his at- tacker about to bring a chair down on his head. Officer seized the man from behind, and detective and prince wrestled him to the floor. The attacker turned out to be another lieutenant at the naval base, with a history of mental illness; following an inquiry, he was committed to a naval hospital. Prince Charles and his detectives were quick to develop and rehearse a set of standard procedures to be adopted in the event of any form of attack.

Until the late 1970s, the Prince of Wales's life tended to be run by older people. (Few company chairmen, indeed, have their mother taking such a close, if ex-officio, interest in the running of their affairs.) From 1970 until May 1, 1979, his private secretary was Squadron Leader David Checketts, an urbane, grammar school–educated public relations man with a distinguished RAF record. Checketts was equerry to the Duke of Edinburgh when he first entered Prince Charles's life, accompanying him to Australia for his six months at school there in 1966. He became equerry to the Prince of Wales the following year, and three years later his first private secretary. He was a pillar in the young prince's uncertain public life, rarely more than six feet from his side, always ready to help him through difficulties and defuse awkward situations. Through the end of his schooldays, his time at Cambridge, his investiture, and his busy service career, Prince Charles owed Checketts a huge debt for the smooth progress of his day-to-day administrative needs and the grand strategy of his emergence into full-time public life. As the uncertain, immature youth, however, grew into a self-possessed, capable young man, he felt a need to surround himself with people more his own age.

Born in 1930, Checketts unavoidably became something of a father figure to the Prince. When both tried to scotch this, his role remained essentially avuncular. Checketts would attempt to curb some of the prince's bolder ideas, urge against his more forthright public statements, express occasional disapproval of his private life. With the prince now very much his own man, a certain friction was bound to set in, and a parting by mutual consent, on the best of terms, became inevitable. After eighteen years' service at the palace, Checketts anyway found fifty an appropriate age at which to return to more lucrative full-time public relations work.

Checketts' place as private secretary was taken by Edward Adeane, nine years older than the prince but a friend of long standing. With his appointment, Adeane's family achieved a century of service to the royal family. His great-grandfather, Lord Stamfordham, was appointed assistant private secretary to Queen Victoria in 1880; he became her private secretary, then private secretary to the Duke of York, later Prince of Wales and King George V, and was still in royal harness when he died at the age of eighty-two. Adeane's father, Sir Michael (now Lord) Adeane, was a page of honor to George V, then successively equerry and assistant private secretary to King George VI (1937–52) and to Elizabeth II, whose principal private secretary he was from her coronation year, 1953, to 1972.

The Hon. Edward Adeane was himself a page to the Queen, and knew the young Prince Charles. A bachelor, he shares the prince's enthusiasm for shooting and fishing, and in recent years has joined the Tryons' summer party in Iceland. To work for the prince, he gave up a lucrative practice as a libel lawyer, with such disparate clients as Lady Falkender and the Tory party, the *Times* and *Playboy* magazine. Educated at Eton and Cambridge, he was plebiscite supervisor in the Southern Cameroons in 1960–61, and was called to the bar in 1962.

Though older than the prince, and indeed a man with a demeanor much older than his years, Adeane is Prince Charles's own appointee, and thus the focal point of the first team the prince has himself established. By the same token the secretary to the Prince of Wales's Office, Michael Colborne, is fourteen years older than Prince Charles; but he was a shipmate aboard HMS *Norfolk*, whence the Prince inveigled him to look after his financial affairs. His press secretaries come and go, but the most successful has been the present one, John Dauth, a thirty-one-year-old Australian diplomat, whose two-year assignment was extended in 1979. Perhaps the most significant appointment, however, was that in 1978 of a thirty-five-year-old diplomat, Oliver Everett, to be assistant private secretary. Everett's birdlike appearance belies his athletic prowess, notably as a polo player of even more accomplishment than his boss; more important, he has organized such initiatives as the Prince of Wales's tour of British industry under the auspices of the National Economic Development Office.

Soon after his thirtieth birthday, therefore, Prince Charles had settled around him a youngish team he had personally chosen. It was the beginning of a not altogether successful attempt to remove himself from beneath the protective wings of older people. Many aspects of his official business were still controlled by mandarin figures, but at least the head office was now in better shape. And the principal subsidiary company, the Duchy of Cornwall, needed only a light hand on the tiller.

The heir to the throne is automatically Duke of Cornwall. Prince Charles is the twenty-fourth since the duchy's creation in 1337, when King Edward III bestowed it on the Black Prince. King Edward's charter, still to be seen in the British Museum, specified that the dukedom should pass to the monarch's "first-begotten son," so that for about half its long history the duchy has been without a duke. Princess Elizabeth, for instance, though first-begotten and heir to the throne, could not inherit the Duchy of Cornwall; it remained vested in the crown, thus enabling George VI to guarantee a handsome income to his younger brother, the Duke of Gloucester. Since Prince Albert reformed its ancient and creaking machinery for his son, the future Edward VII, the Duchy of Cornwall has become an extremely wealthy landowning enterprise, which provides the Prince of Wales with his major source of income. Almost as important, it keeps him out of the now annual brouhaha about the Civil List, the quota of public money voted by Parliament to the monarch and her family.

The duchy owns a total of 131,744 acres in nine counties, which break down impressively: 30,700 in Cornwall, 69,500 on Dartmoor, 3,200 in Devon, 3,700 in Dorset, 1,200 in Gloucestershire, 4,100 in the Scilly Isles, 15,600 in Somerset, 3,700 in Wiltshire, and 44 in Kennington, London. This last, though the smallest, is far the most profitable area. Not only is the prince, as Duke of Cornwall, landlord to thousands of West Country farmers; he controls 850 South London tenancies, with a disparate array of inhabitants. At one end there are the grace-and-favor apartments settled on such faithful retainers as his former nanny, Helen Lightbody; at the other an influx of MPs of all parties, including the imprisoned John Stonehouse and former Prime Minister James Callaghan. Rents are generally lower than elsewhere in London, and access to a Duchy of Cornwall apartment is not always easy.

At the heart of his London estate, the prince owns the Oval cricket ground, leased to Surrey County Cricket Club. Elsewhere, he is the unlikely proprietor of Dartmoor prison (for which he extracts no rent), and owner of such ancient castles as Tintagel, Launceston, Liskeard, Trematon, and Restormel, as well as Exeter's mighty fortress and the rich oyster beds on the River Helford in Cornwall, which yield a million oysters a year. He has a 550-acre farm of his own, the Duchy Home Farm at Stoke Climsland in East Cornwall, where he breeds Devon Red Ruby cattle. It is a model farm, pioneering new agricultural techniques; in like fashion, the extensive flower-growing industry on the Duchy estates includes laboratories for the study of bulb disease.

By ancient statute the prince has first rights on any whale or porpoise washed up on the Cornish beaches; this has proved more of a liability than an asset, as it is also incumbent upon him to dispose of the carcasses. The cargoes of any ships wrecked on the coast are his, as are the worldly goods of any Cornishman who dies intestate and without next of kin (reckoned to be about ten a year). He has the right to extract an annual tithe of three hundred puffins from the inhabitants of the Isles of Scilly, though he has yet to exercise it. Other traditions die hard: on St. George's Day each year the townfolk of Fordington in Dorset roast a sheep and dispatch its most succulent leg to their landlord.

In November 1973, the prince took part for the first time in the archaic ritual of receiving his dues as Duke of Cornwall. On a green beside what remains of Launceston Castle, in a ceremony dating back to the Black Prince's hunting expeditions around his domain, Prince Charles was solemnly presented with his seigneurial rights, to wit: a load of firewood, a gray cloak, 100 old shillings, a pound of pepper, a hunting bow, a pair of gilt spurs, a pound of herbs, a salmon spear resembling Neptune's trident, a pair of falconer's gauntlets, and two greyhounds. With the exception of the greyhounds—which were returned to their owner, Lieutenant Colonel John Molesworth-St. Aubyn—everything was duly put back in the Launceston Museum, ready for the next time. The prince wished his tenants "peaceable and quiet seizin" before going off to lunch with some of his tenant farmers.

There is nothing archaic, however, about the duchy's finances. Its annual turnover runs into several millions of pounds, and a percentage of the profit is plowed back into development of its properties and estates. The net annual profit goes exclusively to the duke. In recent years this has averaged some £250,000 (in 1978 it was a bumper £290,605), to which the Prince of Wales has been entitled since he came of age. By his own decision, following a precedent set by the Duke of Windsor when Prince of Wales, Prince Charles gives fifty percent to the Treasury as a voluntary equivalent of income tax. This leaves him with an annual tax-free income averaging some £125,000 (£145,302.50 in 1978). It has been calculated in answer to parliamentary questions that normal taxation would reduce this to some £10,000; on the other hand, to be left with that kind of income *after* tax would require gross annual earnings in excess of £5 million.

Before Prince Charles became twenty-one, the major part of the Duchy of Cornwall's profits was used to reduce public liability for the Civil List. The Queen retained one-ninth, some £20,000 a year, for her son's education and other expenses, which was increased to a fixed sum of £30,000 on his eighteenth birthday. During those twenty-one years, any surplus was invested on the young prince's behalf, accumulating a nest egg estimated to be worth some £300,000 on his twenty-first birthday; in the same period, the duchy's contributions to the Civil List totaled £2,250,000.

The Duchy of Cornwall is a state-financed government department with a staff of about forty. Its headquarters is a fine Nash-style building next door to Buckingham Palace, and there are five regional offices. The Prince of Wales chairs regular duchy meetings, and likes to be seen as an assiduous and fair-minded landlord. The duchy is run on much more gentlemanly lines than many another property company of the same scale. Land deals are few and far between, although the Prince did in 1959 become the proud new owner of an entire village, Daglingworth in Gloucestershire, including a private boys' school. Prosecutions tend to concentrate on such offenders as ice-cream vendors who disfigure beauty spots. Officially, the Duchy is immune from payment of taxes and the obligation to seek planning permissions; in practice, a sum equivalent to the leviable tax is paid to county and district councils, and any development plans are discussed in advance with planning authorities. One of Prince Charles's innovations has been to set up a scholarship to send the son of a duchy tenant to the sixth form at his old school, Gordonstoun.

The nation's attitude to the Prince of Wales's tax-free income depends entirely on its attitude to the monarchy. Prince Charles undoubtedly appears to need some £100,000 a year to keep himself in the style to which he has become accustomed— the style, moreover, in which his future subjects have become accustomed to seeing him. When a majority wishes to alter the nature and function of the monarchy, that will be the time to start trimming the monarchy's income. The Prince's only other source of income—which *is* subject to normal taxation—is a port-

folio of investments handled on his behalf by a consortium of
three City stockbroking firms. Its value and its holdings at any
given time are a secret as closely guarded as the crown jewels.
He has never accepted any other form of personal income, even
when entitled to it. During his service career, for instance, he
did not draw the salary due to him in the RAF, and donated his
navy pay to the King George's Fund for Sailors.

When he inherits the throne, Charles will become one of
the richest men outside the Arab world. The Queen's fortune has
often been declared incalculable, but is certainly among the
largest in private hands anywhere in the world. Estimates of the
sovereign's personal fortune have varied wildly between $20
million and $140 million. One recent obfuscation came with the
Companies Act of 1976, which was hastily revised to exempt the
royal family from a clause requiring those owning more than
five percent of a public company to disclose their holdings. On
becoming king, Charles will inherit the Duchy of Lancaster, an
even larger property company than the Duchy of Cornwall, with
revenues—entirely free from income tax—about twice the size;
if he still has no son, he will retain the Duchy of Cornwall as
well. Until that heady day, he must pay his staff and personal
expenses—including, rather touchingly, a small sum to his mother
for board and lodging—out of his Duchy of Cornwall income.
One luxury, for instance, is his string of polo ponies, whose up-
keep is estimated at around £12,000 a year; his blue convertible
Aston Martin V8, on the other hand, is eight years old.

As long as the present system holds good, and until he suc-
ceeds to the throne, the Prince of Wales will make no demands
upon the Civil List. He reserves the right to alter his present
arrangement with the Treasury when he marries, and the Civil
List sets aside a theoretical and regularly revised sum, at present
£60,000 per annum, for his widow. At this stage of his life, his
annual income certainly does exceed his expenditure by some
twenty percent, more than enough to make Mr. Micawber
happy. But out of the surplus he is, according to the secretary of
the Duchy of Cornwall, "hideously generous" to charities. Until
the royal family's finances are made publicly accountable, only
the bankers of Coutts Ltd.—who produce special checks imprinted with the prince's coronet, which he signs simply
"Charles"—will know more. For now we will have to make do

with the Buckingham Palace argot: "While the amount retained by His Royal Highness is in excess of his current expenses, it is related to what can reasonably be foreseen in the future. . . . The excess of income over expenditures will permit the gradual accumulation of a reserve fund to cover expenses and contingencies for which there would otherwise be no provision."

The prince's private apartments at Buckingham Palace and Windsor Castle are maintained at state expense. The Duchy of Cornwall, meanwhile, provides him with another tranquil retreat: a three-bedroom cottage on the Scilly island of St. Mary's, where former Prime Minister Sir Harold Wilson is a neighbor. Called Tamarisk after a locally luxuriant shrub, the house is set behind high walls in its own half-acre, just down the road from the local duchy offices, and a few hundred yards from a football field convenient for helicopter landings. But he uses this retreat rarely.

The prince prefers living at home with his parents—as, unlike most young men, he was still doing on his thirtieth birthday. Only when he marries will etiquette force him, reluctantly, to move (though, like his sister after her marriage, he will retain his own suite in the palace). Even then he is most unlikely, despite popular belief to the contrary, to move into his country home, Chevening, in Kent. The prince will be found a London home convenient to Buckingham Palace, where he will retain his office. The most likely candidate—though it is mentioned *sotto voce* in royal circles, for it presupposes the death of Queen Elizabeth the Queen Mother—is Clarence House.

Chevening, which at present he scarcely ever visits, will become a home for country weekends. Set in a three-thousand-acre estate, including a four-acre lake, the mansion dates from 1630 and is in part attributed to Inigo Jones. Some three miles from Sevenoaks, amid the lush North Downs of Kent, its Palladian magnificence far outranks Chequers and Dorneywood, the country residences of the prime minister and the foreign secretary. With its two pavilions, its colonnaded walkways, its thirty-six reception and state rooms, its Italian plasterwork, Waterford chandeliers, and marble floors, Chevening is in the most sumptuous traditions of English country mansions.

Chevening's lawns, the prince has discovered, are a mere twelve helicopter-minutes from the garden of Buckingham Palace.

In the mid-1970s he flew in and out regularly to inspect the progress of the interior restoration, and even talked of producing a book about the house and its glories, as his parents had done after the restoration of Clarence House for them twenty-five years earlier. But since the mansion has been ready for his use, as it was early in 1975 after a renovation costing more than half a million dollars, he has very rarely even looked in at it. Even the shooting rights on the estate, which might well have been thought to be close to his heart, have been sublet to a consortium. Local people are very disappointed, even angry.

As he grows older, as a family grows around him, the prince may come to use Chevening as an alternative to his parents' annual round of January holidays at Sandringham, Easters and Christmases at Windsor, and summers at Balmoral. It would be a sad Princess of Wales whose husband compelled her to spend all their holidays with her in-laws. Prince Charles's independence, which he only began to assert in his late twenties, will perhaps restore some life to what one of its previous occupants called "this most beautiful of English country houses." As a junior court gathers around the prince, Chevening may play host to glittering house parties of a scale to recall the halcyon days when the future King Edward VII was Prince of Wales. Until then it seems likely to remain the object of a magnificent, uniquely royal neglect.

On parade: the Colonel-in-Chief of the Welsh Guards

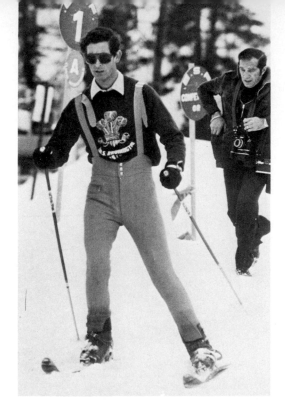

Royal Action Man:
skiing at Klosters

Polo at Windsor . . .

Wind-surfing off Cowes . . .

Fly-fishing at Balmoral . . .   and commando-training with the Royal Marines

Off duty: between chukkas at Windsor

On duty: representing the Queen at the independence celebrations of Papua New Guinea

Stern words from his polo coach, Sinclair Hill, one of the few men allowed to swear at the Prince of Wales

After a fall: royal dignity abandoned

"I'm happiest with my family": with Princess Anne on her twentieth birthday . . .

and his close friend Lord Mountbatten, alias great-uncle Dickie

The royal family at the Montreal Olympics in 1976— the only time they have ever been gathered together abroad

1977: at Elizabeth II's Silver
Jubilee thanksgiving service
in Westminster Abbey

1978: a thirtieth-birthday
portrait at Balmoral

Working prince: a day at Number Ten

The hazards of being a prince:
Pounced upon in the Indian Ocean in 1979

4

God Bless the Prince of Wales

Costly thy habit as thy purse can buy,
But not express'd in fancy; rich, not gaudy;
For the apparel oft proclaims the man . . .
SHAKESPEARE, HAMLET I.iii

THE PRINCE OF WALES spent Saturday, October 3, 1970, out shooting near Paris with the Soames family: Sir Christopher (now Lord) Soames, then the British ambassador to France, and his son Nicholas. Their route home at the end of the day took them through the Bois de Boulogne, a reminder to the prince of the nearby presence of his exiled great-uncle, the Duke of Windsor—King Edward VIII for 325 days in 1936, and Charles's immediate predecessor as Prince of Wales.

On the spur of the moment, the prince asked Sir Christopher to arrange a visit. There was some hemming and hawing. The duke and duchess were still on uncertain terms with the royal family; besides, it was Saturday evening, the switchboard staff were off duty, and people who have been out shooting all day want nothing so much as to relax in a long hot bath. But Prince Charles was insistent. The telephone wires buzzed for a while and later that evening, after dinner, the three were on their way to the rue du Champ d'Entrainment.

When they arrived, by one account, the Windsors' drawing room was "full of appallingly vulgar Americans." But Prince Charles and the duke retreated into a corner together and talked alone for more than an hour. Their respective investitures at Caernarvon—the prince's fresh in his mind from the year before, the duke's nearly sixty years earlier—were one unique mutual

35

ordeal for lighthearted reminiscence. But there were many more, as is to be expected when two of only twenty-one Princes of Wales in more than 650 years get together. Afterwards, the duke politely called the prince "intelligent and perceptive." They parted rather emotionally. Prince Charles was to see his great-uncle only once more: twenty months later, a week before his death.

Their meeting on foreign soil that night, a genteel courtesy from one heir apparent to a fallen predecessor, was in its way a moment of history. The duke, even in absentia, even in death, has played a larger part than most in the unfolding progress of the next Prince of Wales. Britain is more than forty years older, but through Prince Charles's life echoes still the memorable farewell of King Edward VIII to his people in 1936: "I have found it impossible to carry the heavy burden of duty, and to discharge my duties as king as I would wish to do, without the help and support of the woman I love."

Constitutional niceties take little note of social change. The abdication was the British monarchy's greatest trauma this century, and Queen Elizabeth II believes history will remember her for having rebuilt the institution on the foundations laid by her father. December 1936 was a moment of near collapse, when a poll showed that half the British people wanted to seize the chance to do away with the monarchy. The phoenix was not proved risen, to the Queen's mind, until the euphoria of her Silver Jubilee celebrations in 1977 took her completely by surprise. Now more than ever, Prince Edward is held up to the next Prince of Wales as an example of how *nct* to become a king. Prince Charles is a keen student of the history of his office, and equally keen to carve himself a conspicuous niche in the annals of the English Princes of Wales. He knows full well that he will probably pass many more years as prince than as king. With this in mind, many of the precepts he has adopted for his own behavior, both private and public, are designed to eradicate the mixed memories left behind them by his two most colorful immediate predecessors as Prince of Wales, the future Kings Edward VII and Edward VIII. When the time comes for a soap opera on the young life of the present Prince of Wales, the TV companies will be stretched to come up with anything approaching their recent *embarras de richesse*.

Two nights before his abdication, King Edward VIII was in his best form at a dinner party at Fort Belvedere, his Windsor retreat. In the words of his brother the Duke of York, about to become King George VI *malgré lui*, he was "telling the PM [Baldwin] things I am sure he had never heard before about unemployed centers, etc. (referring to his visit in S. Wales)." The duke whispered to his neighbor at table, Walter Monckton, "And this is the man we are going to lose. . . ."

But Edward as king never quite understood why, on a matter like unemployment, there was nothing he could do to force a government's hand; it would have been as unconstitutional as it had been dishonest of him, a few months before, to promise unemployed Welshmen that "something must be done." To his dying day he never really grasped why his choice of bride made abdication inevitable, why the nation and Commonwealth would not accept a divorcée as its queen, consort to the Defender of the Faith. His memoirs, written in 1951, distort the historical facts of the abdication, and later in life he grew ever more convinced that it had all been a sinister plot against him by Baldwin and others. In view of the Duke of Windsor's subsequent flirtation with Hitler and the Nazis, it is perhaps as well he did not remain a king with what he thought should be irresistible political influence.

From Edward's reaction to his investiture as Prince of Wales at the age of sixteen—"I recoiled from anything that tended to set me up as a person requiring homage"—we can see the makings of an unorthodox, probably disastrous king. The monarch of all people should find some point in pomp and circumstance. But an excellent prince, as history has often shown, does not necessarily make an excellent king. No epitaph for King Edward VIII is more fitting than that of Tacitus for the Emperor Galba: *capax imperii nisi imperasset* ("worthy to rule, had he not ruled"). It is as a prince we should remember him.

From the early history of Edward's grandfather, King Edward VII, there are contrasting morals to be drawn. Prince Charles and his parents have always regarded Queen Victoria's son, Prince of Wales for fifty-nine years, as an object lesson in all that can go wrong for the heir of a monarch who comes to the throne young. Charles may well have to wait in the wings, the sovereign's understudy, quite as long as did Prince Albert Edward

("Bertie" to his family). His brief reign turned out to be both popular and successful; but his long years as an idle prince led him into excess and debauchery of a kind that would be anathema to the cozy, domesticated monarchy we have today. Bertie involved the monarchy in gambling and divorce scandals, dragging it down in the popular esteem, making it the butt of some of the cruelest cartooning since Rowlandson and George III. Happily for Prince Charles, the reasons are easy to discern.

Queen Victoria denied her son access to state papers; she refused him any positive role in affairs of state, and even discouraged him from meeting politicians. When the prime minister suggested the prince see cabinet minutes, the queen allowed only—and that with reluctance—that he be informed of cabinet decisions. Gladstone spent two years trying to persuade her to make her son viceroy of Ireland; it would have given him valuable experience of a quasi-monarchical role, and a royal presence in Dublin might have eased the increasingly turbulent Irish question. Victoria would have none of it. Elizabeth II, by contrast, has encouraged her son from his earliest adulthood to take an active part in the constitutional process; he reads cabinet papers, and since becoming a privy councillor in 1977 meets politicians of all hues on an intimate and confidential footing.

In time, when he is married, he may well spend a period as governor-general of a Commonwealth country, Australia being the most likely choice because of his fondness for the place. The idea was mooted several times in the 1970s—ironically enough by Gough Whitlam, the Socialist prime minister who did away with the National Anthem. But the dismissal in 1975 of the Whitlam government by the then governor-general, Sir John Kerr, brought the office too close to politics for princely comfort. By the early or mid-1980s, when there is a Princess of Wales to act as a governor-general's consort, these memories will have healed.

In such ways as this, Prince Charles is constantly exploring new routes toward a more positive role. It is not an easy task, fenced in as he is by the strict political taboo on the conduct of a representative monarchy. As the Duke of Windsor himself put it: "Some princes bend their characters more easily than others to this rule. It was to be my fate to find it at times irksome because I had been endowed with a questioning, independent mind;

and I found it difficult ever to take anything for granted, even my own position."

Prince Charles is endowed with a questioning if not quite so independent mind. He no longer finds it difficult to take his position for granted. He is happier than Prince Edward to adapt his own royal conduct to the style established by his parents, just now and then treading gingerly into pastures new.

Royal links with industry, for instance, are traditional. The Queen's Awards for Exports are only the most familiar of a number of devices of moral encouragement; Prince Philip's "Get your fingers out" speeches are another, though less familiar in his mellower middle age. In his early thirties, Prince Charles has begun to extend those links into the virgin royal territory of the trade unions, as befits the times; in 1979 he attended the annual conference of the Iron and Steel Trades Federation (carefully selected as one of the few unions that had then submitted to the Callaghan government's pay policy). Earlier that year, he too had been telling both sides of British industry to get their fingers out.

By then he had also used—of the pollution of the Welsh countryside—those famous words of the last Prince of Wales: "Something must be done." They are generally remembered as the words of a concerned and dynamic Prince of Wales: in fact, when he said them to a group of unemployed Welshmen, during a tour of the depressed mining valleys of South Wales in 1936, Prince Edward had lately become king and already knew of the likelihood of his abdication. They were dangerous words for Prince Charles to revive, standing as they now do for a memorable moment of betrayal. Already he was trying to right the wrongs of recent history, to show that this was one path down which he would never go.

There are many possible views of the abdication: a dereliction of sacred duty, an easy way out of an unfortunate predicament, visible proof that the monarchy's creaking irrationality is finally outmoded. Wherever the truth lies, there can never be any doubt that Edward was a superb Prince of Wales. Glamorous, energetic, debonair, with a liberal dash of raciness and more than his fair share of charm, he genuinely did care about the less privileged of his father's subjects, and was blessed with a flair for showing that he cared. His impatience with the trappings of royalty, his distaste for protocol and ceremonial, only added—and still do—to his appeal. In 1913, called home from Oxford for a state visit by the king and queen of Denmark, he wrote in his diary: "We stood about in the picture gallery till 11:15 talking to the guests. . . . What rot & a waste of time, money & energy all these State visits are!! This is my only remark on all this unreal show & ceremony!!"

Compare Prince Charles, more than fifty years later: "I would change nothing. Besides ceremony being a major and important aspect of monarchy, something that has grown and developed over a thousand years in Britain, I happen to enjoy it enormously." He is a very different character from his eccentric great-uncle—more cautious, more staid, without a trace of the rebel in him—largely because of his much happier family background. Yet he is highly conscious of Prince Edward's young reputation. In 1978, when the TV series about Edward and Mrs. Simpson provoked arguments around Buckingham Palace, as around every home in Britain, it was the Prince of Wales who sprang to his predecessor's defense. The series concentrated on the events leading up to the abdication, spending little time on the successes of Edward's earlier years; Prince Charles thought this unfair and slapped down those of his household who were critical of television's recalcitrant prince. At the same time, however, he would in no way condone Edward's decision to put his private, personal happiness before his public, inherited obligations. It is thus a confused, in many ways paradoxical example he has to follow.

While emulating Edward's achievements as an industrious, concerned, vivacious Prince of Wales, as much in his private pursuits as his public duties, Prince Charles has gone to some pains to reject the other more colorful traits for which Edward is fondly remembered. In such matters as dress, smoking, drinking, late-night cavorting in clubs and casinos—those personal habits that are very much the man—he has studiously fashioned himself into a complete opposite. Style, although these days an overworked word, precisely pinpoints the quality of Prince Edward that Prince Charles so conspicuously lacks. He is aware of it, and not in the least abashed: "If people think me square," he has said, deliberately using a dated epithet, "then I am happy to be thought square." And again: "I was asked in Australia whether I concentrated on improving my image—as if I were some kind of washing powder, presumably with special blue whitener. I daresay that I could improve it by growing my hair to a more fashionable length, being seen at the Playboy Club at frequent intervals, and squeezing myself into excruciatingly tight clothes . . . but I intend to go on being myself to the best of my ability."

One hundred and twenty years ago, in 1858, the Prince Consort drew up a confidential memorandum on princely behavior, designed to equip the hapless Bertie, Prince of Wales, for the position of "the first gentleman of the country." All requisite qualities, he argued, would stem from "outward deportment and manners," which he discussed under three heads (summarized by Sir Philip Magnus in his biography of Edward VII):

1. *Appearance, Deportment and Dress*
   . . . A gentleman does not indulge in careless self-indulgent lounging ways, such as lolling in armchairs or on sofas, slouching in his gait, or placing himself in unbecoming attitudes with his hands in his pockets. . . . He will borrow nothing from the fashion of the groom or the gamekeeper, and whilst avoiding the frivolity and foolish vanity of dandyism, will take care that his clothes are of the best quality. . . .

2. *Manners and Conduct towards Others*
   The manners and conduct of a gentleman towards others are founded on the basis of kindness, consideration and the absence of selfishness. [A prince must always be scrupulously courteous, attentive, punctual, and on guard against the temptation to use harsh, rude, or bantering expressions.] Anything approaching a *practical joke* [would be impermissible].

3. *The Power to Acquit Himself Creditably in Conversation, or Whatever May Be the Occupation of Society*
   [Gossip, cards, billiards were to be regarded as useless; but] some knowledge of those studies and pursuits which adorn society and make it interesting [was essential. The Prince of Wales must be induced] by persevering example . . . to devote some of his leisure time to music, to the fine arts, either drawing or looking over drawings, engravings etc.,

to hearing poetry, amusing books or good plays read aloud; in short to anything that whilst it amuses may gently exercise the mind. . . .

The memo did not produce the desired effect. So disappointed was Prince Albert with his son's progress that he wrote to his daughter, Bertie's sister: "Bertie has remarkable social talent . . . but usually his intellect is of no more use than a pistol packed in the bottom of a trunk if one were attacked in the robber-infested Apennines." The Prince Consort would scarcely have derived more satisfaction from the subsequent career of his great-grandson, King Edward VIII. In his great-great-great-grandson, Prince Charles, Albert has at last found a convert—apart, perhaps, from the practical jokes.

One hundred and twenty years too late? Prince Charles does not think so: "I daresay many of my views and beliefs would be considered old-fashioned and out of date, but that doesn't worry me. . . . Fashion, by its very definition, is transitory; human nature being what it is, what was old-fashioned at length becomes in fashion and thus the whole process continues."

Recent Princes of Wales have tended to be leaders of sartorial fashion. Edward VII, patron of the dinner jacket and the gray topper, champion of side-creased trousers and the Tyrolean hat, received a continuous flow of advice on the subject from his parents. Prince Albert despaired of his son: "Unfortunately," he told the Princess Royal, "he takes no interest in anything but clothes, and again clothes. Even when out shooting he is more occupied with his trousers than with the game." Queen Victoria took a more fundamental view: "Dress is a trifling matter," she wrote to her son, "but it gives also the outward sign from which people in general can and often do judge upon the *inward* state of mind and feeling of a person. . . . We do not wish to control your tastes and fancies, which, on the contrary, we wish you to indulge and develop, but we do *expect* that you will never wear anything *extravagant* or *slang*, not because we don't like it, but because it would prove a want of self-respect and be an offense against decency, leading—as it has often done in others—to an indifference to what is morally wrong." The queen must have spun in her grave forty-six years later, in the second year of

Edward VII's reign, when the king arrived at Marienbad station wearing a green cap, with a pink tie and white gloves, knee breeches, gray slippers, and a brown overcoat with loud checks. "Loyal subjects must sincerely hope," commented *Tailor and Cutter*, guardian to this day of British sartorial standards, "that His Majesty has not brought this outfit home."

The Duke of Windsor, himself an international leader of fashion, quoted his great-grandmother's homily with approval. He had often wondered, he said, whether to "certain sections of the press, I was not more of a glorified clothes-peg than the heir apparent." The sentiment, like many in his writings, is retrospective and self-justifying. At Oxford Prince Edward popularized plus fours and trouser cuffs. ("Is it raining in *here?*" exclaimed George V on seeing his son and heir wearing turned-up trousers around the palace; thereafter, the duke recalled, "I always kept a pair of old trousers without turn-ups, which I could slip on before I went to see him.") Over dinner one night at La Croe, near Antibes, Prince Edward happened to wear a tartan suit of the kind his father had been wearing in private for fifty years. "One of our guests mentioned the fact to a friend in the men's fashion trade, who immediately cabled the news to America. Within a few months tartan had become a popular material for every sort of masculine garment, from dinner jackets and cummerbunds to swimming trunks and beach shorts. Later the craze even extended to luggage." Later in life the Windsors' secretary, Diana Hood, recalled him in the garden of their home in the south of France one day wearing crimson trousers with a blue shirt and red-and-white shoes, and the next day, bright blue trousers with a canary yellow shirt and blue shoes.

Partly because of recent history's cautionary tales, Prince Charles's sartorial tastes are almost defiantly conservative. In matters of haute couture he is the despair of *Tailor and Cutter*, one of the less likely symbols of the continuity of the British royal family. A century ago Bertie, Prince of Wales, earned the magazine's scorn for helping to popularize the bowler hat—"an abomination in head gear"—while, in the words of his grandson, remaining "a good friend to the tailors of Savile Row, consolidating the position of London as the sartorial shrine for men. . . . When he visited Marienbad, tailors from Paris, Vienna and all parts of the Continent used to gather and follow him around, surreptitiously photographing him and jotting down notes on his clothes."

In our own times *Tailor and Cutter* at first tried to encourage Prince Charles to become a leader of fashion, by voting him one of the world's top ten best-dressed men at the age of four; twenty years later, having received little return on its investment (a Prince of Wales can be very good for business), it denounced his "cult of studied shabbiness." Soon after, invited to be guest of honor at the annual dinner of the Master Tailors' Benevolent Association, the prince rose to the insult by arriving in an old tweed jacket somewhat the worse for wear. After whisking it off to reveal impeccable evening dress, he treated them to one of his better after-dinner jokes: "I am often asked whether it is because of some generic trait that I stand with my hands behind my back, like my father. The answer is that we both have the same tailor. He makes our sleeves so tight that we can't get our hands in front."

Prince Charles looks immensely dashing in any of his numerous uniforms—hats, especially military-style peaked caps, seem to add strength to the shape of his face—but his civilian suits are generally of a style favored by an older generation. His polished toe caps are those of a man steeped beyond his years in service traditions (and lucky enough to have an industrious valet). His refusal even to reflect fashions, let alone to lead them, betokens a man with higher-minded priorities. Dress, as Queen Victoria said, may be a "trifling matter," but it remains an index of character and personality. In Prince Charles's case, it is an outward sign, perhaps deliberate, of his adherence to the values of his parents' generation rather than his own. And it is a conscious rejection of the dilettantism of recent Princes of Wales.

If one cannot require the present prince to be a sartorial trend-setter, no more can one wish alcohol or nicotine poisoning upon him. But he belongs to a generation that looks for chinks in its contemporaries' armor, in his case for some loophole in an otherwise flawless public regime of mental, physical, and spiritual fitness. The Duke of Windsor, himself a lover of manly pursuits, made a pleasant confession about his eighteenth birthday; the fact that he was now eligible to ascend the throne in his own right, without need of a regency, meant rather less to him than "a tangible and satisfying privilege this birthday brought me. Now that I was eighteen my father lifted the ban on my smoking."

A year later he was reassuring his father, in a letter from Oxford, that "I never smoke more than ten cigarettes a day, generally not as many, and then only in the evenings after dinner, with never more than two before tea." If the prince appears to be protesting too much, he subsequently confessed so himself. In another undergraduate letter to his father, he had described the antics of a university dining society, the Bullingdon Club: "Most of them got rather excited and I came back early. There was a good deal of champagne drunk and that accounted for it. It is interesting for me to see the various forms of amusement that undergraduates indulge in." Nearly fifty years later, in his memoirs, he owned up: "I now recall with some shame that the real reason for my early departure . . . was that I was no longer so steady on my feet or so clear in my speech as I was when we sat down to dinner. I hasten to add that this was an unusual occurrence, prompted only by the unwritten law of the Bullingdon Club that the new members should be forced to drink themselves into oblivion."

When offered a cigar by President Tito during his visit to Yugoslavia in 1978, Prince Charles joked that he gave up smoking at school. He is a militant nonsmoker and will drink only at the end of a trying day or when politeness requires it of him. The boldest escapade on record from his university days is a midnight bicycle chase around a courtyard with some rambunctious friends, which earned a complaint about the noise from his director of studies. All his life he has aspired to sober standards of conduct, believing that his office requires him to set a moral example. As he has grown older and more self-conscious about his role, he has not hesitated to inflict these standards on others. In November 1975, at the silver jubilee dinner of the Lord's Taverners, the prince found himself being asked to propose the loyal toast to the Queen halfway through the meal, so that the 1,350 hard-pressed sports and show business guests could begin smoking.

"Do we have to do this now?" he asked the toastmaster,

Bryn Williams, as Williams placed the microphone in front of him. "Why do we have the loyal toast so early? Is this a modern trend?"

"I'm afraid so, sir."

"Well, I don't agree with it. We will have the loyal toast at the right time—after the sweet."

The prince has proved himself a great defender of royal dignity. In July 1973, while captaining the Nassau polo team against Freeport, his game was not improved by the remarks of the commentator over Nassau Racecourse's loudspeaking system. "Now who's he?" labored Tom Oxley, something of a local wag, when the prince got the ball. "He's the son of . . . let's see . . . oh, yes, it's Queen Elizabeth, isn't it? And now who's the other one? Why, isn't it old Philip, Duke of Edinburgh?" Oxley had just told the crowd that his own father and brother had recently played on an American polo team which had beaten an English side including Prince Philip. Charles rode over to the commentary box and strode up its steps. His angry reprimand was broadcast over the loudspeakers to the appalled crowd. "Less of the wise-cracks and stick to the commentary. You're turning the match into a barn dance." The club president, who promptly removed Oxley from the microphone, then recalled that when the same man was commentating at an earlier polo prize-giving, he had referred to the Prince as "Queen Elizabeth's little boy." Charles, it seemed, had remembered the voice.

His sense of humor does not extend to lèse-majesté. In private he can be delightfully witty, with his quick repartée and his gift for mimicry, but he will not gladly suffer any undue familiarity he may inspire. Very rarely can he relax out of his role. He has imposed on himself the sternest obligation of his office.

His public reputation, for a curious combination of bravado and drollery, misses this high seriousness. Yet it is one of the prince's strongest characteristics. If he brings humor to his job, he also brings an inheritance of dour regal solemnity. The Prince of Wales wishes to improve on the records of his immediate predecessors, to avoid their vagaries, their half-truths, their sur-renders to the temptations so vividly conjured up by Walter Bagehot: "All the world and the glory of it, whatever is most attractive, whatever is most seductive, had always been offered to the Prince of Wales of the day, and always will be. It is not rational to expect the best virtue where temptation is applied in the most trying form at the frailest time of human life."

Not rational perhaps, but nor is the institution of monarchy. By taking a different path from his predecessors, this Prince of Wales aims to give purpose to his irrational birthright, and by so doing to reassure himself and his future subjects that the monarchy still works, that a hereditary system can maintain a stable and responsible influence over the affairs of a modern nation. The accident of his birth has indeed laid all the world and its glory at his feet; he is heir to a thousand years of inherited privilege. In return it demands duties which are arduous, monotonous, unavoidable, and often hard to endow with any practical significance.

To take them as seriously as he does is simply to have accepted his fate. The future Edward VII was a Prince of Wales whose enforced idleness left him freer to indulge the perks of his position. The future Edward VIII was a prince who found the price too high; after a gallant attempt, he set a greater value on his personal happiness. Both were by nature more wayward characters, but both were reacting violently to more austere childhoods. Each was taught from birth to accept his role with the utmost gravity and to conduct himself accordingly.

Prince Charles, by contrast, was eased into the strangeness of royalty. His parents wanted him to enjoy his childhood *despite* his position. It did not always prove possible. But his early life was more carefree, more laissez-faire than that of most future kings. He thus grew into his role with equanimity. His solemn awareness of its responsibilities developed late, and so more deeply. All the clues to this curiously convoluted character, with his public braggadocio and his private high seriousness, his sense of self-parody and his insistence on due deference, lie in the tortured decisions made on his behalf throughout his upbringing.

Part II: *Childhood*

5

1948-52 : Prince Charles of Edinburgh

*"From his childhood this boy will be
surrounded by sycophants and flatterers by the score, and will be
taught to believe himself as of a
superior creation."*

KEIR HARDIE ON THE BIRTH OF
THE FUTURE KING EDWARD VIII

THE RUMORS BEGAN, not for the first or the last time, in
Paris. When Princess Elizabeth, elder daughter of King George
VI and heir to the British throne, paid a weekend visit there in
May 1948, those who saw her told each other she did not seem
herself. At divine service in the British Church she looked tired
and listless, rarely raising her eyes from the ground. At a British
Embassy reception in her honor that evening, she had met only
half the guests when her husband led her from the room to rest.
It was less than six months since she had married Lieutenant
Philip Mountbatten, the former Prince Philip of Greece, but that
was time enough. Paris decided that twenty-two-year-old Princess
Elizabeth was pregnant.

Even in 1948, pregnancy was a word that Buckingham Palace officialdom could not quite bring itself to utter in public. On
June 4, the eve of Derby Day, the formal statement simply announced that "Her Royal Highness the Princess Elizabeth,
Duchess of Edinburgh, will undertake no public engagements
after the end of June." The public, left to draw its own conclusions, remembered that the same wording had last been used
eighteen years earlier of the Duchess of York, four months before

she gave birth to Princess Margaret Rose. No announcement at all had been made during the duchess' previous pregnancy; the first the world had known of Princess Elizabeth Alexandra Mary, whom they then little thought would one day be queen of England, was when she entered it by cesarean section on April 21, 1926.

Official confirmation that an heir to the throne was on the way came later that summer in unexpected form. The king, it was announced, had decided to abolish the ancient custom whereby the Home Secretary of the day attended and verified each royal birth. "The attendance of a minister of the crown at a birth in the royal family," said the official statement, "is not a statutory requirement or a constitutional necessity. It is merely the survival of an archaic custom, and the king feels that it is unnecessary to continue further a practice for which there is no legal requirement." In 1948 Mr. James Chuter Ede was thus spared the embarrassment of one of his predecessors, Sir James Graham, who in 1841 had waited uneasily at one end of a huge palace bedchamber while at the other Queen Victoria gave birth to the future King Edward VII. After satisfying himself that all was in order, he approached the bed and intoned: "I congratulate your Majesty most warmly. A very fine boy, if I may say so." From behind the heavy curtains of the four-poster, an indignant voice replied: "A very fine *prince*, Sir James."

The origin of this curiously British tradition is disputed, but it seems to have been firmly established since 1688, when James II's wife, Mary of Modena, was accused of offering a changeling as heir to the throne (known to popular history as "the warming-pan baby") despite the presence of the Lord Chancellor and all available privy councillors at the foot of her bed. In more recent times, it had led rather to embarrassment and farce. In 1926 William Joynson-Hicks had waited uneasily downstairs at 17 Bruton Street, Mayfair, during the operation that delivered Princess Elizabeth; four years later J. R. Clynes, summoned early to Glamis because of a false alarm, spent two weeks kicking his heels at Airlie Castle and was finally in mid-dash between the two when Princess Margaret was born.

Princess Elizabeth's baby was expected in mid-November. The princess and her husband were still living at Buckingham Palace while Clarence House was made ready for them, but much of their time was spent at Windlesham Moor, their then country home near Sunningdale, in Berkshire. There were those who suggested this might be the most peaceful place for her accouchement, but the princess herself decided she would like to have her baby at the palace. On the first floor, overlooking the Mall, a suite centers around the Buhl Room, which Queen Mary had converted into a makeshift palace surgery. Within a few months, this was to be the scene of the first of King George VI's arterial operations, which saved him the loss of his right leg. During the latter stages of his daughter's pregnancy, the king was for the first time becoming aware of the seriousness of his illness. Arteriosclerosis, with a grave danger of gangrene, was diagnosed in the Buhl Room only two days before Prince Charles's birth. But the king gave strict instructions that the princess was to be told nothing. For the present, therefore, it was for a happy event that the room was converted into a lavishly equipped surgical theater.

Despite the distractions of his illness, King George soon found himself confronted by another constitutional problem. Under the edict issued by his father, George V, in 1917, in response to wartime criticisms of the royal family's Germanic titles and connections, the title of prince of the newly established House of Windsor was restricted to the offspring of the sovereign and his sons. As the royals divested themselves of their German titles, and the House of Saxe-Coburg-Gotha surrendered its name to that of the pleasant Berkshire town where it spent its weekends, no thought was given to the offspring of the sovereign's daughters. Thus it was, less than a week before Elizabeth's baby was due, that the king's private secretary, Sir Alan Lascelles, warned him that his first grandchild would not be entitled to the rank of prince or princess.

On becoming engaged to the king's daughter in February 1947, Prince Philip had divested himself of all his Greek and Danish titles, including the rank of prince, and adopted his mother's name of Battenberg, which had been anglicized to Mountbatten. In exchange, this member of the Danish royal house of Schleswig-Holstein-Sonderburg-Glucksburg had received from his future father-in-law the style of Royal Highness, the Order of the Garter, and elevation to the peerage as Baron Greenwich, Earl of Merioneth, and Duke of Edinburgh. "It is a great deal to give a man all at once," the king had written to his mother, Queen Mary, "but I know Philip understands his new responsibilities on his marriage to Lilibet."

According to strict rule, Philip was not reaccorded the title of prince, although George VI always referred to him as Prince Philip and went to his grave believing the rank was automatically conferred with the style of Royal Highness. (In fact, Philip was not formally granted the style and titular dignity of Prince of the United Kingdom until February 22, 1957, when his wife bestowed it on him in recognition of his ten years of service to the country). Thus his and Princess Elizabeth's child, which showed signs of arriving any day, would have to struggle with the help of the Garter King of Arms for a name befitting the king's first grandchild. If it were a boy, the baby would be known simply as Charles Mountbatten, salvaging his infant dignity with the courtesy use of his father's second title: Charles Mountbatten, Earl of Merioneth. If the baby were a girl, she would be known as Lady Anne Mountbatten. And these were the very names with which the genealogists juggled, for Princess Elizabeth and her husband had already decided upon them, although they were to remain a closely guarded secret for another month.

On November 9, less than a week before the child's birth, the king issued letters patent under the Great Seal ordaining that any children born to the Duke and Duchess of Edinburgh would have the title of prince or princess and the style of Royal Highness. In the process, he put paid to another fevered argument among historians and constitutionalists: that on his death, Princess Margaret would have as strong a claim to the throne as her elder sister. The view was based on the legislature's discriminatory failure to establish any rule of primogeniture among females; strictly interpreted, the law as it stood found all daughters of equal rank in the division of inheritance. By placing Princess Elizabeth on the same footing as the sovereign's eldest son, the king had secured her position as his heir and staunched the doubts of worried genealogists the nation over.

Against this heady background, Princess Elizabeth was enjoying a pregnancy so trouble-free she was able to continue an active and varied social life. In October she attended the wedding of her lady-in-waiting, Lady Margaret Egerton, to her private secretary, John Colville, and felt sufficiently well to go to the crowded reception at Londonderry House afterward. Despite her doctor's predictions, she rather hoped the baby might not arrive until her first wedding anniversary on November 20. On November 12, less than forty-eight hours before that hope was to be proved vain, she was still going out in the evenings, on this occasion to dinner with close friends, the Brabournes, in Chester Street. The royal midwife, Miss Helen Rowe, was already installed in the new Buckingham Palace nursery; but it was only when Sir William Gilliatt, president of the Royal College of Obstetricians and Gynaecologists, spent the following night at the palace that the British public knew the waiting was nearly over. Still rationed, still hard pressed, still surrounded by the physical and spiritual aftermath of war, they had followed their princess's pregnancy with an anticipation unusual even for royal births. The doctor's presence was enough to draw a crowd of fifteen hundred to the palace gates that night.

November 14 was a Sunday, and by early morning the throng outside Buckingham Palace had grown to several thousands. The lack of news all day did little to dampen their ardor, despite the dull, chill weather. In the later afternoon, expectations were revived by the sudden arrival of a posse of cars containing medical men; assisting Gilliatt and Sir John Weir, the king's physician, were Mr. (now Sir) John Peel, the obstetrician, and Dr. Vernon Hall, the anesthetist. But there was still no word. Inside the palace, the expectant father grew characteristically impatient. He took off with his private secretary and close friend, Lieutenant Commander Michael Parker, for a game of squash in the palace court. After a swim in the adjacent pool, they were still playing at a quarter past nine when the king's private secretary, Sir Alan Lascelles, ran in with the news that a prince had been born.

Philip took the stairs three at a time. He rushed into the Buhl Room to find his wife still under anesthetic; it had been a forceps delivery. After speaking with the doctors, he was taken to the nursery to behold his infant son, and to share a handshake and an embrace with his parents-in-law. When the princess awoke, her husband was at her side with a bouquet of carnations and roses. In an outer room, he had already been opening bottles of champagne for the medical and household staff. By this time the palace post office was hard at work: prepared telegrams, the word "prince" written into the blank space, were being dispatched around the world to kings and presidents, governors and ambassadors—the first, by another "archaic custom," carried by the rather less archaic means of motorcycle dispatch rider to the Lord Mayor of London.

Mr. Chuter Ede, though not at the bedside, was waiting by a telephone, for he it was who had to sign the notices to be posted outside the Home Office in Whitehall and the Mansion House in the City. The wording was the same as in that secured to the palace railings by the Colville cousins: Sir John ("Jock"), private secretary to Princess Elizabeth (and previously to Neville Chamberlain, Winston Chuchill, and Clement Attlee at 10 Downing Street), and Commander Richard, press secretary to the king (and later to Elizabeth II). Richard Colville had proudly written the announcement in his own hand: "Her Royal Highness the Princess Elizabeth, Duchess of Edinburgh, was safely delivered of a Prince at 9:14 o'clock this evening. Her Royal Highness and the infant Prince are both doing well."

By that time, however, the news had already drawn Londoners from their homes, their restaurants, and their nightclubs to swell the crowd outside Buckingham Palace. John Snagge, the BBC Home Service announcer, had in his excitement offered the nation's "royal" rather than "loyal" greetings; the version now in the BBC archives was rerecorded for posterity two days later. It had been nicely timed, however, to launch closing-time celebrations in pubs all round the country, to start guns firing and bonfires blazing, to turn the fountains in Trafalgar Square blue for a boy (as they stayed for a week), and to draw four thousand telegrams of congratulations to the palace post office that night.

The first the growing crowd outside the palace knew of it was very soon after the event itself, when those who had climbed to the top of the Victoria Memorial saw a blue-liveried palace footman emerge to whisper into the ear of a policeman—one of the many trying to protect the palace guard, then still on the pavement outside the railings, from being trampled underfoot. "It's a boy!" bawled this privileged officer, and the cry was taken up around the Mall, growing to a roar which lasted several hours, punctuated by occasional chants of "For he's a jolly good fellow," "We want Philip," and, from the prescient Welsh contingent, "Land of Our Fathers."

Every car going in and out was fiercely scrutinized, none

more so than that of the king's mother, eighty-one-year-old Queen Mary, who arrived at 11 P.M. to inspect her first great-grandchild. Despite the aftereffects of a bout of influenza, the old lady stayed until after midnight, by which time the crowd outside had grown larger and noisier than ever. Up on the first floor of the palace, on the Mall frontage, was a young woman exhilarated by the birth of her first child and the enthusiasm of her family, but in need of sleep. The well-wishers outside were keeping her awake. At the princess's behest, therefore, Michael Parker and a colleague walked across the forecourt to try and quiet them. As they struggled to make themselves heard, one recipient of the princess's message was none other than David Niven, already at that time a well-known and eminently recognizable figure. "I was pinned against the railings and, being unable to move, I was the recipient of the message hissed in my ear by the man from the palace. I had my coat collar turned up and was huddled inside the garment, hoping not to be recognized and asked for autographs on that particular location. However, I turned round and did my best to shush those nearest to me, which did little good as everyone was far too excited and happy." Police loudspeaker vans had to be called in to disperse the crowd. Thus did the princess fall asleep to the strangest of lullabies.

The seven-pound six-ounce infant so warmly welcomed was the first royal child to be born at Buckingham Palace for sixty-two years (the last being the daughter of Arthur, Duke of Connaught, and so niece of Edward VII), and the first royal baby in direct succession to the throne since the birth of the future Edward VIII in 1894. Princess Elizabeth was only the fourth heiress presumptive in British history to have given birth to a male child. In 1133 Matilda, daughter of King Henry I, bore the future King Henry II; in 1566 Mary Queen of Scots (the undeclared heiress presumptive) bore Prince James; and Queen Anne had a number of children, none of whom survived childhood.

The prince, as yet unnamed, could be declared fifth in descent from Queen Victoria, thirty-second from William the Conqueror, and thirty-ninth from Alfred the Great. He was described as the most Scottish prince since Charles I and the most English since Henry VIII; eleventh in descent from the Electress Sophia, through whom the present royal family's claim to the throne is established under the Act of Settlement, he could claim descent from the Yorkist kings through William I and the Lancastrian kings through John of Gaunt. Thirteenth in descent from James I and VI, his Scottish ancestry included Robert the Bruce and St. Mary of Scotland through James's mother, Mary Queen of Scots; through Henry Tudor, his Welsh ancestry could be traced back to Llewelyn-ap-Gruffydd, the last native prince of all Wales. Through his maternal grandmother, he was the first potential Prince of Wales ever to be a direct descendant of Owen Glendower; through his father, he had the blood of Harold, last of the Anglo-Saxon kings. Genealogists stretched the line almost to the crack of doom: on one side Charlemagne, Cadwallader, and Musa ibn Naseir, an Arab sheikh born in Mecca in 660, on the other plainer names such as John Smith, Frances Webb, Mary Browne, and Peter Checke, a sixteenth-century Essex innkeeper. (See Appendix C.)

Next morning, the world acknowledged the news. The British fleet, wherever it happened to be, was dressed overall; in Australia, the Melbourne town hall carillon somewhat prematurely played "God Bless the Prince of Wales"; forty-one-gun salutes and peals of bells awoke New Zealand and South Africa; in Kenya the news was broadcast in seven native languages; from Key West, Florida, President Truman sent a telegram of congratulations; and from South Africa, Premier Jan Smuts cabled: "We pray that the prince will be a blessing to our Commonwealth and to the world." In republican New York the *Herald Tribune* declared that freedom in Britain had "grown and been safeguarded under the ancient institution of the monarchy." In Athens, where it was not forgotten that Philip had been a prince of Greece, hundreds of his compatriots carried their greetings to the British Embassy; on the island of Tenos, where she was engaged in charitable work, Philip's mother, Princess Andrew of Greece, was roused from her sleep by the arrival of her telegram.

In London there was special pageantry as the King's Troop, Royal Horse Artillery, rode in full dress from St. John's Wood to Hyde Park, drawing six guns to fire a forty-one-salvo salute. The bells of St. Paul's pealed almost without interruption from 9 A.M.; those of Westminster Abbey took three hours to complete a peal of five thousand changes, then did it all again. On the

Thames, barges and small craft were gaily festooned with flags and bunting; at the top of the Mall, cars and taxis passing the palace kept up a constant hooting of horns; at Plymouth, the U.S. warships *Columbus* and *Hamel* joined with the battleship *Vanguard* in a twenty-one-gun salute; guns were fired in Edinburgh and Rosyth, Cardiff and Windsor; beacons were lit along the Welsh mountains. In towns the length and breadth of the kingdom, the day was marked by the constant firing of guns and pealing of bells. By evening, another crowd had gathered outside the palace gates, this time to sing a succession of somewhat raucous lullabies.

Inside the palace, the cause of it all slept in the same cradle used by his mother and aunt in their infancy. His crib, trimmed in advance in ambiguous yellow, was a splendid cast-iron four-poster used by the king's family for more than one hundred years. The palace nursery was of course affected, if less than many others, by postwar austerity; silk and lace had been dug out of old trunks at Windsor to be reused, and Prince Philip even came up with some of his own baby clothes for repair. Unlike most other homes, however, the palace had received an avalanche of gifts from around the world, notably a ton and a half of diapers from the United States, which were distributed from a special operations room to other expectant mothers around the country. The Linen and Woollen Drapers Institute, of which the princess was patron, had presented a layette of fifty-five garments, produced by the cottage industry of twenty-five retired dressmakers; within a few weeks, the prince was earning his first dollars for Britain as replicas of his baby clothes sold in US stores. It was within his first few hours of life, however, that he received his first family gift: an ivory-handled rattle from his grandmother, the queen, which she had once given her own first child, and since kept in hope of this day.

The BBC marked the occasion by commissioning "Music for a Prince" from three prominent British composers, Gordon Jacobs, Herbert Howells, and Michael Tippett, to be performed at a special Albert Hall concert two months later. No less speedy in his inspiration was the poet laureate, John Masefield, whose quatrain "A Hope for the Newly Born" had the laureateship's authentic limp:

May destiny, allotting what befalls,
   Grant to the newly-born this saving grace,
A guard more sure than ships and fortress-walls,
   The loyal love and service of a race.

A week after Charles's birth palace staff were allowed in to coo over him in groups of five, as shortly afterward were select members of the Privy Council. His mother had begun breast-feeding him, as she did for several weeks. The princess did not leave her bed for the first ten days, but her son was soon being walked in a second-generation pram, which Elizabeth had sought out in Royal Lodge, her parents' Windsor retreat. It was so enormous that Charles claims he can still to this day remember lying in its vastness, overshadowed by its high sides.

Information as to his looks was at a premium. His mother's first day out of doors, November 29, was to have been the occasion for a newsreel film of her wheeling him around the palace gardens, to be shown at the Royal Command Performance. But fog ruled this out. So the first word came from the queen's sister, Countess Granville, who told a convention of Girl Guides in Northern Ireland that "he could not be more angelic looking. He is golden-haired and has the most beautiful complexion, as well as amazingly delicate features for so young a baby. . . . The queen says that she thinks the baby is like his mother, but the duke is quite certain that the baby is very like himself." Princess Elizabeth, whom the countess described as "wonderfully well and radiantly happy," soon wrote to a friend: "Don't you think he is quite adorable? I still can't believe he is really mine, but perhaps that happens to new parents. Anyway, this particular boy's parents couldn't be more proud of him. It's wonderful to think, isn't it, that his arrival could give a bit of happiness to so many people, besides ourselves, at this time?" To her former music teacher, Miss Mabel Lander (known to the princess as "Goosey" Lander), she wrote: "The baby is very sweet and we are enormously proud of him. He has an interesting pair of hands for a baby. They are rather large, but fine with long fingers —quite unlike mine and certainly unlike his father's. It will be interesting to see what they will become. I still find it hard to believe I have a baby of my own!"

Visiting the palace to take the first official photographs, Cecil Beaton was also struck by the child's "remarkably long and pointed fingers." His eyes, Beaton told the world, were like his mother's, and he had a tuft of fair hair: "He looks like Queen Mary." Queen Mary herself, looking through an old family album, decided the baby looked remarkably like his great-great-great-grandfather Albert, the Prince Consort. Princess Elizabeth herself began to tell friends he had his father's smile; his father told *his* friends the baby resembled nothing so much as a plum pudding.

Such tiny morsels were eagerly snapped up because no pictures of the child were released, nor was any announcement made of his name, until the day of his christening, December 15. The unusual delay prompted some criticism—in fact, it was the first of his parents' many moves to protect him from undue publicity—which quickly turned to surprise when the names were finally made known. All the pundits had been proved wrong, especially those who believed that Elizabeth and Philip would not be the first royal generation in a hundred years to defy Queen Victoria's wish that all her descendants should bear her or her husband's name. (They remedied the matter in 1960 by christening their second son Prince Andrew Albert Christian Edward.)

The choice of Charles Philip Arthur George, with the emphasis on Charles, was said by the palace to have been made by the baby's parents for "personal and private reasons." The surprise about Charles was that the two English kings who had borne the name had had such miserable reigns that it had been abandoned by the royal family for nigh on three hundred years; its only other royal holder, Bonnie Prince Charlie, was notorious for his insurrection against the House of Hanover. It was widely interpreted, especially when the prince's younger sister was christened Anne almost two years later, as a deliberate revival of the names of the royal Stuarts; the only immediate explanation was that it was in tribute to the baby's godfather, King Haakon of Norway, who had been Prince Charles of Denmark until he acceded to the Norwegian throne in 1905. In truth even this had scarcely occurred to Elizabeth and Philip; they had called their son Charles simply because it was the male forename they liked best. Another of the prince's godparents, Princess Margaret, greeted the news with a surprised "I suppose I'll now be known as Charley's Aunt."

He was named Philip, of course, after his father, and George after his grandfather, who also bore the name Arthur. But Arthur is one of the most traditional royal names. Apart from its romantic associations with the Arthurian legend, it has been borne by many heirs to the throne: for instance, the eldest son of Henry VII, Arthur, Prince of Wales, whose premature death led to the succession of Henry VIII and deprived England of its first post-Conquest King Arthur. It was also chosen for a closer family association: Princess Elizabeth's godfather had been Arthur, Duke of Connaught, third son of Queen Victoria, who had in turn been named after his own godfather, the then elderly Arthur Wellesley, first Duke of Wellington.

The names were duly registered by Prince Philip with Mr. Stanley Clare, senior registrar of Caxton Hall in the City of Westminster, who called at the palace on the morning of the christening. The ceremony that afternoon would have been held at Windsor, where all such family occasions usually take place, had it not been for the king's health. As it was, the palace chapel had been destroyed by the Nazi bombers in September 1940, so the baptism was performed in the white-and-gold music room, whose great crimson-curtained bow window looked out onto a wintry palace garden.

The Archbishop of Canterbury, Dr. Geoffrey Fisher, officiated, assisted by the Precentor of the Chapel Royal, the Reverend Maurice Foxell. The golden Lily Font, designed by Prince Albert for the christening of his and Victoria's children, had been brought up from Windsor for the occasion. By Dr. Fisher's account the infant prince, dressed in a robe of Honiton lace and white silk used by all Victoria's children, remained "as quiet as a mouse" as he was bathed in water specially brought from the River Jordan, a royal tradition dating back to the Crusades. The baby was held by his youngest godparent, Princess Margaret. His other sponsors were the king and queen; the queen's brother, David Bowes-Lyon; the king of Norway; the Duke of Edinburgh's grandmother, the Dowager Marchioness of Milford Haven; his uncle, Prince George of Greece; and his cousin, Earl

Mountbatten's elder daughter, Lady Brabourne. Of the eight, only King Haakon and Prince George, both in their late seventies, were unable to be present. By Charles's thirtieth birthday in 1978, indeed, only three of his godparents—the Queen Mother, Princess Margaret, and Lady Brabourne—were still alive.

The half-hour ceremony, which began with a piano rendition of Handel's Water Music by the organist of the Chapel Royal, was attended by the closest circle of the royal family. So the room contained four granddaughters of Queen Victoria—the Dowager Marchioness of Milford Haven; Princess Marie Louise; Princess Alice, Countess of Athlone; and Lady Patricia Ramsay —all of whom had themselves worn the same christening robes. But the princess had not forgotten others close to her. As the two magnificent crystal chandeliers glinted in the firelight, lighting up the golden splendor of Prince Albert's font, watching between the music room's massive purple pillars were the princess's own nurserymaid, Margaret MacDonald ("Bobo," since 1952 the Queen's dresser), and the domestic staff from Windlesham Moor, including the cook, Mrs. Barnes. She had baked one of the three christening cakes which afterward graced the party in the White Drawing Room, where the guests presented their lavish array of christening presents. Queen Mary's seems to have stolen the show; that night she noted in her diary: "I gave the baby a silver gilt cup and cover which George III had given to a godson in 1780, so that I gave a present from my great-grandfather to my great-grandson 168 years later."

Thus Prince Charles of Edinburgh formally entered the Protestant Church of England, a solemn prerequisite of one day ascending the British throne. At the same time, being a newborn postwar baby, he received his ration card and milk allowance. Miss Rowe's work complete, she yielded her place in the nursery to two Scottish-born nurses, Helen Lightbody and Mabel Anderson. Miss Lightbody had been "passed on" to the princess by her aunt, the Duchess of Gloucester, whose two sons she had brought up; as the senior of the two palace nurses, she was given the courtesy title of "Mrs." Miss Anderson, the young daughter of a policeman killed in the Liverpool blitz, had placed an ad in the Situations Wanted column of a nursing magazine, and been pleasantly surprised to find herself summoned to Buckingham

Palace for an interview with the princess. In time, she was to find herself in charge of Anne, Andrew, and Edward as well; now she is nanny to Princess Anne's son, Peter Phillips.

Five days after the christening, Dr. Jacob Snowman of Hampstead, London, then in his eighties, visited the palace to circumcise the baby. It was the week before Christmas, and a festive tree adorned the dressing table of Charles's first nursery, a converted guest room to which he had now been moved from his mother's dressing room. Though no one could predict it then, the baby's first Christmas and New Year were the last for several years that he would spend with both his parents at his side. The family was, for the first time in many years, to spend Christmas in London, as the king's doctors had advised against the seasonal journey to Windsor. Only two days after the birth, in fact, they had insisted that the king announce the cancellation of a Commonwealth tour through Australia, New Zealand, and Canada. It had been the first his daughter knew of the extent of his illness, and it cast the only shadow over the annual celebrations.

Early in January, however, the king was sufficiently recovered to lead a family expedition to Norfolk, and by January 18 was out shooting on his beloved Sandringham estate. Miss Lightbody was back in familiar territory, having spent many hours in the country nursery with Prince William and Prince Richard. Suddenly she found herself more than ever in sole charge of Charles, as his mother contracted measles and was not allowed near her month-old baby for three weeks.

By March the family was back in London, and the princess sufficiently recovered to resume public engagements. For the king, however, the prognosis was much more dispiriting. Since the November diagnosis, he had led the life of a virtual invalid; his doctors now advised that he must always continue to do so, or face an immediate operation to ease blood constriction in his right leg. For a man of his temperament, there was no choice. The operation, performed in the Buhl Room on March 12, was so successful that he was able to hold a Privy Council meeting by March 29, to be undertaking public duties again by May, and to attend the Trooping of the Colour in June. But he and his wife had already realized that he could not have long to live.

By July, when her father seemed in much better spirits after a week's rest at Balmoral, Princess Elizabeth was at last able to move with her husband and child into their first family home. The renovation of Clarence House had dragged on much longer than expected, and it was a great relief to leave the lonely vastness of the palace for a more compact, centrally heated home with all modern conveniences. Clarence House, just across the Mall from Buckingham Palace, had been the home of the Duke of Clarence before his accession as William IV in 1830. Later it had been the London home of the princess's godfather, the Duke of Connaught, until his death in 1942 (although in old age he rarely used it). During the Second World War, George VI had given it to the British Red Cross as office space. Now it housed a chintz-curtained nursery, with white walls and blue-for-a-boy moldings, which looked out across its one walled and private garden beyond the Mall to St. James's Park. The family moved in on July 4—as Prince Philip aptly pointed out, "Independence Day."

From Clarence House, the two nurses could wheel the baby round the park with little fear of recognition. The only identifying features, which sometimes drew the curious to peer into the pram, were the private detectives following discreetly behind and the Edinburghs' noisy little terrier, Shandy. The infant Prince Charles's daily routine has been described in meticulous detail, but it comes down to an unsurprising round of playpens, teddy bears, torn-up books, and regally soiled nappies. One of its few distinguishing features was that the enormous pram would sometimes be wheeled to nearby Marlborough House, where visits to Queen Mary (whom her great-grandson called "Gan Gan," as Edward VIII had Queen Victoria) provide another of Charles's earliest memories. He has a vivid picture of the dignified old lady sitting bolt upright, her legs culminating on a footstool, surrounded by the array of precious objects that formed her famous collection. History relates that the previous generation of royal infants, the Princesses Elizabeth and Margaret, were never allowed to go near the jade, the silver, the crystal in their magnificent display cabinets, whereas young Charles was permitted to play around with whatever priceless object took his fancy. Since the princesses' infancy, however, Queen Mary had lived through the deaths of her husband and two of her sons, and had seen another abandon the throne for an American divorcée.

Now another son, she knew, was dying. In the child by her foot-stool lay the future of the dynasty of which she was matriarch.

Charles's first year of life had been one of royal indulgences: his mother had been spared all but a few royal duties, and his father had been based at the Admiralty in London rather than on active naval service. By his first birthday that November, however, the normal working life of what George VI called "the firm" had been resumed. Princess Elizabeth gave a small tea party at Clarence House, and Prince Philip flew in a present from Malta, where he was serving as a lieutenant aboard HMS *Chequers*. Before joining her husband out there for their second wedding anniversary the following week, the Princess authorized the release to the press of the latest Charles statistics: age one year, weight twenty-four pounds, hair gold and shiny, teeth six and pearly. Already he was taking his first steps, with the aid of Jumbo, a much-loved fluffy blue elephant on wheels.

His father was also away for Christmas, which was spent with the king and queen at Sandringham. Cinema audiences at the festive season enjoyed the first newsreel film of the happy young royals, playing with their baby in the garden of Windle-sham Moor. The public had been taken further into the family's domestic life with the publication of a book illustrating the reno-vations at Clarence House. That Christmas, however, there was another secret of which they were to know nothing until a palace announcement the following May. During her anniversary visit to Malta, spent with her husband in the seclusion of the Mount-battens' Villa Guardamangia, Princess Elizabeth had conceived her second child.

Princess Anne was born at Clarence House on August 15, 1950—just before midday, in midsummer, in the mid-year of the century. Prince Charles was one year and nine months old. His father, who had returned from Malta for the event at the end of July, told him over lunch that Tuesday that he had a baby sister, and most unusually allowed him to get down from the table to go and take a look at her. Photographs of the period quickly show the tiny signs of bewilderment on the face of a young child no longer the epicenter of his parents' attention. Charles could scarcely yet have been aware that straits and islands around the world had been named after him, though he took more than a usual childish interest in the sheets of stamps that bore his face. He was too young to know that the visitor for whom he had been taught to say *"Bonjour"* the previous March was the president of France. But his young world was already, as it was to remain throughout his childhood, one much more of adults than of children his own age; and it may not have been simply the fondness of his parents that already credited him with a certain maturity, as he took "a most watchful, protective interest" in his sister from the first.

With two children installed, and their parents' lives again busy and public, the royal nursery settled into a more rigid daily regime than before. Charles and Anne were got up each day at seven sharp, dressed, fed, and played with in the nursery until nine, when they enjoyed a statutory half hour with their mother. Fresh air was the order of every day, and mornings were spent in the park. Lunch, Charles's favorite menu being boiled chicken and rice, was at one, followed by more outings until four thirty, at which time Princess Elizabeth would hope to have cleared two hours in her day. She insisted on bathing the children herself whenever her schedule permitted, and distinguished visitors were rarely allowed to distract her. The man who arrived with a splendid fleet of metal battleships, marvelous on the nursery floor but disappointingly leaden at bathtime, was King Frederik of Denmark. The lady perched on the bathroom chair, wiping splashes of water from her dress, was Queen Louise of Sweden. No one was spared Charles's incessant batting of an old saucepan with a wooden spoon. Only two royal personages insisted on a certain decorum. Even before his third birthday, Charles had learnt to bow before offering his cheek for a peck from "Gan Gan" Mary, and not to sit down unbidden when in the presence of his grandfather the king.

By Christmas 1950 Prince Philip had his own naval command. Gazetted lieutenant commander on the day of his daughter's birth, his ship was the frigate *Magpie*, again in Malta, where Elizabeth again flew to spend the holiday with him. Charles and Anne were left in their grandparents' care at Sandringham, with their Aunt Margaret deputizing for their mother at bathtime. The young prince enjoyed his first experience of constitutional monarchy that Christmas, when the Lord President of the Council, Herbert Morrison, shut the door of a Privy Council meeting in his face. "Sorry, young fellow-me-lad," said

Morrison, "but I'm afraid you can't go in there. We've got a meeting with your grandfather, and it's very, very secret. Ever so secret. Some day . . . well, you'll learn about that in due course."

On New Year's Day there was the excitement of a phone call from his mother aboard the *Magpie*. She had received a letter from her father at Sandringham, saying: "Charles is too sweet, stumping around the room. We shall love having him at Sandringham. He is the fifth generation to live there, and I hope he will get to like the place."

Charles was visibly happier when the domestic routine settled back to normal at Clarence House that spring. And so might the princess's happy family life have continued, as she dearly hoped, for another ten or fifteen years before being blighted by the burden of monarchy. But the king's health was growing worse. His wife and daughter knew, though as yet he did not, that he had cancer. In July an increase in the young couple's royal duties on the monarch's behalf forced Prince Philip to give up his one brief naval command. In October, their departure delayed for two weeks by another operation on the king, they left for a tour of North America and Canada. Included in the princess's luggage was a sealed envelope of documents she would have to sign if her father died during her absence.

So Elizabeth and Philip missed their son's third birthday, which was spent with his grandparents and Aunt Margaret at Buckingham Palace. Charles's one memory of his grandfather dates from this day: an impression of sitting on a sofa with him, this much larger person, while another man dangled something bright and shiny in front of them. Colville, the press secretary, was waving his pocket watch to try and keep the boy still while he had his photograph taken with his grandfather. The resulting picture (following p. 98) has since become famous. It stands, and has always stood, on Queen Elizabeth II's desk, uniting one of her last memories of her father with one of her first of her son.

There were more phone calls from his absent parents, one from the White House, where they visited President Truman. Three days after his birthday, Charles made one of his first formal public appearances when he was taken to London Airport to greet their return. Control tower staff made his day by allowing him to switch on the runway lights in front of the incoming aircraft. And back at Sandringham, this second long absence was more than compensated for by the cowboy and Indian outfits it bestowed on him. He little knew the significance of a ceremony on December 4, when the king made the Duke and Duchess of Edinburgh members of the Privy Council. It was all by way of momentous preparation, which to Charles only meant a Christmas rather spoiled by the news that his parents would soon be off traveling again. His mother took him to visit Father Christmas at Harrods, perhaps meditating that a particular wheel had come full circle. At the time of Prince Charles's birth, the king had had to cancel a Commonwealth tour; by Christmas 1950, it had been rescheduled for early 1952. Now, again because of his health, it was to be undertaken for him by his daughter and her husband.

On January 30, 1952, the king took them to *South Pacific* at Drury Lane Theatre, and next morning to London Airport to see them off to the Commonwealth. Charles and Anne had already said their good-bys. The pictures of the king at the airport, a frail and shadowy figure seemingly buffeted by the breeze, were a shock to the nation. It was Elizabeth's last moment on British soil as a princess. Her life in the wings, protecting her children from the center-stage spotlight of monarchy, was at an end.

6

1952-54: Duke of Cornwall

The heir, as long as he is a child,
differeth nothing from a servant.

GAL. 4:1

FEBRUARY 5, 1952, was "Keeper's Day" at Sandringham, and King George VI enjoyed a particularly good day's hare shooting before spending a late teatime playing with his grandchildren. As the queen followed them up to the nursery, to supervise bathtime and hear them say their prayers, the king sent notes of thanks and congratulations to each of his keepers, and planned the next day's shooting. He was contented and relaxed over dinner that evening. After retiring to his room at ten thirty, he worked on papers until midnight, when a watchman saw him close his bedroom window. In the early hours of February 6, the king died peacefully in his sleep.

Charles and his sister were kept unusually late in the nursery that morning. When the boy noticed one of the maids in tears, he asked Nurse Lightbody: "Why is everybody crying?" Because his grandpa had gone away, he was told, which made him wonder why his grandpa had not said good-by. He asked to see his grandmother, but was told he must wait. When Queen Elizabeth at last did come to the nursery, she took Charles on her knee and listened for a while to his chatter, telling him that his mama and papa would soon be home, sooner than expected. But Charles again asked where his grandpa had gone, and Queen Elizabeth broke down. When Charles said gently, "Don't cry, Granny," the nurses too were in tears.

At about that time, 11:45 A.M., in a hunting lodge called

Treetops overlooking the Sagana River in Kenya, Charles's mother learned that she was queen. Michael Parker had taken a phone call from Martin Charteris, the private secretary, who was in a hotel across the valley. A reporter from the *East African Standard* had told him of a news agency wire announcing the king's death. Parker tried to tune in to BBC news bulletins, but could find only solemn music, which seemed confirmation enough. Careful not to be seen by Elizabeth, he signaled the Duke of Edinburgh to step out of the lodge's long sitting room. Prince Philip himself broke the news to his wife.

As Parker and the prince worked out the fastest route back to London, Elizabeth calmly set about her first duties as queen: messages to all the Commonwealth countries she would not be able to visit, the summoning of the traditional Accession Council, and the announcement that she would style herself Queen Elizabeth II. Monarch at twenty-five, she had suddenly lost her already restricted freedom and family life; her father was dead at fifty-six, fourteen years younger than his father George V, and as it was to prove twenty-two years younger than his brother Edward VIII. Even less prepared for accession on this journey than on her last, she left for the urgent flight home in a brightly patterned dress and white hat. As she said good-by to the grief-stricken servants at the door of the lodge, her chauffeur knelt on all fours to kiss her shoes.

London and the nation, very personally shocked by the suddenness of the king's death, plunged into official and ritual mourning. At the request of the prime minister, Winston Churchill, all but a defiant few wore dark clothes for three days and observed a nationwide two minutes' silence on the day of the funeral. Shop-window displays were draped in black; a rush-hour crowd emerging from an underground station was observed to divide into two streams, to avoid treading on a fallen newspaper placard saying THE KING IS DEAD.

On February 7, when the Argonaut *Atalanta* bore the new Queen home to London Airport, Prime Minister Winston Churchill, the Leader of the Opposition (Clement Attlee), and the Foreign Secretary (Anthony Eden) were there to meet her, with other members of the cabinet and the late king's brother, the Duke of Gloucester. Crowds stood silent along the Mall as the royal motorcade approached Clarence House, where Queen Mary waited to greet her new sovereign. As the Queen's car drew up, the royal standard was raised on the flagstaff for the first time in Elizabeth II's reign.

Heir apparent at three years old, Prince Charles was now Duke of Cornwall, Duke of Rothesay, Earl of Carrick and Baron of Renfrew, Lord of the Isles and Great Steward of Scotland. "That's me, Mummy," he was soon to cry on hearing the Duke of Cornwall's name mentioned in church among the prayers for the royal family. Contrary to popular belief, he was not yet Prince of Wales. That is a title the sovereign may bestow on the heir apparent (if male) at whatever moment he or she deems appropriate.

From his point of view, of course, little had changed. He was scarcely aware that flags would now fly throughout the land on his birthday. His family was still living at Clarence House; daily routine was much the same, apart from the absence of his grandfather; he saw no difference in the mother who still supervised his bathtime—to which end, the Queen had asked the prime minister, Churchill, to put back his weekly appointment with the monarch by one hour. It was Charles's mother who, in time, explained his grandfather's disappearance as far as any Christian parent can to a three-year-old child. Charles was kept strictly away from all the rituals of obsequy; he had been taken for a walk to the other side of the Sandringham estate as the funeral cortege left for London, and he was sent back to Sandringham for two days during his grandfather's funeral and burial ceremonies.

Easter was spent, as usual, at Windsor, though with the court still in mourning it was a subdued holiday. When it was over, Charles was confronted with the first outward sign of change. His grandmother and Aunt Margaret had moved into Clarence House, the family home so recently prepared for him and his parents, who in turn moved back into Buckingham Palace. The second-floor nursery suite had been carefully redecorated, to seem as much like the Clarence House nursery as possible. There was his box of toy soldiers, his cuckoo clock, his ten-foot-high mock-Tudor doll's house, his toy cupboard (his particular favorite being a model steam shovel); he had a new, full-size bed, made for him by students of the Royal College of Art, but still the same horsehair pillow. The only room in the palace forbidden to him was his mother's study on the floor below.

Passing it one day, Charles urged his mother to come and play. "If only I could," said the new Queen, gently closing the door. Forbidding this territory to Charles and Anne—by the childhood of Andrew and Edward, she was sufficiently experienced to relax the rule—was one of the few impositions the Queen allowed her new role to place on her family life at home. But it was a sign of a new era in family monarchy that she refused to allow her children to bow and curtsy to her, as tradition decreed, and as she and her sister had been instructed when their father had unexpectedly become king. Such decorum was still maintained at Marlborough House, where Queen Mary did not altogether approve of these new dispensations. Elizabeth, however, knew how much it had upset her father to see his children suddenly take to performing acts of fealty when they entered the room. It had been Queen Elizabeth, equally reluctantly, who had insisted on it, to help her husband acquire the essential aloofness of sovereignty which was so little in his nature.

As the months went by, Charles had no reason to think his childhood any different from any other little boy's. When he joined his family on the palace balcony, or at the Trooping of the Colour, his eyes were those of an excited member of the crowd, watching the colorful displays. It was puzzling when some people seemed to prefer to look at him. All the palace staff, at the Queen's insistence, called him simply "Charles"; when he heard himself referred to as "Prince Charles," the prefix seemed no different from that of his friends Master Norton (Knatchbull) or Lady Jane (Wellesley). He had a penchant for collecting the plastic gifts then given away in cereal packets, but was dismayed when the palace butler would open only one packet at a time. Coming across a valet one day, he said: "Those are my daddy's clothes. Where are you taking them?" When he misbehaved, he was punished, the palm being administered to the royal hindquarters as much as by his nanny as his father. He had to learn to take his toffee out of his mouth before the royal car stopped, and not—as he once did, to general popular delight—to press his half-sucked sweet into his mother's hand. Prince Philip once spanked him for sticking his tongue out at the crowd watching him drive down the Mall. In such painful ways did Prince Charles begin to learn about the unusual accident of his birth.

His parents were particularly anxious to ensure that the

deference all around the young Charles would not affect his character. When he omitted to call the Queen's detective "Mister," simply using his surname, as he heard his mother and father do all the time, he was rebuked and told to apologize. When he slipped an ice cube down a footman's neck, he was punished. Once, when he left a door open and a footman rushed to shut it, Philip stopped the servant, saying, "Leave it alone, man. The boy's got hands." His father also once found Charles pelting a Sandringham policeman with snowballs, while the hapless officer took his punishment, unsure whether to reply in kind. "Don't just stand there," shouted the Duke of Edinburgh. "Throw some back." Also at Sandringham, the Queen once sent Charles back out of the house, not to return until he had found a dog lead he had lost in the grounds. "Dog leads," she told him, "cost money."

Such was the pattern throughout his childhood. But in the later months of 1952, as he began to master the rudiments of the Queen's English, Prince Charles began almost by accident to discover the meaning of the lavish home life he otherwise took for granted. Meeting a private secretary in a palace corridor, a few weeks before his fourth birthday, Charles asked his usual question: "What are you doing here?"

"I'm going to see the Queen," explained the secretary.

"Oh yes?" said Prince Charles. "Who's she?"

On being told the Queen was his mother, Charles appeared extremely puzzled. The courtier felt a qualm of guilt, "as if I had given away the secret of Father Christmas."

Other outward signs began to impress upon him what he was much later to call "the ghastly, inexorable" truth. No longer could he ride around London in the back of the family car, with his father at the wheel. These favorite excursions had suddenly stopped, and now—aged three—he had his own car with his own chauffeur. He also had his own footman, an eighteen-year-old palace servant named Richard Brown (whom he once "knighted" with his knife when he stooped to pick up some food the young prince had dropped). "Why haven't you got a Richard?" asked Charles when out to tea with a friend one day. His friend didn't have a Mr. Kelly, either—to be precise, Sergeant Kelly, Charles's newly assigned private detective, the first in a long line who would shadow him for the rest of his life. It was thanks to Kelly that Charles soon met another change of routine. No more could he go for walks through Green Park and St. James's Park, across the road from his home. Public curiosity had grown too intense. Instead, Mrs. Lightbody took the royal children on excursions to Putney Heath, Richmond Park, and Wimbledon Common—with the faithful Kelly discreetly in attendance.

Looking back on all this nearly twenty years later, Prince Charles was unable to pinpoint any particular moment when he realized he had been born to be king. "I didn't suddenly wake up in my pram one day and say 'Yippee.' I think it just dawns on you, slowly, that people are interested . . . and slowly you get the idea that you have a certain duty and responsibility. It's better that way, rather than someone suddenly telling you 'You must do this' and 'You must do that,' because of who you are. It's one of those things you grow up in."

Part of growing up, as Charles's distinctive character began to emerge, was to develop some sort of childish working relationship with his sister. The Queen, looking back, is emphatic that all four of her children showed very different personalities at the earliest ages, and it was already clear that Charles and Anne were totally unalike. He was much more like their father in appearance, already aping some of his public mannerisms: the hands behind the back, the erect bearing, the habit of looking an interlocutor fixedly in the eyes, often causing uneasiness. She was much more like their father in character: extroverted, self-confident almost to a fault, occasionally temperamental. Charles took after his mother, who in turn took after George VI: instinctively shy and retiring, yet overcoming it with a deliberate effort of will, which in time sowed the seeds of a driving sense of duty. The solemnity on Charles's face in some of those early pictures, contrasting with the evident mischievousness of Anne's, is that of the camera-shy, not of the humorless, child.

It was Anne, the Mall contingents noted, who waved confidently, after the fashion of her mother, long before her elder brother could summon the gall to do the same. It was Charles, by contrast, who kept reminding his sister, often in vain, that she must curtsy when entering Gan-Gan's drawing room. It was Charles who pulled Anne along the platform to say thank you to the engine driver when the royal train delivered them to Sandringham. But it was Anne who first discovered, and exploited, the wonderful palace game discovered by her mother before her: if you walked past a sentry, he would make a very satisfying clatter coming to attention and presenting arms. To walk back and forth past a sentry box provided hours of childish entertainment, to the chagrin of the long-suffering guards on duty. Charles, when he discovered that he too was one of the privileged few who could produce this startling effect, steered clear of sentry boxes. It was somehow embarrassing.

Charles's fourth birthday that autumn was the first his father had ever spent with him. It was the occasion for a grand palace party; marble busts and other ornaments were cleared from the corridors—at two hundred feet long, they were ideal for races and games—and the palace rang with the laughter of young children for the first time since the parties of Queen Victoria's offspring a century before. Among the guests were Charles's Gloucester cousins; the Knatchbulls (children of the Brabournes, grandchildren of Lord Mountbatten); the Charteris children; James Dawnay, son of the Queen Mother's private secretary; Nicholas and Simon Renton, grandchildren of Sir Alan Lascelles; and Lord Ipswich and Lady Henrietta Fitzroy, children of Lord and Lady Euston. The band of the Grenadier Guards played a selection of nursery rhymes, interspersed with "Happy Birthday to You" and the young prince's favorite, "The Teddy Bear's Picnic."

The coronation of Elizabeth II was by now set for the following June. The Duke of Cornwall, as senior royal duke and head of the peerage, would be obliged to take an oath of allegiance to the new monarch; but it was the first time in British history, at least since the creation of the dukedom in 1337, that a sovereign with so young an heir was to be crowned. The Queen was reluctant to put Charles through such an ordeal, and knew that worries about his behavior would stretch her own already taut nerves. At Sandringham and Balmoral, he had had to be taken out of the parish church for fidgeting during the sermon. As a test, two days before his birthday, the Queen accompanied her son on his first public appearance: to one of Sir Robert Mayer's concerts for children in the Royal Festival Hall. Alas, boredom set in halfway through the program, and he had to be taken home.

So it was decided to spare Charles the solemn oath of allegiance, and a decision was postponed on whether he would attend the coronation at all. In the meantime, there was much for him and Anne to enjoy in the preparations for the event—marred only by the death of Queen Mary in March, though again the prince was too young to be touched by his great-grandmother's sudden disappearance. As June approached, Charles was much amused to find that a part of his mother's magnificent robe was called a train; courtiers and visitors alike were roped in to coronation games. Looking out the window one day Anne declared excitedly that the coronation had begun, only to be informed rather haughtily by her brother that it was just the changing of the guard. Charles remembers a large man with a large hat and a large cigar—Winston Churchill, who had developed a rather emotional affection for his young new Queen—coming and going with great ceremony. He had a ride in the coronation coach as it was put through its trials in the Palace Mews, causing royal commentators to announce excitedly that he had become the first future monarch in history to ride in the coach before his own coronation.

By the day itself, June 2, a gray summer's day even by London standards, there had been a last-minute change of heart. Prince Charles's name did not appear in the official coronation program, indicating that the Queen had thought it best to leave him, like Anne, at home. But he begged to be allowed to come. A white satin suit was prepared, his hair was slicked down with brilliantine (see pictures following p. 98), and he watched his parents drive through the cheering Mall crowds in the glass coach of George III. After the mile-long procession had disappeared, Mrs. Lightbody saw him into a plain car which took a side route to Westminster Abbey. The heir apparent entered holding his nanny and a Grenadier Guard officer by the hand. Quietly he joined his grandmother and Aunt Margaret in the royal box, where he stood on a footstool to watch the solemn coronation rites of his mother.

The ceremony was well under way, and had just reached one of its most splendid moments: the anointing of the sovereign with consecrated oil, as the choir sang Handel's anthem "Zadok the Priest." It was a worrying moment for the child: he saw his mother divested of her ornate finery, in the plainest white robe, surrounded by men in extravagant uniforms; four of them, Knights of the Garter, held over her head a canopy of cloth of gold, while the Archbishop of Canterbury prepared to anoint her hands, breast, and head with oil. For all her preoccupation, the

Queen was seen to look up and give her son a reassuring little smile.

Those eyes that remained on Charles saw him spread his arms wide in admiration of the gold plate on the altar. And amid his constant questions to the Queen Mother, he kept smoothing his hair with his hand, then offering her his palm so she could smell his new hair oil. Only once did she have to restrain him as he leaned over the balcony for a better view. But he was allowed to stay longer than anticipated; he was ushered out shortly before the peers' oaths of allegiance—which it might anyway have been constitutionally improper for him to attend without taking part. Mrs. Lightbody saw him out through a side door and home for lunch.

That afternoon, like the rest of a nation newly equipped with sets for the occasion, Charles watched his parents' triumphant progress through the West End of London on television. When they returned to the palace, the Queen went out on the balcony alone for a few moments, still wearing her robes and crown. Then Prince Philip led the children forward, to renewed cheering. It was Charles's first experience of mass adulation, which might be thought likely to turn the head of a four-and-a-half-year-old child. But scarcely anything of that day has lodged at all vividly in his memory.

For the slightly bewildered young boy, all the coronation really meant was that his parents would soon be going away again—for much longer than ever before. For a few months, the Queen's presence at home was interrupted only by excursions around the country, to show herself to her new subjects. But in late November she and Prince Philip were again to undertake that postponed and interrupted Commonwealth tour, this time in their own right. They would be away for six months.

The days until November passed happily enough. Charles had swimming lessons from his father and Michael Parker in the palace pool; at Balmoral, he learnt to ride on an old Shetland pony called Fum. In June, the young Duke of Cornwall's five-year-old bull Supreme—just a year older than its owner—was named Supreme Champion at the Bath and West Show. He was always more passionate about animals than things mechanical: the palace nursery had by now become a veritable menagerie. Apart from his two corgis, there were a hamster named Chi-Chi, a rabbit named Harvey, and two South American lovebirds (a gift from his grandmother), which he called David and Annie, after Davy Crockett and Annie Oakley.

The coronation had led to the first full flush of publicity about the royal children, which their mother decided was not in their best interests. They had never been allowed to see too many of the newspapers that carried their photographs; but she now began to impose further restrictions, for the children's own good. In late June, the palace officially announced that Charles—still only four—would not be undertaking any official engagements. By way of a sign, the Queen canceled plans for the youngest member of the Duke of Cornwall's Light Infantry to present Charles with a set of model soldiers to mark their 250th anniversary.

For several months following the Trooping of the Colour on June 11, no photographs at all were issued of the royal children. There had been criticism that they were already becoming over-exposed to the public's unremitting interest; the *Daily Express* calculated that in the twenty-three weeks of 1953 up to June 11, it alone had published fifty pages of royal photographs. Nor was there any special celebration of Charles's fifth birthday in November. His parents stayed at Sandringham, finalizing their plans for the tour, while Charles spent the day at Windsor with his grandmother and Aunt Margaret. Much of it he passed aping the guards, with the helmet and sword given him by his mother for his birthday. His grandmother—providentially, in view of the months ahead in her care—gave him a miniature set of gardening tools.

A week later, however, came the moment of parting. One of Prince Philip's last acts before leaving was to see the nursery staircase at Buckingham Palace safely covered over with netting, so boisterous was Charles growing. The Queen again took herself off to Harrods, returning with a red-white-and-blue glider and some mud pie molds to be stored away for her son's Christmas presents. Then, on November 23, they waved good-by to their children. The royal yacht, *Britannia*, had been launched only in April and was still undergoing trials. So they flew to Jamaica to join the converted cruise liner *Gothic*, a cardboard cutout of which was added to Charles's already voluminous scrapbook. The night before the Queen had tucked her children in, and Charles had spontaneously promised "to look after Anne." Once out of the

room, Elizabeth II—still feeling inadequate to the role suddenly
thrust upon her—melted into tears.

As much as Charles resented these partings, he was already
aware of the need for them. "Mummy has an important job to
do," he told a friend who asked where the Queen was. "She's
down here." He pointed out Australia on the globe newly installed in the nursery, on which he followed his parents' progress.
Letters and phone calls kept them in touch, with a special message from New Zealand on Christmas Day. The Queen had anyway planned to link up with *Britannia* for the leg home from Tobruk. She promised Charles and Anne that they could sail out in
the new yacht to join her there.

It was the royal children's first trip abroad, and it remains
Charles's earliest memory of his sister. On April 5 Queen Elizabeth
took them down to Portsmouth, where she handed them into the
care of Mrs. Lightbody and Miss Anderson. The Queen Mother
was happy to see that the royal crew had risen to the occasion:
already installed on deck were a sandpit, a slide, and a model of
Britannia mounted on a pedal car frame. It was a somewhat unorthodox maiden voyage, with the heir to the throne rolling up
his corduroy dungarees and swabbing the decks with the four
young ratings assigned to keep an eye on him. With films and
other entertainments provided, the week's sailing to Malta was
quickly over, and Charles was reunited with his favorite uncle,
Dickie—Lord Mountbatten, based on the island as commander in
chief of the Mediterranean Fleet. There followed a further week
of play and sightseeing, with some crab fishing in the rock pools
of Gozo, punctuated by a day aboard the visiting aircraft carrier
Eagle, where Charles was seen to snap to attention and salute with
all the gravity of his great-uncle.

Then, on May 2, the Queen was piped aboard at Tobruk.
Only with difficulty was Charles restrained from joining the line
of dignitaries waiting to shake hands with her. "No, not you,
dear," were Her Majesty's first words to her son after their six-
month parting, before she took him off to the state rooms for a
private and very emotional reunion. The young prince seemed to
have grown up beyond recognition during the long separation,
and the rest of the voyage was a joyous holiday of rediscovery.
The interval at Gibraltar, where Charles encouraged the Barbary
apes to jump on his sister's shoulders but was visibly horrified

when they treated Miss Anderson with similarly scant respect, remains one of the family's treasured memories.

At the time, there was a permanent reminder in the shape of a model train set, presented to the royal children by the Gibraltar garrison. Most of Prince Charles's many unsolicited gifts of toys and games were passed on to children's hospitals, but this one took pride of place back in the palace, in what had been King George VI's schoolroom. Prince Philip, like all fathers, spent perhaps more time than his son racing it round the pâpier-maché rock. For Charles, it came second only to his favorite childhood possession, a powder-blue Austin pedal car, which to this day you still walk past when you take the Queen's Entrance out into the Buckingham Palace garden.

Thanks to Winston Churchill's sense of occasion, the royal yacht sailed home up the Thames to the Pool of London. There the royal family transferred to a stately barge and continued their triumphant progress—with the prime minister on board—through a wildly enthusiastic throng to Westminster. There were great celebrations at the palace homecoming that evening, but next morning the prolonged holiday for Prince Charles was finally declared over. It was time for his education to begin in earnest.

7

1954-57:
"Mispy" and Hill House School

"The difficulty in the education of a prince, especially of the heir to the throne, is that he is forced too early into life, and that too much is expected of him."

FREDERICK WAYMOUTH GIBBS,
SENIOR TUTOR TO THE FUTURE
KING EDWARD VII

O N HIS FIFTH BIRTHDAY the previous November, Prince Charles had reached the age at which the law requires every English child to begin a formal education. The Queen and Prince Philip had already decided, some time before, to alter the traditional patterns of royal tutelage; they wished their children, especially the heir to the throne, to grow up as far as possible like other people's. The plans they had in mind were in their way revolutionary, but as yet still strictly secret. Charles did not seem quite ready to be sent, as some MPs were demanding, to the state primary school around the corner. For a five-year-old, the rather plump little boy was socially mature, as was only to be expected of one living in a world of adult and formal behavior. But he did not seem particularly bright.

He could write his own name, in carefully etched capital letters, he could count to a hundred, and he could tell the time. His mother herself had taught him that much. But he could scarcely read at all, despite hours of enjoyment being read—and committing to memory—the works of Beatrix Potter and A. A. Milne, and the Babar the Elephant books. He enjoyed his dancing classes, for which a mixed group of young aristocrats joined him at the palace each week under the instruction of the celebrated Miss Marguerite Vacani; at Windsor, he had graduated to a Welsh pony called William under the instruction of Sybil Smith, who had taught the Queen to ride, but he already showed less enthusiasm than his sister. The prince attended a London gym class and had started piano lessons with Miss Hilda Bor. He showed some musical aptitude, singing nursery rhymes with his mother and driving some palace staff to distraction with his love of military marches, especially "The British Grenadiers." But, thus far, the only other formal instruction he had received for the arduous royal years head was to be made to stand still for long periods of time.

Before leaving for her Commonwealth tour, the Queen had engaged a governess for Prince Charles: Miss Catherine Peebles, another Scotswoman (the nursery staff became known as "the Scottish Mafia"). A small and spry woman in her mid-forties, "Mispy" had previously had charge of the widowed Duchess of Kent's two younger children, Princess Alexandra and Prince Michael. She had no formal training, no university or college degree, and no revolutionary ideas on the upbringing of children; but the Queen had noticed in Miss Peebles a mixture of common sense and kindly strictness which echoed her own attitudes. The one rule Her Majesty imposed on her son's governess, knowing the child's uncertainty of himself, was "No forcing."

The Queen had pondered the idea of inviting other children to join Charles's classes, but decided his temperament urged against it. If his world so far had been one of adults, it had also been one of female adults—and distinctly genteel ones at that. Apart from his father, who was so often away, Charles had spent most of his time with the Queen, the Queen Mother, Princess Margaret, Mrs. Lightbody, Miss Anderson, and his sister. The difficulty of establishing normal dealings with other children just yet might distract him. It was decided that Charles would have his lessons alone. Even Anne was forbidden to disturb his morning with Miss Peebles in the palace schoolroom, where a desk and blackboard had now joined the more familiar globe. When the time came for Mispy to teach Charles's three younger siblings, other children did join the classes. Looking back, the Queen is sure she judged the difference in Charles correctly.

Miss Peebles became one of the select few to receive a copy of the Queen's daily engagement card. Each morning, when possible, Charles still spent half an hour with his mother at nine. Then the day's instruction began, lasting initially until eleven thirty, noon when he was a little older. Mispy confirmed the Queen's concern for Charles as a nervous, oversensitive child. "If you raised your voice to him, he would draw back into his shell and for a time you would be able to do nothing with him." Mabel Anderson agreed: "He was never as boisterous or noisy as Princess Anne. She had a much stronger, more extrovert personality. She didn't exactly push him aside, but she was certainly a more forceful child." Anne could always find something to amuse herself, while Charles often needed to be entertained. She was also better with her hands; Charles was all "fingers and thumbs."

Charles's shyness was in part due to some dawning awareness of his position. He knew how to behave, if not yet exactly why. When he visited a friend's farm, it was noticed that he took a polite interest in everything to be seen—almost as if he were on a royal visit—rather than showing a child's quick and selective enthusiasms. The spectacle of a little boy so aware of proprieties can become almost pathetic: when encouraging his corgi or another pet to perform its tricks, he would always add a most polite "please."

On a rewards-for-effort system, Miss Peebles began to draw out his special interests. After beginning each day with a Bible story, Charles was allowed to indulge his fondness for painting, at which he has since developed some of his father's skill. Geography was a natural source of fascination; it was Miss Peebles who installed the globe on which he followed his parents' travels, and he was soon able to tell visiting ambassadors the precise whereabouts of their country. History was more of a problem when trying to educate a future king to think of himself as a normal child. But Miss Peebles carefully developed a course she called Children in History, in which great figures were traced right back to their origins, whether regal or humble. The only subject that completely baffled him, and has continued to ever since, was arithmetic. The Queen smiled indulgently, for like her mother she has always had the same blind spot.

The afternoons were taken up with educational excursions. Down the Mall to the shipping offices in Cockspur Street, for a talk from Miss Peebles on the trade routes. Up to Highgate Hill to trace the steps of Dick Whittington and his cat before a visit to the pantomime. To the Tower, to be shown round by beefeaters; to St. George's Chapel, Windsor, to see Winston Churchill installed as a Knight of the Garter; to Madame Tussaud's, to laugh at the wax effigies of his parents.

In that first year Charles quickly learned to read, but still had some difficulty with his writing. After Christmas 1955—celebrated with a party for forty children at the palace, and a visit to Harrods to ask Father Christmas for a bicycle—Charles began to learn French. The afternoon excursions became more rigorously instructive, with visits to the various London museums. But by now the press had caught on to the routine, and all too often the outings had to be abandoned for a straightforward nature walk through Richmond Park.

The Queen began to doubt whether it was possible for her son to enjoy a normal education. If the press would not allow him to visit the British Museum in peace, what chance of privacy would he have at a normal school? And would his presence disturb the education of his fellow schoolchildren? Her cherished plans seemed in danger, but she was determined not to abandon them lightly. On April 11, 1955, her press secretary, Richard Colville, sent a personal letter to all newspaper edtiors:

> I am commanded by the Queen to say that Her Majesty and the Duke of Edinburgh have decided that their son has reached the stage when he should take part in more grown-up educational pursuits with other children.
>
> In consequence, a certain amount of the Duke of Cornwall's instructions will take place outside his home; for example, he will visit museums and other places of interest. The Queen trusts, therefore, that His Royal Highness will be able to enjoy this in the same way as other children without the embarrassment of constant publicity. In this respect, Her Majesty feels that it is

equally important that those in charge of, or sharing in, the instruction should be spared undue publicity, which can so seriously interrupt their normal lives.

I would be grateful if you will communicate the above to your members and seek their cooperation in this matter, informing them at the same time that they are at liberty to publish this letter if they so wish.

The request caused a lull (it was to prove only temporary) in press attention, but had the unwelcome countereffect of persuading editors to satisfy public demand with totally fictitious stories. One popular paper, for instance, had Charles cruising down the Rhine, complete with photograph (in fact, of the son of a British naval officer). Moved only in the direst straits to issue denials, the palace had to put up with it. At least Charles and Mispy remained comparatively unmolested when they visited London Zoo and the Planetarium; Charles was soon an expert in recognizing constellations, proof to his mother that, like her, he was at heart "a country person." They even managed a ride on the underground, Charles apparently passing unrecognized as the son of inconspicuous parents (Mispy and the prince's detective). It was to be some years yet, however, before he realized his childhood dream of riding on a double-decker bus.

Extracurricular activities included charades, field sports, more riding, and Charles's initiation into the curious rites of his countrymen's national game, cricket. The first was especially popular: if you happen to be a member of a family that enjoys dressing up, there can be fewer places with better-equipped wardrobes than Buckingham Palace and Windsor Castle. At Sandringham, Charles had already helped to round up the hounds before a hunt, and at Balmoral his Welsh pony had been replaced by an Irish roan. He played his first game of cricket in the summer of 1956, and that autumn his first game of soccer; but neither was to prove an abiding interest. Under his tuition of one of the Balmoral stalkers, Charles meanwhile developed his life-long love of fly-fishing. His father had begun to teach him boxing, but had reluctantly, with some irritation, abandoned the idea after a chorus of public protest.

"The Duke of Edinburgh," Mabel Anderson recalled, "was a marvelous father. When the children were younger, he always used to set aside time to read to them, or help them put together those little model toys." As they grew, he also encouraged practical jokes, something of a family tradition. The last two Princes of Wales, Edward VII and Edward VIII, set the precedents: the one was known for concealing dead birds in guest beds, the other for once feeding his French tutor, M. Hua, a tadpole sandwich. In time, Charles would develop his own eccentric style—at its height during his service career. For now, to his father's delight and Mrs. Lightbody's dismay, he contented himself with more traditional pranks such as artificial ink stains, and a "whoopee cushion" upon which the Bishop of Norwich once sat while visiting Sandringham.

By that autumn, 1956, the Queen was sufficiently pleased with Prince Charles's progress to take the next major step she had in mind. In October, soon after the start of the school term, Colonel Henry Townend, founder and headmaster of a smart London day school for boys, was pleasantly surprised to find himself invited to tea with Her Majesty at Buckingham Palace. Hill House, the colonel's small establishment in Hans Place, just behind Knightsbridge (conveniently near the palace), had been recommended to Charles's parents by friends and acquaintances who sent their own sons there. One had particularly pleased Her Majesty by informing her that it was the only school in London outside which the pavement was washed and the railings dusted every day. The school's philosophy is to this day trumpeted on the busy noticeboard beside its front steps, open for inspection to any casual passerby: "A sense of rivalry has to be encouraged and a boy must be led to discover something in which he can excel. He must be trained to react quickly in an emergency, have a good sense of balance and control, have the strength and ability to extract himself from a dangerous situation—and the urge to win."

Colonel Townend was naturally flattered when the Queen asked him to accept her son as a pupil, but alarmed by the enormous double responsibility, both to the heir to the throne and to his other pupils. It was mutually agreed that, for the present, Charles would simply join the other boys for their afternoon recreation.

Lessons with Mispy continued in the morning, then Charles would don his school uniform and be taken to Hill House to join the daily march along the King's Road to Chelsea. School games were played in the grounds of Duke of York's Headquarters, the military depot named after that very duke who "marched his men to the top of the hill and marched them down again." Newspaper editors, of course, also marched their men to the top of the playing fields, once the prince's new afternoon schedule—which had been successfully kept secret for several weeks—was discovered. But one picture of Charles playing soccer looked much like another, especially as he did not join in the game with much enthusiasm, and the novelty soon wore off. As the Queen and Colonel Townend had hoped, he quickly merged into the crowd of schoolboys walking in line down the street, recognizable only when politely raising his school cap to passersby. It was not as if he were yet a fully fledged schoolboy.

That, again amid tight security, was being planned for the New Year. Over Christmas, meanwhile, official duties again took Prince Philip abroad, to open the Olympic Games at Melbourne and to tour the Antarctic, so it was thought necessary to provide Prince Charles with some male company to offset the petticoat regime. Michael Farebrother, a thirty-six-year-old former Guards officer and headmaster of St. Peter's School, Seaford, joined the royal household at Sandringham as "tutor-companion" to the prince. They roamed the estate together, visited Brancaster Beach, kicked a rugby ball around the Sandringham gardens, and talked about the great figures of history. Farebrother's special subjects were Latin and history, but little academic work was done. Charles's favorite occupation that Christmas, according to his new companion, was watching *The Lone Ranger* and *Champion the Wonder Horse* on TV.

Farebrother's brief spell coincided with Catherine Peebles' Christmas holiday, but it also marked the end of her supervision of Prince Charles. Though Mispy was to stay at the palace to take charge of Princess Anne, Charles was to miss her sorely. With the retirement not long after of Helen Lightbody (Miss Anderson also stayed on to look after Anne), he was suddenly deprived of the two main guardians of his childhood, with whom he had spent considerably more time than with his parents. As he moved into a suite of his own at the palace, Charles kept in close touch with both, writing them long letters and visiting Miss Lightbody in her grace-and-favor Duchy of Cornwall flat in Kennington. But the shock of their departure drove home the awesome prospect of his first day at school with other children. Although his parents had striven to prepare him for it, he was simply not equipped to be wrenched from his sheltered environment.

Not long before the news of Colonel Townend's establishment was broken to him, Prince Charles had asked the Queen: "Mummy, what *are* schoolboys?" For all the Queen's thoughtful care, for all the down-to-earth influence of Prince Philip, by no stretch of anyone's imagination was eight-year-old Prince Charles an ordinary child. He had grown up in palaces and castles. Ships and soldiers, objects of fantasy and imagination to other boys his age, were to Charles everyday realities. He had seen his parents, and on occasion himself, treated with awe and reverence. People became nervous and ill at ease in the presence of his family. At the ring of a telephone, his nanny—and he had no reason to suppose that all children did not have nannies—would abandon whatever was happening and take him along to see his mother. At the age of four, he had been named one of the world's Top Ten Best-Dressed Men. (The citation, in *Tailor and Cutter* magazine, praised his taste in "baby bows, farm stalkers, and double-breasted woollies. . . . His velvet-collared topcoat also follows a popular current trend.") On the list with Prince Charles were Marshal Tito and Bulganin, General Sir Frank Browning, Billy Graham, Fred Astaire, Charlie Chaplin, and Adlai Stevenson. He made the Top Ten again two years later, aged six, along with Harold Macmillan (then housing minister), Sir Hartley Shawcross ("easily the best-dressed Socialist"), Rocky Marciano, Stewart Granger, and Captain Cecil Boyd-Rochfort, the Queen's racehorse trainer.

The prince had never handled money; when eventually he did, it turned out to be puzzling discs of bronze and cupronickel bearing a picture of his mother. He had never been shopping. He had never been on a bus. He had never got lost in a crowd. He had never had to fend for himself.

Nevertheless, on January 28, 1957, Prince Charles made British history by becoming the first heir to the throne ever to go to school. At 9:15 A.M. a black Ford Zephyr driven by a palace chauffeur, with Charles and Miss Peebles in the back, pulled up at the school entrance, where Colonel Townend was waiting to greet him. In the school uniform of cinnamon-colored jersey and corduroy trousers, Charles ran up to the man he had previously known as a football referee. Inside he hung up his coat—distinctive for the velvet collar so admired by *Tailor and Cutter*—and plunged straight into the morning's routine.

The new boy was No. 102 on the school roll of 120, the sons of well-to-do professional men, lawyers, doctors, military men, and politicians. One fellow pupil was the grandson of the new prime minister, Harold Macmillan. There were a number of foreign children, the sons of diplomats stationed in London. It was a school for privileged children, still young and self-confident enough not to be in awe of him. The headmaster had warned them to make no special fuss of the distinguished new face in their midst, but their upbringing anyway equipped them to take Charles's arrival in their stride. All of which was little more help to him at Hill House than it would have been at Dotheboys Hall.

Opened only five years before, the school very much reflected the personal philosophy of Colonel Townend, a former gunnery officer of forty-seven, who had been an Oxford football blue and England athlete. There was no corporal punishment, and the predominantly female staff taught a syllabus broad by preprepatory school standards. It even included elementary anatomy lessons from Mrs. Townend, a state-registered nurse who had once been operating theater sister at Guy's Hospital to Sir John Weir, Gilliatt's assistant at the prince's birth. The school doors were equipped with automatic devices to prevent trapped fingers; all the furniture had rounded edges. The fees were £27 a term (lunch 2s 6d a day extra) and the school motto was taken from Plutarch: "A boy's mind is not a vessel to be filled, but a fire to be kindled."

Charles's first day began with the school song, for which Townend had chosen a hymn called "Schooldays" by the little-known composer Jonathan Battishill (1738–1801):

> Help us that with eager mind
> We may learn both fact and rule,
> Patient, diligent and kind
> In the comradeship of school.

Prince Charles to the staff, plain Charles to his fellow members of Form Six of Middle School, he was given no special escort that first morning, but left to make his own way. Highlight of the day was a visit to the school "madhouse," a gymnasium with padded walls, for basketball. After lunch—beef and carrots, followed by apple pie—he painted a picture of Tower Bridge, and signed it Charles. At three thirty it was time to go home, and the black Zephyr was waiting at the door. As the prince told the Queen all about it that evening, she felt a great sense of relief. The experiment, it seemed, was going to work.

Next morning, however, the crowd outside Hill House was so enormous that she hesitated to let him go. It was not just that the press had set up a constant vigil; local residents who had read of the new recruit in their morning newspapers were all but choking the street. After telephone consultations with Townend the Queen relented, and Charles arrived at school thirty-five minutes late. He had to run the gauntlet of sightseers and photographers to get inside. It was the same when he left.

On the third morning, Townend again telephoned the palace to warn them of a large crowd. It became clear to both the headmaster and the royal parents that this could not go on. Unless the news hounds could be called off, the monarchy's experiment in liberal education might have to be abandoned. The Queen kept her son at home, while her press secretary went into action.

A detective reported back to him with the identities of all the members of the press waiting outside the school, and the news that they intended to wait all day. Colville then personally telephoned each of the newspaper editors involved, reminding them of the Queen's plea of eighteen months before. Within an hour all the Fleet Street representatives had been recalled, and Charles was able to go to school. Thus might his first term have continued in comparative normality had he not contracted tonsillitis the following day, and taken to his bed for three weeks.

By the end of February, he had settled back into everyday school routine more smoothly than those watching over him dared to hope. Swimming and wrestling (which took the place of boxing at Hill House) became his favorite pastimes, and he continued to show promise with watercolors. In the classroom, he remained something of a plodder.

This worried nobody. The purpose of sending Prince Charles to school was not to sow the seeds of a giant intellect, but to help him meet people his own age and learn to live among them. More important, perhaps, it was also to help him develop normal relationships with people older than himself—people other than courtiers and aristocrats. In this it succeeded admirably. Charles was, if anything, politer to the staff than most of the other children; if not yet wholly aware of his station in life, he had been sufficiently drilled at home to treat those around him, however deferential, with the utmost respect. Moreover, Townend's philosophy was to instill discipline in a family rather than an institutional context. Though the boys called him "sir," and though he did not eat his meals with them, the geography of the cramped, converted six-story building was such that they constantly ran in and out of his private quarters at will. It all helped Charles to understand status as a functional necessity, not a matter of arbitrary rank and privilege.

To run into the headmaster's dining room while he was entertaining guests was no crime. To disgrace the school uniform in public, however, was the cardinal sin, meriting the ultimate punishment: loss of the school tie. Townend allowed healthy chaos to exist behind the school doors, but insisted on utterly correct decorum in public. Charles, he later recalled, was usually to be found in the thick of any high-spirited mélée. But he never lost his tie.

The climax of that first term was the school's Field Day. Townend was insistent that it should not be called Sports Day, as there was less emphasis on competition than on keen participation, in the Olympic tradition. The Queen and Prince Philip attended with Anne, after first making it clear that no fuss was to be made of them. Following a recent school outing to the Royal Tournament, Townend included on the program the dismantling and reerection of a military-style field gun. The prince was practice-perfect at this event, though he did not otherwise shine as an athlete. Nonetheless, he remembers how bucked up he was to hear his father's stentorian "Well done, Charles" ringing across the field. For the Queen, it was a day of great importance. As she watched her son set to with a will, anxiously looking to her every so often for fond maternal approval, she was moved by the apparent success of her initiative. And as Charles gravely introduced her to the members of his class—Andrew Smith, son of an air marshal; Michael Carpenter, son of a Westminster canon; William Ladd, son of a diplomat; Edward Lankey, son of a senior Foreign Office civil servant; Andrew Starling, son of an architect; Nicholas Lamb, son of an army officer—she shooks hands with them as earnestly as if they had been the Privy Council. Perhaps the heir to the throne could, after all, grow up like any other little boy from a "good" family background.

His end-of-term report was certainly ordinary. Hill House made a practice of not sending exam results to parents; they were posted on the board and could be viewed by those who wished to. The royal parents did not bother, and Charles himself has perhaps conveniently forgotten how he fared. His school report, however, has been preserved for posterity:

Lent 1957, Upper VI.

READING: *very good indeed; good expression.*

WRITING: *good, firm, clear, well formed.*

ARITHMETIC: *below form average; careful but slow, not very keen.*

SCRIPTURE: *shows keen interest.*

GEOGRAPHY: *good.*

HISTORY: *loves this subject.*

FRENCH: *shows promise.*

LATIN: *made a fair start.*

ART: *good, and simply loves drawing and painting.*

SINGING: *a sweet voice, especially in the lower register.*

FOOTBALL: *enjoying the game.*

GYMNASTICS: *good.*

Hidden behind the familiar vernacular of the schoolteacher, anxious not to cause too much trouble at home, was a reassuringly average start.

The summer term began, like the first, with an attack of tonsillitis, but this time the tonsils lost. They were removed in the Buhl Room at the palace by James Crook of Great Ormond Street Hospital for Children, and Charles insisted on keeping them in a jar on his bedroom mantelpiece. During a few days' recuperation in Great Ormond Street, he sent a message to the eight-year-old daughter of a hospital porter: "To Maureen, with love from Charles." Maureen wrote back, but the romance ended there. Charles was sent to convalesce in Norfolk, at Holkham Hall, home of the Earl of Leicester. It was conveniently near Sandringham and the coastline he knew so well, and he was soon romping in the sand dunes with the Leicesters' twelve-year-old daughter, Lady Sarah Coke. In late May, he was back at Hill House.

By the end of term, the assessment remained much the same:

determined but slow. He was, perhaps generously at that stage, credited with "above average intelligence," and showed signs of a creative bent scarcely evident in either of his parents. Arithmetic was still a major problem, painting his favorite pursuit. At Balmoral that summer, twenty-seven-year-old Mlle Bibiane de Roujoux was imported from Paris on the recommendation of the Queen's former teacher, Madame Untermeyer, to help with his French, which for a while was the only language spoken at the royal dining table.

By August he was enjoying his first yacht racing at Cowes, though seasickness made his first outing with his father in *Bluebottle* something of an ordeal. Once he got over it, however, he shared Prince Philip's exhilaration at the closeness to sea and wind, and the distance from the press. Earlier that summer, his father had forked up ten shillings after betting Charles he could not swim two lengths of the palace pool; later that summer he ticked him off for fidgeting at the highland games at Braemar, observed by a crowd of twenty thousand people. The prince was wearing his first kilt, of Balmoral tartan—to the Scots a sure sign that he was growing up.

The nation had already received another sign that summer, with the announcement that Prince Charles was to be sent away to a prep school.

Part III: *Education*

8

1841-1957: The Education of Princes

Poor little Wales,
Sure the saddest of tales
Is the tale of the studies
With which they are cramming thee.
Punch ON THE YOUNG BERTIE,
PRINCE OF WALES

IN THE EARLY YEARS of her reign, Elizabeth II's sense of inadequacy to the task suddenly thrust upon her was capable of reducing her to tears. For the first ten years of her life, after all, there had been no prospect of her becoming queen of England; she was taught the decorum befitting a king's granddaughter and niece, not the sophistication and know-how befitting a king's daughter and heir. Even after King George VI's reluctant accession, when his daughter's prayers that he might yet have a son proved vain, her father thought *Punch* magazine the best way of introducing her to political arguments and personalities. Occasionally he would mark an article for her to read in the palace copy of the *Times*, in those days still a special edition printed on superior paper.

From Elizabeth and Margaret Rose's governess, Miss Marion Crawford ("Crawfie"), we have received a chatty and detailed account of the little princesses' upbringing, which makes it clear that preparations for the burdens of monarchy were the last thing on the Duke and Duchess of York's curriculum for their children. "I had the feeling," wrote Miss Crawford, "that the Duke and Duchess, most happy in their own married life, were not over concerned with the higher education of their daughters. They

97

wanted most for them a really happy childhood, with lots of pleasant memories stored up against the days that might come out and, later, happy marriages." Even their grandfather, King George V, was concerned about nothing so much as their hand-writing. "For goodness' sake," he told Crawfie, "teach Margaret and Lilibet to write a decent hand, that's all I ask you. None of my children could write properly. They all do it exactly the same way. I like a hand with some character in it."

Their mother's aspirations for them summed up the princesses' education: "To spend as long as possible in the open air, to enjoy to the full the pleasures of the country, to be able to dance and draw and appreciate music, to acquire good manners and perfect deportment, and to cultivate all the distinctively feminine graces." Thus Elizabeth II, not surprisingly, would have preferred to the life of a queen that of "a lady living in the country with lots of horses and dogs." Which, for somewhat less than half her waking hours, is precisely what she is. But over twenty-five years and more she has also, after that uncertain start, become the shrewdest and most deft of monarchs, inching the institution closer to its people while preserving the essential, mystical gulf between the two.

Such skills are innate in her; they owe little to the lessons in the constitution that she started at the age of thirteen with Sir Henry Marten, vice-provost of Eton, and which became a correspondence course when she was sequestered at royal country residences during the war. Marten religiously imbued the teen-age princess with the precepts of Walter Bagehot, on which her grandfather, George V, had been raised, despite the aspersions occasionally cast on his father. Bagehot's definition of the British constitutional monarchy, with its famous summary of the monarch's rights vis-à-vis the prime minister, "to be consulted, to encourage and to warn," remains largely unchallenged. But the representative family monarchy of the later twentieth century, as acclaimed by its people in Silver Jubilee Year, 1977, is much more the personal creation of Elizabeth II.

One uncharted course in which she showed a hand both firm and innovative was the education of her eldest son. In the long and painstaking series of decisions it involved, she relied heavily on the rough-hewn good sense of her husband. If, in retrospect, it seems inevitable that Prince Charles should have gone to the

"Safely delivered of a Prince":
the first picture by Cecil
Beaton, November 1948

Four generations: with his
mother, his grandfather,
King George VI, and his
great-grandmother, Queen
Mary, at his christening

The birth certificate

92	Fourteenth November, 1948 Buckingham Palace	Charles Philip Arthur George	Boy	His Royal Highness Philip, Duke of Edinburgh	Her Royal Highness The Princess Elizabeth Alexandra Mary, Duchess of Edinburgh	His Royal Highness The Duke of Edinburgh (Lieutenant, R.N.)	*[signature]* Buckingham Palace, S.W.1	Fifteenth December, 1948	*[signature]* Registrar
93									
94									

First year:
on the lawn
at Windlesham Moor

Aged two, at Clarence House

Watching the parade go by:
on the garden wall of Clarence House

Third birthday: a walk in
the park with Nanny Lightbody

En route for Sandringham:
Princess Anne's first public appearance

With "Grandpa England":
Elizabeth II's favorite
portrait of her father
and her son, which still
stands on her desk at
Buckingham Palace

Duke of Cornwall:
The new Queen with
her family at Balmoral,
September 1952

The favorite pedal car,
now a palace *objet d'art*

. . . and is kept in order by
Grandmama and Aunt Margot

Coronation, 1953:
the heir apparent
arrives at the Abbey . . .

First "balcony job": enjoying the coronation fly-past

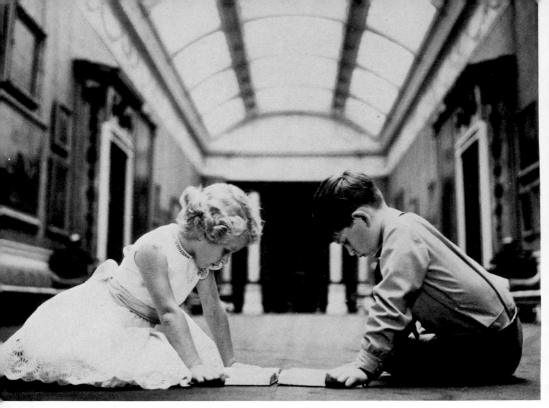

Royal siblings: a study by the future Lord Snowdon

Making new friends at Sandringham . . .

and Windsor

Hill House: the first heir apparent ever to be a schoolboy

Sports Day at Hill House, under the watchful eye of Colonel Townend

One boy who can't be an engine driver when he grows up

same schools as his father, these were far from foregone conclusions in the first few years of his life. The young Duke of Cornwall showed little of the self-confidence one of his rank would need to survive in the brutal, amoral world of young schoolboys away from home. But the Queen and Prince Philip had pooled their own very different experiences, hers the traditionally sheltered royal education at the hands of a governess and tutors, his a disrupted progress through private schools in France, England, Germany, and Scotland. They were determined to make a bold departure from the pattern established by their forebears, and their every effort with the young Charles was directed toward it. They wanted the heir to the throne to be educated outside his home, in the company of other boys his own age, from the earliest possible moment.

The education of Princes of Wales has throughout British history provided a forum of argument, experiment, and even intrigue, resulting as often as not in unhappiness and failure. From the time of Edward I, who was sent to France to be educated, most monarchs have tried to create supermonarchs in their own image; others, such as the Hanoverians, have been more intent on defusing the threat posed to their own rule by their own heir. But it was the last hundred years that provided the most instructive examples, all too familiar to Queen Victoria's two great-great-grandchildren in the 1950s. Elizabeth II and her consort were above all concerned to learn from the mistakes made by Victoria and hers.

Elizabeth and Philip's supreme good sense was to realize that a contemporary constitutional monarch needs a good, all-round education much more than any form of special training. Since the death of George IV in 1830, when monarchs have reigned rather than ruled, the one essential requirement of a sovereign has been that he command the respect of his people. It would be absurd to expect consistent ability, even competence, of any office passed on by heredity. Given a character that his people can respect, from a distance, any sovereign can survive; without it, the monarchy would be in its nearest danger of collapse, as it was in 1830, and as it would have been in 1936 had not the Duke of York quickly grown into the breach left by the abdication of his elder brother. King George VI was a historic example of a monarch who started out with respect, if few other qualifications, and was subsequently enlarged by his office. Prince Charles himself has said: "There isn't any power. There can be influence. The influence is in direct ratio to the respect people have for you."

Of his upbringing he has also said: "I've learnt the way a monkey learns—by watching its parents." Prince Philip has always been cogent on this: "Training isn't necessary. They do on-the-job training, so to speak, and learn the trade, or business, or craft, just from being with us and watching us function, and seeing the whole organization around us. They can't avoid it. What is much more difficult is bringing them up as people." Victoria and Albert saw things precisely the other way round.

Who Should Educate the Prince of Wales? was the title of a provocative and anonymous pamphlet published in 1843, when the future King Edward VII was just two years old. His mother, Victoria, was as intent as the pamphleteer and his huge readership on producing a model prince—ideally, to her, a working model of her beloved husband. The queen was aware of the inadequacies of her own education, thanks in part to the plain speaking of her uncle, the king of Hanover: "She was more ignorant on her accession than any girl of her age in the world." But she was more anxious, as were her subjects, to eradicate the memory of George III's lecherous sons, her other uncles, of whom she shared Shelley's view ("the dregs of their dull race") rather than Lord Melbourne's ("jolly fellows"). The plans she and Albert laid for their son's upbringing, even before he was born, were partly by way of atonement. More important, they constituted an elaborate effort to secure a shaky and discredited monarchy, and to lay the foundations for its survival into a more democratic age.

The educational treadmill they devised for poor Bertie was founded on a fundamental misreading of history, swallowed wholesale from their overtrusted German confidant Baron Christian von Stockmar. He persuaded them that the mistakes of George III's sons were caused by their inadequate education, and that this had been largely responsible for the gradual shift of executive power from the monarch to the monarch's ministers. But their education had been excellent: George IV, if not William IV, was one of Britain's most cultivated kings. The alteration in the unwritten constitution owed much more to the industrial revolution and the nineteenth-century electoral reforms which followed it than to the character of the sovereign. The growth of diverse political parties, and the alternatives thus available to a more broadly enfranchised nation, forced the monarchy into its now familiar nonpolitical role. The alternative, and the only way to retain executive state powers, was for the king to identify himself with political factions, which would have ensured his downfall with theirs. He could not, as Sir Lewis Namier observed, "in turn captain opposite teams."

Victoria was plainly surprised by the limits to her constitutional powers, and constantly attempted to exceed them. Prince Albert was himself a man of considerable ability, whose intellect and imagination were quite the match of most of his wife's ministers. He was, as Lord John Russell put it, "an informal and potent member of all cabinets," and he believed that his son would need similar qualities to ensure the monarchy's survival. So, with Stockmar, Prince Albert personally devised a comprehensive program designed to drum them into him.

At the age of seven, the prince was handed from the nursery to a formidable team of tutors. Their principal, a thirty-year-old Eton master aptly named Henry Birch, was instructed quite simply to fashion an "executive Governor of the State . . . the respository of all the moral and intellectual qualities by which it is held together, and under the guidance of which it advances in the great path of civilisation." Lessons in the palace lasted at first six, then seven, hours a day, six days a week. Bertie worked longer hours and enjoyed shorter holidays than any of his schoolboy contemporaries. Birch had orders to ensure that he was thoroughly exhausted by the end of each day; among other physical pursuits, he was drilled daily by a drill sergeant to deflect his budding skills at dancing. Even the tutors began to think the regime too demanding. "You will wear him out too early . . . Make him climb trees! Run! Leap! Row! Ride!" the French master, Dr. Voisin, urged Birch's successor. "In many things, savages are much better educated than we are." But Albert and Stockmar would have none of it. The results were disastrous.

Before he was ten, the prince was on the edge of a nervous breakdown. Days of utter lethargy began to follow a few of intense activity. There were outbursts of destructive rage. He would stand in a corner screaming and stamping, or hurl things against walls and through windows, before falling into a state of complete physical collapse. His father devised a series of punishments for this behavior, but none, however severe, could curb it.

The young Bertie's world was entirely one of adults. At one stage he was sent to attend meetings of Pop, the Eton debating society, but behaved with such boorishness, and displayed such ignorance, that he was quickly withdrawn from the society of his fellows. When he was finally sent out into the world, to Oxford, his father was insistent that "his position and life *must* be different from that of other undergraduates." He wore the distinctive gown and gold-tufted cap of the nobleman; professors came to his home to teach him and six hand-picked aristocrats; students had to rise whenever he entered a lecture hall or common room. Prince Albert at this time dismissed him as a "thorough and cunning lazybones," and Queen Victoria even told friends that he was mentally deficient. But his tutors found in him powers of application and qualities of openness and honesty that his regimented life had all but suppressed.

Thanks to a liberating tour of America in 1860, and a happier time at Cambridge, Bertie gradually began to escape the shadows of his youth and adolescence. He grew from an overweight, oversexed, utterly repressed Prince of Wales into a mature, diplomatic, and immensely popular king. Over forty years as the pillar of a glittering London court, he eroded memories of the gambling and marital scandals with which his youth had besmirched the monarchy. On his thirtieth birthday, soon after giving evidence in the Mordaunt divorce case, he lay apparently dying from typhoid; his sudden recovery six weeks later had the nation, surprised at its own fickleness, demanding a day of national rejoicing. His strength of character ensured his security and success, thirty years later, on the throne. Some legacies of his upbringing, notably those fits of rage, never left him. But he was aware of it, and took pains to see that his own sons were spared such suffering.

King Edward VII was a grandfather four years before he acceded to the throne. As Prince of Wales, he had had to cope with his widowed mother's intransigence when setting about the education of his own heir. His initial plan was to send Prince Albert Victor ("Eddy" to his family) to public school and university, and his second son, George, to Dartmouth and a naval career. But at only seven months Prince Eddy was diagnosed a weak baby, and soon showed himself a backward child. The tutor engaged by their father, the Reverend John Neale Dalton (father of the Labour politician Hugh Dalton), found that only Prince George's company could inspire Eddy's constitutional lethargy to any interest in anything. He advised that they should on no account be separated.

Their grandmother had set her heart on sending Prince Eddy to Wellington, a school with a military slant of which the Prince of Wales was a governor. She was content for George to enter the navy, but Eddy was to be king and should not be allowed to acquire the rough habits and nationalistic attitudes of service life. It took all her son's and Dalton's ingenuity to dissuade her; the palace memos that flew on this subject are themselves full of cautionary tales for anyone contemplating the education of a monarch. The Prince of Wales's first concern was that his sons should grow up, unlike him, with people rather than books, out of doors more than in classrooms, left to find their own levels rather than programmed for perfection. But thanks to Dalton, he was now even more intent on keeping them together. Victoria was coaxed into permitting them both to attend Dartmouth "as an experiment."

King George V later recalled: "It never did me any good to be a prince, I can tell you, and many was the time I wished I hadn't been. Dartmouth was a pretty tough place and, so far from making allowance for our disadvantages, the other boys made a point of taking it out of us, on the grounds that they'd never be able to do it later on. There was a lot of fighting among the cadets, and the rule was that if challenged you had to accept. So they used to make me go up and challenge the bigger boys—I was awfully small then—and I'd get a hiding time and again."

It may have made a man of George, but it just about destroyed poor Eddy. Dalton reported to the Prince of Wales that Eddy "fails not in one or two subjects, but in all." His "abnormally dormant" disposition made it impossible for him "to fix his attention to any given subject for more than a few minutes consecutively." And even that was achieved only thanks to the reassuring presence of his younger brother. Plans to part their ways were again abandoned, and Eddy was sent to join

George aboard HMS *Bacchante*. Between 1879 and 1892, accompanied by Dalton and a team of tutors specially chosen to assist his backwardness, Eddy accompanied George on three extended world cruises, the one brother still fading away, the other growing to the full flush of manhood. Those years, wrote King George V's biographer, Harold Nicolson, developed in him "a quality more forceful than ordinary manliness—a categorical sense of duty . . . which became the fly-wheel of his life."

In 1892, their ways did at last part. After a brief sojourn together in France, Prince George was back in the navy as a midshipman, while Prince Eddy was being crammed for Cambridge. "I do not think he can possibly derive much benefit," the head tutor reported to Dalton. "He hardly knows the meaning of the words 'to read.' " After Cambridge, Eddy served a bored term in the Hussars, then began to devote what energies he had to a life of somewhat scandalous dissipation; to this day, theories survive that Prince Eddy was Jack the Ripper. For once, Queen Victoria and the Prince of Wales were agreed: his only chance of salvation was "a good sensible wife with some considerable character." She was found in Princess May of Teck, to whom Prince Eddy proposed in December 1891. A month later, aged twenty-seven, he was dead of influenza.

For all his lack of promise, Prince Albert Victor in death stirred his family and the nation to paroxysms of grief. His brother George, robbed of the only human being with whom he could enjoy an absolutely equal friendship, was desolated. "No two brothers could have loved each other more than we did," he wrote to his mother, Queen Alexandra. "Alas! It is only now that I have found out how deeply I have loved him." The prince's devastation was compounded by the fact that he was now heir to the throne and would have to abandon his naval career for a study of the constitution. His standard of education, as he himself readily admitted, was "below that of the average country gentleman educated at a public school." The navy had given him a strict sense of duty, orderly habits, a strong instinct for command and obedience, and a deep feeling for conservative orthodoxy. But he was woefully ignorant, for instance, of contemporary domestic and foreign politics; his main interests were yachting, shooting, stamp collecting, and the management of the Sandringham estates. Even after falling in love with and marrying his brother's fiancée, Princess May (who later became Queen Mary), he remained emotionally immature.

His father came to the rescue. Edward VII took a great delight in endowing his virtuous son with all the fatherly companionship he himself had been denied. "We are more like brothers than father and son," he wrote to him. He made George, created successively Duke of York and Prince of Wales, privy to all state secrets, again a reversal of his own parents' policy, and instructed him in the ways of the world. But he could do nothing about that emotional deficiency. King George V conspicuously failed to recreate this happy and productive relationship with his own children.

George told his friend Lord Derby: "My father was frightened of his mother, I was frightened of my father, and I am damned well going to see to it that my children are frightened of me." Throughout his life, he treated his family as if it were a ship's company, of which he was both master and martinet. His eldest son, when Duke of Windsor, recalled in his memoirs: "We were, in fact, figuratively speaking, always on parade, a fact that he would never allow us to forget. If we appeared before him with our Navy lanyards a fraction of an inch out of place, or with our dirks or our sporrans awry, there would be an outburst worthy of the quarterdeck of a warship. Another greeted the appearance of one of us—it may well have been me—with hands stuffed into trouser pockets. Lala [their nanny] was immediately summoned and ordered to sew up the pockets of our sailor suits, a royal command which, despite some inward reservations, she did not dare to disobey."

George V deeply detested change, and decreed that what had been good enough for him would be good enough for his sons. A senior tutor, H. P. Hansell, was therefore engaged to prepare Prince Edward and Prince Albert (known to their family as David and Bertie, later respectively King Edward VIII and King George VI) for entry to Dartmouth. Hansell urged that they be sent to preparatory school, where, he argued, they would benefit from the stimulus of competition and gain valuable early experience of community life. "My brother and I," George replied, "never went to preparatory school. The navy will teach David all he needs to know."

This time it was the younger brother who lagged behind.

Prince Edward, though slight, was physically robust; his natural charm, combined with his quick brain and genuine modesty, ensured easy success. Prince Albert was more diffident, suffered from a stammer, and was invariably bottom of his class. "One could wish," wrote his tutor to the king, "that he had more of Prince Edward's keenness and application." King George VI's biographer, Sir John Wheeler-Bennett, quotes a contemporary's judgment that "it was like comparing an ugly duckling with a cock pheasant." Through a characteristic effort of will, however, Bertie later began to make up lost ground, and was to enjoy a happy and successful naval career after his elder brother had been diverted to training for kingship.

Edward was sent to France and Germany, to learn their languages and study their politics, and thence, reluctantly, to Oxford. At Magdalen he insisted on living in his own rooms in college—a happy precedent for Prince Charles—and was soon known around the university as "the Pragger-Wagger." He beagled, kept a string of polo ponies, played roulette, and frequented the college steward's bar, "Gunners." (Gunstone, the steward, was in the habit of inserting a banana in the neck of a bottle filled with burning paper, so that the banana would be pulled inside. This more than anything else impressed the king on his one visit to his son in Oxford. "By God," he said, "that's one of the smartest tricks I've ever seen.") This routine Edward recalled in his memoirs as "tranquil, sober and serious" days. "Bookish he will never be," reported the college president, Sir Herbert Warren, to the king, "not a 'Beauclerk,' still less a 'British Solomon.' " George V was not in the least concerned.

Edward VIII, in fact, seemed in later life to think education a positive disadvantage for a prince. Remembering how little he had learnt from his tutor, Mr. Hansell, and being "unable to recall anything brilliant or original that he ever said," the Duke of Windsor commented: "No doubt, in view of the restraints laid upon the Monarchy, this was all for the best. To have put a prince in the direct line of succession under a bold and opinionated teacher might well have led to the one conflict with which the constitutional system cannot cope." At least Oxford taught him something of his fellow man. "All the time," according to Warren's report, "he was learning more and more every day of men, gauging character, watching its play, getting to know what

Englishmen are like, both individually and in the mass. . . ."

This would have stood him in good stead at Dartmouth, where he had been mercilessly ragged. The other cadets were fond of dyeing his hair red, and on one occasion "guillotined" him in a window frame to remind him of his heritage. "Nothing I had ever learnt under Mr. Hansell," he wrote, "seemed to supply a solution" to such problems.

Prince Edward did not risk taking a degree at Oxford. Nor did Prince Albert when he spent a year at Cambridge after the 1914–18 war—in which both saw service, though not as active as either would have wished. In the early 1920s, Albert was content to build up a solid reputation at home, particularly in industrial welfare and youth work, while the Prince of Wales scored a series of dazzling personal triumphs overseas. It was this cautious, determined conscientiousness that stood the Duke of York in such good stead in 1936, when his brother's abdication suddenly pitchforked him into a job for which he was totally unprepared.

George VI's daughter and her husband thus had a lengthy chapter of accidents from which to learn. Elizabeth II also knew that she herself had met few beyond the palace walls before the age of eighteen, when she had persuaded her father to let her sign on as a second subaltern in the wartime ATS. She and Prince Philip were all too aware of the disadvantages of sequestering their eldest son at home. But they had equal evidence that it was no use expecting him to melt inconspicuously into the life of a boarding school, like any other child. Simpering royal commentators were cooing in column after column that Charles and Anne were "ordinary" children being brought up in a "normal" way, but it was obvious to their parents that this was impossible. No one put the problem better than the Duke of Windsor, whose memoirs were published at this time (1951): "The pleased incredulity with which the public reacts to the elementary demonstrations on the part of Royalty that they are, after all, like other people is matched by the public's firm refusal to accept them as such."

The best Elizabeth and Philip could hope for was to guide Charles, by their own fond attentions, into sharing the lives of other children without himself unduly suffering. Prince Philip put this forcefully to his biographer, Basil Boothroyd, when Prince Charles was already at public school.

> People talk about a normal upbringing. What is a normal upbringing? What you really mean is: was I insisting that they should go through all the disadvantages of being brought up in the way other people are brought up? Precisely that—disadvantages. There's always this idea about treating them exactly like other children. In fact it means they're treated much worse, because they're known by name and by association. . . . It's all very well to say they're treated the same as everybody else, but it's impossible. I think that what is possible, and in fact necessary, is that they should realise they're not anonymous. This has got to come at some stage.

The first step with Prince Charles—and an innovation of more consequence than the common sense behind it suggests— was to treat him exactly the same as his younger sister and brothers. All four were introduced at the earliest ages to the widest possible choice of pastimes: swimming, sailing, shooting, fishing, go-karting, polo. In Charles's case, fishing, shooting, and polo became abiding passions, at all of which he in time became more proficient than his father. "I've always tried to help them master at least one thing," said Prince Philip, "because as soon as a child feels self-confidence in one area, it spills over into all the others. You even notice that if they feel they've made a real personal accomplishment of that kind, then this is immediately reflected even in their academic performance."

He never cared too much, however, about academic prowess. Like any other parent, Prince Philip went through school reports, but there were rarely recriminations. "I don't really take them frightfully seriously. I say: 'Look, I'm only going to bother if you're permanently bottom. I really couldn't care less where you are. Just stay in the middle, that's all I ask.' " He has always, anyway, disapproved of the importance attached to examinations. "Children go through enormous changes. For a time they're in phase with life around them, then they go out of phase and become unlivable with, and everything they do is wrong and cross-grained and maddening. Then suddenly it all comes right for a bit. Then they go off on another tack. It's impossible at any point to say 'This is what they're going to be like.' The pendulum's got to swing a lot more before it settles down."

Prince Philip is not the strict, disciplinarian parent that has been painted. His idea of a major family crime is dishonesty—"by which I mean that if you ask them a question, they must give you an honest answer." Nor has he been an overinquisitive father. "There are often questions you'd like to ask, but it's much better not to unless it's really necessary." His children's behavior, he told Boothroyd, had been average to good. "I think they do silly things occasionally, but it's nearly always satisfactorily resolved, more by discussion than anything."

Thus Prince Charles was consulted about his own education at every stage after his prep school. "From the beginning," said his father, "I was careful not to make a rigid plan—I haven't for any of them—until some sort of foreseeable situation arose. I said, 'Well, here are the alternatives: you've seen Eton, you know the place, it's right on our doorstep [at Windsor], you can more or less come home any time you like. Its disadvantages are that every time you hiccup you'll have the whole of the national press on your shoulders. Also, Eton is frequently in the news, and when it is it's going to reflect on you. If you go to the north of Scotland you'll be out of sight, and they're going to think twice about taking an airplane to get up there, so it's got to be a major crisis before they'll actually turn up, and you'll be able to get on with things.' And we had a general discussion, and I said, 'Well, it's up to you.' "

The Prince of Wales has repaid the compliment: "My parents were marvelous in this way. They'd outline all the possibilities, and in the end it was up to you. My father had a particularly strong influence, and it was very good for me. I had perfect confidence in his judgment."

Family decisions are still taken on a committee basis, one member, one vote. Again, Elizabeth II and her husband have learned from their family's recent history. As Prince Philip put it: "It's no use saying do this, do that, don't do this, don't do that. You can warn them about certain things—that's about the most you can do—or you can say, 'This is the situation you are in, these are the choices, on balance it looks as if this is the sensible one, go away and think it over, and come back and let me know what you think.' " There were times, of course, when the children's wishes were overruled. "It's very easy, when children want something, to say no immediately. I think it's quite important not to give an unequivocal answer at once. Much better to think it over. Then if you do eventually say no, I think they really accept it."

Prince Philip's freewheeling nature has also propelled him, of course, into expansive pronouncements on such subjects as education in more general terms. "The art of education," he once said, "is to combine formal training with as wide a variety of experiences as possible, including some which involve a calculated risk. I think education is intended to produce intelligent, morally strong, self-sufficient human beings willing and capable of improving the machinery of living which man has created for his enjoyment." On a visit to the USA in 1956, he was a little more specific. "The Queen and I want Charles to go to school with other boys of his generation and learn to live with other children, and to absorb from childhood the discipline imposed by education with others." The royal couple had already been making a series of visits, private and public, to British boys' schools, and had entertained a number of headmasters socially at Buckingham Palace. But Philip's announcement brought forth a predictable shower of advice.

In the forefront was Lord Altrincham (now John Grigg), whose attack on the monarchy in the August 1957 edition of his journal, the *National and English Review*, had earned him a televised slap in the face and lasting public obloquy. In England it is now generally forgotten that Altrincham was a self-declared monarchist, and that the rest of his review's special edition on the monarchy was devoted to glowing assessments by such passionate loyalists as Dermot Morrah, Prince Charles's previous biographer. Altrincham protested that he made his criticisms in the Queen's own interests; there were few, however, who bore this in increasingly apoplectic mind as they read how the monarchy had "lamentably failed to live with the times" and that the court, unlike the society it was supposed to reflect, remained "a tight little enclave of English ladies and gentlemen." The name of Altrincham—though renounced long since by its owner, a reluctant peer—has ever since stuck in the gullet of the English patriot.

The Queen's already announced decision that Prince Charles would go to a private preparatory school was one topic to which Altrincham addressed himself. "Will she have the wisdom," he wrote, "to give her children an education very different from her own? Will she, above all, see to it that Prince Charles is equipped with all the knowledge he can absorb without injury to his health, and that he mixes during his formative years with children who will one day be bus drivers, dockers, engineers etc., not merely with future landowners or stockbrokers?" A minority of socialist MPs joined him in the cry that the heir to the throne should attend a state school and mix with the less wealthy and less privileged of his future subjects.

The feeling at the palace was not that such a course was impossible. Indeed, it had obvious cosmetic advantages at a time when Elizabeth II was concerned to bring the monarchy into closer touch with a broader cross-section of her people. (She had recently introduced palace luncheon parties with more democratic guest lists, abolished the presentation of debutantes at court, welcomed the introduction of life peerages, and opened part of Buckingham Palace to the public as the Queen's Gallery.) But would not the pupils, perhaps even the staff, at a London secondary or grammar school be even more in awe of the heir to the throne than the sons of the well-to-do? Would not a private boarding school, enclosed in its own grounds, afford a greater chance of privacy than a school open to the streets of the capital? If Charles were to be the first heir to the throne in British history to be sent away to school so young, might it not be done by degrees, rather than by so abrupt and melodramatic a gesture toward democracy?

If this reads like special pleading, so it was. Apart from any such considerations, the Queen and Prince Philip, like a large proportion of the British public, were convinced that the standards of private education were still higher than those of state schools. They were about to make their son suffer quite enough, they could tell, without risking substandard tuition to undermine his future. And, given a system that permitted freedom of educational choice to the wealthy, they had as much right as any other well-heeled British couple to make their own decision.

A boarding school, and a private one, it was to be. Prince Charles was too young to be consulted about his first school, and had anyway made it more than clear—like any other child his age—that he was reluctant to leave home at all. But the Queen and Prince Philip had looked over a number of preparatory schools, including the one Philip had himself attended. It had moved since the 1930s, and was scarcely the same school. But it provided everything they were looking for. And, despite himself, Prince Philip found the idea of sending his son to his old school downright satisfying.

9

1957-62: Cheam

He is still a little shy, but very pop-
ular . . . passionately keen on and
promising at games . . . academi-
cally, a good average. . . .
PRINCE CHARLES'S FIRST END-OF-
TERM REPORT FROM CHEAM

JUST BEFORE THE First World War Prince Louis of Battenberg, then First Sea Lord, had occasion to be impressed by the
manners of two midshipmen under his command. He asked them
where they had been educated. On discovering they were both
ex-pupils of Cheam preparatory school, the Duke of Edinburgh's
grandfather decreed that henceforth all male members of the
Battenberg family would go there.

When Prince Philip enrolled at the school in 1930, it had
been established for more than two hundred years in the Surrey
town from which it takes its name. But the school from which it
grew has an even longer history, giving Cheam its claim to be
England's oldest prep school. The pupils of the Reverend George
Aldritch, founder of a small private establishment in London for
the sons of the gentry, can be traced back to the reign of Charles I;
the records of Caius College, Cambridge, show one of them
matriculating in 1650. The Great Plague of 1665 forced Aldritch
out of London to Cheam, where he joined forces with a local
school in a house called Whitehall, which still stands (it is now
an antique shop) in the High Street. After several further moves
within the town limits, Cheam School settled itself in 1719 onto
the thirteen-acre site it still occupied on Prince Philip's arrival

in 1930. By then, however, a railway station had materialized nearby, and urban London was fast encroaching.

Thus in 1934, the year after Philip's departure, it moved again: to a sixty-five-acre site in the village of Headley, near the Hampshire downs. Though now in the county of Hampshire, the school's postal address was in Berkshire, and it was still named after a small town in Surrey. The rest of Cheam's pedigree was equally quixotic, thanks particularly to two colorful headmasters among the fourteen the school had had in some three hundred years. In 1752, when there were just fifteen pupils on the school roll, Cheam was bought by a reforming young clergyman called William Gilpin, who went on to become vicar of Boldre and achieve modest renown as the author of a series of illustrated travel books. He is better known to posterity as the original for Dr. Syntax, in whose adventures Rowlandson and William Combe parodied Gilpin's literary style. He may also have been the model for Mr. Jennings, the schoolmaster in Smollett's *Peregrine Pickle*. At Cheam, he is best remembered for a very un-eighteenth-century aversion to corporal punishment; he introduced a system of fines and detentions, firmly enshrined on paper in case his rage got the better of his judgment. An equally eccentric nineteenth-century successor was Robert Stammers Tabor, who took over the school in 1856 (and, like Gilpin, handed it on to his son after him). Tabor, something of a snob, initiated a new system of address for the aristocratic pupils which Cheam always seems to have attracted: a peer was called "my darling child," the son of a peer "my dear child," and a commoner "my child."

Tabor would have enjoyed working out a new category for the pupil who joined Cheam School on September 23, 1957: Charles, Duke of Cornwall, the first heir apparent to have been sent to a preparatory school in British history. The joint headmasters, Peter Beck and Mark Wheeler, both Cambridge graduates, contented themselves with continuing the Hill House tradition, as requested by the Queen: he would be "Charles" to his fellow pupils, "Prince Charles" to members of staff, whom he in turn would address normally as "sir."

The school's most distinguished old boy was the new recruit's father. Prince Philip's cousin, the Marquess of Milford Haven, had also been there. Among other former pupils were numbered one prime minister; one speaker of the House of Commons; two viceroys of India, one of them Lord Hardinge of Penshurst, friend of Edward VII and father of the private secretary to Edward VIII and George VI; Sir Ian Hamilton, military commander of the ill-fated Gallipoli expedition; Lord Dunsany, the Irish writer of plays, prose, and verse; and Lord Randolph Churchill, father of Sir Winston, who according to his son was "most kindly treated and quite content" at the school.

Charles had already visited Cheam with his parents and his sister. "You won't be able to jump up and down on *these* beds," the Queen told him as he gazed with dismay upon the two-hundred-year-old springless wooden frame and its unyielding hair mattress. Beyond the lily pond was a happier sight: a swimming pool. As the royal family roamed the tranquil school grounds, the peace disturbed only by jets from the nearby US air base, they agreed that the sixty-five acres should provide the required insulation from the outside world of sightseers and journalists; its copious undergrowth, however, would also provide excellent cover for intruders, so it was decided that the young prince's detective should accompany him and live in the grounds. Beck and Wheeler further complied with the Queen's wishes by sending a letter to all parents before the beginning of that autumn term:

"It is the wish of the Queen and Prince Philip that there shall be no alteration in the way the school is run and that Prince Charles shall be treated the same as other boys. . . . It will be a great help if you will explain this. His parents' wishes are that he should be given exactly the same education and upbringing as the other boys at the school."

Once again, however, it was impossible for anyone to expect Charles to merge inconspicuously into the beginning-of-term throng. He remembers those first few days at Cheam as the most miserable of his life. His mother recalled him shuddering with horror as they began the long overnight train journey from Balmoral to London, to be followed by the sixty-mile drive to Headley. On arrival, in his gray school uniform, Charles raised his blue school cap politely to Mr. Beck, then watched his parents drive away. A few hours later the mathematics master, David Munir, who had been detailed to keep a special eye on the prince, looked out into the school grounds. One small boy, "very much in need of a haircut," stood conspicuously apart, a solitary and utterly wretched figure. Cheam boys were sufficiently older than the Prince's fellow pupils at Hill House to be unable to accept the heir to the throne as just another of the twelve new boys, despite—perhaps because of—their parents' urgings. Charles himself had no experience at all of forcing his way into a group of strangers, winning the acceptance of his peers. The Cheam boys couldn't quite believe he was among them. Nor, for that matter, could Prince Charles.

Cheam had one hundred pupils between the ages of eight and fourteen; Prince Charles's school number was 89. The day began at 7:15 A.M. with the rising bell, followed by prayers at seven forty-five and breakfast at eight. For the first time in his life, Charles was sharing an uncarpeted room with other boys, making his own bed, cleaning his own shoes, waiting on others at table, and keeping his clothes in a wicker basket under his bed (known to the boys as "the dog basket"). Lessons began at nine and continued, with a break, until lunch at one. There were half holidays on Wednesdays and Saturdays; on Sundays there was an extra half hour in bed before the school parade to the nearby parish church of St. Peter's.

Charles happily wrote the compulsory minimum of one letter home per week and was always among the first to snap up his weekly half-pound allowance of sweets. Though he was losing his puppy fat, the prince was still a plumpish boy. When the change to a school diet prompted a few stomach upsets, he confided to the first-year teacher, Miss Margaret Cowlishaw, that he wasn't used to all this rich food at home.

No "tuck" boxes were allowed, as at most such schools, but sweets were "bought" out of the boys' recommended pocket money of twenty-five shillings a term; in fact, the boys did not handle the money themselves, using instead a system of credits. So the young prince was still denied experience of coin of the realm, itself enough to render apocryphal one of the first Cheam stories to make the British newspapers. Charles, it went, was kept short of pocket money by his parents, so had held an auction of his personal belongings to raise money for more sweets. For once, he learned that newspaper fictions can have their rewards. As the story wended its way into the American press, the Association of Retail Confectioners of America, then in conference in San Francisco, voted to send across a massive food parcel containing everything from bubble gum and jelly beans to peanut butter and Tootsie Rolls. "We were told the prince was short of candy," said the accompanying note, "so our committee unanimously passed a resolution to the effect that we ought to pitch in and help him out of a jam."

It did him no harm in the school popularity stakes. According to Peter Beck, Charles quickly became a good mixer. A special friend was the headmaster's daughter, Mary Beck, the only girl at the school. Charles's loneliness, indeed, may have been only in his own mind; he was already aware that other children might befriend him for the wrong reasons. It was often the nicest boys, he recalls, who hung back, not wishing to be seen "sucking up" to him; those who forced their attentions on him were often those whom he liked least. Throughout his life, he has felt the need to make an extra effort in such company. He knows the heir to the throne is by definition the focal point of any room's attention; to justify that attention, he has to try to appear more than usually interesting. It is a tricky psychological problem, which must account in large degree for the painful shyness of the eight-year-old schoolboy. As he strove to overcome this, his fellows marked him down as a bit of a lone wolf.

At Cheam, furthermore, he began to be haunted by another shadow which has pursued him ever after: that of his father, an outgoing, gregarious man who had never had to cope with such problems. At Cheam, after all, Philip was prince of Greece and Denmark, not of England or Wales. The press were not pursuing him from bush to bush, and the other boys looked on him with no awe. While academically undistinguished, he had shone on the sports field (first team goalkeeper and captain of the cricket eleven) and Charles knew his father was hoping for some such achievement from him.

Charles's lessons at Cheam were of course geared to the Common Entrance Examination taken before admission to most British public schools (although as it transpired, he was to attend one which did not require it). History remained an abiding interest, not least because he now knew it concerned his ancestors and was already preparing to receive him. In geography he also shone, again because his parents' tours had made the globe a familiar place. Math remained an utter mystery, closely followed by Latin and Greek. Before the afternoon lessons there were games, about which he remained unenthusiastic (despite evidence to the contrary in his end-of-term reports), or other outdoor activities such as camping or wildlife study, very much modeled on the precepts of Lord Baden-Powell, though the school had no Boy Scout troop as such. As at Hill House, the Cheam gymnasium became one of Charles's favorite haunts, where athletic rough-and-tumble often developed into a mild schoolboy fracas. Charles soon had a reputation for giving as good as he got. He was particularly sensitive to jokes about his plumpness, and took days to recover after hearing the boy beneath him in a collapsed rugby scrum cry, "Oh, do get *off*, Fatty." The school was visited regularly by a barber from Harrods, Cecil Cox, who once saw an older boy douse Charles's head under a cold tap; the visitor watched impressed as the prince filled a bath with cold water, wrestled with his assailant, and finally forced him in fully clothed—only to be pulled in himself.

This was one of many Cheam anecdotes, some truer than others, which found their way into the press during Charles's first term. "Even the school barber was in the pay of the newspapers," snorted Prince Philip.

Frequently, and not surprisingly, there had to be complex inquiries before school crimes apparently to be laid at Charles's door were found to be the work of others. Within a week of his arrival at the school, for instance, Charles's name had been deeply carved in the back of a pew in the parish church. This was one of the stories the newspapers got hold of, but Peter Beck made them print corrections when other boys at last admitted their guilt.

In an attempt to head off journalists' intrusions, Beck and Wheeler had held a press visit to the school before term began, and made a special plea to be left thereafter in peace. But of the eighty-eight days of term, there were stories in one newspaper or another on sixty-eight. Again, the effects were unpleasant. Rumors abounded of boys and staff accepting bribes from newspapermen. They were never proved true, but a tense atmosphere of mutual suspicion developed. Morale at the school began to suffer. Although the prince's detective coped with most intruders, there were occasionally more dramatic incidents. One night he aroused the headmaster after seeing a prowler on the roof of

Charles's dormitory; a lengthy search was conducted, but no one found; only much later did a young friend of Charles's, David Daukes, confess to getting back into bed seconds before the search party arrived. Even schoolboy pranks were becoming worthy of the police incident book. Once again, the Queen decided to safeguard her son's education by direct action.

In the Christmas holidays her press secretary, Richard Colville, invited all newspaper editors to a meeting at Buckingham Palace. Peter Beck told the gathering of the disruption their employees were causing at his school. Bribes had been offered, though none to his knowledge accepted. Everyone felt they were under constant surveillance. The prince's first term had ended unhappily for all. Recalling the pleas he had made before and during Charles's time at Hill House, Colville spoke plainly to the editors. Either it stopped, and the press printed only those stories of genuine significance, or the Queen would abandon her cherished plan to educate her son at normal schools and withdraw him behind the palace walls to the care of tutors—and it would be the fault of the press.

Duly sobered, British editors ensured that Cheam was little more molested during Charles's four years there. Only the foreign photographers persisted, climbing over the newly heightened walls and building hides in the undergrowth; on one occasion Mary Beck, drawing her father's attention to an unseasonal fireworks display in the garden, unwittingly assisted in the capture of one intruder, who had been using infrared equipment to take pictures after dark.

Six months later, however, there was a story "of genuine significance" to be written. It was the summer term of 1958, the end of Charles's first year at Cheam, and the Commonwealth Games were being held in Cardiff. The Queen had been due to perform the closing ceremony at Cardiff Arms Park on July 26, but a sinusitis operation enforced her absence. The Duke of Edinburgh took her place, and introduced a tape-recorded message from Her Majesty, which was played over the loudspeakers of the packed stadium. Charles and a few friends filed into Peter Beck's study to watch the event on television. After Prince Philip's opening remarks, they heard the Queen's voice say: "I want to take this opportunity of speaking to all Welsh people, not only in this arena, but wherever they may be. The British Empire and Commonwealth Games in the capital, together with all the activities of the Festival of Wales, have made this a memorable year for the principality. I have therefore decided to mark it further by an act which will, I hope, give as much pleasure to all Welshmen as it does to me." There was a buzz of anticipation; many in the arena had guessed what she was going to say. "I intend to create my son Charles Prince of Wales today."

The tape had to be stopped as an enormous cheer convulsed the stadium, and 36,000 Welsh voices broke into "God Bless the Prince of Wales." When the clamor died down, the Queen's voice continued: "When he is grown up, I will present him to you at Caernarvon."

The scene in Beck's study at Cheam might have given the Queen a moment's pause. The headmaster, who with Charles had known what was coming, watched a look of dire unease cloud his face as the other boys spontaneously joined in the clapping and cheering. For a mother trying to bring her son up as much like other boys as possible, aware that his own emerging character had still far from mastered its environment, it was an odd piece of timing. The Queen now perhaps numbers this moment among the mistakes she has confessed to having made in Charles's upbringing. His own memory of the occasion is vivid. "I remember being acutely embarrassed when it was announced. I heard this marvelous great cheer coming from the stadium in Cardiff, and I think for a little boy of nine it was rather bewildering. All the others turned and looked at me in amazement. And it perhaps didn't mean all that much then; later on, as I grew older, it became apparent what it meant."

In the headmaster's study that afternoon, Charles automatically also became Earl of Chester and Knight Companion of the Most Noble Order of the Garter. They go, as it were, with the job. The Earldom of Chester is the oldest of all the dignities of the heir to the throne, dating from 1254, when it was bestowed on the future Edward I. Since then it has always been conjoined with the title of Prince of Wales—though both, unlike the Dukedom of Cornwall, are life peerages, which merge into the crown when their holder becomes monarch, to be bestowed at his discretion upon his eldest son. The monarch and the Prince of Wales are the only two ex-officio of the twenty-six Knights of the Garter, Europe's oldest secular order of chivalry; the Prince of Wales's pew, by ancient tradition, is the second in rank (though the first on the left) in St. George's Chapel at Windsor, but may not be occupied until he has been formally dubbed and installed by the sovereign. The Queen, perhaps having reflected on her son's re-action at the age of nine years and eight months, did not per-form this ceremony (which also entitled him to wear the Garter's resplendent robes and insignia) for another ten years. By that time, June 1968, it was part of the buildup to his investiture at Caernarvon and his emergence into full-time public life.

Those days were still, however, mercifully distant as Charles enjoyed his summer holidays at Balmoral and shrugged off his weighty new honors for the return to another school year at Cheam. In August he had trodden Welsh soil for the first time since becoming Prince of Wales, at Holyhead, where a plaque now marks the event. But his new honors seemed a slight dis-tinction compared with the year's superiority he could now ex-ercise over the incoming new boys.

His school progress was steady but undistinguished. Peter Beck later summed it up by saying that Charles was above aver-age in intelligence, but only average in attainment. By this he did not mean that the boy was bright but idle; rather, he was confirming the natural advantage Charles possessed in general knowledge. He was much better informed about the world—the outside world and its ways—than his contemporaries; he had, after all, by this time met many of the people who ran it and engaged them in polite conversation. This strange species of maturity, fostered by the formal conduct around him at home, also meant that he spoke and wrote the Queen's English with above-average clarity and style, at times tending to a precocious use of long words. In other ways, he was much less mature than his fellows, and remained so for many years. He joined in their schoolboy crazes—at that time for pogo sticks, hula hoops, and roller skates—with the intense enthusiasm of one unaware of such excitements at home. But the Queen's caution in not providing everything he requested led to embarrassments. When he asked for a boat to sail on the school pond, his was conspicuously the smallest to be seen. At least he had the good sense not to waste his time sharing his friends' love of stamp collecting; at home, he knew, the collection he would inherit from his great-grand-father, George V, was the finest and most valuable in the world.

He continued his piano lessons, the first steps in a love of music unparalleled in the royal family since Prince Albert. He sang in the school choir and piped a clear treble solo in the end-of-term concert attended by the Queen. He continued to show promise at painting and a passing talent at woodwork: Charles produced a coffee table which for many years remained one of Princess Anne's most treasured possessions. He dominated one end-of-term exhibition with a grim construction entitled "Gallows and Stocks." He also began to join with a will in many of the school entertainments devised and produced by David Munir. Like his mother, who with her sister had starred in wartime Windsor pantomimes, he seemed to find such enforced public display one way of conquering his shyness. In a way, this was an apt preparation for the many bizarre public roles required of royalty. One such Cheam production certainly was: a Shakespeare compilation, under the title *The Last Baron*, which told the tale of the Duke of Gloucester, later Richard III. The time-honored understudy's dream came true when the boy cast as Richard fell ill; Charles hurriedly took over the part. In front of an audience of parents, he had to deliver with due gravity such lines as "And soon may I ascend the throne." The drama critic of the *Cheam School Chronicle* wrote: "Prince Charles played the traditional Gloucester with competence and depth; he had a good voice and excellent elocution, and very well conveyed the ambition and bitterness of the twisted hunchback." His "traditional Gloucester" was modeled on Laurence Olivier's performance as Richard III. Before the Cheam production, the young prince listened intensely and repeatedly to a recording of the Olivier production. (In 1978, on learning of this from the author, Lord Olivier repaid the compliment: "I have a great hero-worship of the Prince of Wales and have found him utterly charming and thoughtful in discussion and conversation. I hope his history will not be visited by the same kind of miseries as were, willy-nilly, visited upon his great-great-grandfather. It would be delightful, would it not, for Charles III to be the first artistic king since Charles II.")

The star's mother, unusually, was not in the audience, as she had been the previous Christmas for her son's minor-role debut in a Munir entertainment called *Ten Little Cheam Boys*. Her absence that night was soon explained by the headmaster, who interrupted the performance to come onstage and announce that the Queen had given birth to another son (Prince Andrew). It was February 19, 1960. Charles's delight at having a baby brother, and the enthusiasm with which he relayed the latest news from home, impressed on the Cheam staff that he would always be much happier in the bosom of his family. As Mabel Anderson had said of Charles: "He felt family separation very deeply. He dreaded going away to school." His only link with home was the unlikely figure of his detective, Detective Constable Reg Summers, who provided a reassuring presence around the school grounds and behind the Sunday march to church. The Queen felt the distance equally keenly, and denied herself as well as her son much pleasure by resisting the temptation to call him home for royal occasions. Later that summer, however, a special dispensation was granted for him to attend the wedding in Westminster Abbey of his Aunt Margaret to the photographer Tony Armstrong-Jones. The Earl of Snowdon, as he became the following year, quickly formed an especially warm friendship with Prince Charles—founded as much as anything else on mutual admiration—which lasts to this day.

The Queen was careful to visit her son no more frequently— three times a term—than other parents, and to ask for no special privileges beyond the fact that cameras should be put away in her presence. Princess Anne enjoyed coming for the annual sports day, and always entered the younger sisters' race, unfortunately achieving no higher a position than fourth. She could take comfort in her brother's generally undistinguished record on the sports field. Never much of a team player, he was bored by cricket, although he eventually made the first eleven, and not the most mobile of rugger players: "They always put me in the second row," he complained, "the worst place in the scrum." His reluctant best was soccer, and in his last year he was made captain of the first team. Unhappily, the team lost every match that season, with a final tally of four goals scored against their opponents' eighty-two. This time, the *Cheam School Chronicle* was not so kind: "At half," wrote the soccer coach, "Prince Charles seldom drove himself as hard as his ability and position demanded."

Looking back, the staff remember Charles fondly for his uncertainty of himself, and for a few little incidents which showed promise of the man in the making. "Most of the time," said one of Charles's teachers, "he was very quiet. He never spoke out of turn. Sometimes his voice was so low that it was difficult to hear him. But he was a boy who preferred action to noise. When there was a task to do, he got on with it quietly. No fuss." David Munir remembered once catching Charles downstairs, finishing off his daily chores, when he should long since have been in bed. Munir warned him that he would be getting himself into trouble with the matron. "I can't help that, sir," the boy replied. "I must do my duties."

Charles's extreme gentility was particularly marked on the football field, where he caused general amusement by his habit of apologizing chivalrously to anyone he felled with a perfectly proper tackle. But it was endearing to find him so embarrassed by the standard prayer for the royal family, including the Duke of Cornwall, at Sunday morning service in St. Peter's. "I wish," he said, "they prayed for the other boys too." When someone gave Charles a "doodle-master," a then newfangled drawing toy, he was happy to lend it around until every other locker had its own. And he took his corporal punishment—the edicts of Gilpin had long since been abandoned—with the maturity beyond his years of one who "would rather get things over with."

These are the kind of school details for which the press hunger, but which tend not to emerge for many years—as is illustrated by two parallel father-and-son anecdotes. When Prince Philip visited the school for its tercentenary celebrations in 1947, one of his first public engagements after his betrothal to Princess Elizabeth, he introduced his fiancée to his former headmaster, the Reverend Harold Taylor: "This is the man who used to cane me." In 1974, during an Australian tour, Charles met Peter Beck's son Philip, by then a reporter for an Australian newspaper, beneath a canvas shelter deep in a Tasmanian forest. "I remember your father well," Charles told him. "He caned me once—no, twice—for ragging."

By the end of his time at Cheam, Charles had scored more credits than black marks for his house, Canada (the others appropriately enough, being Australia, New Zealand, and, until recently, South Africa). School life had been considerably disrupted—most notably in 1959, when Scotland Yard unearthed a plot by an Irish terrorist group, Fianna Uladh, to kidnap Charles and hold him hostage against a United Ireland; for days, the school grounds had swarmed with police. But Charles had emerged at worst an average pupil, and the obvious benefits of his presence had outweighed the disadvantages.

In the holidays, meanwhile, his parents found that he was growing fast, and advanced his home education accordingly. Michael Farebrother had been called in again as companion, and a French-Canadian tutor, twenty-seven-year-old Lieutenant Jean Lajeunesse, had taken up the work of Mlle de Roujoux. Father and son had grown ever closer as Charles developed Philip's enthusiasm for field sports; from taking him out shooting at Sandringham to teaching him to drive a Land-Rover while only twelve, the Duke of Edinburgh was intent on advancing his son beyond his years. At Christmas 1958 they went off on their first expedition together, to a coot shoot at Hickling Broad, near Sandringham; it turned into something of an adventure when their rented bungalow was flooded, and the royal pair shook the locals by applying for a room at the nearby Pleasure Boat Inn.

That same Christmas, Charles at his own request toured the British Sugar Corporation plant in King's Lynn—his first look inside a factory, and his first solo public engagement. His parents were well pleased with his progress. In the spring of 1962, in the absence abroad of Prince Philip, the Queen asked Charles to take his father's place as host at one of the luncheon parties she had introduced as a means of meeting a broader cross-section of her subjects. The thirteen-year-old prince held his own quite happily in conversation with a dozen or so guests, including the editor of the *Church Times*, an industrialist, a choreographer, a trade union leader, and the chairman of the BBC.

Cheam had also disposed of a number of the other chores of childhood: Charles's first broken bone (his ankle, falling down the school stairs), measles (urgent telegrams to his parents in Pakistan), chicken pox, and his appendix (which came out at Great Ormond Street Hospital for Children in February 1962). But the school had never quite won his whole-hearted enthusiasm. The jolt of leaving home had caused bruises he still nursed. If he had grown accustomed to life away from home, he was still miserably aware that he was not—and could never be—quite one of the boys. Peter Beck emphasizes that "the job of a preparatory school is what it says: to prepare, and not to produce a finished product." But Charles had only just mastered his new environment when he was abruptly removed from it. The last thing Cheam had prepared this particular pupil for, in a way, was the unwelcome translation even farther from home to the chilly wastes of north Scotland, and Gordonstoun.

10

1962-65: Gordonstoun

QUESTION TO PRINCE PHILIP: *"How's he getting on?"*
ANSWER: *"Well, at least he hasn't run away yet."*

WAS GORDONSTOUN the right choice? Those who advised Elizabeth II on Prince Charles's education, among them the Queen Mother, Lord Mountbatten, and Robert Woods, then Dean of Windsor, are still divided. The Queen and Prince Philip—and now that it's all over, their son—are in no doubt that it was. Charles's younger brothers, Andrew and Edward, went to the school after him, and there is every reason to expect the Prince of Wales, in time, to send any sons of his own there. The overwhelming argument in 1962 was that it was Prince Philip's old school, and that he had been very happy there. But, as we have already seen, bringing Prince Charles up in Prince Philip's mold was not a logical exercise. Where Philip was outgoing, Charles was introspective; where Philip gregarious, Charles awkwardly sociable; and where Philip had been an obscure European prince, of the kind not unfamiliar to many British public-school boys, Charles was the heir to the throne.

The Queen and her mother had favored Eton—to many commentators also the obvious choice. They had a friend who was a housemaster there, Giles St. Aubyn, younger son of Lord St. Levan, occasionally drafted as an older childhood companion for Charles. Speculation had been fueled in April 1959 when the prince's other childhood companion, Michael Farebrother, had taken Charles round the school during the Easter holidays at Windsor. The press assumed, incorrectly, that his name had been put down for Eton at birth (causing his father much amusement: "They'd have found it difficult to turn him down, wouldn't

127

they?"). There was a wave of criticism in the Sunday opinion columns, much of it from Old Etonians, more of it from socialist politicians, that it would be positively dangerous for the future king to go to Eton. His fellow-pupils would scarcely be a representative cross-section of his future subjects; and he would probably find, as king, that all his old school chums comprised the Tory cabinet. (The same argument was applied, this time about a future Labour cabinet, when Winchester was suggested.) Prince Philip would not hear of Eton, using much the same antielitist arguments. It might be happily close to Windsor, he told his wife and her mother, but it was also unhappily close to Fleet Street. The Queen and her husband went on an extended tour of British public schools, visiting among others Repton, Mill Hill, Fettes, and Charles's own suggestion, Charterhouse, where some of his friends were going from Cheam.

But as early as 1959, three years before any announcement was made, Philip was clearly forcing the pace in the family argument. That July, he subscribed £1,000 toward a rebuilding program at Gordonstoun, saying to his brother-in-law, Prince George of Hanover, a former headmaster of the school's "twin," Salem, in Germany: "Wouldn't it be nice if my son could take advantage of all these improvements?" That October Dr. Kurt Hahn, Gordonstoun's founder-headmaster, came to London from his Salem headquarters to address the Parents' National Education Union; the meeting was chaired by Lady Brabourne, Prince Philip's cousin, and the vote of thanks was proposed by Lady Rupert Nevill, one of the Queen's closest friends. Sitting inconspicuously at the back was James Orr, Prince Philip's private secretary—and himself a Gordonstoun old boy.

By Charles's thirteenth birthday in November 1961, it was time for a decision. The Queen, on balance, confessed that the world of boys' schools remained largely a mystery to her, and was happy to be guided by her husband. So Gordonstoun it was, as a palace statement announced on January 23, 1962, agreement having been reached with the school's warden, Henry Brereton, and the headmaster, Robert Chew, some weeks before.

Chew had paid a secret visit to Peter Beck, to find out more about his new pupil. Gordonstoun does not require the Common Entrance Examination, leading some to conclude that Charles was going there because he couldn't pass it. Particularly stung by one suggestion that the school was "a kind of academic *salon des refusés*," the Queen insisted that her son take a version of Common Entrance anyway, to staunch any self-doubt as much as to silence further criticism. Mr. Chew was more than satisfied. Charles, who would start in May, thought the place sounded "pretty gruesome." Lord Rudolph Russell, younger son of the Duke of Bedford, had recently run away, declaring: "Gordonstoun is no place for me."

The school has been painted as a remote Spartan outpost providing some sort of Germanic assault course toward manhood. Its life is tough, to be sure, with an unusual emphasis on outdoor and physical attainment. But its ways are far from brutish; every item on the school curriculum, every eccentrically named rung up the school status ladder, is based on a rigorous educational code founded in pacifism. It was formulated in the wake of the First World War by Prince Max of Baden, last chancellor of the Kaiser's Imperial Germany, and refined by his successor and disciple, Kurt Hahn. Gordonstoun parents are well aware what they are letting their sons in for.

The school is modeled on that founded in 1920 by Prince Max in his castle-monastery at Salem, on the north shore of Lake Constance, in southern Germany. The prince, to whom Hahn was private secretary, had been intimately involved in the collapse of Germany and set himself the personal task of rebuilding his nation's manhood. "Let us train soldiers," he said, "who are at the same time lovers of peace." Prince Max was given to somewhat grandiose statements which, by appointing his private secretary the school's first headmaster, he expected Hahn to put into effect: "Build up the imagination of the boy of decision and the willpower of the dreamer, so that in future wise men will have the nerve to lead the way they have shown, and men of action will have the vision to imagine the consequences of their decisions."

What he really sought, Hahn realized, was the combination of stamina and leadership that had defeated Germany, the very combination bred in the English public schools—of which he had gained some experience when a Rhodes scholar at Oxford before the war. Hahn's two great influences were Plato (particularly *The Republic*) and Dr. Thomas Arnold of Rugby, both of whom he was given to quoting copiously. "I will call the three views of

education the Ionian view, the Spartan view, the Platonic view.
. . . Those who hold the first view believe that the individual
ought to be nurtured and humored regardless of the interests of
the community. . . . According to the second view the individual may and should be neglected for the benefit of the State.
. . . The third, the Platonic view, is that any nation is a slovenly
guardian of its own interests if it does not do all it can to make
the individual citizen discover his own powers: and further, that
the individual becomes a cripple from his or her own point of
view if he is not qualified by education to serve the community."

The selection process at Salem was quite as elitist as at Eton.
Only children from the upper layers of German society were considered; even then, Hahn fiercely scrutinized their strength of
character, far more important to him than their academic prowess, before admitting them.

In the Germany of the 1930s, after the death of Prince Max,
Hahn was accused of anglicizing German education. He also
happened to have been born Jewish. In 1933, when Hitler took
power, he was arrested and the school closed. His stand was un-
compromising. He wrote to the old boys of Salem: "It is a question now in Germany of its Christian morality, its reputation, its
soldierly honor: Salem cannot remain neutral. I call on all members of the Salem Association who are active in the SA or SS to
terminate their allegiance either to Hitler or to Salem." The rise
of Nazism made him feel more urgently "the need to educate
young people in independence of judgment and in strength of
purpose when following an unfashionable cause, to teach the
protection of the weak, the recognition of the rights of the less
fortunate, and the worth of a simple human life." The children
of 1930s' Germany were surrounded by "three decays: the decay
of adventure and enterprise, of skill and care, and of compassion."

On his release, Hahn fled to England, where he fell ill. An
Oxford friend, William Calder, invited him to recuperate on his
estate in Morayshire, where he met up again with another university contemporary, Evan Barron, then owner and editor of
the *Inverness Courier*. Hahn told them of his plans to recreate
the Salem experiment in Britain, and they took him to see the
Gordonstoun estate, near Elgin. A lease was available on the
eighteenth-century mansion house, complete with pepperpot
turrets and balustrades, and its three hundred acres. Hahn took

it, and in the summer of 1934 opened the school with a clutch of masters (including Robert Chew) and just thirty boys, one of them Prince Philip. (The lease lasted until 1947, when the property was purchased from the Gordon Cumming family. By ironic coincidence, Gordonstoun had been the home of Sir William Gordon Cumming, lieutenant colonel of the Scots Guards, who had involved a previous Prince of Wales, the future Edward VII, in the famous Tranby Croft gambling scandal. Prince Charles's great-great-grandfather had been dealing the cards when Gordon Cumming was accused of cheating at baccarat. He lost the subsequent slander action—in which the Prince of Wales, to Queen Victoria's and the nation's dismay, had to give evidence—and was drummed out of society and the army in disgrace.)

The Gordonstoun philosophy was based on that of Salem, but Hahn added two important new dimensions. One was to carry across from Germany the altruistic traditions of the Cistercian monks, who had ministered to the vicinity of Salem centuries before. The other was to counteract the scholastic emphasis of other British schools. "I estimate," he said, "that about sixty percent of boys have their vitality damaged under the conditions of modern boarding schools." His aim was "to kindle on the threshold of puberty nonpoisonous passions which act as guardians during the dangerous years."

He was now accused of Germanizing English education, but all Hahn's philosophy came down to was a version, more literal than in most public schools, of Juvenal's *mens sana in corpore sano*. To protect his pupils from their increasingly urbanized home environment, he wanted them to pit their young physical resources against the forces of nature on land and sea. Like Baden-Powell, he aimed to inspire a sense of purpose and self-reliance, aligned with one of duty and service. Boys, said Hahn, should be taught "to argue without quarreling, to quarrel without suspecting, and to suspect without slandering." Apart from a special concern for late developers—a boon to its new recruit—Gordonstoun's purpose, enshrined in the school motto, *Plus Est En Vous* ("There is more in you"), was not markedly different from the traditional British public school ideal. But the method was. (So were the fees. The minimum total—at more than $1,250 a year, higher than at Harrow or Eton—was based on a standard fee plus a contribution assessed by parents themselves in one of twelve categories graded according to wealth and income. Another disadvantage, perhaps, of being the royal family.)

Physical fitness was something of a cult; it remains so with the Prince of Wales to this day. Boys were frequently dispatched on testing expeditions, over land and water, designed to stretch initiative and physique to their limits. Public services was instilled by participation in four local activities: firefighting (the school's auxiliary is a recognized branch of the Elgin fire service); manning a coast guard station, complete with rockets and lifesaving equipment; a mountain rescue team, which has in its time saved climbers' lives; and an ocean lifesaving team. Hahn introduced the Moray Badge as a selective reward for achievement in these fields. It proved the inspiration for the Duke of Edinburgh's own nationwide award scheme, whose silver medal Prince Charles was to win in his last term.

On the day it was announced that Charles would be going to Gordonstoun, Hahn was by coincidence delivering a lecture in Glasgow. "A sick civilization," he said, "is throwing up five kinds of young people: the lawless, the listless, the pleasure and sensation addicts, the angry young men, and the honorable skeptics." The antidotes were "simple physical training, expedition training, and rescue service training." With garbled versions of Hahn's precepts and the school's strenuous regime appearing in the British press, it was no wonder the thirteen-year-old prince felt daunted. Again he paid a private visit to the school with his parents, to find conditions even more Spartan than at Cheam: unpainted dormitories with bare floorboards, naked light bulbs, and spare wooden bedsteads. Life appeared to be lived in huts, as exposed to the North Sea gales as were the boys' knees in their short trousers. It was a cheerless sight, and Charles was unenthusiastic about what he called his "imminent incarceration." He remained unaware of a goodwill gesture from his future fellow pupils: Radio Luxembourg, then the favorite channel for public school pop music followers, had played Bobby Darin's "Goodbye Cruel World" at the request of a group of Gordonstoun boys, "as a welcome to Prince Charles." The joke turned sour when the headmaster, Mr. Chew, expressed considerable annoyance; the second line of the song, he had been informed, was ". . . I'm off to join the circus."

Prince Philip flew his son north on May 1. The locals could

tell they were coming: on the school gate stood naval guards with fixed bayonets, and tradesmen (and parents) were required to produce passes to get in. The Queen's consort, not the new boy, was accorded an official welcome by Brereton and Chew, with Captain Iain Tennant, chairman of the governors, and Peter Paice, the head boy. The only privilege accorded Charles was a private lunch with his father and the headmaster before Prince Philip left. He drove back to his aircraft at Lossiemouth, then flew over the school before heading south again, dipping his wings in a farewell salute to his son. Charles watched with a sinking heart.

His arrival at Gordonstoun, he remembers, was even more miserable than at Cheam. As he was shown to Windmill Lodge, the asbestos-roofed stone building he was to share with fifty-nine of the four hundred other boys, the prospects seemed even worse than he had expected. Not merely had he been rudely yanked from an environment to which he had just grown accustomed; all his dogged progress up the Cheam hierarchy had now come to naught. He was an underprivileged new boy again, and at a school where the boys' older years altered their attitude to him. Where at Cheam he had found diffidence, at Gordonstoun he came up against adolescent malice. The only boys he knew, apart from Lord Mountbatten's grandson, Norton Knatchbull, were his cousins Prince Welf of Hanover, whom he had visited with his father in Germany earlier that year, and Prince Alexander of Yugoslavia. Even they, for befriending him in his first few days, were labeled "bloodsucker" and "sponge" by their contemporaries.

The Gordonstoun day began with the cry of the "waker" at 7 A.M., followed by a run round the garden in shorts and singlet. Then came the first of the day's two cold showers; Charles and his fifty-nine housemates shared a washroom containing six showers and one bath. He had to make his own bed and clean his own shoes before breakfast.

The rest of the new boys' day, in an official summary prepared for public consumption by Mr. Chew (who died in 1970), ran as follows:

8:15: Breakfast and surgery.
8:55: Morning prayers.
9:10: Classwork begins. There are five 40-minute pe-

riods in the morning but for every boy one of
these, on several days in the week, is a training
break (running, jumping, discus- and javelin-
throwing, assault course, etc.) under the Physical Training Master.

1:20: Lunch. After lunch there is a rest period (20 minutes): music or reading aloud to boys relaxing on
their backs.

2:30: Afternoon activities. On three days a week there
are either games (rugger or hockey in winter;
cricket, lawn tennis, or athletics in summer), or
seamanship, or practical work on the estate. The
proportion of time spent on each depends upon
a boy's interests and development. One afternoon
a week is allocated to the Services: Coast Guard
Watchers, Sea Cadets, Army Cadets, Scouts, Fire
Service, Mountain Rescue and Surf Life Saving.
One afternoon and evening a week are given to
work on boys' individual projects which are ex-
hibited and judged at the end of each year. On
Saturday afternoons there are matches and opportunities for expeditions.

4:00: Warm wash and cold shower. Change into evening school uniform. Tea. After tea, classes or
tutorial periods.

6:20: Supper, followed by preparation in Houses or by
"Societies."

9:15: Bedtime; silence period of five minutes.

9:30: Lights out.

When not occupied by this formidable schedule, boys were
at liberty to wander at will around the countryside and down to
the sea, though the town of Elgin was out of bounds. Charles took
full advantage of this freedom; visitors noticed that he tended to
take them for walks around the countryside rather than show
them around the school. He developed nodding acquaintanceships with the fishermen and shopkeepers of the nearby village
of Hopeman, and occasionally—but only occasionally, for fear
of singling himself out—accepted invitations to Sunday lunch
or a day's shooting with Captain Tennant, who was also the lord

lieutenant of Morayshire, or the vice-lieutenant, Lieutenant Colonel Kenneth Mackessack. It was in the countryside that he preferred to relax; school games he did not much enjoy, and he shunned his peers' illicit activities in Elgin's Pete's Café.

But Charles quickly took to all maritime activities. Having already taken the helm of his father's yacht, *Bluebottle*, at Cowes, and become a proficient swimmer in the Buckingham Palace pool, he was almost more self-confident in the water than on terra firma. He and Welf teamed up as a lifesaving unit, and they received their proficiency certificates on Charles's fourteenth birthday. One of his earliest exercises, a canoe expedition from Hopeman Beach to Findhorn Bay, turned ugly even by Gordonstoun standards when a storm blew up shortly after they were out to sea. The twelve-mile journey took all day, and the prince arrived back at school exhausted. In true British public school spirit, he went out to dinner that night with Captain Tennant and told him he was eager to repeat the adventure.

Other early duties included carting about the school trash cans and tidying up their trail of refuse. By the end of his first term he had qualified for his school uniform, the gray sweater and shorts to which all blue-uniformed new boys aspire. The winning of his school uniform also involved the new boy, by time-honored rite, in a ducking in a cold bath, fully clothed. It seems strange that the Gordonstoun boys hesitated over putting the Queen's son through this traditional humiliation; but one boy, who left soon after to sell his story to a Sunday paper, explained: "How can you treat a boy as just an ordinary chap when his mother's portrait is on the coins you spend in the school shop, on the stamps you put on your letters home, and when a detective follows him wherever he goes?" He went on: "Most boys tend to fight shy of friendship with Charles. The result is that he is very lonely. It is this loneliness, rather than the school's toughness, which must be hardest on him."

It was. "It's near Balmoral," his father had told him. "There's always [the estate manager] there; you can go and stay with him. And your grandmother goes up there to fish. You can go and see her." Charles did, whenever he could. At Birkhall, her home on the Balmoral estate, the Queen Mother heard from Charles of his homesickness, his loneliness, the impossibility of blending into school life like other boys. She provided a sympathetic shoulder to cry on, literally, and was especially moved by all the qualities of her late husband so evident in her favorite grandchild. More than Charles's parents, perhaps, she understood the ordeal of the quiet, uncertain child in a harsh and alien world. "He is a very gentle boy, with a very kind heart," she said, "which I think is the essence of everything." But she would not, as he asked, intercede with the Queen and Prince Philip to take him away from Gordonstoun. She would try, she said, to help him through an ordeal he must face. It was another early lesson in duty.

At the end of the first term, Mr. Chew reported to the Queen that Charles was "well up . . . very near the top of his class." The Christmas holidays, after family festivities at Sandringham, provided the first in a new and traumatic wave of trials by newspaper. It was New Year 1963, and Charles traveled alone to Bavaria for a winter sports break with his "uncle," Prince Ludwig of Hesse, and his family. The crowds of press photographers, which in turn attracted crowds of sightseers, quite simply ruined it. After two or three chaotic days in the resort of Tarasp, he was forced again to retire into an artificial world: the private slopes of the Hesse *schloss*. Even there he needed a bodyguard of Swiss police, themselves patrolling the property on skis.

His resentment was only forgotten the following summer, when a much greater ordeal overwhelmed him. The Cherry Brandy Incident, now a fondly remembered, amusing milestone of Prince Charles's childhood to most Britons, was much more than that to the boy at the time. It upset him deeply, leaving scars that lasted several years, notably a mistrust of the press which has never really left him.

On his arrival at Gordonstoun, as at Cheam, an appeal had been made to the press to leave him in peace: "The added strain and burden of publicity upon a young boy of the Prince of Wales's age, on joining a public school for the first time, can readily be understood by all parents. For this reason, Her Majesty and His Royal Highness hope that editors personally will be able to co-operate. . . . When publicity was reduced at the end of the first term at Cheam School, it became possible for the whole school to function in the normal way, and therefore the Prince of Wales was able to receive a normal education. This was only possible because neither he nor any of the other boys and staff were subjected to publicity, which is most unsettling and which, of course, singles His Royal Highness out as different in the eyes of all other boys of the school. . . ."

By his third term at Gordonstoun, press coverage of his progress was minimal. By then, June 1963, he had received the next—and coveted—stage of school promotion, membership in the Junior Training Plan. It entitled him to more freedom of choice over outdoor training activities, one of which was the expedition aboard the school yacht, *Pinta*, which brought him to Stornoway, on the Isle of Lewis, on Monday, June 17. As usual his detective, Donald Green, accompanied the party of Charles and four other boys ashore. Green went off to make arrangements at the local cinema—Jayne Mansfield was to be the Junior Training Plan's subject of study that evening—leaving the boys to wait in the Crown Hotel. A crowd quickly gathered once word of Charles's arrival got around, and the young prince soon found a sea of faces pressed against the hotel windows, peering and pointing at him. "I thought 'I can't bear this anymore' and went off somewhere else. The only other place was the bar. Having never been into a bar before, the first thing I thought of doing was having a drink, of course. And being terrified, not knowing what to do, I said the first drink that came into my head, which happened to be cherry brandy, because I'd drunk it before when it was cold out shooting. Hardly had I taken a sip when the whole world exploded around my ears."

What had happened, as he took that first sip, was that into the bar had come Frances Thornton, a twenty-two-year-old free-lance journalist, known ever after to Charles as "that dreadful woman." The Prince of Wales was fourteen, under the legal age for purchasing alcoholic liquor. Within twenty-four hours the story had gone around the world. Coming soon after other recent public criticisms—of Charles shooting his first stag the previous autumn, of his "invading the Lord's Day" by skiing in the Cairngorms on Sundays—it caused uproar. Even the Profumo Affair, then at its height, could not keep it off the front pages. To make matters worse, Buckingham Palace at first issued a denial, after misunderstanding Green's telephoned account of the incident. The following day, after further inquiries, they were forced to retract it, thus keeping the story bubbling along. There followed the carpeting of Green by Superintendent Albert Perkins, the

Queen's senior detective (soon after which Green resigned), and the question of school punishment for Charles. The *Times* itself felt moved to inform its readers that the headmaster kept a cane for such misdemeanors.

As leading articles called on the head to act, Charles was summoned to Mr. Chew's study, where after cross-examination he was deprived of his membership in the Junior Training Plan. It was a punishment much more devastating than the cane. Reduced to the ranks, he had again had his life complicated by unwelcome and undue attention. For so trivial an incident to have had so disproportionate an effect now seems absurd; the Queen was able to laugh at the episode, later concluding that it was a good lesson in the necessary restraints of royal conduct. Charles, though to many newspaper readers a more endearing and human figure, was thoroughly unsettled and unable to laugh about it at all for several years.

And there was to be only brief respite. As his Gordonstoun life grew more varied and self-confident—a stint at HMS Vernon, the naval training camp at Portsmouth, his first archaeological digs around Morayshire, a bout of pneumonia after one camping expedition to Balmoral—he won his way back into the Junior Training Plan and further up the scale. A year later, he proved something to himself and many others by passing the General Certificate of Education at "Ordinary" level in five subjects: Latin, French, history, and English language and literature, though math and physics still eluded his grasp. The summer of 1964 passed happily enough, at Balmoral and Cowes, with the added bonus of an excursion to King Constantine's wedding in Athens, where he had the satisfaction of ducking a raftload of prying French photographers. By the time he returned to school that September, he had found a new equilibrium. But life was very quickly to turn sour again.

An exercise book was missing from his classroom. That sort of thing had happened before: forgeries had been hawked around Fleet Street, and one genuine one, culled from a wastepaper basket, had proved to be the work of another boy. Name tags taken from Charles's clothes had proved popular on the school's "black market," and books inscribed with his name had disappeared. But this time the olive-green book in which Charles wrote his essays had been stolen from the pile on his form master's desk, and the headmaster issued an appeal for what he called "a collector's item." Too late. It had already reached Fleet Street.

The trial proved mildly fascinating. A Gordonstoun boy (he was never identified) was reputed to have got £7 for the book from a Gordonstoun old boy, an officer cadet, who had then sold it to a Scottish journalist for £100. Rumors of offers as high as £5,000 abounded in London for some time until the book was traced to St. Helen's, Lancashire, and the offices of Terence Smith of the Mercury Press. It had taken Scotland Yard six weeks to get the book back, and Smith promptly sued the Metropolitan Police Commissioner, Sir Joseph Simpson, for the return of "goods wrongly taken." As those goods were stolen property, his case didn't get very far.

The police seizure, however, itself prompted the next stage. The German magazine *Der Stern*, which with *Life* magazine and *Paris-Match* possessed photostats, had been unconvinced about the authenticity of the documents. The police action, it said, "made it clear they were genuine"; the magazine bought the rights for £1,000 and on November 17 published the essays in full (in German), illustrated by the handwritten text in English— complete with the form master's comment "Quite well argued." Buckingham Palace, biding its time until authenticity was beyond doubt, said: "If these reports are true, it is highly regrettable that the private essays of a schoolboy should have been published at all in this way."

So it was; but it could have been a deal worse. Charles emerged with credit from worldwide exposure which would have daunted any schoolboy. Though published under the headline "The Confessions of Prince Charles," what little the essays revealed showed the sixteen-year-old prince a liberal and original thinker, reasonably mature for his age. *Stern* managed to miss the point on the piece about which it got most excited: a dissertation on the corrupting effects of power. Its views were not those of the future king of England but of the nineteenth-century historian William Lecky, a section of whose *History of England in the Eighteenth Century* the class had been told to précis.

The *Times* quoted with approval from another piece on the subject of Democracy. The prince professed himself "troubled by the fact that the voters today tend to go for a particular party and not for the individual candidate, because they vote for the politics of a party." He thought it wrong, for instance, that a below-par Conservative candidate should win votes simply because he toed the party line against nationalization or the abolition of the public schools. In another, on the press, he emerged from his recent ordeals surprisingly unsoured: a free press, he argued, was essential in democratic society "to protect people from the government in many ways, to let them know what is going on—perhaps behind their backs."

A fourth essay was a ten-minute exercise to name the four items he would take to a desert island if evacuated during a nuclear crisis. Charles opted for a tent, a knife, "lots of rope and string," and a radio, both to keep in touch with developments, and to monitor any hope of rescue. He did add, however, that such an emergency would have him "in a frightful panic."

The matter might have ended there, had not *Stern* thought of adding a last, gratuitous paragraph: "Prince Charles became short of pocket money at Gordonstoun at the end of August. It then occurred to him that some collectors paid good money for original handwritten manuscripts. He sold the work to a schoolmate for thirty shillings." *Time* magazine decided to follow up this intriguing tidbit and the following week published its version of the saga under the headline "The Princely Pauper." The palace now lost patience and issued one of its extremely rare denials. "There is no truth whatever," the Queen's press secretary, Colville, wrote to *Time*, "in the story that Prince Charles had sold his autograph at any time. There is also no truth whatever in the story that he sold his composition book to a classmate. In the first place he is intelligent and old enough to realize how embarrassing this would turn out to be, and second, he is only too conscious of the interest of the press in anything to do with himself and his family. The suggestion that his parents keep him so short of money that he has to find other means to raise it is also a complete invention. Finally, the police would not have attempted to regain the composition book unless they were quite satisfied that it had been obtained illegally." In their own unique style, *Time*'s editors headlined the letter "Moneyed Prince Charlie," and added beneath it: "The royal family's press officer mounts a princely defense in his belated offer to clarify the case."

There was another diversion from that autumn's strains: a mock election, a common practice in many British schools, to coincide with the British general election of October 1964. Charles was to be seen wearing a Scottish Nationalist Party rosette around Gordonstoun, and speaking vehemently in favor of what has since become known as devolution. When one opponent gently reminded him he was Prince of Wales, he cried: "Independence for Wales, too! That's for the next election!" It is a measure of the breeding of British public-school boys that the Conservative Party romped home with 140 votes. The Scottish Nationalist Party polled 129; but Labour—with 16—trailed behind the Liberals and the Irish Independents, at a time when they were winning their first British general election for thirteen years.

The affair of the exercise book dragged on into the Christmas holidays, marked by the delivery of a "beat group" kit—a guitar with amplifier, and an electric organ—to Windsor Castle, to complement Charles's much-worn Beatle wig. After New Year at Sandringham, he and Anne were again dogged by the press on a skiing holiday in Liechtenstein. Through his hosts, Prince Franz Josef and Princess Gina, he reached an accommodation with the photographers—who were mostly foreign; British editors were still attempting to respect the Queen's wishes. Photographers would be welcome on the slopes in the afternoons, if they would leave him alone in the mornings. To everyone's surprise it worked, and he was able to continue his progress toward becoming the proficient skier he is today.

Back at Sandringham it was the usual round of field sports, in unusually severe winter weather. "The whole family," said Mabel Anderson, "goes out in weather most would think mad." Prince Charles had become, his family noticed, more contemplative of late, in part because he was due to be confirmed at Easter. He was again aware of his father's shadow. With his sometimes too unquestioning young seriousness, Charles had long since accepted the tenets of Christianity with due solemnity. But he was aware that his father thought sixteen perhaps too young for confirmation, and had had doubts about his own faith. Prince Philip's tortured progress from the Greek Orthodoxy of his childhood through Salem's German Protestantism to the formal Anglicanism of his adopted life had bred a disenchantment, even a cynicism; there had been a time—though he had now in middle age reverted to Anglican orthodoxy—when he had classed himself agnostic, perhaps atheist. Again, Charles was not in the same mold. During his preconfirmation talks with the Dean of Windsor, Robert Woods, he displayed a sound grasp of his undertakings, and his faith has not since wavered. At Easter 1965, however, Prince Philip was not quite so sure, and was anyway of the view that the then Archbishop of Canterbury, Michael Ramsey, was a very tiresome preacher. Throughout his son's confirmation service in St. George's Chapel, Windsor, Prince Philip conspicuously read a book—his Bible being the nearest to hand.

"Come and have a drink," said Woods to Ramsey afterward. "Thank you," said the Archbishop. "Bloody rude, that's what I call it."

Charles's progress at Gordonstoun had been interrupted by only one recall to London on official duty: earlier that year, for the state funeral of Sir Winston Churchill. He was nearing the end of his fourth year, had moved from Senior Training Plan, to Colour Bearer (prefect), and had finally managed to satisfy the O level examiners of a modest grasp of mathematics. He had graduated from piano to trumpet, and taken part in several concerts in Elgin town hall and St. Giles's Cathedral, Edinburgh. He had also had his first taste of two enduring, if contradictory, passions, polo and the cello, and was to crown his last full year at the school with boldness in a field in which his father never shone: for the school play at Christmas 1965, Prince Charles undertook the role of Shakespeare's Macbeth. Thirty years before, Prince Philip had qualified only for the role of an attendant lord, Donalbain.

Charles took the part very seriously, treating his six weeks of research into the character as an expedition into those realms of human nature questioned and explored at the time of his confirmation. A fortnight after their son's seventeenth birthday, the Queen and Prince Philip flew north to see him strut and fret his few hours in front of Gordonstoun's version of Glamis Castle, ancestral home of his grandmother's family, the Bowes-Lyons. A schoolboy's picture of the false-bearded prince performing the famous dagger soliloquy (following p. 162) again went around the world, earning the Gordonstoun photographic society some £500. It raised only this paltry sum because, in deference to the royal family, the picture was distributed through the "normal channels" of the Press Association; had it been sold through a freelance agency, according to a contemporary estimate, it would have earned more than £10,000. The prince looked so convincing that the Gordonstoun thespians were accused of importing London makeup expertise for the occasion. Not so; the royal chin experienced the familiar schoolboy agonies of tufts of crepe hair stuck on with glue.

One small amendment was made in Shakespeare's text. For the benefit of the Queen, it was decided to dispense with the stage direction: "Reenter Macduff with Macbeth's head." Otherwise, Charles's satanic thane stoutly endured the eloquent nagging of fourteen-year-old Douglas Campbell as Lady Macbeth, and raised an impromptu buzz in the audience only when the three witches cried: "All hail, Macbeth, that shalt be king hereafter!" The *Gordonstoun Record* did him proud: "Prince Charles was at his very best in the quiet poetic soliloquies, the poetry of which he so beautifully brought out, and in the bits which expressed Macbeth's terrible agony of remorse and fear. In the second part of the play, he equally well expressed the degenerative hardening of Macbeth's character, the assumption of cynicism in an attempt to blunt the underlying and too painful moral sensitivity."

A local triumph, the high point in a year during which school life had become, after those early trials, somewhat monotonous. That Christmas, the question of a university career was already under discussion in the royal family. Charles had not yet completed his span at Gordonstoun, but was in the mood for a change, the familiar mood of those young school-leavers who take a year out in the wide world between school and university. He wanted a break. On the condition that he would return to Gordonstoun later, to finish the business he had begun there, the Queen and Prince Philip agreed.

II

1966-67: Geelong and Gordonstoun

"Australia opened my eyes. Having a title, and being a member of the upper classes, as often as not militates against you there. . . . Australia conquered my shyness."

D URING HER CORONATION TOUR of Australia, Queen Elizabeth II had undertaken to "send my eldest son to visit you, too, when he is older." The promise seemed long overdue in that autumn of 1965, when a Commonwealth school was one of the suggestions under consideration for Prince Charles's break from Gordonstoun. The Australian prime minister, Sir Robert Menzies, visited London that autumn, and found himself invited to spend a weekend at Balmoral, for an intensive grilling on his country's better schools. Others involved in the consultations included the dean of Windsor, Dr. Woods, whose brother was archbishop of Melbourne, and the then Australian high commissioner in London, Sir Alexander Downer, an old boy of Geelong Church of England Grammar School, in Menzies' State of Victoria.

Between them, they decided on Geelong, suggesting that its country outpost, Timbertop, might provide exactly what Prince Charles and his parents were looking for. Geelong School itself, often described as "the Eton of Australia," is very near Melbourne, but Timbertop is some two hundred miles to the north, and two thousand feet above sea level, in remote but accessible countryside on the slopes of the mountain from which it takes its name. Geelong sent its boys for an outdoor year of exercise and self-reliance at Timbertop, which immediately made Charles fear it was simply an Australian Gordonstoun. Not so; its philosophy is

144

less heavy-handed, more homespun. By self-reliance, the school meant literally that: there were a handful of masters *in loco parentis*, but the boys were mainly younger ones in the charge of their seniors, who would appeal to the staff only in the event of emergency. Theirs was a rural life of comparative self-sufficiency, each boy having broad freedom to spend his time as he liked. It was an exercise in getting to know people, from which the young Prince of Wales could only benefit. As he was of the age of the older boys, he would also undertake the responsibility of having a younger group in his direct care. Unlike his fellows, he would have to spend some time working for his GCE "Advanced" levels in history and French, scheduled for his return to Gordonstoun, but the rest of the time would be more or less his own, in excellent fishing and walking countryside. Though made famous by Nevil Shute in *The Far Country*, the gum forests around Mount Timbertop were otherwise undiscovered by the rest of humanity.

This was the deciding factor stressed by Menzies on his return home, when a Labour member of the Australian parliament raised the same questions about Geelong as had English critics over the choice of Cheam and Gordonstoun. Geelong, he charged, was "generally accepted" as the most exclusive school in Australia. "Why did the prime minister not suggest that Prince Charles, like the great majority of his future subjects, should attend one of the excellent state high schools?"

"It is not difficult for people to understand that a school with a rural branch has attractions in this instance," replied Menzies. "I would be very sorry for the young prince if he were at a school in the middle of a crowded city in Australia, with people gazing at him, with people trying to make him a raree-show. This isn't what he will be here for."

Charles left for Australia at the end of January 1966. He was just seventeen. Though it was nearly nine years since that first dark day at Cheam, he had still not conquered his fears of new, unknown situations, and again remembers being very apprehensive. It is in this curious respect that he perhaps most resembles his grandfather, George VI, and perhaps other, less likely royal predecessors. George V, for instance, a man by no means daunted by his role, nevertheless expressed surprise at the warmth of his reception during his Silver Jubilee parade through London in 1935: "I had no idea they felt like that about me. I'm beginning to think they must really like me for myself." To Charles, as to his great-grandfather, such warmth remains a surprise. He sees no reason why affection should be spontaneous, unearned. He had heard that Australians were "critical," and expected a mixed reception. Even more unnerving, this was his first trip abroad without either of his parents.

He did, however, have reassuring company in his detective, Detective Inspector Derek Sharp, and Squadron Leader David Checketts, the then thirty-five-year-old equerry to Prince Philip, and already a familiar figure to Charles. A former public relations man with a distinguished RAF record, Checketts was to prove a mainstay of Prince Charles's life for the next thirteen years. In Australia, he set up house with his wife and family at Devon Farm, some 120 miles from Timbertop, and acted as a kind of business manager to the prince. The farm became a headquarters for dealing with all press and administrative inquiries, and for entertaining Charles over many an Australian weekend. The prince was like a member of the family, coming down to breakfast in his dressing gown, making his own bed, doing his share of the household chores, acting as elder brother to the Checketts' young children. It was the beginning of a firm friendship; in time Checketts was to become his equerry, and later the Prince of Wales's first private secretary.

Checketts has said of those seven months in Australia: "I went out there with a boy, and returned with a man." Many others, including Charles himself, have testified that this is the period in which he suddenly shed the burden of "late development" and grew to manhood.

At first the Australians did, as he expected, receive him with caution; there were, of course, the usual official receptions and enthusiastic crowds, but it was the acceptance of his school fellows he wanted to win. One night at Timbertop, after taking a walk in the rain, he knew he had succeeded. He returned to his dormitory duties carrying a rolled umbrella and was delighted to hear a cry of "Pommy bastard."

It was the first time for forty-five years that a Prince of Wales had set foot in Australia, and the press were rampant. (Within minutes of his arrival in Canberra, while driving to Government House, the Prince saw the all too predictable kangaroo by the roadside; local residents believed enterprising newsmen had planted the animal there for his benefit.) Checketts headed off the threat of constant harassment by arranging an open day when Charles arrived at Timbertop. All day the press followed him around the school and the surrounding countryside, on the strict condition that they then withdraw for the rest of term. And so they did. Checketts fielded myriad telephone calls at Devon Farm, releasing what information he chose. But even he, not noted for his love of the press gangs around the prince, saluted the Australian newspapers' behavior as "wonderful."

Timbertop boys live together in a compound of nine huts, each containing about fifteen and each supervised by an older boy described as "a sort of NCO." One such was Charles, who shared a room in the masters' quarters with a sheep farmer's son named Stuart Macgregor, a former head boy of Geelong who had come out to Timbertop to study in peace for his university entrance. Here Charles, too, worked by himself for his A levels. He did not attend what few classes there were at Timbertop, but had to spend some of his time supervising the younger boys in such chores as woodcutting, boiler stoking, and (again) trash-can emptying. He joined with a will in the strenuous hikes and cross-country runs which were compulsory most afternoons and on weekends; on one occasion, David Checketts gamely joined in a sixty-mile hike across arduous mountain terrain. Charles earned popularity by rather neglecting his studies for the life of the outback; a familiar figure silhouetted against the horizon with his fishing rod, he was occasionally late with the essays he took down to supervisors at Geelong. His Australian hosts were introducing him, quite deliberately, to a university style of tuition, not knowing whether he would ever again have the chance to enjoy this type of academic life.

Excursions farther afield became more exotic: sheep shearing and pig swilling, gem hunting and panning for gold. Charles felled trees, took part in a scheme to help war widows, and was introduced to the exotic local ornithology.

He was thoroughly enjoying himself. Timbertop, he found, was as stimulating as Gordonstoun had become monotonous. He was popular among his fellows for himself, not for his rank, and he had never known such freedom to wander the great outdoors unobserved. He had originally come to Australia for one term, but the Queen had privately directed that he might stay on for a second if he wished. The choice was to be left entirely to him. He decided, without hesitation, to stay.

Charles's enjoyment of Timbertop is best expressed in his own words, written under the heading "Timbertop: or Beating about the bush" for the *Gordonstoun Record*. With boyish enthusiasm, he chronicles the delights of each busy day:

"Almost everyone, master and boys, enjoy themselves up here. One never seems to stop running here and there for one minute of the day, from 7:30 A.M. breakfast—and no morning run, though there's worse to follow—until the lights go out at 9:15 P.M., having had tea at the unearthly hour of 5:30. If you have done a cross-country at 4:45 P.M. and arrived back at 5:05 P.M., it's difficult to persuade your stomach to accept food. . . ."

Wood chopping was "essential as the boys' boilers have to be stoked with logs and the kitchen uses a huge number. The first week I was here I was made to go out and chop up logs on a hillside in boiling hot weather. I could hardly see my hands for blisters. . . . Each afternoon after classes, which end at three o'clock, there are jobs which . . . involve chopping and splitting wood, feeding the pigs, cleaning out fly traps (which are revolting glass bowls seething with flies and very ancient meat), or picking up bits of paper round the school. . . ."

Of weekend expeditions into the bush, he wrote: "You can't see anything but gum tree upon gum tree, which tends to become rather monotonous. . . . You virtually have to inspect every inch of the ground you hope to put your tent on in case there are any ants or other ghastly creatures. There is one species of ant called Bull Ants which are three-quarters of an inch long, and they bite like mad! Some boys manage to walk fantastic distances over a weekend of four days or less, and do 130 or even 200 miles. The furthest I've been is 60–70 miles in three days, climbing about five peaks on the way. At the campsite the cooking is done on an open fire in a trench. You have to be very careful in hot weather that you don't start a bush fire, and at the beginning of this term there was a total ban in force, so that you ate all the tinned food cold."

Each Wednesday there was a tug o' war "or, if it's hot, there is swimming, or perhaps someone is feeling sufficiently cruel to organize a race that involves carrying half a tree for a certain distance." If those boys who returned from weekend hikes were indulging in a little royal leg pulling with their claims of "130 or even 200 miles," Charles was evidently able to give as good as he got. "I almost convinced one or two Australians outside the school that we rustled kangaroos at Timbertop, and that we performed this art by creeping up on them behind, grabbing them by the tail and flicking them over on their backs, where you had them at your mercy." Rather more authentic was his account of a sheep-shearing expedition: "I made rather a mess of it, and left a somewhat shredded sheep."

A pleasant interruption to the prince's first term at Timbertop was an Australian visit by the Queen Mother. Charles received permission to go and meet his grandmother in Canberra, and they spent two days together in a cabin in the Snowy Mountains. Queen Elizabeth was delighted to hear, and to see for herself, how much happier Charles was than during those early days at Gordonstoun. She was able to return home with news and snapshots to reassure the Queen that a second term at Timbertop was in Prince Charles's best interests.

An unexpectedly important moment in the prince's life came at the end of that first term, when he joined a party of thirty boys making Geelong's annual visit to the missionary stations in Papua and New Guinea. With the headmaster, Thomas Garnett, they flew over Prince of Wales Island to Port Moresby, with a refueling stop near Brisbane. It was here that a vast and unexpected crowd had gathered on the tarmac to see the prince, who had never before confronted such a throng in his own right. His instinct was to stay on the aircraft and hope it took off again as soon as possible. But David Checketts urged him to go and talk to them. Checketts, as both remember it, had more or less to kick the prince off the plane; Charles walked across the tarmac to the ecstatic assembly with very mixed feelings. Once he reached them, however, and found how easy it was to talk to people even in such difficult circumstances, he began to enjoy the experience. Since that day, he says, he has never been nervous of big crowds.

The final stage of the journey was by launch across Goodenough Bay to the village of Wedau, near Dogura Cathedral. There was a reception committee of thousands, Australians and Papuans, in school uniforms, nuns' habits, grass skirts, and feather headdresses; as the southern sun set over the beach, it was an intensely dramatic sight. The bishop, Dr. John Chisholm, led

Charles forward, and there was a huge chorus of *"Egualau"*—
Wedauan for "welcome."

For four days Charles and his friends toured the area, seeing
the mission's schools, hospitals, churches, and charitable outposts.
Again he wrote his own account, this time for the Geelong school
magazine, in which it is possible to read the dawning of his interest in anthropology. "I can't help feeling that less and less interest is being taken by the younger Papuans in the customs and
skills of their parents and grandparents, because they feel that
they have to live up to European standards, and that these things
belong to the past and have no relevance to the present or future.
This may be a completely false impression, but I was given one or
two presents by young people, and when I asked if they had made
them, they said their mothers or aunts had. No doubt, however,
in the years to come, when there are new generations of Papuans,
they will consider these ancient skills of use. . . ."

One evening he watched dancers "in magnificent headdresses
of bird of paradise feathers, cassowary feathers, hornbill beaks,
and chicken feathers," and then joined in the dancing, himself
leading "a somewhat hilarious reel." In the year following his
confirmation, however, it was the work of the Anglican mission,
in the middle of nowhere, which most caught his young and re-
flective imagination: "I would like to mention how fresh and sincere I found the Church at Doguar. Everyone was so eager to take
part in the services, and the singing was almost deafening. One
felt that it might almost be the original Church. Where Christianity is new, it must be much easier to enter into the whole
spirit of it wholeheartedly. . . ."

He spent the rest of that holiday exploring the east coast of
Australia with David Checketts, bobbing from one friend's house
to the next, fishing, playing polo, and at Eidsvold in Queensland
driving twenty head of cattle back and forth through the stock-
yard gates—for the benefit of the press, who had by now caught
up again. At the Melanda reserve near Cairns, he met seventy-
year-old Davey Douglas, an aborigine, the oldest living man to
have been convicted of cannibalism (in the 1920s). "I kept my
hands behind my back," wrote Charles, "but he assured me he has
lost his taste for humans." At Sydney he had his first sight of
surfing, at North Bondi, but conditions were too hazardous for

beginners. He has since more than made up for this first disappointment.

After visiting the Outward Bound School on the Hawkesbury River, it was back for a few days to Devon Farm, during which brief visit Mrs. Checketts gave birth to another daughter. Charles was delighted; he has always been rather soft about babies. (After the early childhood of his two young brothers, there was only his increasing collection of his godchildren to coo over, until the birth in 1977 of Princess Anne's son.)

Then back to Timbertop, where life had changed only with the seasons. It was now June, midwinter in Victoria, which gave him a chance for some skiing. But his main preoccupation was still with the A levels looming on his return to Gordonstoun. In the course of his history studies, more urgent than his French, he decided to give his fellow pupils a lecture on the subject of King Charles I. This "saddest of all kings" was a particularly vivid figure to Charles, who had made a special study of his two historical namesakes, and had grown up with Van Dyck portraits around him on the familiar walls of the state apartments of Buckingham Palace. Later, he was to find Cromwell a more impressive figure: "I realized that Charles I was not entirely splendid and innocent, as I had always thought."

Charles and Checketts returned to England by way of Tahiti, Mexico City, and Jamaica, where they joined Prince Philip and Princess Anne at the Commonwealth Games—always, to Prince Charles, the anniversary of his creation as Prince of Wales. Before he left Australia, Geelong's headmaster, Mr. Garnett, had said of him: "Leaving aside the question of royalty, we have really enjoyed having Prince Charles at the school. Before his visit, most Australians had very hazy and possibly erroneous ideas of him, if they had any ideas at all. They probably thought of him as just a distant, uninteresting figurehead. In future most of them will know him as a friendly, intelligent natural boy with a good sense of humor, someone who by no means has an easy task ahead of him in life."

Charles insisted on repaying the compliment. His six months in Australia had been "the most wonderful period of my life," and he was himself aware of the self-confidence and maturity he had developed. The freshness and directness of the people had excited him; there was little of the servility or sycophancy to which he had grown so used at home. "In Australia you are judged on how people see you and feel about you. There are no assumptions. You have to fend for yourself." He was to make a point of returning to Australia (and Geelong) whenever possible, and has always regarded it as his favorite home away from home.

Before leaving, the Prince wrote a few sentences which he asked David Checketts to read aloud to the reporters and well-wishers gathered at the airport: "It would be difficult to leave without saying how much I have enjoyed and appreciated my stay in Australia and how touched I have been by the kindness of so many people in making these six months such a worthwhile experience. The most wonderful part was the opportunity to travel and see at least some of the country (I hope I shall be able to come back and see the rest) and also the chance to meet so many people, which completes the link with a country I am very sad to be leaving. And yet I shall now be able to visualize Australia in the most vivid terms, after such a marvelous visit."

Three terms back at Gordonstoun seemed an unwelcome extension to the prince's schooldays, but they were to provide new opportunities of some moment. His arrival back at the school was considerably more impressive than his first appearance there, on his father's coattails, four years earlier; this time Prince Philip sat in the back as Charles drove himself up to the school gates, six-year-old Prince Andrew at his side in the front passenger seat. (His father's presence in the car was legally required because Charles had only a provisional license; he passed his driving test in his mother's Rover 2000 the following April.)

His fellows at Windmill Lodge had elected him "Helper," or Head of House, and the following term Charles was chosen as Guardian. In becoming head boy, he had followed his father in one role close to both their hearts; Prince Philip had been Guardian in 1938–39. The job was really a matter of liaison between the headmaster and the boys. There was no power to inflict corporal punishment, only to urge or advise the headmaster in administrative or disciplinary matters—not unlike the relationship, as defined by Walter Bagehot, between monarch and prime minister. Prince Charles on one occasion exercised his rights by trying to persuade Mr. Chew not to expel two boys caught in a serious misdemeanor; his advice was listened to but not acted upon.

Though it failed, his stand was respected by headmaster and fellow pupils alike. Basil Boothroyd, the Duke of Edinburgh's biographer, made the mistake of suggesting to the dean of Windsor that Charles's appointment as Guardian was a "put-up job." "No, no," came the reply, "he was streets ahead of the lot of them."

As Helper, Charles had graduated to his own individual study, which set him more than ever apart from his fellows in Windmill Lodge. As Guardian, he moved out to a small bed-sitting room in the flat of Bob Waddell, the Gordonstoun art master (who had also directed the prince as Macbeth). Waddell was relieved to find that the music blasting through the communal wall was, for once, more classical than pop. He had been gratified that the prince had chosen one of his subjects, pottery, as his special project throughout his time at Gordonstoun. The master and the prince became close friends, and still remain in touch.

Prince Charles's eighteenth birthday that November was spent carrying out his duties and preparing for his A levels. As he gave a small tea party in the Guardian's room, bells tolled in London and judges at the Old Bailey wore their finest scarlet robes in honor of the occasion. The day carried a special significance of which the prince was well aware. He had now reached the age at which he could reign as king in his own right. If any disablement befell the sovereign, there would no longer be the need for a regent to act in his place. For the first twelve months of Elizabeth II's reign, any such regency would have passed to Princess Margaret; by the Regency Act of 1953, however, Parliament, at the sovereign's request, transferred the powers to the Duke of Edinburgh. Had any mischance befallen the Queen before her son's eighteenth birthday, Prince Philip would have reigned in her place.

The regency, like the monarchy, had traditionally been a hereditary privilege. In King George VI's reign, under the Regency Act of 1937, the Duke of Gloucester would have acted as regent until Princess Elizabeth's eighteenth birthday. The reason for this departure from tradition in 1953, given that Prince Philip was well down the line of succession, was quite simply to implement a father's right to be responsible for the upbringing of his son. This was made clear in the Queen's message to Parliament, read by the Home Secretary, Sir David Maxwell Fyfe: "The uncertainty of human life leads me to put you in mind of the possibility that a child of myself and my dear husband may succeed to the throne whilst under the age of eighteen years. And I would recommend to your consideration whether it be no expediency to provide that, in that event and also in the event of a Regency becoming necessary during my lifetime, whilst there is no child or grandchild of ours who can be the Regent, my husband should be the Regent and be charged with the guardianship of the person of the Sovereign."

That day, moreover, Prince Charles qualified to act as the senior counsellor of state in the Queen's absence abroad. The following July, he was named as one of four such counsellors (the others being the Queen Mother, Princess Margaret, and the Duke of Gloucester) empowered to act during the Queen's and Prince Philip's six-day visit to Canada. Had there been any urgent legislative business, he could have conducted a Privy Council meeting or given the royal assent to parliamentary bills. He could have made peace or declared war. Perhaps to the disappointment of one preparing for exams, there was no such emergency to call him away from Gordonstoun.

To his own satisfaction more than anyone else's, that summer brought the news that Prince Charles had satisfied the A level examiners. He was awarded a grade C in French, and a B in history, with a distinction in the optional special paper, thus giving him an S ("Scholarship") level. Prince Charles had proved that he could win a university place in his own right, unlike any other heir to the throne before him. His own delight was exceeded perhaps only by that of Mr. R. M. Todd, secretary of the Oxford and Cambridge Schools Examinations Board, who got quite carried away when discussing the results in the *Times*. The optional paper, he said, was "the one which marks out the high flyer as regards judgement, initiative and historical acumen. If a boy has done well in this paper—and the Prince got a distinction—it is a very good guide to university prospects." Only six percent of the four thousand candidates had gained such distinctions. "I consider that his performance was extraordinary, especially when you consider that he was digging about in Australia and that kind of thing beforehand. He has so many things to do, he must have worked like a demon. I should hesitate to take the paper myself. . . ."

In his last days at Gordonstoun, Prince Charles also developed his skills on the cello, explored the music of Bach and Mozart, and followed his success as Macbeth by singing the Pirate King in Gilbert and Sullivan's *Pirates of Penzance*. Again, in the presence of his parents, there was an unfortunate line: "We yield at once, with humble mien . . . Because with all our faults we love the Queen." As before, he was graduating to a major role from a minor; he had played the Duke of Exeter in *Henry V* before taking on Macbeth, and he had sung a guardsman in Gilbert and Sullivan's *Patience*. But it was the musical element that most appealed to him—quite apart from his being, against theatrical tradition, the prince who wanted to play a clown. Music was becoming a passion. A good sight-reader, he had sung in Benjamin Britten's "St. Nicholas," in Elgar's "Dream of Gerontius," in Bach's B Minor Mass. He was playing the cello quite well—better, for sure, than he had the trumpet. "There was a wonderful German lady who had been there for years; she was there when my father was there [Frau Lachmann, a refugee from Nazi Germany whom Hahn had given a job]. She kept turning around in the middle of the orchestra and saying: 'Ach ze trumpet, I cannot stand ze trumpet.' So I decided to give it up." Inspired by hearing Jacqueline du Pré play the Dvořák concerto in the Royal Festival Hall, the prince took cello lessons for several years, though pressure on his time eventually forced him to give it up.

"I'm glad I went to Gordonstoun," he said later. "The toughness of the place is too much exaggerated by report. It was the character of the general education there—Kurt Hahn's principles; an education which tried to balance the physical and mental with the emphasis on self-reliance to develop a rounded human being. I did not enjoy school as much as I might have, but that was because I am happier at home than anywhere else. But Gordonstoun developed my will-power and self-control, helped me to discipline myself, and I think that discipline, not in the sense of making you bath in cold water, but in the Latin sense—giving shape and form and tidiness to your life—is the most important thing your education can do."

In this last year, curiously perhaps, Gordonstoun had developed more than anything else Charles's growing fondness for the arts. Other penchants were becoming clearer. Unlike his father, he showed no interest in matters scientific or technological; his preoccupations seemed to lie in the past rather than the future,

and the time he had spent in the caves of Morayshire, bats flutter-
ing around his head, was to be followed up in a close study of
archaeology at Cambridge and thereafter. He had played his last
team games—apart from polo, much more an individualist's sport
anyway—and had only a broken nose to show for his time on the
rugger field. His natural introspection had much more to feed on.

At home, too, he had made significant advances. On becoming eighteen, he had attended his first meeting of the Duchy of
Cornwall. He had taken part in his first full-scale public engagement with his parents: a large garden party at Holyroodhouse in
Edinburgh, prompting a headline special to the *New York Times:*
PRINCE CHARLES A SOCIAL SUCCESS: HE'S JUST A CHIP OFF THE OLD
BLOCK. He had been granted his own coat of arms, and thus his
own ensign. And a date had now been announced for his investiture as Prince of Wales at Caernarvon: July 1, 1969. He had just
two more years before his emergence, fully fledged and much
trumpeted, into public life.

He was to spend them enjoying a brief taste of a unique kind
of freedom, the freedom of university life, which to most who
have known it retains a distinctive flavor throughout all their subsequent metamorphoses. Charles was more than ready for it. He
may have been pleased he went to Gordonstoun, but he was even
more pleased to leave. "He's looking forward to leaving school,"
said his father. "There comes a time when you've had enough
of it."

12

1967-69: Trinity and Aberystwyth

*"I'm one of those stupid bums who
never went to university . . . and
I don't think it's done me any
harm."* PRINCE PHILIP

ON DECEMBER 22, 1965, the Queen and Prince Philip
held a dinner party at Buckingham Palace with the express purpose of discussing the Prince of Wales's future. Gathered around
the table were the prime minister (Harold Wilson), the Archbishop of Canterbury (Michael Ramsey), Earl Mountbatten (representing the services, as Admiral of the Fleet), the Dean of Windsor, the chairman of the Committee of University Vice-Chancel-
lors (Sir Charles Wilson), and the Queen's private secretary, Sir
Michael Adeane. Adeane had briefed all the guests beforehand
on the subject for discussion—who was not himself invited.

Over breakfast next morning, Prince Charles learned from
his parents that the conversation had continued into the small
hours. He had already indicated his own wish to go to university,
and the dinner party had gone right through the pros and cons
of ancient, "red brick," and modern. These in turn were weighed
against the services: Dartmouth, Cranwell, Sandhurst. Soft drinks
and beer were served after dinner, plus a brandy for the prime
minister, who urged Mountbatten to speak his mind. "Trinity
College," said Charles's great-uncle Dickie, "like his grandfather;
Dartmouth like his father and grandfather; and then to sea in
the Royal Navy, ending up with a command of his own." The pattern was hard to resist.

But there would again be innovations. If he were to go to
university, Charles was insistent on living in college—like Edward

157

VIII at Oxford, but unlike Edward VII and George VI at Cambridge, both of whom had lived in large town houses, their tutors traveling to them. None of the three had stayed at university the full three years, or taken a degree. This remained a matter of debate between the prince and his parents, who postponed a decision. Charles himself was at first in favor of a multidisciplinary course of study, perhaps including a dabble in medicine and other such curiosities, which would have made a final examination impossible. Prince Philip kept his son's options open for him: "I don't think his course should be constrained by the absolute need to take a degree." Some advisers supported this view, telling his parents: "For God's sake, don't let him risk exams."

Prince Charles himself opted for Cambridge, preferring the old to the new wherever possible, and valuing his family's links with the University. Edward VIII had been the only Prince of Wales to go to Oxford, where he had won a reputation as a gay blade. The more academically minded Charles had no such aspiration: he wanted to seize the chance for some peace and quiet, and to devote his last years free from royal duties to the kind of studies for which he would never again have time. Besides, Cambridge was closer to Sandringham, where he now had his own home. An old gray stone cottage on the estate, known locally as Dr. Ansell's house because it had for years been the home of the Queen's Sandringham physician, had been converted for the prince's use and rechristened Wood Farm. It would make the ideal weekend retreat.

The choice of college took slightly longer. The Dean of Windsor, Dr. Woods, was asked by the Queen to look at the possibilities, and traveled to Cambridge for discussions with a number of heads of colleges. He delivered a written report to Her Majesty outlining the merits and demerits of a short list of five, and finally opting for Trinity—his own college, where his elder son, Robert (whom the prince knew), was already an undergraduate and his younger son, Edward, would be a contemporaneous freshman. The royal family was pleased. Trinity was the college of the Queen's father, King George VI, and his brother the Duke of Gloucester, of King Edward VII and his ill-fated son Prince Eddy, Duke of Clarence, quite apart from Bacon and Dryden, Marvell and Thackeray, Byron and Tennyson, Newton and Rutherford, Balfour and Baldwin, Melbourne, Grey, Campbell-Bannerman, and the composer Ralph Vaughan Williams. King George V had visited the college when its master had been Henry Montagu Butler, great-uncle of the recently installed master, the newly ennobled Lord Butler of Saffron Walden. As R. A. ("Rab") Butler, the Conservative Chancellor, Foreign Secretary, and Home Secretary, often described in England as "the greatest prime minister we never had," he had been much involved with the royal family over the years and was a valued and trusted friend.

Over Christmas 1966, Charles invited Butler to tea at Buckingham Palace and told him of his interest in archaeology and anthropology. The master suggested he pursue the subjects at Trinity. Against some urgings, Butler saw no point in the young prince's spending his youth trying to master the British constitution. There would be plenty of time for that. Let him study something he was genuinely interested in; if it gave him some understanding of the structure of society, perhaps even of the ritual adulation offered a monarchy by its people, so much the better.

Early in the New Year, Charles and his father returned the visit, driving over from Sandringham to meet Trinity's senior tutor, Dr. Denis Marrian, who was also to be the prince's individual tutor. Marrian conducted a standard entrance interview and made the assessment that "he was capable enough and interested enough to take an Honours Degree." Marrian explained that a special course could be arranged, but could not lead to a degree of any kind. If the prince spent his first year studying for the Part One Tripos, in archaeology and physical and social anthropology, he would then have three options: continue to the Part Two exams, switch to another subject for Part Two, or abandon the idea of taking a degree—and dabble. If he started out on a specially tailored course of studies, there would be no chance to turn back to a degree syllabus. Partly because of this, because he might be thought to be avoiding public assessment, the prince opted for the "ark and anth" degree course, reserving the option to switch to history for Part Two. He was thus embarked upon the hazardous course of attempting to become the first heir to the throne ever to win university honors.

That day, the prince and his father inspected his "set" of rooms, number six on Staircase E of New Court, a quiet corner of the college beside the River Cam and the Cambridge "backs." The Queen later paid a private visit herself, and had a long chat in her son's rooms with forty-seven-year-old Mrs. Florence Moore, "Mrs. M." to the students, who was to be Prince Charles's "bedder" (room cleaner). She also had a look at the college sick bay and met its overseer, Sister Custerson. Behind Her Majesty came a train of Sandringham workmen, bearing carpets and curtains for the new royal abode. At Butler's suggestion, the prince was to allow himself the luxury of a telephone and a small kitchen area in his rooms; Trinity meanwhile protested that a new bathroom suite installed on the staircase that year had anyway long been scheduled. The prince's set was one flight up, to prevent inquisitive noses pressing against his window, and gave easy access to Cambridge's river walks and, in summer, punting. As Charles walked back through the Grand Gate with his father, past the statue of the boy Prince Charles (the First), he relished the prospect of a temporarily cloistered life. It would be "marvelous to have three years when you are not bound by anything, and not married, and haven't got any particular job."

His arrival as a freshman that October, in David Checketts' red Mini, was chaotic. He was twelve minutes late, thanks to city-center traffic jams, leaving Lord Butler and Dr. Marrian standing outside the college entrance with the huge crowd that had gathered to greet him. All he could see from the Mini on arrival were "serried ranks of variously trousered legs, from which I had to distinguish those of the master and the senior tutor." His most vivid memory of that day is of "several burly, bowler-hatted gentlemen [the college porters] dragging shut those magnificent wooden gates to prevent the crowd from following in. It was like a scene from the French Revolution."

Someone in the crowd shouted "Good Luck!" "Thanks," Charles shouted back, "I'll need it." That evening, Robert Woods showed him around the college, and he dined in Hall with the first sitting of freshmen. But Lord Butler had perhaps been prescient in suggesting that Charles have his own kitchen. He had intended to dine in college with his fellow students as often as possible, but it soon became something of an ordeal. As at Cheam and Gordonstoun, people tended to hang back, even to avoid him; at Cambridge, moreover, in the "student protest" era of 1968, it was not always fashionable to be seen in the company of princes. On one occasion, Charles found himself locked out of the college late at night, along with another nervous young freshman; together they had to ring for the porter to let them in. It was the kind of modest adventure which sometimes sparks undergraduate friendships. Next night in Hall, however, as Charles wandered down the aisle looking for someone to sit with, he saw the face of his coconspirator turn away in sheer embarrassment. Nobody wanted to be thought too anxious to become his friend.

If he did strike up any pleasant acquaintanceships it was hard to follow them up, as people tended to disappear into their own corner of university life for days or weeks on end. There were, at least, his Gloucester cousins to visit. But rather to Butler's disappointment, Charles tended to befriend such groups as the polo-playing fraternity (he quickly won his half-Blue), or public-school–educated boys from the country gentry (with some of whom he founded an all-male dining club called the Wapiti Society), rather than the grammar school products who comprised three-quarters of the college's population.

Butler proved himself a staunch ally and counselor. He turned a blind eye when Charles went off in his detective's Land-Rover to collect his new MGB, complete with bull horn, from the city outskirts; undergraduates were not allowed cars in their first year, and even after that were forbidden to drive them within the city limits. More important, he cleared forty-five minutes before dinner each evening, and gave Charles his own key to a side entrance to the Master's Lodge, which led by way of what he liked to call "my secret staircase" directly into his study. He found Charles "talented—which is a different word from clever, and a different word from bright." Though still a plodder academically, the prince had a relentless curiosity about the ways of the world, which the master was more than qualified to gratify. "He grew," says Butler. "When he arrived, he was boyish, rather immature, and perhaps too susceptible to the influence of his family." Those evening chats, over Charles's three years at Trinity, were among the most important he had ever had in broadening his experience and understanding of his fellow man.

They were not, however, without their tricky moments. Charles arrived one evening to tell Butler of a long chat he had had with Hywel Jones, an economics student from Cardiff with rooms on the same staircase. Jones had read Marx at fourteen; an eloquent socialist, he was destined to become president of the Trinity student union. "Do you think it would be all right if I joined the University Labour Club?" Charles asked the master. "Hell, no," said Butler, and patiently explained that he must never show allegiance to any individual political party. But he urged the prince to pursue his political arguments with Jones, in private, and both prince and republican now believe they modified each other's views. Any brief flirtation with the left was anyway, perhaps, only a product of Charles's immaturity, his susceptibility to ideas he had never before heard cogently argued; in his twenties, living at home again with his parents, he quickly reverted to their orthodox conservative attitudes.

Before the prince's arrival at Trinity, Marrian had met both the local and national press, who had agreed to leave Charles in peace as much as public demand would allow. But happily for a Prince of Wales, the town of Cambridge anyway makes a point of treating celebrities with scant ceremony. He was able to bicycle around the town at will, those who recognized him letting him go on his way with a knowing grin, though a Land-Rover bearing his detective ("Oddjob" to the students) was never far behind. He could, for once in his life, go shopping: he was a familiar figure at the vegetable market, and on one occasion complained (correctly) that he had been shortchanged. Without attracting crowds, he could visit the coffeehouse opposite Trinity, the Whim-at-Eleven, soon rechristened by its clients the "Him-at-Eleven." With Robert Woods, he joined the college Madrigal Society, and played his cello in a public concert. He went to a club showing of the Marx Brothers in *A Night at the Opera*, signing himself in as Charlie Chester—which, as Charles, Earl of Chester, he had every right to do. He even joined adult education classes in pottery, one evening a week, at the Cambridge College of Arts and Technology.

Cambridge did, however, prompt the Prince of Wales to don a disguise—to avoid public recognition—for the first and only time in his life: he wanted to attend a student demonstration "to see what they were like." He came away unimpressed. "I do try and understand what they're getting at, but I can't help feeling that a lot of it is purely for the sake of change, and for the sake of doing something to change things—which, from my point of view, is pointless." The prince also disapproved of less fundamental revolutions. "Change for the sake of change" was his verdict on Trinity's relaxation of its "gate laws." Traditionally,

Balmoral: last days of holiday freedom before . . .

Cheam School: the Sunday two-by-two to church

President Eisenhower learns the royal walk

1958: created Prince of Wales
at nine years old

1960: returning with the Queen and the Queen Mother
from Princess Margaret's wedding to Tony Armstrong-Jones

1962: first steps
at polo

The new arrival at Gordonstoun
meets his headmaster, Robert Chew

1963: a skiing holiday, and a
first taste of pursuit by press

1966: leaving London Airport for school in Australia.
Between Prince Philip and Prince Charles is David Checketts.

In his father's footsteps:
"He's taught me a great deal."

In the heir apparent's seat
beside the throne at his first
State Opening of Parliament, 1967

"All hail Macbeth, that shalt be King hereafter!"

Two undergraduate Princes of Wales: the future King Edward VII at Oxford,
1859, and the future King Charles III at Cambridge, 110 years later

The actor manqué; scenes from the Trinity revue

Two Princes of Wales invested at Caernarvon: Prince Charles, 1969,
and Prince Edward (later King Edward VIII and Duke of Windsor), 1911

At the castle gate: presented to the people of Wales
(and a television audience of 500 million)

The contemporary monarchy: go-carting with five-year-old Prince Edward

High seriousness: an unconventional twenty-first-birthday portrait

Degree Day: the first heir apparent in British history to win university honors the college door had been closed at eleven, and guests had to leave by midnight; the times were now put back two hours. "It was a great challenge to climb in over the wall," said the disappointed prince. "Half the fun of university life is breaking the rules."

Charles's first year at Cambridge saw the twenty-first birthday of *Varsity*, the undergraduate newspaper, and he agreed to a request from its then editor, David Taylor (now deputy editor of *Punch*), to contribute. For him, he wrote, life at Trinity meant "every modulation of light and weather, like the orange-pink glow from the stone of the Wren Library in the last rays from a wintry sun"; it meant "the everlasting splashing of the Great Court fountain" and the everlasting sound "of photographers' boots ringing on the cobbles." In the early morning, there was also the noise of the world coming to life beneath his window. "This is something I find hard to accustom myself to, particularly the grinding note of an Urban District Council dust lorry's engine rising and falling in spasmodic energy at seven o'clock in the morning, accompanied by the monotonous jovial dustman's refrain of 'O Come All Ye Faithful' and the head-splitting clang of the dustbins." Some have greatness thrust upon them: within a few days the singing dustman in question, an ex-Coldstream Guards sergeant named Frank Clarke, was a national celebrity, and had been signed by a record company. And—the perks of being a prince—the UDC put back the collection time of Trinity dustbins to 9 A.M.

On Charles's nineteenth birthday that November, the bells of the University Church of Great St. Mary's pealed, as usual, in honor of the occasion; this year, for once, the Prince of Wales climbed the 123 steps to the belfry to thank the twelve ringers. Prince Charles was not much in evidence around Cambridge, as he was taking his work rather seriously. He was keen to endow his anthropology studies with practical significance: "If more people can be assisted to appreciate and understand their own social behavior, the better and more healthy our society will be." His director of studies, Dr. John Coles, reported to Dr. Marrian: "He writes useful and thoughtful essays, although sometimes they are a little rushed. He is interested in discussion, and likes to draw parallels between the peoples we study and ourselves." His archaeology, also supervised by Dr. Glyn

Daniel of modest television renown, took him in the spring to the Dordogne region of France. A few members of the Cambridge Archaeological Society, with Coles, Daniel, and David Checketts, had the rare privilege of being flown to France in a Heron of the Queen's Flight, with the Duke of Edinburgh at the controls. From the primitive cave paintings of Les Eyzies, the party traveled north through the Loire to Brittany, and thence to Jersey, where the expedition climaxed in a weekend under canvas. "Believe me," said Charles's long-suffering detective, "this was no holiday. It's one of the hardest few days I've ever spent. I'd like to lie in the sun for a week to recover."

At the end of the following term, enthusiasm and diligence had their reward: a place in division one of Class II in the first-year Tripos Exams. When Charles had gone to Cambridge, the National Union of Students had debated a motion of protest at his admission with only two A levels (the usual requirement being three); others, ran the counterargument, may have been better qualified, but a Prince of Wales is entitled to benefit from the best British education, and this one was at least trying to win his academic spurs. Now Prince Charles had conspicuously won himself an above-average result, on merit. That June he was formally installed as a Knight of the Garter; after the ceremony in Windsor Castle, he walked in public procession, plumed and robed, with such figures as Mountbatten, Alexander, and Montgomery. Photographs of the occasion show a new strength in his features: the hard-won self-confidence of a prince who for the first time has placed himself in open competition with his fellows and not been found wanting.

For his remaining two years, Prince Charles decided to turn his attention to history.

"Why?" asked Butler. "If you stick to archaeology or anthropology, you might get a First." But Charles was determined: Trinity had partly been chosen because of its strong history side, and he had always found it as much a pleasure as a duty to inform himself about his ancestors. He also wanted to begin a study of the British constitution.

"Why?" asked Butler again.

"Because I'm probably going to be king," replied Charles.

Butler was disappointed. "You've got years for all that. Enjoy yourself while you can." But the prince was not to be budged. He had just attended his first state opening of Parliament, supreme moment of the monarch's majesty, and for the first time taken the heir's traditional place on the sovereign's right. His sense of history was high in his mind, as intimations of the royal duties ahead began to crowd in on him.

There were, in the meantime, other pleasures to be sought. During one of their preprandial chats, Butler encouraged Charles to take part in the activities of the Dryden Society, Trinity's drama club. The prince had displayed a taste for the stage at school, and now the master advised him that more experience would prove invaluable for all kinds of royal public occasions, notably appearances on television. Thus it was, at the beginning of Charles's second year in the autumn of 1968, that the nation thrilled to the sight of the Prince of Wales having a custard pie thrust in his face. He had auditioned for (mime, improvisation, prepared speech) and secured the part of the padre in Joe Orton's *Erpingham Camp*. The production, for which he borrowed the Dean's "dog collar," also required him at one point to be pelted with pork pies.

Trinity's modest amateur production received fuller (and more fulsome) reviews than any West End opening that week. Charles was evidently good box office, and three months later he was making his debut in satirical revue. His love of the Goons (a long-running anarchic radio comedy series starring Spike Milligan, Peter Sellers, Michael Bentine, and Harry Secombe) was evidence of a rather childish sense of humor, but then undergraduate comedy is scarcely of the most mature. His talent for Goonish funny voices, beloved of so many products of the British public schools, wowed the journalists at a special press preview, and had the black market in four shilling tickets active in Paris and Germany. Prince Charles took part in fourteen of the forty sketches in *Revulution*, impersonating the Duke of Wellington, mimicking Lord Butler, and declaring beneath an umbrella: "I lead a sheltered life." Most popular moment, perhaps, was his appearance in a Sherlock Holmes sketch as Sir Cummerbund Overspill; the Prince of Wales escorted a young lady offstage, a lascivious look in his eye: "I like to give myself heirs." The best remembered image, however, is that of the Prince of Wales sitting in a trash can (following p. 162). Trash cans seemed to have become a recurring feature of his young life.

In the role of "Reg Sprott," Singing Dustman, the prince charged £5 for interviews with the press, and rendered his chart-topping version of 'O Come All Ye Faithful.' The final Sunday performance had to be canceled—the disadvantages of being a prince—because of protests from the Lord's Day Observance Society. "Very silly," said Charles, rather daringly. "It made me very angry."

The Prince was beginning to take an interest in wine—an extracurricular topic of discussion with his tutor. Seeing Dr. Marrian climbing out of the iron grating above his wine cellar one day, bottles in hand, Charles said: "I've always wondered where the senior tutor lived." In his Trinity rooms, meanwhile, he was developing something of a reputation as a homespun chef, entertaining the Butlers more than once to his specialty, goulash, and roasting a chicken for a private dinner with the Queen. His history studies were progressing under a new director of studies, Dr. Anil Seal, a modern historian specializing in India and other non-European countries. One vacation saw the first of the Prince's now familiar whistle-stop tours around government and industry—a call on Barbara Castle at the Department of Employment, down a coal mine, around a newspaper, over a power station—where he met another Trinity student, doing a vacation job. "That," said Charles, "makes two of us."

But other royal duties were increasingly intruding into Cambridge life and work, to the considerable annoyance of Lord Butler, who referred to them scathingly as "balcony jobs." The approach of Charles's investiture at Caernarvon made its own demands: on a visit to the Welsh Office in Cardiff, he had a foretaste of the animosities in store—eggs, smoke bombs, and shouts of "Go home, Charlie." Confessing afterward to "slight butterflies," he approached the demonstrators to seek their complaints, only to be roundly abused. "You're not too brilliant, are you?" declared one nationalist (later fined for throwing a smoke bomb). "You got into university on just two A levels." Charles remembered: "This chap was holding a placard in Welsh, and I asked him what it meant. I hadn't learnt much Welsh then. He just hurled abuse, so after more questions I gave up. There was no point."

Back at Trinity, there was a knock at the door of his rooms one evening, and he thought he must be disturbing someone with his cello practice. On opening the door, however, he found two rather scruffy and menacing individuals, and feared for a moment it might be a kidnap attempt. They turned out to be two students from Aberystwyth University. "We were in Cambridge collecting for our rag week, and we thought we'd come and see what you were like." The prince invited them in, gave them a contribution, and let them take a look at him. They returned home converts.

The occasion for such strange visitations was the announce· ment, on November 1, 1967, that the Prince of Wales would spend the summer term of 1969—immediately prior to his investiture—studying Welsh at the University College of Wales, Aberystwyth. There had been a chorus of protest from Welsh Nationalists, then growing in strength, and they had not been alone; such Englishmen as A. J. P. Taylor, the historian, complained of "this sordid plot to exploit Prince Charles," saying: "The move is being made for political reasons, and what is worse, for reasons of party. . . . Mr. Wilson is imposing on Prince Charles a sacrifice which he would not dream of imposing on his own son."

Charles himself was not entirely happy about the move. Like Lord Butler, who was furious, he regarded it as an unwelcome interruption to his Cambridge studies, which were still going well. But he could see the need for it. He knew well, as few others did, that in the two years since the date of the investiture had been announced, his entire life had been geared for these last few months before his emergence as a public figure. He had made his first public speech (on December 10, 1968, as chairman of the Countryside in 1970 Conference, in Cardiff); he had attended his first Buckingham Palace garden party; he had now attended his second state opening of Parliament—to listen, ironically enough, to a Queen's Speech proposing the abolition of hereditary honors.

He had held two cocktail parties for journalists, on June 24 and 25, 1968, after the palace had requested each newspaper to assign one of its staff to take an interest in him. (They dubbed themselves the FOPCs, Followers of Prince Charles, and scarcely rose to their task: Mary Kenny of the London *Evening Standard* emerged from the palace calling Charles "a sweet virgin boy.") He had given his first radio interview on St. David's Day, 1969, and was limbering up for his first TV and newspaper interviews. The BBC-ITV joint production, *Royal Family*, was already well under way, and David Frost had been assigned to make a film about Charles for investiture time.

The entire program was being carefully organized from Buckingham Palace by two men: William Heseltine, then the Queen's press secretary (today her deputy private secretary), and David Checketts. In consultation with the Queen, Prince Philip, and Prince Charles, they intended to use the investiture as an appropriate moment to "relaunch" the monarchy, as well as to launch Charles. Aberystwyth was part of the plan.

Heseltine, an Australian, had originally come to London in 1960 to join the palace staff as an assistant information officer. Returning to Australia two years later (where he moved from the prime minister's to the governor-general's office), he was struck by the difference between the reserved, almost sullen monarch in the popular mind, and the jaunty, witty lady he had got to know. Returning to the palace in 1965, Heseltine determined to do something about it. Checketts, who had experience of public relations as a director of Neilson McCarthy, was at the same time pondering the problem of sending Charles forth into society. The success of the radio interview had surprised everyone. The prince talked naturally and easily about his schooldays, about Australia, about his parents and his early life, and did some of his funny voices from *Revulution*, then in production. When the television companies subsequently applied for an interview, permission was granted warily but the success repeated. Charles was even prepared to answer an unscheduled question about his thoughts on the subject of marriage.

Had this deliberate packaging of the Prince of Wales been more widely perceived early in 1960, as Charles prepared to brave the wrath of his reluctant principality, protest might have been yet more vociferous. Even as it was, bomb attacks on public buildings began. The Queen told her prime minister, Harold Wilson, that she feared for her son's safety. Thus the Home Office held a conference of police chiefs, chaired by the chief inspector of constabulary, Sir Eric St. Johnston, who called in a number of Welsh officers and the head of the Special Branch, Commander Ferguson Smith. It was decided to set up an intensive security operation to guard the prince throughout his period in Wales that year, and Detective Superintendent Jock Wilson was promoted chief superintendent to command it. An operational headquarters was set up in Shrewsbury.

This merely inflamed the controversy. It was argued that the unit should have been commanded by a Welshman, and based in Wales. Many Welsh-born police officers loyal to the crown were disappointed, and even more dismayed when heavy security blankets descended somewhat crudely on Aberystwyth and Caernarvon, turning them into what the Nationalists could and did call "garrison towns." Another mistake, it seemed at the time, was in the very choice of Aberystwyth, a stronghold of nationalism, whose dowdy mid-Victorian architecture had come to symbolize the unwelcome English invasion. Cardiff or Swansea universities, neither so fiercely Welsh, would have provided quite as good a grounding in ethnic language and culture in a much less hostile atmosphere. There would have been no need to cause further resentment, as the security unit soon did, by billeting some seventy police officers in the town's hotels and infiltrating undercover men into the university as kitchen staff, cleaners, and even as students.

Furthermore, the choice of Aberystwyth meant that Prince Charles's tutor would be Edward Millward, lecturer in Welsh language and literature, who was also vice-president of Plaid Cymru, the Welsh Nationalist Party, which had declared itself opposed in principle to the investiture. When four Aberystwyth students went on a week's hunger strike in protest against the prince's imminent arrival at the university, Mr. Millward congratulated them.

It was not an enviable prospect. When Charles paid an advance visit to the campus with David Checketts on April 1, the university bookshop was selling copies of a satirical university poster of him captioned *Arwr, Sant Carlo*—"Hero, Saint Charles." Carlo, a common Welsh name for a dog, had become a popular derogatory nickname for the prince. In that spring of 1969, the leader of the Welsh Language Society, Dafydd Iwan, had risen to the top of the Welsh charts with a song entitled "Carlo," which ran:

> I have a friend who lives in Buckingham Palace,
> And Carlo Windsor is his name.

> The last time I went round to his house
> His mother answered the door and said:
> "Carlo, Carlo, Carlo is playing polo today,
> Carlo is playing polo with his Daddy."
> So come all ye serfs of Wales
> And join in the chorus:
> At last you have a prince in this land of song.

"We don't need a royal circus," said Dafydd Iwan. "We need roads, industry, schools, indoor lavatories and water laid on." Said one of the hunger strikers: "We have nothing against Charles personally, but we are protesting against the political machine which is using him as a pawn." Even the English-born president of the Aberystwyth student union declared: "The investiture is a cheap shoddy political gesture, and if I were Welsh I would feel incensed." Strong opposition to the English Prince of Wales, it was calculated, was confined to some three hundred of the thousand Welsh students at Aberystwyth, themselves less than half the total student population. But it was the voice of protest, unsurprisingly, which drowned all other arguments.

Around the Welsh hills, caches of gelignite and machine guns were unearthed by Jock Wilson's men. A time bomb destroyed an RAF radio post near Aberystwyth. On the day of the prince's arrival, April 20, young Welsh bloods attempted to saw the head off the statue of another Prince of Wales, the future Edward VIII, on the town's promenade. To make matters worse, the security team had dictated that the prince could not live in Ceredigion Hall, the sea-front hostel for students of Welsh; instead, he was given Room 95 in Pantycelyn, a modern hall of residence for English students. That first day Windsor C., as he was in the university register, disarmed all protest by wandering openly around the town on a shopping expedition for coat hangers and picture hooks. He had taken the precaution of learning a few words of Welsh during his vacation, from the then secretary of state for Wales, George Thomas, and he sprinkled them liberally among the crowd who followed his every move. Even more sensibly, he thereafter confined himself conscientiously to the university language laboratory; he knew he had only eight weeks before a major speech in Welsh at an Eisteddfod—quite apart from another a month later, at his investiture, before a television audience of 500 million. The prospect concentrated the prince's mind wonderfully, and the crowds soon melted away from the entrance to Pantycelyn. His fellow students there, on one occasion, dispersed a group of noisy Nationalist demonstrators by emptying buckets of water over their heads. But the weeks, on the whole, passed quietly, as he had anticipated in his St. David's Day broadcast: "Once I have been there for eight weeks, things might improve."

They did. It was a lonely time—"I haven't made many friends, there haven't been many parties"—and it had begun apprehensively: "Naturally, misgivings had built up, but one had an exaggerated view of the situation." He turned down an invitation to meet nationalist students in the local milk bar, saying he would choose his own location, but from Millward he learnt "a great deal about nationalist ideas and aims and policies." During his television interview, he declared his sympathy: "If I've learnt anything in the last eight weeks, it's been about Wales in particular, and its problems, and what these people feel about Wales. They're depressed about what might happen if they don't try and preserve the language and culture, which is unique and special to Wales. And if something is unique and special, I think it's well worth preserving." One measure of his acceptance by fellow students is that a continental magazine found no takers for its offer of £5,000 for a photograph of the Prince of Wales being slapped in the face by a Welsh Nationalist. After he left, the number of students applying for places at Aberystwyth rose by twenty-five percent.

When he met the mayor of Llanelli, Charles was able to "fill his eye with saliva" by pronouncing the name of his town correctly. His ingenuous charm, and his evident eagerness to please, had won most Welsh hearts. To the majority he was "Carlo bach"—a term of endearment as significant in Wales as "pommy bastard" had been in Australia. It was a not immodest personal success, much admired by his father—"He came, saw, and conquered the Welsh," Prince Philip confided to a friend— and a source of great relief to David Checketts, whose admiration of his young master grew by the day. As Checketts' plans for the "unveiling" of Charles neared fruition, he had one great source of strength: by hitherto protecting the prince as far as possible from personal publicity, he had also concealed the fact that this young man was more than equal to the tasks ahead of him. He was alert, shrewd, and solemnly aware of his role. All of which would come as something of a surprise to the great British public, who in the palace's view could have been forgiven for thinking—after the cherry brandy incident, the Goonish theatricals, and the initial inability to handle Welsh protest—that the prince was just another upper-class half-wit.

But if Charles had defused Aberystwyth, he knew that he had as yet won less than half the battle. Just before going there, he had honestly—if foolishly—asked a banner-carrying Welsh Nationalist who Llewelyn was, candidly confessing he didn't yet know much Welsh history. Now he did. Llewelyn-ap-Gruffydd, he knew only too well, was the last Welsh Prince of Wales, killed in 1282 by the English invader, Edward I. The following year, after, for good measure, having hanged, beheaded, disemboweled, and quartered Llewelyn's brother David, Edward had captured Caernarvon Castle. There, in 1284, he had declared his infant son the first English Prince of Wales. And there, the following month, Charles was to undergo the private and public ordeal of investiture as the twenty-first English Prince of Wales, but only the second in nearly seven hundred years to be invested at Caernarvon.

He hadn't conquered Wales yet.

13

1967-69: Investiture

"Your friends will understand that as a prince you are obliged to do things which may seem a little silly."

QUEEN MARY TO HER SON EDWARD, PRINCE OF WALES, BEFORE HIS INVESTITURE AT CAERNARVON IN 1911

DURING THE SUMMER OF 1969, while Prince Charles was weathering the storm at Aberystwyth, Welshmen slightly farther north were enjoying another unusual glimpse of their monarchy in action. Out in Caernarvon Bay the Queen's brother-in-law, the first Earl of Snowdon, was living in a handsome launch lent him by a Welsh industrialist. With him were two friends, both designers: Carl Toms, already well known for his work in theater, ballet, and film design, and John Pound of the Ministry of Works design team. At six each morning Snowdon would go water-skiing around the bay, then breakfast with his colleagues in the morning sunshine, discussing the problems of the day ahead. Charles's investiture as Prince of Wales, they were determined, was not going to be just another piece of predictable royal pageantry. Snowdon, still something of a Bohemian figure to be a member of the Royal Family, was intent on dragging royal ceremonial into the Swinging Sixties, of which he was very much a representative figure; to Americans, the era is perhaps best remembered for Carnaby Street, the Kings Road and other focal points of "Swinging London." Snowdon had just designed a futuristic aviary for London Zoo, and was determined that the new materials, the new aesthetic, the not-so-radical chic

173

then dominating the visual arts in Britain would all play a part. Above all, he argued, he was designing a television production for 500 million viewers. With Snowdon's theatrically minded team ranged against Garter King of Arms's traditional protocol experts, and the Duke of Norfolk acting the genial referee, Caernarvon Castle was staging another in its long history of Welsh-English battles royal.

Snowdon is, of course, a Welshman himself. The young Tony Armstrong-Jones grew up only three miles from Caernarvon at Plas Dinas, his father's home in the village of Bontnewydd, and as a boy had often played in the castle grounds. He had not lost touch when his London career as a photographer began to flourish in the 1950s; among many memorable royal studies was Prince Charles's official seventh birthday portrait in 1955. So when he married the Queen's sister in 1960, it seemed logical that he should take his title from his homeland—and that three years later, on the death of Lord Harlech, the Queen should invite him to become constable of Caernarvon Castle.

When creating her son Prince of Wales in 1958, Elizabeth II had promised the Welsh people that she would one day "present him to you at Caernarvon." There were times she subsequently regretted the commitment. The decline of the British economy, the rise of Welsh nationalism, and the advent of an era of violent protest all conspired to make such a ceremony seem at best a political blunder, at worst a positive danger to its protagonist's life. So there was much discussion as to timing, the approach of Charles's twenty-first birthday being balanced against the depressed mood of late-sixties Britain. Five years after the initial announcement, with Snowdon's appointment as constable, interested parties thought he must know the date the Queen had in mind. He did not. She had not yet decided herself. No announcement was to be forthcoming for another four years.

The only previous investiture at Caernarvon was that of the last Prince of Wales, the future King Edward VIII, in 1911. It was David Lloyd George, then Chancellor of the Exchequer, who had foisted this flagrantly political device on King George V less than a year after he had ascended the throne. Alfred Edwards, bishop of St. Asaph (and later the first archbishop of Wales), had told Lloyd George of his vain attempts to persuade Queen Victoria and Edward VII of the need for some ceremony demonstrating Anglo-Welsh unity during the painful days of the dis-establishment of the Welsh church. As MP for Caernarvon, constable of the Castle, and a born opportunist, Lloyd George talked the king into mounting a ceremony that could only enhance his own political prestige and appease the opponents of his constant assaults on inherited privilege. The Duke of Windsor himself recalled how shocked George V and his family had been "only a few years before" by Lloyd George's famous Limehouse speech.

History has embalmed the myth that Edward I displayed his infant son to the Welsh barons at Caernarvon in 1284, thus creating the long line of English Princes of Wales. The story seems to be pure invention, but it provided the only "precedent" for the 1911 ceremony. For more than six hundred years, monarchs had been content to invest their eldest sons in Parliament, in royal palaces, or in English towns. Caernarvon, to the Welsh, remained the symbol of English usurpation of their sovereignty. Nonetheless, the king decided that such a spectacle would provide a fitting climax to his nationwide coronation tour. Lloyd George had his way and scored a momentous political triumph. To this day he stands in aggressive bronze splendor in the Castle Square, his back turned on the ancient battlements—"the alternative, I suppose," as Charles himself pointed out, "to turning his back on the people."

For the future Edward VIII, then a seventeen-year-old naval cadet at Dartmouth, popular enough to be nicknamed "Sardine" by his fellow midshipmen, it was an appalling prospect. "The ceremony I had to go through, with the speech I had to make, the Welsh I had to speak, were, I thought, a sufficient ordeal for anyone. But when a tailor appeared to measure me for a fantastic costume designed for the occasion, consisting of white satin breeches and a mantle and surcoat of purple velvet edged with ermine, I decided things had gone too far." As Lord Anglesey supervised the restoration of the ruined castle, using stone from the same quarries mined six hundred years before, the young prince refused to wear the "preposterous rig." There ensued what he called "a family blowup." He complained that he would become a laughingstock to his friends in the navy, but his mother talked him into acquiescence: "It will be only for this once."

His memories of that sweltering July day, nevertheless, remained miserable. "Within the vast ruin of Caernarvon Castle, with Winston Churchill as Home Secretary mellifluously proclaiming my titles (he told me afterward that he rehearsed them on the golf course), my father invested me as Prince of Wales. Upon my head he put a coronet cap as token of principality, and into my hand the gold verge of government, and on the middle finger the gold ring of responsibility. Then leading me by the hand through an archway to one of the towers of the battlements, he presented me to the people of Wales. Half fainting with heat and nervousness, I delivered the Welsh sentences that Mr. Lloyd George, standing close by in the ancient garb of constable, had taught me." In his diary that night, the king recorded: "The dear boy did it all remarkably well and looked so nice." But the prince wrote: "I got the impression that if I did what was asked of me, it would help Papa in his dealings with the difficult Mr. Lloyd George."

These memories were all revived in the summer of 1967, during Prince Charles's last term at Gordonstoun, when it was announced that his investiture would be held at Caernarvon two years later. By autumn, the date had hardened to July 1, 1969, and the scale of the operation had become frighteningly apparent. When Charles attended the first meeting of the Investiture Committee, at St. James's Palace on October 26, he was astonished to find around the vast mahogany table no fewer than fifty-three members, ranging from Lord Cobbold, the Lord Chamberlain, via the chairman of the Welsh Tourist Board to the Reverend E. Gwyndaf Evans, Archdruid of Wales. The chairman was, of course, Bernard, Duke of Norfolk, who as hereditary Earl Marshal and Chief Butler of England was a past master of state ceremonial, his finest hour having been the stage management of Elizabeth II's coronation in 1953. His two most vociferous lieutenants were Snowdon and the secretary of state for Wales, Cledwyn Hughes (succeeded the following year by George Thomas). Charles was relieved to see the reassuring presence of David Checketts.

With a budget provisionally fixed by the government at £200,000, an office for the investiture was established in Northumberland Avenue. Subcommittees began to proliferate, discussing music, protocol, heraldry, the religious service, and of course design. Snowdon conceived and chaired one of his own, under the auspices of the Council of Industrial Design, to pass on all official souvenirs for the occasion. Over the next eighteen months, 166 out of 450 designs submitted—goblets and cruets, pendants and paperweights, dolls, rugs and even pie funnels—were approved by a team including Mary Quant, the fashion designer. Strict rules were laid down for the marketing of approved souvenirs: none were to be sold before January 31, 1969, or manufactured after December 31, 1969, and all heraldic devices were to be based on a choice of fifty officially made available to industry by the College of Arms.

Protests began at once. Emrys Hughes, a Welsh republican representing a Scottish seat, launched a sustained House of Commons campaign by denouncing the entire "mini-coronation." It was quite inappropriate, he told the House, to hold a ceremony "in a castle built by Welsh slave labor under the orders of the intruder, the conqueror." The forty-thousand-member Welsh Nationalist Party, Plaid Cymru, had one MP—its president, Gwynfor Evans, who two years earlier had won Camarthen from Labour (in the shape, ironically enough, of David Lloyd George's daughter Megan). "Not unnaturally," said Evans, "I am enthusiastic about this. The situation would be quite different if Wales had Commonwealth status, in which case the Queen of England would be the Queen of Wales, as she is the Queen of Canada, Australia, and New Zealand when she goes to those countries."

Plaid Cymru dissociated itself from what it called "a piece of English trickery," and began a long campaign of peaceful protest. The more extreme Welsh Language Society, claiming eight hundred members, took to the roads. English-language traffic signs all over Wales were defaced; Welsh, and occasionally revolutionary, slogans appeared on roads and bridges. But both groups also dissociated themselves from the sterner forms of protest which began on November 17. As Lord Snowdon and the secretary for Wales were arriving in Cardiff for a planning meeting with 450 Welsh delegates, a time bomb exploded in the building, unhappily named the Temple of Peace. There was extensive damage, but no one was hurt. It was the first of a succession of fifteen bomb attacks on government and military buildings, post offices and pipelines, which would culminate on the morning of the investiture itself. "If this doesn't stop, someone is going to get killed," said Cardiff's chief constable, and he was to be proved right.

For the time being, however, there was the financial battle to be waged. In Parliament that Christmas, another Welsh Labour MP, Elystan Morgan, suggested that the true cost would be closer to £2½ million. For the first time it was publicly made clear that the Queen herself had asked for every economy to be made, offering to save expense by forgoing her own elaborate procession to the castle with the Windsor grays, and personally vetoing the originally proposed estimate of £500,000. This never deterred Emrys Hughes, who in his subsequent book *The Prince, the Crown and the Cash* wrote: "Although the secretary for Wales took the view that the main purpose of the investiture was to boost the Welsh tourist industry, there was another view: that it would give a boost to the Prince, and Royalty, preparatory to a campaign for an increase in the Civil List."

At a time of national austerity, confusion reigned as to exactly what the cost would be. The minister for Public Buildings and Works, Robert Mellish, insisted that it was a maximum of £200,000, and the Duke of Norfolk explained the misunderstandings in a letter of apology to the prime minister, Harold Wilson. "It was meant to be a help, not a hindrance. I said that from what I'd heard it might come to more than £200,000, and we may have to have—what's the phrase—a supplementary estimate." Throughout the dispute, Norfolk preserved an endearing line in no-nonsense banter. He moaned about the limited funds, saying that £1 million would have given his brainchild "a spot of glamour," and he insisted that all the rehearsals were held in London "because Caernarvon is such a hell of a place to get to."

To defuse the growing chorus of protest, it was thought prudent for Charles to begin a series of meetings with Welshmen, and Cledwyn Hughes hosted a luncheon in his honor for Welsh academics, politicians, rugby players, opera singers, actors, and Goons. The next target, however, was the £55,000 budget set aside for the preparation of the castle, £7,650 of which was allotted to Snowdon's design team. Emrys Hughes suggested in the Commons that the money might be better spent on housing and education in the principality. Had he known what Lord Snowdon and his friends were planning, he might have adopted even more acerbic tones.

Attempting to ignore the protest campaign, Snowdon took himself off to Caernarvon with his Aston Martin, his motor bike, and his speedboat, and mused upon the Victorian motto which has always been his artistic creed: "Never construct decoration; only decorate construction." The castle, in other words, was to be left as spare and uncluttered as possible. Whatever constructions and embellishments were necessary would be kept classically simple and elegant. By rejecting the serried array of heraldic banners prepared by the College of Arms in favor of a simplified Carl Toms motif repeated around the towers and battlements, Snowdon deprived the college of considerable revenue and further distanced himself from Garter King of Arms and his traditionalists.

Toms, aesthetically, was a romantic, Pound a modernist. Sitting between them on train rides to and from Caernarvon, Snowdon had to find a balance. When the three had finally agreed in principle on a massive perspex canopy over the central royal dais, Pound suggested that it should be held aloft by balloons. Snowdon pointed out that it needed only one Welsh Nationalist marksman, or even a mischievous child with an air rifle, to bring the whole edifice down on the royal heads beneath. He opted instead for giant steel pillars, raked slightly outward to give the canopy the look of a medieval tent. A model of the structure was tested in the British Aircraft Corporation's wind tunnel, for resistance to 60 mph gales, which had already caused havoc with some of the Toms heraldic banners. Wind was one of Snowdon's constant worries.

Another was rain. He had further enraged "Garter" (Sir Anthony Wagner) by refusing to countenance any red carpets, making the revolutionary suggestion that the Queen should walk across the grass. Garter pointed out that if it rained, her heels would sink into the fifty tons of specially laid turf; so Snowdon consulted Her Majesty, who happily agreed to avoid stilettoes. Had there been any rain in the few days before the ceremony, however, he was well aware that the royal procession would have got bogged down. Even the grass itself caused another disagreement, this time happily settled by compromise. The traditionalists wanted it one inch above the paved walkways; Snowdon's team wanted it flush. When the turf was laid, it was slightly raised, contoured down at the edges to meet the paving stones.

Furthermore, Snowdon had insisted to the television and press representatives that he did not want cameras filming each other. Positions were allocated so that no one got in each other's frames; television cranes were reluctantly persuaded to descend out of view between shots. With the enthusiastic support of the TV crews, Snowdon overruled plans for striped awnings to protect the royal party as it proceeded to its central position. With only the perspex canopy rising above ground level, the cameras had clear views of the ceremony from every possible angle. The cameramen appreciated having a photographer in charge: light-meter readings were constant all over the site.

Snowdon's aesthetic also called for as few microphones as possible obscuring the Queen and the prince as the various speeches were delivered. Snowdon decided on a maximum of two, concealed behind an elegant pillar of Welsh slate and fed by underground wires. Again, rain—and the failure of either microphone—could have deprived the watching world of sound with its pictures. For aesthetic reasons, Snowdon was taking quite a lot of risks. He was also, to Garter's further horror, refusing any kind of shelter to the VIP guests. In this, as in all, Norfolk gave him invaluable support. "What happens if it rains?" Charles himself asked the duke one day. "We get wet," replied the Earl Marshal.

In 1911, the central investiture ritual had taken place in a striped yellow crusader tent, so that few of the eleven thousand notables present could see a thing. Snowdon's theatrical design eased that problem, but he caused further consternation by insisting that the audience be reduced to four thousand, so that they presented a decorous, well-behaved assemblage for the cameras. Even so, there were some whose view of the proceedings would be obscured by a castle wall. Snowdon installed closed-circuit TV, but it proved invisible in sunlight. So he commissioned a series of giant plastic mirrors to reflect the scene. When they were in place, he realized he had made a fundamental error: they worked for only one vertical segment of the audience. So he took them down again and installed them as cheery decor in the waiting room—a converted dungeon—he was making ready for the prince. He then designed a series of convex plastic balloon mirrors to reflect the scene to the unsighted, and on investiture morning he got the royal trumpeters to blow them up.

Pound and Snowdon then began to think about the design of the four thousand guests' chairs. They again flouted convention by refusing to accord different styles of seat to different grades of guest and rejecting Garter's request for specially designed, very costly chairs for VIPs. So it was that royalty entered the era of the utility throne. Made of Welsh slate, those of Prince Philip and Prince Charles were backless, for the benefit of the TV cameras, while the Queen's had a low back for reasons of status rather than comfort. Each throne was tailored to its occupant's every ergonomic need. For the rest, there were simple, elegant chairs of laminated plywood, painted scarlet, the seat covered in red Welsh tweed. Adhering to his policy that every material and manufacturer should be Welsh, Snowdon commissioned Remploy Ltd. (who employed only disabled people) to produce them so economically that they could afterwards be sold to their occupants for £12 each. Thus they would be self-financing, like many items on his design budget (which after the event came close to breaking even). By the morning of the investiture, Remploy had sold just six chairs—all to Lord Snowdon, the dining table of whose country home they still adorn. By the end of the day, they could have sold twice the four thousand they had made.

Imperial Chemical Industries meanwhile began the manufacture of the giant perspex canopy. Twenty-five feet wide at the front, tapering downward to nine feet six inches, and weighing over a ton, it was the largest perspex object ever made. Snowdon had decided to attach a giant version of the Prince of Wales's three feathers insignia, molded in expanded polystyrene and painted gold, to the canopy's underbelly. But he could not find, from all the many available versions, a design combining the simplicity and sophistication he sought. Regular drinkers at the Prince of Wales pub in Notting Hill Gate, London, were surprised one evening to find the Queen's brother-in-law taking minutely detailed photographs of the pub's Victorian windows. The feathers were delicately etched, but still (he thought) rather bland. Then in Caernarvon Castle itself, in the regimental museum of the Royal Welch Fusiliers, he found a Cader Idris belt buckle with exactly what he was looking for. The right-hand feather sloped elegantly back, and the *Ich Dien* scrolled motto curled gently from feather to feather. Large photographic reproductions were made, and the nine-foot polystyrene version hand-carved. It was the dominant motif of the day.

On July 16, 1968, just under a year before the appointed date, Prince Charles traveled incognito with Snowdon on the overnight train from London to Holyhead. The constable thought it important that the central figure of the drama should have some feel of the place, and had shrouded their excursion in total secrecy. They motored across Anglesey and joined the tourists in the castle; as they proceeded from the Water Gate along the proposed route of the procession to the central dais, news of the royal presence spread around Caernarvon, throwing the borough council into a panic. The mayor and the town clerk were out of town for the day on business, so their deputies hurried along to offer an official welcome. Then the press caught up, and Snowdon's hopes of a quiet preview for Charles were ruined. He managed to escape by taking the prince along to meet Evan Lloyd, boatman to his late father, Ronnie Armstrong-Jones, who took them for a trip around the bay on the Harbour Trust launch, *Cadnant*. At Snowdon's suggestion, the boatman then simply took the prince home to meet his wife, Nellie. Number 3 Balaclava Road, Caernarvon, thus became the first Welsh household in which the Prince of Wales ever set foot.

During the following year, the prospect of Charles's investiture roused both town and principality to fever pitch. When the date had been announced, eighteen months ahead of time, every hotel room and inn in Caernarvon and for twenty miles around was declared booked within forty-eight hours. As much as a year before the day itself, grossly inflated offers for accommodation from overseas visitors and desperate journalists were being turned down. The borough council tried to keep control, but Caernarvon knew it was in for a giant one-night spree. Investiture fever soon spread through the rest of Wales, as plans were laid for a week-long program of celebrations under the title *Croeso 69* ("Welcome 69"). The Welsh Tourist Board was about to receive the greatest boost in its history. Snowdon's hopes of keeping all souvenirs decorous proved, not to his surprise, vain. Visiting Caernarvon on investiture eve, Nicholas Tomalin of the *Sunday Times* wrote of Prince Charles: "You can sit on him, wear him, stand on him, drink out of him, dry your dishes with him, even hold your oven casseroles with him." Shopkeepers had decided, however, that plans to put "God Bless The Prince of Wales" through special sticks of Welsh rock candy were "inappropriate."

The Caernarvon council authorized its private householders to take in paying guests during the investiture period, and issued several tons of free paint to its citizens—in carefully selected, noncontroversial colors—as an incentive to spruce the place up. A Welsh property owner did brisk business with Americans when he offered 500,000-foot-square plots of land in Snowdonia for sale at £4 each; their particular attraction was that the Queen owned mineral and sporting rights to the territory, so each lucky purchaser received an illuminated title deed proving joint ownership with Her Majesty.

The political protests continued. Charles laughed off the suggestion that he was "a political tool," but the bombing went on. The investiture was giving a brief new lease on life to a thin line of anarchists calling themselves the Free Wales Army. They claimed close relations with the provisional IRA, then a year into a renewed campaign of violence in Northern Ireland, but were fortunately much less well organized. (Nine self-confessed members were arrested in February 1969; after a four-month trial, which ended on the morning of the investiture, two were sentenced to nineteen months imprisonment.) The Welsh Language Society, organizing a series of anti-investiture rallies, declared that "Prince Charles has never done anything for Wales, and has no right to call himself its prince."

A majority of Plaid Cymru members voted to boycott the ceremony, although the party's initially united opposition had now broken down in an embarrassing public split. The two groups were fairly evenly balanced: on the one side, implacable opponents who viewed the investiture as an English plot to be resisted at all costs; on the other, the more moderate upholders of party policy, which called for an independent Wales under the crown. The common ground was perhaps the most paradoxical: to oppose the investiture of a prince who was taking the trouble to learn Welsh seemed illogical in view of the party's official allegiance to the crown, yet to support the ceremony seemed somehow supine. The consensus eventually reached the undignified public posture of ignoring the whole thing, seemingly in the hope that it would go away.

The polls were not much more helpful. The *Western Mail*, Wales's national morning newspaper, came up with some daunting figures: 44 percent of the Welsh people thought the investiture and its accompanying celebrations "a waste of money"; as many as 86 percent believed that the Prince of Wales did not mix informally enough with the Welsh people, and 73 percent wanted him to have an official residence in Wales.

Six months later, defending the royal family's decision in a Welsh television interview, the Duke of Edinburgh felt confident enough to say: "The governing factor was that it was quite obvious that a very large proportion of Welsh opinion favored having the investiture." Having agreed that there might well be further terrorism, and thrown in a characteristic sideswipe at student demonstrators, Prince Philip confessed that "the doubts were not so much about allowing the prince to take part at all, but perhaps to what extent this sort of virtually medieval revival is relevant." Charles himself took a more conciliatory tone: "I don't blame people demonstrating like that. They've never seen me before. They don't know what I'm like. I've hardly been to Wales, and you can't expect people to be overzealous about the fact of having a so-called English prince come amongst them and be frightfully excited about it." He wasn't surprised it had become "a friction point" for so many people.

He also admitted to sharing his great-uncle's dread of the occasion, pointing out that he himself had the advantage of being three years older. "It would be unnatural if one didn't feel any apprehension. One always wonders what's going to happen in this sort of thing. But I think if one takes it as it comes, it'll be much easier. . . . As long as I don't get covered too much in egg and tomato, I'll be all right." He would be glad, he said, when it was over.

Six months before the appointed day, at the height of the bombing and protest campaign, a small but persistent caucus of of the Investiture Committee favored cancellation or postponement. The secretary of state, George Thomas, called a representative meeting, at the Welsh Office in Cardiff, which has remained a closely guarded secret to this day. The arguments for postponement were reluctant, but there was an irresistible fear that the prince's life was in genuine danger. Thomas himself had received letters threatening his life, but it was his speech from

the chair, the eloquence of a Welshman sharpening the shrewdness of an experienced politician, which swayed the meeting. "If
we postpone the investiture," he said, "we will be canceling it—
putting it off forever. There should be no part of the United
Kingdom where the royal family cannot go." He went on: "It will
require great moral courage from that young man, but he has
already displayed it in considerable quantities." He told the
meeting of the day he had accompanied Prince Charles through
noisy demonstrators to the Welsh Office. Looking out at them
through the window, the prince had said to the secretary of state:
"I'm going to talk to them."

Thomas had said: "I would advise against it, sir."

"I know you would, but I'm going."

"In that case, sir, I'm coming with you."

The caucus was persuaded, and the meeting had officially
never taken place. Those still in doubt as the investiture approached were mightily cheered three weeks before the event,
when Prince Charles himself dramatically changed the atmosphere. His speech in Welsh to Urdd Gobaith Cymru, the Welsh
League of Youth, at its eisteddfod in Aberystywth, was a triumph.
Three hundred well-pronounced, unfluffed words proved that
this English Prince of Wales could speak Welsh quite as well as
those few Welshmen who could speak any. "I have found time to
read Dafydd ap Gwilym in bed," he said of an amorous Welsh
bard well known to the locals, "and now I know something of
the girls of Llanbadarn." All that was needed was a promise to
fight for the preservation of the language, and his reception was
tumultuous. The Plaid Cymru split widened in the moderates'
favor, and a majority statement from its executive called for an
end to the Welsh graffiti protest campaign. The Welsh Language
Society remained undeterred, and announced anti-investiture
rallies for the week before the ceremony. But Charles had won
Welsh hearts. The token eight weeks in Aberystwyth had more
than justified the risks involved; by his own steadfast and cautious efforts, he had converted an apparent political blunder into
something of a personal triumph.

The open-hearted Welsh, after all the bluster, realized what
an impossible position Charles had been placed in, and what a
decorous exit he had made. "If anybody lays a finger on that
lad," a self-declared Nationalist was heard to announce in an

Aberystwyth pub, "they'll swing from the nearest tree." A mid-Wales trade unionist opined: "I'm not a Royalist. I'm a Socialist. But I tell you this: that young man has done more for Wales already than we could dream of." It was, however, the mayor of Caernarvon, Ifor Bowen Griffiths, who scaled the true Welsh heights of English hyperbole: "Charles is the ace in our pack. When he stood up at the eisteddfod and started to speak in Welsh, he wasn't just a boy. He was a prince. You could have put a suit of armor on that lad and sent him off to Agincourt."

The prince found further evidence of his hard-won acceptance later that week in Cardiff. Receiving the freedom of the city on behalf of the newly formed Royal Regiment of Wales, of which he had just been installed colonel-in-chief, he also received a huge and very personal ovation—not least, according to the local paper, for "speaking better Welsh than the Lord Mayor." George Thomas added to Charles's kudos by making his own rather endearing Welsh error: by addressing the Lord Mayor as "Arglwydd Fawr" instead of "Arglwydd Faer," he had hailed him as God Almighty. (Thomas also noticed a strong strain of nationalism in the prince's remarks—the influence, he assumed, of Edward Millward at Aberystwyth. Later that year, at a banquet in London to celebrate the centenary of the *Western Mail*, he was relieved to hear him return to more orthodox sympathies.)

In the newly designed colonel-in-chief's uniform he wore that day in Cardiff, Prince Charles had chanced upon a welcome alternative to the satin breeches which had so mortified his great-uncle. His investiture regalia was at last decided. But over the military uniform, protocol decreed, he would indeed wear a purple surcoat trimmed with ermine. Snowdon was disappointed. He had designed for himself a sharp tail suit of military green, zip fastened to its roll-collar neck, which was trimmed with the three-feathered insignia in mirror images. He had hoped the Prince would wear a similarly simple cloak over his military gear. But he had the consolation after the event that his own outfit, for all its traditional military touches, was perhaps the most satirized item on display.

He did not, however, approve of the coronet to be worn by the prince. Snowdon, again, had wanted a classically simple band of plain gold around Charles's brow. But this time the College of Arms won the day, and a carefully contemporary version of the Prince of Wales's traditional crown was commissioned from Louis Osman. (Charles was amused to hear that Osman had previously found renown by designing a big top for Billy Smart's circus.) As the goldsmith imprinted his hallmark on the Osman coronet, a tiny flaw was discovered; were it to fall from Charles's head on the big day, it would shatter ominously before the watching millions. So a second gold crown was fashioned, and the seventy-five diamonds and twelve emeralds hastily transferred, the platinum trimming renewed. The finished object was to be worn once before, like Edward VIII's regalia, finding its way into a Welsh museum.

Charles wore his crown around the palace for a few days, to get used to it. Down the road at Kensington Palace, Lord Snowdon was at much the same time inviting visitors to try out the three royal thrones sitting waiting in his hallway. He took one of the £12 chairs around to Clarence House for his mother-in-law, Queen Elizabeth, to try. There were other vicarious entertainments for Londoners during those months: those passing Buckingham Palace atop a double-decker bus could see the royal family being shunted by the Duke of Norfolk through a rehearsal ground of white markers and measuring tapes. When the Queen congratulated Bernard Norfolk on his plans, he told her he'd had his best ideas in the bath.

The day before the ceremony, a dress rehearsal (without the royal family) was held at Caernarvon. Journalists were surprised to find themselves given every courtesy and facility: evidence indeed, as one of them put it, that the monarchy was "going into overdrive." A vogue joke in somewhat bad taste— "What time is it by your bomb?"—was of little consolation to Lord Snowdon that week, as he traveled in his speedboat to an investiture party at the home of Lord Newborough, high above the Menai Straits. He was delighted to see the assembled guests gathered on the clifftop to greet his arrival, and not displeased when a cannon salute heralded his approach. Several seconds later, however, a cannon ball whacked into the spray, a yard from his bow. "What a pity you didn't sink him," one of the guests told Newborough. "Think what an honor it would have been for our lifeboat boys to have rescued him." (This particular eccentricity seems to run in Lord Newborough's family. In 1911, a stray shot from the loyal salute of one of his ancestors nearly sank the royal yacht.)

On investiture eve, the Queen's progress north with her family in the royal train was interrupted for an hour just outside Chester. A bomb had been found beneath the bridge which carries the railway across the River Dee. It turned out to be a hoax: three sticks of plasticine, attached to an alarm clock, in a cardboard box. A few hours later, around dawn on July 1, two men were attempting to position a real bomb against the wall of a local government office in Abergele, thirty miles from Caernarvon. It exploded as they were priming it, killing them both. In London the previous afternoon a group of Charles's teachers and friends and others had foregathered in a BBC television studio to record their personal tributes to the Prince of Wales—to be broadcast in the event of his assassination next day.

The train and its occupants spent the night in a special halt built in the railway siding of Ferodo Ltd. near Bangor, close enough to Plas Newydd, the Marquess of Anglesey's home, for some convivial hospitality. Next morning the Lord Lieutenant of Caernarvonshire, Sir Michael Duff, escorted the family to Vaynol, his elegant Queen Anne mansion overlooking the Menai Straits. This was the royal rendezvous point. "Do you realize," said the Duke of Beaufort, "that so many royals have never been under one nonroyal roof before?"

Charles spent much of the morning wandering nervously around the Duff estate. Each time he returned to the house he found his television interview being replayed on one or other of the channels. "It's always me," he complained. "I'm getting rather sick of my face." After lunch, the Queen wished him a slightly tense "Good luck" as he left with the advance party. George Thomas and David Checketts shared the coach in which he made his triumphal progress through the crowds to the castle. A loud bang was heard in the near distance, and Charles asked Thomas what it was. Both knew very well it was another bomb.

"Oh, that's a royal salute, sir."

"Peculiar sort of royal salute."

"Peculiar sort of people up here," said the southern Welshman of his northern compatriots. The carriage continued its way through the narrow streets of the city, overhung by many an open window which would have made an assassin's work easy. But the Special Branch had been thorough. Thomas, nevertheless, remembers being much more nervous than the prince. "You felt safe once inside the castle, but far from safe outside its walls."

The prince and his companions arrived to see his personal banner unfurled on the battlements, and to hear a deafening rendition of "God Bless the Prince of Wales." Thomas joined in, but could not get beyond the first verse. As he lah-lahed his way through the rest of it, the prince gently chided him. "You must remember," Thomas replied, "the last time I sang this was for your great-uncle."

He and Checketts accompanied the prince to the waiting room, where Snowdon's young children ran into Charles's arms and made him forget his nerves for a while. For twenty minutes he watched his relatives' arrival on television. On the table was a good luck note from Lord Snowdon, asking Charles to sign the central table with a felt-tip pen. This he did, and the signature is now immortalized there in stainless steel.

Outside, a boom had been stretched across the harbor entrance, which was patrolled by two minesweepers. Snowdon had wanted *Britannia* to hover dramatically in the estuary, but the naval authorities had calculated that she would probably run aground in the shallows; so the royal yacht waited up the coast off Holyhead, where frogmen regularly checked her hull for limpet mines. Back in Caernarvon, police patrolled the straits in launches and rubber dinghies, helicopters scanned the crowds from three hundred feet, and closed-circuit TV relayed the watching faces to a police control center. The town was sealed off from all traffic. Even Princess Margaret was asked for proof of her identity. As the Queen's carriage approached the castle, a banana skin was thrown beneath her horses' hooves. Watching police had to extract the offender quickly from the angry crowd, who appeared about to lynch him.

The tension surrounding the day ahead had even infused the words of the poet laureate, C. Day Lewis, who had made a break with tradition by presenting his celebratory verse to that morning's *Guardian*, rather than the *Times*. The *Times'* editor, William Rees-Mogg, professed himself "undismayed," for reasons we can only surmise:

Today bells ring, bands play, flags are unfurled,
    Anxieties and feuds lie buried
Under a ceremonial joy. You, sir, inherit
    A weight of history in a changing world,
Its treasured wisdom and its true
    Aspirings the best birthday gift for you.

Coming of age, you come into a land
    Of mountain, pasture, cwm, pithead,
Steelworks. A proud and fiery people, thoroughbred
    For singing, eloquence, rugby football, stand
Beneath Caernarvon's battlements
    To greet and take the measure of their prince.

But can they measure his hard task—to be
    Both man and symbol? With the man's
Selfhood the symbol grows in clearer light, or wanes,
    Your mother's grace, your father's gallantry
Go with you now to nerve and cheer you
    Upon the crowded, lonely way before you.

May your integrity silence each tongue
    That sneers or flatters. May this hour
Reach through its pageantry to the deep reservoir
    Whence Britain's heart draws all that is fresh and young.
Over the tuneful land prevails
    One song, one prayer—God Bless the Prince of Wales.

Lord Plunkett knocked on the Water Gate, which was opened by the constable, Lord Snowdon, bearing a fifteen-inch key: "Madam, I surrender the key of this castle into Your Majesty's hand." The Queen, in a yellow Norman Hartnell dress and hat, touched it, saying: "Sir Constable, I return the key of the castle into your keeping." The royal party made its way across to the central dais (heels not sinking into the grass, though rain threatened). Prince Charles was summoned, and the ceremony was at last under way.

Charles's procession was more splendid than anything he will know again before his own coronation. Flanked by the secretary of state for Wales, the Welsh Herald Extraordinary, and two lords-in-waiting, he was followed by five Welsh peers carrying his insignia. Earl Lloyd George of Dwyfor bore the same silver-gilt sword used by the last Prince of Wales, Lord Heycock the golden rod, Lord Maelor the gold ring embellished with two dragons and an amethyst, Lord Harlech the mantle of purple velvet and ermine, and Lord Ogmore the coronet. To Snowdon's horror, a few drops of rain began to fall. At this climactic moment, however, the four thousand were not to be disturbed. Only one, before the watching millions, disrupted the scene by maneuvering himself into a raincoat: Mr. Jeremy Thorpe, then leader of the Liberal Party.

The Queen handed the letters patent to the Home Secretary, James Callaghan, himself by happy chance the member for a Welsh constituency. Almost entirely lacking punctuation, they were something of a mouthful:

> "Elizabeth the Second by the Grace of God of the United Kingdom of Great Britain and Northern Ireland and of Our other Realms and Territories Queen Head of the Commonwealth Defender of the Faith. To all Lords Spiritual and Temporal and all other Our Subjects whatsoever to whom these Presents shall come Greeting Know ye that we have made and created and by these Our Letters Do make and create our most dear Son Charles Philip Arthur George Prince of the United Kingdom of Great Britain and Northern Ireland Duke of Cornwall and Rothesay Earl of Carrick Baron of Renfrew Lord of the Isles and Great Steward of Scotland Prince of Wales and Earl of Chester And to the same Our most dear Son Charles Philip Arthur George have given and granted and by this Our Present Charter do give grant and confirm the name style title dignity and honor of the same Principality and Earldom And Him Our most dear Son Charles Philip Arthur George as he has been accustomed We do ennoble and invest with the said Principality and Earldom by girding him with a Sword by putting a Coronet on his head and a

Gold Ring on his finger and also by delivering a Gold
Rod into his hand that he may preside there and may
direct and defend those parts To hold to him and his
heirs Kings of the United Kingdom of Great Britain
and Northern Ireland and of Our other Realms and
Territories Heads of the Commonwealth for ever. . . ."

As Callaghan struggled on, the Queen formally invested
Charles with the insignia, and both waited while the Charter
was read again in Welsh, this time by George Thomas. Then
came the climax of the ceremony. Kneeling before his mother,
the Prince of Wales intoned the oath he had been too young to
swear at her coronation. Placing his hands between the Queen's,
he declared: "I, Charles, Prince of Wales, do become your liege
man of life and limb and of earthly worship, and faith and truth
I will bear unto you to live and die against all manner of folks."

At the same moment, across the world, three men were
preparing to land on the moon. But this archaic ritual, watched
with mixed emotion by the Duke of Windsor in his Paris home,
had a vital saving grace. In the week before the investiture, the
TV film *Royal Family* had at last been shown, giving the British
people an unprecedented peep into the private life of their
royals. The majestic hands now raising Charles to his feet had
last been seen wielding a barbecue fork; Prince Philip, watching
solemnly in his field marshal's uniform, had just rowed a complaining Prince Edward into the Balmoral sunset; Her Majesty's
"liege man of life and limb" had endangered his younger
brother's by snapping a cello string in his face. Charles, particularly, had been discovered in every home that week, through
interviews and special films, to be every parent's ideal son. The
royals may not have been a family just like any other, but they
were a family who did relatively normal things in relatively
normal ways. For once, the pomp and circumstance of royalty in
public ceremonial perhaps took second place, in the minds of
those watching, to the private family cracking jokes around the
breakfast table. Paradoxically, the ancient ritual crystallized a
new era of family monarchy, which would reach its climax
eight years later in Elizabeth II's Silver Jubilee.

As Charles listened to George Thomas' rolling Welsh phrases, his coronet balanced uncertainly on his head, his left hand encumbered with a scepter, he realized, appalled, that he was sitting on his speech. The TV record of the occasion shows him fumbling urgently beneath the folds of his purple mantle, trying to dislodge those vital words of Welsh without at the same time dislodging his crown. Success; a relieved smile; and he launched into a carefully phrased vow to fight for the preservation of all things Welsh—unstuffy enough to number "a memorable Goon" [Harry Secombe] among them. There followed a short service, a Welsh Bible reading, and the Queen was soon presenting her son to his people at three gates of the castle. Fanfares sounded, the RAF flew past overhead, and all Welsh doubts were staunched in an irresistible tide of loyal emotion.

"Oh, Mr. Thomas," said the Queen to the secretary of state, "it's been a wonderful day."

Said the secretary of state: "I don't want to be guilty of the Welsh sin of exaggeration, but it was a far greater triumph than we had a right to expect. He really was the Prince Charming. Wales has been in a state of euphoria, and at least half a million dollars came to Caernarvon itself." George Thomas, a hardened political veteran (now the Speaker of the House of Commons), says he has never known such an overwhelming sense of relief as he felt at the end of that day.

Back at the Ferodo siding Charles bid farewell to his parents and repaired to the royal yacht for "an evening's rest" (a high-spirited ball for young friends). For the next four days, as he toured his principality, he could do no wrong. From Conway to Montgomeryshire, from Fishguard to Swansea, from the Rhondda to Newport, and finally to Cardiff, he prompted scenes of rejoicing which belied the past two years. An icon in his own right (the stamps, the commemorative medals, the souvenirs, the TV presence), he baffled people into hysterical submission. "I touched him," was a familiar cry from teen-age girls. "I *saw* him," was enough for most. The Prince of Wales was himself elated. Only on the final day did a last, ugly outrage turn his week sour: in Caernarvon an eleven-year-old schoolboy playing football set off a booby trap bomb and lost his leg. Before leaving for a holiday in Malta, Charles launched a fund for the child; he wanted to visit him, but was told his condition was too grave. The boy recovered, yet Charles's hostess in Malta, Lady Dorman, testifies that the event clouded his few days' respite.

Not a happy ending. But the prince had, despite it all, conquered Wales.

14

1970-76: The Services

*"There is no more fitting preparation
for a king than to have been trained
in the navy."*

PRINCE LOUIS OF BATTENBERG
TO THE FUTURE KING GEORGE V

PRINCE CHARLES'S twenty-first birthday found him hedged around with young seriousness. He posed for an official photograph at the controls of an aircraft (following p. 162): unconventional by royal standards, but in his eyes shone the uncluttered idealism with which the emotional period of his investiture had fired him. Early on the morning of his birthday, he escorted his grandmother to the Chapel Royal of St. John, in the Tower of London, for a service of thanksgiving and dedication for his future life. Of *Ich Dien* ("I serve"), the motto he had inherited from Edward, the Black Prince, he said: "It means just that. It is the basis of one's job: to serve other people. If you have a sense of duty, and I like to think I have, service means that you give yourself to people, particularly if they want you, and sometimes if they don't." He was soon to put it to practical, and literal, use by a prolonged stint in the armed services. First, however, he had to finish his university degree.

On the night before November 4, 1969, a group of Trinity students climbed two eighty-foot towers, the highest points of the dining hall and the college chapel, to sling between them a three-hundred-foot banner proclaiming "Happy Birthday, Charles" in gold letters three feet high. Their spectacular gesture was, alas, in vain, as unknown to them the prince had already left for London, where a grand birthday party was to be held at Buckingham Palace. Again, young seriousness was to the fore:

he had asked Yehudi Menuhin and the Bath Festival Orchestra to play a Mozart violin concerto, and Maurice Gendron to follow with a Haydn cello concerto. Fireworks lit the London sky, and four Oxford undergraduates managed to gatecrash the proceedings, enjoying long chats with the prime minister (Harold Wilson), the Leader of the Opposition (Edward Heath), and their "host" himself before being ejected. Four hundred guests—including the Queen, who kicked off her shoes with gay abandon—danced until a kedgeree breakfast at 3 A.M.

The Royal Warrant Holders Association, that select group of traders entitled to use the "By Appointment" tag, presented the prince with a £700 polo pony called Freckles, no doubt to encourage him to start issuing warrants of his own. He decided to postpone this until 1980. But the birthday did prompt another step forward into the life of what King George VI liked to call "the firm"—and Prince Charles prefers to call "the family firm." On February 11, 1970, with the Princesses Anne, Alexandra, and Margaret watching from the balcony, and the Lords Mountbatten and Snowdon lending moral support in the chamber, the Prince of Wales was formally introduced into the House of Lords.

Prince Charles had hoped to make an earlier debut in the Lords, and the Queen had asked her staff to investigate the precedents as early as 1964, when he was fifteen. But the Clerk of the Parliaments gave a disappointing reply to her private secretary:

> The question has proved rather more intricate and has involved more research than I expected. . . .
> House of Lords Standing Order No. 2 says that: "No Lord under the age of one and twenty years shall be permitted to sit in the House." This Standing Order dates from 22nd May 1685 and since that date no Prince of Wales has been introduced under the age of twenty-one. It seems, I must say, a little odd that the Prince of Wales could inherit the crown without being subject to a Regency at the age of eighteen and yet does not qualify (if that is the fact) for a seat in the House of Lords. But so far as the precedents since 1685 go, it seems clear that the Prince of Wales has been treated as if the Standing Order applied to him.
> There have, in fact, been only six introductions of

a Prince of Wales since 1685, four in the eighteenth
century, one in the nineteenth, and one in the twentieth.
. . . Three out of the six, namely the Princes of Wales
who subsequently became George III, George IV, and
Edward VII, were introduced as Prince of Wales within
a few months of becoming twenty-one. . . .

So he had had to wait. But this heady background to the
occasion made it the more worthwhile. Preceded by his coronet
on a velvet cushion, Charles strode into the chamber with such
self-confidence that he looked to the *Times* correspondent "as if he
owned the place." Sponsored by the Duke of Kent and the Duke
of Beaufort, he had beforehand stood between them in the full
regalia of ermine-collared purple robe, cupping his hands to his
mouth to mimic a town crier. Once inside, however, he treated
the occasion with due solemnity, even when declaring an oath
of loyalty to himself: "I, Charles, Prince of Wales, do swear by
Almighty God that I will be faithful and bear true allegiance to
Her Majesty Queen Elizabeth, her heirs and successors, so help
me God." The formalities over, he slipped out again to disrobe,
and returned to the chamber in a plain suit to listen, appropriately enough, to a debate on youth and community service.

Back at Cambridge, Charles now had new and grander rooms
on Staircase P of Great Court, including a paneled sitting room
dating from the seventeenth century, on whose chimneypiece he
duly carved his initial. It was to be an interrupted year, he knew,
so he largely withdrew from Cambridge society and, in Denis
Marrian's words, "got his head down." In view of his looming
deadline, he even took a course in speed-reading—which has since
proved invaluable to one who so dislikes paperwork, yet must get
through so much of it. He joined the Cambridge Union and attended a couple of debates, but his main concern was that his
success or failure in the final Tripos exams the following summer
would be worldwide public knowledge. A bad degree would be
disastrous.

Nonetheless, there were some indulgences he could not resist. In the spring term of 1970 he was back onstage in another
revue, this time called *Quiet Flows the Don*. To spare him a repeat of the worldwide interest in *Revulution*, tickets were limited
to members of Trinity and their guests. Among these were the

Queen and Princess Anne, who dined with the prince in his rooms before attending one of the five performances. Charles took part in four sketches, notably as a weather forecaster in flippers and gas mask: "By morning promiscuity will be widespread, but it will lift, and may give way to some hill snog. . . . As William of Orange said, here come the pips." At a dress rehearsal, to which the poker-faced press were admitted, the prince raised the biggest laugh of the evening by forgetting his lines. "What the hell comes next? It doesn't happen like this on the BBC."

The Easter vacation, to a long sigh from Lord Butler, took the Prince of Wales on an extended tour of New Zealand and Australia with his parents to celebrate the 200th anniversary of Captain Cook's voyage, and onward to Japan on his own. He returned to Cambridge barely a month before his examinations. The six three-hour papers included such questions as "How and to what extent did George III exercise control of his ministers before 1784?"; "What role in politics and society was the Prince Consort able to exercise?"; and "Was Winston Churchill an unsuccessful peacetime prime minister?" There was a question, appropriately enough, on Machiavelli's *The Prince*, and, almost as close to home, "In what sense is it true to describe Louis XIV as 'King of the Vile Bourgeoisie'?"

The prince's answers to these and other apposite inquiries will be known to posterity, as his exam papers are already lodged in the Royal Archives at Windsor for an official biographer to inspect after his death. As a last-minute thought, Denis Marrian also rescued his file on the prince's progress from the pulping machine and placed it in the Trinity archives. For now, all we know is that Prince Charles won a B.A. honors degree in Class II Division 2. Sandwiched in the list of results between Vaux J.F.G. (Selwyn College) and Walker J.N.G. (Caius), Wales, H.R.H. Prince of, had made royal history. The fact that it was a "II-2," an absolutely average result, helped to convince the skeptical that the prince's papers were written beneath an anonymous number and did not bear his name.

Lord Butler believes the prince might have achieved a II-1 had royal duties not intruded so much on his last year's work. He also believes Charles would have stood "a damn good chance of a First" had he stuck to archaeology or anthropology, and not gone to Aberystwyth. Be all that as it may, the three years had

more than satisfied the Prince of Wales. He had successfully
emerged as a public figure, ridden the Welsh storm, and at the
same time become the first heir apparent in British history to
win a university degree. Said Lord Butler: "I think I can say we
have done a good job at Trinity." And Dr. Marrian: "It is a
good thing for the country to be able to see that the heir to the
throne is able to start and finish an extremely difficult task like
this."

And so to the final dose of Lord Louis's prescription.

"It is pointless and ill-informed to say that I am entering a profession trained in killing. The services in the first place are there
for fast, efficient, and well-trained action in defense. Surely the
services must attract a large number of duty-conscious people?
Otherwise who else would subject themselves to being square-
bashed, shouted at by petty officers, and made to do ghastly things
in Force Ten gales? I am entering the RAF and then the navy
because I believe I can contribute something to this country by
so doing. To me it is a worthwhile occupation, and one which I
am convinced will stand me in good stead for the rest of my life."

It was a week before the Prince of Wales was due to check
in as a graduate entrant at RAF Cranwell, and he was thanking
the City of London for making him a freeman. It was scarcely
the most solemn of occasions: Charles had enjoyed hearing it
proclaimed that he was the son of "Prince Philip, Duke of Edinburgh, Citizen and Fishmonger of London, and that he was born
in lawful wedlock . . . his son so reputed and taken to be, and
so they all say." But he had been irritated by suggestions in the
press that the services no longer provided appropriate training for
an heir to the throne; he entirely shared the views of his family,
both living and of recent memory, that an officer's career in at
least two of the three was an indispensable discipline and
adventure.

The maritime traditions of his family go back a long way on
both sides. Prince Charles's great-uncle, Lord Mountbatten, was
a naval cadet at the age of thirteen and a First Sea Lord at fifty-
five, having spent the better part of all the intervening years at
sea. Lord Mountbatten's father, Prince Louis of Battenberg, was
also First Sea Lord in 1914, when the approach of war with Germany forced him to resign his German name and titles, becoming

the first Marquis of Milford Haven. And Prince Louis's great-grandson, Prince Philip, Duke of Edinburgh, had taken British citizenship in February 1947 as a means of continuing his career in the Royal Navy—not, as was thought at the time, to smooth his path toward his forthcoming marriage. As Prince Philip of Greece, he had already distinguished himself in HMS *Valiant* in 1941; he was mentioned in dispatches by his commanding officer, Admiral Cunningham, for his handling of the search-lights at the Battle of Matapan. In time, he had his own com-mand, of the frigate *Magpie* in the Mediterranean in 1950–51 — cut short by the last illness of King George VI, and a call to royal duty. But there were sterner precedents for that.

On his mother's side, Prince Charles's great-grandfather, King George V, had also just enjoyed his first command (of the gunboat *Thrush*) when the death of his elder brother, Prince Eddy, Duke of Clarence, cut short his naval career in 1892. In the words of his son, the Duke of Windsor, the loss of his life at sea affected him deeply. "He did love the navy . . . and long after he had taken up his work ashore, the habits and outlooks he had formed in the navy continued to regulate his daily routine. He retained a gruff, blue-water approach to all human situations." The king's other son, George VI, Prince Charles's grandfather, saw active service at the Battle of Jutland when a twenty-one-year-old acting lieutenant. At the time, he too had no thoughts of ascending the throne. After his elder brother's abdication in 1936, the reluctant new king confided to Lord Mountbatten: "Dickie, this is absolutely terrible. I never wanted this to happen; I'm quite unprepared for it . . . I've never seen a State paper. I'm only a naval officer. It's the only thing I know about." Mountbatten replied: "This is a very curious coincidence. My father once told me that, when the Duke of Clarence died, your father came to him and said almost the same things that you have said to me now, and my father answered: 'George, you're wrong. There is no more fitting preparation for a king than to have been trained in the navy.' "

With every awareness of this heritage Prince Charles was about to devote to the navy, and to the naval arm of the RAF, the major part of his next five years, the prime of his young man-hood. The nine months since Cambridge had meanwhile taken him around the world again: to Canada and the Arctic, to the

Nixon White House in Washington (see Chapter 17), to Fiji and the Gilbert and Ellice Islands, to the 350th anniversary of the Bermudan Parliament, and to Kenya, on televised safari with Princess Anne. Nineteen years to the day after his mother's accession to the throne, he had visited the site where she had heard the news of her father's death—to find that Treetops Lodge had been destroyed by fire and a modern motel had risen in its place. He had celebrated his twenty-second birthday with another cello concerto (plus a harp concerto performed by Osian Ellis); lunched with the prime minister, Edward Heath; and addressed the Institute of Directors at the Royal Albert Hall: "Whoever invited me exploited my extreme ignorance. I assumed you were a small business organization. Little did I know that I had agreed to speak to five thousand whiz-kids, tycoons, industrial giants. . . ."

Flight Lieutenant the Prince of Wales rather saucily flew himself to RAF Cranwell on March 8, 1971. Having left Windsor by helicopter, he changed at RAF Benson to a twin-engined Bassett, in which he had already won his pilot's license (Grade A) and clocked some eighty flying hours. Charles had begun flying lessons during his first year at Cambridge, starting in a Chipmunk, as had his father before him. On June 13, 1968, a team of doctors from the RAF Central Medical Establishment visited Buckingham Palace to give him his physical, and by the end of the month he had sampled the first of a series of air experience flights at RAF Tangmere in Sussex. A special training unit was meanwhile established under the aegis of the Queen's Flight at RAF Benson, near Oxford; in command was the Captain of the Queen's Flight, Air Commodore A. D. ("Archie") Winskill. Flight Lieutenant (now Squadron Leader) Phillip Pinney, a New Zealander, was assigned from the RAF Central Flying School to see the prince through to his first solo flight. Six months later, on January 14, 1969, after only fourteen and a half hours' instruction in nineteen dual sorties, the big moment had come at RAF Bassingbourn, in Hertfordshire: "I taxied and took off, wondering whether I could do it, and the moment I was in the air it was absolutely marvelous. . . . Fortunately, I landed first time. I had visions of myself going round and round until eventually the fuel ran out."

In the following ten months, the prince accumulated some

sixty flying hours, about twice as many as he would have achieved as a member of an RAF University Air Squadron. On August 2, 1969, he had received his preliminary flying badge and was ready to graduate from the Chipmunk to the twin-engined Beagle Basset. With its more advanced controls and communication system, the Basset was an ideal aircraft for the prince to fly himself to and from official engagements. The RAF made one over to the Queen's Flight on June 27; the Prince made his first flight in it on October 10, and has been using it ever since.

The Duke of Edinburgh, though so closely identified with the navy, says instinct would have taken him into the RAF. For Prince Charles the prospect of a career in both, apart from carrying on a type-cast family tradition, provided the chance of hours of unwonted freedom. To fly an airplane is in itself an exhilarating experience, more so if it is one's only chance to escape from a womb of advisers and observers. Similarly, the prince's time at sea was to prove perhaps the most "natural" of his life. No press, no sightseers, no private secretaries, no red boxes—even, for the only time in his life, no private detective, as the navy took over responsibility for security while the prince was off terra firma. Added to which, there was the camaraderie of life in the services, which made him more genuinely than at any other time in his life "one of the boys."

He was not pleased, therefore, when his five-month jet conversion course at Cranwell was christened Operation Golden Eagle. To hear the station commander describe him as "a precious piece of the nation's property," and to know that the two Mark V jet Provosts set aside for his personal use had been specially modified was not to his liking. He had specifically asked not to be provided with special privileges or safety systems: the extra warning lights on the Provost control panel and the improved ejector seat beneath him were as irritating as they were reassuring. It was perhaps because of this unfortunate start that he went on to attempt more reckless and dangerous feats quite unnecessarily. "I'm stupid enough to like trying things. Perhaps I do push myself too hard."

He had a natural talent for flying, and the five months saw him proceed effortlessly to the winning of his wings, under the expert tuition of Squadron Leader Dick Johns. He shunned the Cranwell revue, preferring to clock up another eighty hours in

Provosts, some twenty-four of them solo, as well as going through ejector-seat training, ditching drill, and all the irksome paperwork of navigation. He lived in normal Cranwell quarters with three other officer cadets, each with his own private bedroom, but was still uneasy that as Golden Eagle his path had been somehow made smooth. It was not enough to have played a role in operational "front-line raids" over the North Sea and to have co-piloted supersonic Phantom and Nimrod jets, "attacking" Royal Navy submarines and flying the length and breadth of Britain in eight-hour sorties. Although he was spared parades and drills, because he was completing a twelve-month course in five, it was not enough to have perfected the handling of his aircraft at high, medium, and low levels, flying by day and by night, by instruments and in formation. It was not enough to have taken courses in aerodynamics, airmanship, meteorology, navigation, aviation medicine, safety equipment, survival and rescue, and instrumentation. Before the passing-out parade in August, he announced, he wanted to make a parachute jump. Needless to say, this too was something no heir to the throne, indeed no member of the royal family, had undertaken before him.

The Queen was not enthusiastic, but she knew she could not talk him out of it. Hearts in Whitehall also skipped a few beats as the Prince of Wales found another way of testing and proving himself. The Gordonstoun ethic had stuck deep. He had already experienced a "near miss," ironically enough while copiloting the modest Bassett with his father in 1970; they were three seconds from collision with a Piper Aztec over Sussex. Now he took himself off to the RAF Parachute Training School at Abingdon, near Oxford. He went through all the ground simulation exercises in preparation for the big day, July 28, 1971—when, of course, something *did* go wrong.

Twelve hundred feet over Studland Bay in Dorset, the prince watched as two senior officers jumped from the Andover ahead of him. "You're the chap who pushes me out, I suppose?" he said to Flight Sergeant Ken Kidd beside him. "Oh, no, sir," said Kidd. "We don't do that. We just help." Kidd thought the prince looked nervous, so he gave him a Polo mint. On the command Charles jumped, and found the slipstream stronger than he had expected. It was 6:20 P.M.; at 3 P.M. that afternoon, the wind speed had been recorded at 9 knots, 0.3 above the RAF's maximum strength permissible for parachute jump safety. The Prince of Wales flipped over onto his back, and looked up to see his feet caught in the rigging over his head.

He recalls the moment with nonchalance. "It was very odd. Either I've got hollow legs or something. It doesn't often happen. The first thing I thought was 'They didn't tell me anything about this.' Fortunately, my feet weren't twisted around the lines, and they came out very quickly. The Royal Marines were roaring around in little rubber boats underneath, and I was out of the water within ten seconds. . . . A rather hairy experience."

The prince's Cranwell report just glowed: "He will make an excellent fighter pilot at supersonic speeds . . . a natural aptitude for flying . . . excelled at aerobatics in jets . . . all-round ability." He had completed the first-year graduate course in five months, and had even managed to leave the characteristic little memory of which he is so fond. On April 1, the prince persuaded the college caretaker, Joe Sylvester, to announce over the loudspeaker system that all regulation-issue officers' shoes should be handed in as the manufacturers had found the heels to be faulty. Several dozen shoeless officer cadets thereupon proved themselves April fools.

While at Cranwell he traveled around the station on a bicycle, like everyone else. But he had also swapped his MGB for a dark blue Aston Martin DB6 Volante, which whipped him off to polo matches and weekend retreats at Sandringham. Charles had also taken advantage of the anonymity of the RAF uniform, never given a second glance in that corner of Lincolnshire, to indulge in some inconspicuous sightseeing. Two favorite memories: a high-level bombing attack by Vulcan on his unsuspecting future subjects in Doncaster, where he scored a "direct hit" on the railway yard; and the Philipesque flourish, a week before his parachute jump, of shattering the regal July air over Balmoral as he flew himself by Phantom into the exclusive Ten Ton Club (more than 1,000 mph). On August 20 the marshal of the RAF, a proud father indeed, saluted his son before watching him receive his wings from the air chief marshal, Sir Denis Spotswood. The parade band struck up "God Bless the Prince of Wales," and Prince Philip told photographers: "I'll stand on my head if you like."

A month later Acting Sublieutenant the Prince of Wales took

up residence at the Royal Naval College, Dartmouth, attended by his father and grandfather before him. It had been at the Captain's house, now occupied by Captain Allan Tait, that the young Prince Philip of Greece had first met thirteen-year-old Princess Elizabeth, heir presumptive to King George VI, in 1939. That year, Prince Philip had won the King's Dirk as the best cadet, following the tradition set by his uncle, Lord Mountbatten. Charles had a lot to live up to in six short, intensive weeks of basic training in seamanship, navigation, marine and electrical engineering, administration, man-management—all the duties of a divisional officer—plus a brief stint at sea aboard the minesweeper *Walkerton*. Even when he treated himself to a weekend off in Cornwall, his companions found him studying his naval manuals on the beach.

When he too pulled off a royal coup—top in navigation and in seamanship, "all," as Lord Mountbatten declared, "we seamen care about"—his father was in Berlin, and unable to attend the passing-out parade. Mountbatten telephoned Tait: "I think the family should be represented. I'm flying down." With proprietorial pride, Uncle Dickie afterward took his nephew home by helicopter to lunch with the Queen.

At Dartmouth, Charles had lived in Cabin A30, a handsome first-floor room overlooking the River Dart, and shared his brief course with twelve other graduates his own age. He had worn a naval uniform for the first time, his RAF wings conspicuous on his arm. Now, pausing only to attend a conservation conference in Merthyr Tydfil and the state opening of Parliament at Westminster, he was off to sea in earnest. The next nine months were to be spent as an officer of Her Majesty's guided-missile destroyer *Norfolk*.

The services had, for a while, ridden roughshod over the fact of his royalty. There may have been huge holiday crowds on the cliffs near Poole to watch his parachute jump the previous July, but the press had been granted few facilities at Cranwell and Dartmouth, and Charles had achieved proportionately more in a very short time. One of the irritants of being a prince had marked his arrival at the Royal Naval College. He had driven down from Balmoral the previous night to dine with Captain Tait, but because of a large and formal welcoming committee next morning, had had to slip out of a back entrance and pretend to arrive again. "Sorry I'm late, sir," he said to Tait, after enjoying his late sleep for some considerable time. "I've had a long drive."

A greater disadvantage soon became apparent when he flew out to join the *Norfolk* in the Mediterranean on November 5. The 56,600-ton vessel was on routine NATO exercises, of the kind that would help the prince to his watchkeeping and naval competence certificates—but it just happened to be berthed at Gibraltar. As soon as the Prince of Wales set foot there, the Spanish foreign minister lodged a note of protest: the prince's presence, it said, "caused uncalled-for injury to national sentiment and stirs up Spanish public opinion." The British Embassy in Madrid countered that His Royal Highness's movements as a serving officer were "subject to normal operational requirements, and purely a matter for Her Majesty's Government." The chief minister of Gibraltar, Major Robert Peliza, felt moved to write to the *Times* in protest that he had received no advance warning of the prince's visit. Far from preferring to play down the distinguished arrival, as the press had suggested, he would have considered it "a profound honour to have been allowed to have received and welcomed Prince Charles in our homeland on behalf of a people who, notwithstanding many years of economic, political, and psychological harassment caused by the hostility of the Spanish dictatorial government, almost unanimously resolved in the 1967 referendum to remain under the British crown." Merely by attempting to carry out his naval duties, the prince had reopened an old and particularly sore wound. The Ministry of Defence advised the *Norfolk*'s captain not to put in, as planned, at Malta, whose relations with Britain were then at their most strained. Thus did protocol deprive the prince of a chance to see the Maltese prime minister, Dom Mintoff, with whom he had struck up a particular jaunty friendship in 1969. Thereafter, the course charted by HMS *Norfolk* was always a matter of political nicety for NATO.

Unknown to the prince, other arguments raged around him in Whitehall. The old naval school thought it demeaning that the heir to the throne should have been posted to a ship as large as *Norfolk*, where the duties of a sublieutenant carry little responsibility. Behind the move, however, lay the traditional beliefs of the Admiral of the Fleet himself, Earl Mountbatten, who felt that one of the "capital" ships carried the appropriate status for Charles's first posting. It had already been decided that a year later he would join HMS *Minerva*, a Leander class frigate, with only seventeen officers in the ship's complement as opposed to *Norfolk*'s thirty-three. On *Minerva* he would carry considerable responsibility, including the welfare and, when necessary, punishment of a proportion of the crew. A preparatory year aboard a larger ship would ease him into this unaccustomed and not altogether congenial role.

Cabin 36 on the starboard side of HMS *Norfolk*'s 01 deck was a mere seven feet square, the first of a series of such confined spaces that the Prince of Wales would be calling home. Cramped between its steel washbasin, wardrobes, bunk, and desk, Charles had to compile the junior officer's journal as well as continue all the paperwork of the apprentice officer. Life aboard was more mechanized than he had envisaged, more so indeed than either his father or his great-uncle had experienced. The prince's twenty-third birthday was celebrated off Sardinia, keeping watch in a Force Ten gale. By day, his duties included a humble role in the complex control room, and an assistant's position at the ship's wheel.

After only six weeks he was home for Christmas at Windsor, then quickly back to paperwork—communications, bridgework, and gunnery courses—at the shore base, HMS *Dryad*. That January also took in another unenviable royal "first": underwater escape practice in the hundred-foot training tank at HMS *Dolphin*, the Gosport shore base. The Prince of Wales's staff were as apprehensive as the naval top brass, who filmed the whole event for recruitment purposes, as Prince Charles made three separate escapes, from 30, 60, and 100 feet. The occasion is preserved in the TV film *Pilot Royal*, in which the Prince's face provides evidence enough of the genuine dangers involved, and his awareness of them. Though some five thousand officers and men complete this routine training each year—the Prince of Wales had rejected all suggestions that he should give it a miss— the next two years were to see the death of two ratings in separate underwater escape accidents.

If he was insistent on shirking none of the less pleasant aspects of training, there were other areas in which Prince Charles's wishes were overruled. Later in his service career, his request to fly Buccaneer strike aircraft at sea would be vetoed as simply too dangerous for the heir to the throne. For the same reason, he never fulfilled his wish to pilot Sea King antisubmarine helicopters. Political considerations prevented his serving aboard Polaris nuclear submarines, their missiles supposedly trained on Moscow. The 1974 defense cuts ruled out the posting he would have then preferred aboard the commando ship *Bulwark:* it was thought unseemly for the Prince of Wales to serve aboard a vessel due to be scrapped within eighteen months. Similarly, he was never allowed to serve aboard the aircraft carrier *Ark Royal*, as one of his position would be unsuitably submerged in so large a crew; for political reasons, he could never be transferred to any of the frigates patrolling the fishing waters off Iceland during the so-called cod wars or blockading Beira in the earlier days of economic sanctions against Rhodesia.

In the meantime, the prince got through quite enough to satisfy the less aspiring. "I have to try that little bit harder," he conceded, "to be as professional as possible, to assimilate all the vast problems rather more quickly." *Dryad* and *Dolphin* were followed by three weeks aboard the Fleet Air Arm frigate *Hermione*, engaged in mock attacks upon "Portlandia" (Portland). Back aboard *Norfolk*, May saw the Prince of Wales donning civvies to tour Toulon's red-light district with brother officers, before joining his mother on her state visit to France. With the Queen, Prince Charles spent a night in Provence before returning to Paris, where they paid a visit to the ailing Duke of Windsor at his home in the Bois de Boulogne. Eight days later, as a reprieved *Norfolk* enjoyed a summer visit to Malta and Dom Mintoff, Charles was called home by the news of the duke's death. It was the Prince of Wales who escorted the Duchess of Windsor, for the first time in her life accorded Buckingham Palace hospitality, to see the body of her husband lying in state at Windsor.

The following month, with *Norfolk* back at Portsmouth, the Queen paid her son a visit aboard "while I still have the chance." His nose was embellished by sticking plaster, after a polo mishap, as Charles showed his mother over the ship before giving her tea in the officers' mess. His watchkeeping and competence certificates secured, he was now embarked on courses at the naval signals school, *Mercury*, in Hampshire, and back at *Dryad* for a study of nuclear, biological and chemical weapons. That summer he flew by helicopter with his grandmother to the wedding of his cousin, Prince Richard of Gloucester. Within a month, when it had already been announced that Prince Charles was to return to Cranwell for a Provost refresher course, Richard's brother Prince William was killed in a light aircraft crash.

The Queen's anxieties were again aroused. It was a doubly unhappy coincidence that a Jet Provost Mark 7, of the type her son would be flying, had also crashed a week before. But by now the prince had an irresistible momentum. At Cranwell he flew the new Hunter jet fighter as well as the Provost. He then had a brief foretaste of helicopter flight at the navy's Yeovilton base— to which he would later return with renewed enthusiasm—before returning to Portland for a ten-day course aboard the minesweeper *Glasserton*. And so down to Portsmouth, to join the 2,450-ton *Minerva*.

This hectic routine was interspersed, naturally enough, with calls away on royal duty. That October: to Germany, to visit the Prince of Wales Division (where as a new officer he was required to eat a raw leek and sing an unaccompanied song—he chose the Goons' "Ying Tong Tiddle-i-po"), and to attend a reception in his honor at the West German Senate; to southern Spain, for a shooting holiday on the Wellington estate. In November, just before going to *Minerva*, Charles organized and hosted a private dinner party to mark his parents' silver wedding anniversary. At his behest, the English Chamber Orchestra played the Wedding March, and the Bach Choir sang anthems from the service twenty-five years before. The day had begun with a thanksgiving service at St. Paul's and a "walkabout" in the new Barbican development, about whose architecture he was rather rude; it ended with a lively after-dinner speech from Charles, and the four royal children offering a barbershop quartet version of "Happy Anniversary" for their delighted parents.

Minerva's first commission took Prince Charles and his crewmates to the West Indies. In further token of his growing stature, Charles had been encouraged to double diplomatic and naval duties, so that courtesies were exchanged with local dignitaries at each port of call, in many of which he also managed to fit in a game of polo. For his shipmates, this new dimension of life at sea brought welcome perks: everywhere she went, *Minerva* attracted all kinds of welcome attention. In Bermuda, the Prince of Wales spent a long evening with the governor, Sir Richard Sharples; after dinner they took a stroll around the garden, continuing their discussion of the effect on the Caribbean of the Bahamas' imminent independence. Taking the same stroll around the same garden a week later, Sir Richard and a young aide, Captain Hugh Sayers, were assassinated.

At first it was thought that one of the bullets might have been intended for the prince. His departure from the island might have escaped the gunman's notice, the theory went, and Sayers had been mistaken for Charles. Either way, Sir Richard was an alternate symbol of British imperialism as acceptable to the gunman's purpose. The prince's visit may well have stirred the growing anti-British feelings of Bermuda's small but militant group of independence fighters. Within a couple of years, rioting and civil disobedience on the island had grown to such a pitch that a royal commission under Lord Pitts recommended that independence be granted.

The assassination's immediate effect was that Prince Charles was transferred to the survey ship *Fox*, working out of Antigua. *Minerva* was due to revisit Bermuda for repairs and maintenance work, and no one was going to risk returning the prince with her. His brief stay on *Fox*, a small hydrographic workhorse, was not uneventful: within a few days he was involved in her attempts to refloat a 55,000-ton Swedish freighter, *Ariadne*, which had hit a reef while en route from Virginia to Japan. There was a further touch of drama when *Fox* had to withdraw her divers as man-eating sharks moved in.

Back with *Minerva*, now promoted to acting lieutenant, the prince as second gunnery officer was responsible for the vessel's 4.5-inch weapons and Seacat missiles. It was the climax of a very happy period. The ship bobbed from one to another of the world's most attractive islands: the Leewards, the Windwards, the Virgins, and the Bahamas, in the last of which Charles represented the Queen at the independence ceremonies, taking a delighted ship's company ashore with him for the exotic celebrations. He discovered the pleasures of deep-sea diving, gathering pieces of eight from an old Spanish wreck in an underwater world resembling "some vast green cathedral filled with shoals of silver fish." In Nassau, he joined with a will in a spectacular local dance called the *merengue;* in Caracas, he danced in a night club until 5 A.M., with *Minerva* due to sail again at six-thirty.

Relations aboard ship were perhaps the closest he had known. As his father has said: "At sea you learn to live with people." Out on the ocean for days on end, with no distractions beyond the calls of naval duty, he was required as much as anyone else to reminisce of life at home. It was part of his job as an officer to take an interest in the crew's welfare, and thus their tales about wives and girl friends, but he managed to keep his own royal counsel to an extent tantalizing for his companions. The best tidbit they brought ashore was the gallery of pinups ingeniously hidden behind the bulkhead shaft over his bunk; other royal gossip gleaned they none. "We learned a lot about the prince," said one brother officer, "but nothing about the rest of his family."

Furthermore, what they did pick up they kept to themselves, in the best naval tradition. There was much talk of practical jokes and other such high jinx, but no detail beyond the Prince of Wales's penchant for cooking his shipmates bread-and-butter pudding, laced with "lashings of rum." He was also said to be fond of blowing up balloons for target practice with an air rifle; yet a much traveled story that one rating slipped in a contraceptive, which the prince had begun inflating before realizing what it was, may be discounted. It is true, however, that during this period he compiled a German-English phrase book, entitled *A Guide to the Chatting Up of Girls*, for the men of the Royal Regiment of Wales, of which he is colonel-in-chief. In his monthly newsletter, he had received complaints from the squaddies, stationed in Germany, that language difficulties were inhibiting their progress with the local ladies. Charles obligingly drew up a list of useful gambits, which David Checketts helped him translate into German. The resulting two-page dossier is said to have increased the Anglo-German marriage rate during the regiment's tour of duty.

Charles left *Minerva* when it docked at Chatham in September 1973, and had four months before his posting to another frigate, HMS *Jupiter*, in January. He threw himself into his first sustained stint of royal duties, including for the first time the receiving of ambassadors as senior counsellor of state during the Queen's absence in Australia. On one notable day he ended a program of engagements in Luxembourg by attending a charity dinner for the Lord's Taverners back in London, telling the comedian Jimmy Edwards he had "always wondered what it was like to do two shows a night." There was another state opening of Parliament, by now a familiar occasion, and Princess Anne's wedding. Charles took much care and trouble choosing appropriate gifts: for his sister a spectacular diamond brooch, and for his new brother-in-law, Captain Mark Phillips, a pair of leather gun cases. They were married in Westminster Abbey on November 14, Prince Charles's twenty-fifth birthday. Captain Phillips, like Tony Armstrong-Jones a commoner marrying into the royal family, had been Princess Anne's equestrian friend and team mate, winner of a gold medal at the 1972 Olympic Games in Munich, but to growing subsequent dismay showed little interest in anything else. It is said to be from soon after his engagement to Princess Anne that Captain Phillips was saddled with the royal family's nickname for him: "Fog"—"because he is thick and wet." He hit back with a nice stroke of self-parody in November 1977, when Princess Anne gave birth to their first child: "Well, at least I've done *something* right."

On January 4, 1974, the Prince of Wales joined the frigate *Jupiter*, which had two things in common with *Minerva:* it belonged to the same Leander class, and it quickly became the most popular ship afloat. The Prince of Wales's presence on board guaranteed enthusiastic receptions wherever *Jupiter* called, which in the first few months of 1974 included Australia, New Zealand, Suva, Samoa, Hawaii, Fiji, and California. There was one night of drama at sea, when *Jupiter*'s communications officer, Lieutenant the Prince of Wales, played a central role in the rescue of the crew of the tug *Mediator*, which had gone aground in ferocious weather with two heavily laden barges in tow. Otherwise, *Jupiter*'s landfalls were rather more eventful than its progress at sea.

During the ship's stopover at Brisbane, a member of the Prince of Wales's signals staff, Neil Race, was killed by a hit-and-run motorist. In accordance with naval tradition, the dead man's belongings were auctioned, to benefit his next-of-kin. Neil Race's personal effects raised the astonishing sum of £1,500, thanks largely to the prince's generosity. He set the bidding standards by paying £100 for a tired old suitcase and £60 for a pair of socks.

While at Brisbane Prince Charles took the chance for some surfing, and made telephone contact with his father, then en route to open the Commonwealth Games at Christchurch, New Zealand. When *Jupiter* docked in Christchurch on January 29, its communications officer could be seen sprinting along the dock to the royal yacht, *Britannia*, six berths away; it was barely dawn, and Charles was anxious to surprise his father by carrying in his breakfast. The following day the Queen and the young newlyweds, Anne and Mark, joined them after flying from London via the Cook Islands.

Their ways soon parted again, the royal yacht to the New Hebrides, and Charles in *Jupiter* to San Diego, where he played a (for him) rare game of golf with the then U.S. ambassador to London, Walter Annenberg. In Hollywood he took tea with Barbra Streisand, who professed herself bowled over by "this real English gentleman," and at the San Diego yacht club he met an admiral's daughter named Laura Jo Watkins, who was to occupy his attention for several months (see Chapter 15).

It was during this short leave, on March 24, that he heard by telephone of the attempt to kidnap Princess Anne in the Mall. The princess and her husband, just back from the royal tour, were returning to Buckingham Palace from an equestrian charity film show when a Ford Escort swerved across the path of their car, forcing it to a halt. Its driver (subsequently found to be mentally ill and ordered by the Lord Chief Justice to be detained "without limit of time") shot and wounded the princess's detective and chauffeur, plus another policeman and a passerby, in his attempt to abduct her. At one point, after Captain Phillips had closed the car door on the assailant, he fired straight at the princess; but her detective, James Beaton, already shot in the stomach, put his hand over the muzzle of the gun and deflected the bullet. Beaton was later awarded the George Cross.

During the phone call, Prince Charles was at first intent on flying straight home. But his sister reassured him that she was recovered, if shaken. She would hear none of it. At her behest, Charles continued to enjoy himself. When a posse of photographers arrived on the quay in pursuit of him, they shouted their inquiries to a scruffy, unshaven sailor leaning over the ship's side. "Prince Charles?" he shouted back. "Oh, he won't see you. He's a pretty nasty piece of work, you know." The newshounds departed reluctantly, little knowing they had been talking to their prey.

The long voyage home gave the prince a chance for some

painting, some reading (Solzhenitsyn and Cecil Woodham-Smith's biography of Queen Victoria), and time to plan another practical joke. His brother officers had normally known how to conduct themselves toward the royal heir in their midst; occasionally, and inevitably during a 46,000-mile around-the-world voyage, they had overstepped the bounds of familiarity. Attempting on one occasion to "debag" him, they removed his trousers to find another pair beneath; after removing those to find a third, they gave up. Not so much on his dignity at sea, Charles had responded by threatening them with the Tower. "I can send you there, you know. It's quite within my power." When *Jupiter* docked at Devonport that April, a black naval minibus waited on the quayside; emblazoned on its side in nine-inch letters was HM TOWER OF LONDON FOR OFFICERS OF HMS JUPITER. The communications officer, it appeared, had been radioing ahead.

One of the prince's duties on *Jupiter*'s home voyage, as flight deck officer, had been supervising the landing and takeoff of Fleet Air Arm helicopters. At Devonport he waved his "ping-pong bats" for the benefit of the press, excited by the prospect of his next posting: to master helicopter flight himself, back at Yeovilton. Prince Philip had gained his helicopter license at the age of thirty-five; Charles was now intent on winning his ten years younger. Again it involved an intensive, truncated course: 105 hours instruction in forty-five days, comprising 50 hours of ground instruction, 40 of flight training in dual-control aircraft, and a minimum of 15 solo flight.

Endowed with another somewhat melodramatic call sign, Red Dragon, the prince undertook all the emergency training procedures—including landing damaged and blazing helicopters—and awkward routine operations such as carrying heavy loads. He also went to the Royal Marine School at Lympstone for a fearsome commando-training program, on the theory that helicopter pilots should familiarize themselves with the skills of the marine commandos they support. In camouflage gear, his face blacked, he was asked by one press photographer, "When does His Nibs arrive?"

It was "very exciting, very rewarding, very stimulating, and sometimes bloody terrifying." But he had found his true métier. "I adore flying, and I personally can't think of a better combination than naval flying—being at sea and being able to fly." In an introduction to a history of the Fleet Air Arm, he wrote: "Pride swells in my heart when I recall the part played by my great-grandfather, Prince Louis of Battenberg, in the formation of the Royal Naval Air Service in 1914. Without his interest and enthusiasm, and his determined support of the aeroplane versus the airship, the Naval Air Service might quite literally have had great difficulty in getting off the ground." During his forty-five days at Yeovilton, spread over the last three months of 1974 and much interrupted by royal duties, Charles managed to complete 105 flying hours, 26 of them solo, in his Wessex V helicopter code-named Whisky Alpha.

On December 12, he passed out as a fully qualified pilot, winning the Double Diamond award for the trainee who had made most progress. It was 707 Squadron's tenth anniversary, and the prince led a celebratory fly-past, his personal standard streaming from the winch-wire beneath his aircraft. His fellow officers, who had enjoyed his company on pub crawls around Somerset in search of "scrumpy," the powerful West Country cider, presented him with a pen stand made from a piece of helicopter rotor blade. One of his most valued possessions, it still sits on his desk at Buckingham Palace.

If Charles had at last discovered his favorite service activity, he was well aware that it had been one of the most dangerous, and that his position might prevent him keeping it up. "I hope and pray there'll be a chance for me to continue," he told his fellow Red Dragons in a farewell speech, "but we shall have to wait and see." He was also aware that special precautions had again surrounded his training; throughout his solo flying time, he had been shadowed by an auxiliary machine with firefighting and other emergency equipment. Just as well: in his twenty-six solo hours aloft, the prince was forced to make three emergency landings, due respectively to computer failure, engine failure, and a broken fragment of engine cover lodging in his engine. Shudders passed between Whitehall and Buckingham Palace, but the Ministry of Defence, still keen to use the prince as a recruiting agent, mentioned only "precautionary landings" in its press statements. Through it all, Charles was still resentful that the most hazardous thrills aloft, in Buccaneers and other supersonic jets, were implacably denied him: "If you're living dangerously," he declared, "it tends to make you appreciate your life that much more, and to really want to live it to its fullest."

His enthusiasm did, however, win him a postponement of his return to shore studies at Greenwich. Instead he joined 845 Naval Air Support Squadron aboard the aircraft carrier *Hermes*, bound for NATO exercises in the Atlantic, en route for the West Indies. In April, he was called away to royal duties in Canada, but seized the chance to travel north and sample the icebound life of the Northwest Territories. The newspapermen ever at the prince's heels were beginning to feel the strain of following so insatiable an adventurer, and life in the Arctic brought prince and press unusually close together. For those who had lugged their cameras that far, however, he turned in a princely tour de force after diving beneath the North Polar ice with Dr. Joe Mac-innis, a young scientist based at the underwater research station at Resolute Bay.

The ice had closed over their heads as soon as they disappeared beneath it; in a temperature of 28.5° Fahrenheit, it was six feet thick, over water thirty feet deep. Returning to the surface after half an hour underwater, Charles inflated his orange diving suit with compressed air until he looked "like Michelin Man," then let it deflate again until he was merely "an orange walrus." As he bowed to the ecstatic TV cameras, he knew the whole scene would be enjoyed by his family back home.

Hermes then took him to a month's helicopter training with the Royal Canadian Air Force at the inaptly named Blissville, New Brunswick, where he shared two weeks of life under canvas in subzero temperatures. The cameras followed him even to this desolate spot, where Charles felt sufficiently remote and at ease to give on-camera interviews unshaven—on his way, as it transpired, to a "full set." The beard, which reminded many of that of the young Duke of York, his grandfather, is preserved for posterity in the TV film *Pilot Royal.* Charles directed his own sequence at Blissville, in a sepia parody of silent films in which he at last takes his revenge on his instructor, Lieutenant Commander Alan Mac-Gregor. Still to be seen in *Pilot Royal*, the royal film alternates between faintly embarrassing Goonery and a passing imitation of Laurel and Hardy.

The beard became even more famous when it flew home with its owner for his installation as a Great Master of the Order of the Bath, ranking third to the Garter and the Thistle among British knighthoods. In the car home from Heathrow with David Checketts, Charles joked about returning from a bathless month under canvas to receive that particular dignity. He also wondered what his mother would say about his beard. That was clear next morning. The beard had gone, and Prince Charles sported only a mustache as he proceeded with his mother through Westminster Abbey and vowed "to defend maidens, widows, and orphans." Even the mustache had gone by the following morning, when he flew back to *Hermes*; naval regulations stipulate a "full set" or nothing. But the beard is a fond memory. The only jarring note was a *vox populi* exercise in one of the popular newspapers, in which a loyal subject declared that she liked the prince's beard "because it hid his rather weak chin." Of all the many millions of words written about him, that remark has always stuck in Prince Charles's mind. It rankles still.

His service career was to end in style, with a command of his own. On February 9, 1976, after completing captaincy courses at Greenwich and Portsmouth, the Prince of Wales took command of the minehunter HMS *Bronington*, at 193 feet and 360 tons one of the navy's smallest ships, with a complement of four officers and thirty-three ratings. The wooden-hulled vessel—named, appropriately enough, after a Welsh village—was built in the 1950s, and based on Rosyth. Its new commander was just twenty-seven years old, two years younger than his father had been when given command of the frigate *Magpie* in 1950.

Bronington was not renowned as a particularly stable vessel. Her outgoing captain, Lieutenant Commander Harry Bates, said she rolled "even on wet grass." Known in the navy as "Old Quarter Past Eleven"—her pennant number was 1115—she had a young crew: the first officer, Lieutenant Roy Clare, was twenty-five, and the ratings' average age just nineteen and a half. The captain's cabin, nine feet by ten, with a folding bunk, a desk, chair, and faded green carpet, was situated next to the ship's deep freeze. In rough weather, the best lunch available was stew from a pot tied to the galley stove.

For ten months, Prince Charles and *Bronington* patrolled the North Sea locating mines and assisting naval divers to dispose of them. Not an immensely exciting schedule, and not immensely pleasant in a ship so much at the weather's mercy. Charles later confessed that command had "aged" him—and that, after five years in the navy, *Bronington* was the first ship aboard which he had been seasick.

On *Bronington*'s return to Rosyth, its commander proudly welcomed the Admiral of the Fleet, his father, on board, and entertained him with tea and cucumber sandwiches in the cramped wardroom. But his finest hour came in mid-November, when he sailed his ship into the Pool of London just in time to be home for his twenty-eighth birthday. He was to enjoy just one more month on the bridge. Nineteen seventy-seven and Elizabeth II's Silver Jubilee, in which the Prince of Wales was to play a central role, loomed large. On December 14, he jumped two ranks in both the services in which he had served, promoted to wing commander in the RAF (skipping David Checketts' rank of squadron leader) and commander (skipping lieutenant commander) in the Royal Navy. The following day, his crew "pushed" him back into Civvy Street in a wheelchair, a lavatory seat slung like a laurel wreath around his neck. "See you behave yourself, lads," were the commander's parting words, to which "Doc" Kevin Ryan, *Bronington*'s medical assistant, countered, "See you keep your bowels open, sir." An inelegant farewell, but one in keeping with the navy's cherished traditions (previous captains had been hoisted aloft on cranes to mark their departure), and boorish enough to appeal to the broader side of the prince's sense of humor.

The services had proved a successful, if conventional, end to twenty-four years of otherwise unprecedented royal education. Elizabeth II and her consort had long since realized that their gamble had paid handsome dividends. Their son had had opportunities unprecedented for an heir to the throne to share the life of his fellow men. He had been allowed to go much further in hazardous personal adventure. What had started for him as a bad dream had developed into a glimpse of a freer world he was reluctant to leave.

But, as his father reminded him, duty called. And the Duke of Edinburgh added a compliment which touched his son: "What a great relief it is when you find that you've actually brought up a reasonable and civilized human being."

Part IV: *I've Danced with a Man Who's Danced with a Girl Who's Danced with the Prince of Wales*

My word, I've had a party,
My word, I've had a spree!
Believe me or believe me not,
It's all the same to me!
I'm wild with exaltation,
I'm dizzy with success,
For I've danced with a man who—
Well, you'll never guess!

I've danced with a man who's danced with a girl
Who's danced with the Prince of Wales!
I'm crazy with excitement,
Completely off the rails!
And when he said to me what she said to him
The Prince remark'd to her,
It was simply grand!
He said, "Topping band!"
And she said, "Delightful, sir!"
Glory, glory hallelujah,
I'm the luckiest of females,
For I've danced with a man who's danced with a girl
Who's danced with the Prince of Wales!

—*Popular song by Herbert Farjeon*
and Harold Scott, 1928

15

The World's Most Eligible Bachelor

"I have not yet met the girl I want to marry."

THE PRINCE OF WALES ON JUNE 17, 1977, THE DAY THE *Daily Express* "OFFICIALLY" AN-NOUNCED HIS ENGAGEMENT TO PRINCESS MARIE-ASTRID OF LUX-EMBOURG

IN AUGUST 1861, Bertie, Prince of Wales, the future King Edward VII, was nearing the end of an unhappy three-month military training stint at the Curragh Camp, near Dublin. An ill-conceived postscript to Prince Albert's rigorous scheme of education for his son, the course was designed to fit Bertie within one month for the command of a battalion, thus justifying his honorific promotion to the rank of colonel. The prince was as glum as his commanding officer, Colonel Percy, and indeed his mother the queen, when by the end of the third month he fell short of requirements. When Victoria and Albert paid a visit of inspection, their son suffered the humiliation of performing a mere subaltern's duties in his colonel's uniform. "You are too imperfect in your drill, sir," Colonel Percy told him. "Your word of command is indistinct."

History might tactfully have forgotten this miserable episode had it not been for one eventful summer night that August. The prince's brother officers, through curiously mixed motives of charity and mischief, smuggled into his quarters a young actress whose company they had all enjoyed, one Nellie Clifden. Thus was Bertie expertly initiated in a subject distinctly not on Prince Albert's curriculum.

It is the fate of kings and princes to have this, perhaps the most private moment of their lives, trumpeted to posterity as gleefully as their other, more public conquests. Most, happily, are spared it in their own lifetimes. For Bertie, however, the incident proved disastrous. As Queen Victoria noted painfully in her diary, Nellie Clifden "bragged" after the encounter had become an affair. The story was soon a favorite in the gentlemen's clubs, and was thence brought to court by a new lord-in-waiting, Lord Torrington, described equally painfully by Victoria as "one of the great gossips of London." Prince Albert traveled to Cambridge to remonstrate with his son, and returned home with the subject closed, the transgression forgiven. He also returned home, however, depressed and exhausted. Within a week he had collapsed, with what was diagnosed as typhoid fever, and twelve days later he was dead. Victoria, distraught, immediately blamed the loss of her beloved husband on the "fall" of their eldest son. "Oh, that boy," she wrote to her daughter, the Crown Princess of Prussia, "much as I pity, I never can or shall look at him without a shudder."

In the century since Bertie's "fall," social attitudes in the loftiest circles have altered as much as in society at large. But one of the lasting, distinctive qualities of the English upper classes is their discretion about each other, a code of self-preservation which has kept them cohesive during the drift toward a classless society. In the exuberant Prince of Wales-ship of Edward VII, once Nellie Clifden had launched him on his way, his many and varied affairs were well known and discussed throughout high society, whose members were outlawed only if they gossiped beneath themselves. By the 1930s and the brief, heady youth of the future Edward VIII, princely dalliance was an accepted and well-guarded secret long before he met Wallis Simpson. His friendships with Lady Furness and Mrs. Freda Dudley Ward were the talking point only of his own charmed circle, the same well-born elite which has since changed its outward show but not its inward dealings.

Certain members of today's aristocracy could, if they chose, noise abroad salacious detail of the present Prince of Wales's private life, notably of those country weekends which do not appear in the court circular. Those gentry who occasionally open their gates to the public these days are careful to shut them more firmly than ever the rest of the time.

But Prince Charles is the first Prince of Wales to have grown up in the era of the rampant mass media, when the royal family as much as anyone else has had to adapt to insatiable public curiosity about its private life. On more than one occasion in the late 1970s a senior member of the royal circle felt free, in what he thought the prince's best interests, to talk beyond the family of "Charles popping in and out of bed with girls." But the present Prince of Wales is by nature less of a libertine than either of his immediate predecessors. Unlike Edward VIII he would not contemplate abandoning his public duties, let alone his crown, for a woman. Unlike Edward VII, he will not contemplate taking mistresses after he has taken a bride; Prince Charles's religious and moral convictions on the sanctity of marriage are firmly held.

Paradoxically, it is the major common factor of his and Bertie's lives which most distinguishes them: That dauntingly long wait in the wings, as understudy to a revered and longeval sovereign, earns Prince Charles all the parental indulgences denied his great-great-grandfather. He intends to marry in the next few years; he would not wish to be too old a father to his children, and his own happy family background is the single most important component of his life so far. But only his duty to breed heirs will compel him to marry in his thirties. Until that day, the prince's amorous exploits may cause an occasional family row and earn the avuncular disapproval of his former private secretary, but they are scarcely likely to change the course of history. Elizabeth II may have wished her son had married younger; she hopes, and has on one occasion attempted to ensure, that he can find someone of royal blood to love. But she has always behaved more as his mother than his queen.

Nevertheless, the Prince of Wales regards it as something of an achievement that he reached the age of thirty unmarried. Throughout his twenties, the pressures on him to choose the nation and the Commonwealth its future queen—constant from the press and public, intermittent from those close to him—were almost as daunting as the family precedents. His parents married when his father was twenty-six, his mother twenty-one. His grandfather, King George VI, married at twenty-seven; his great-grandfather, George V, at twenty-eight; his great-great-grand-father, Edward VII, at twenty-one. Of Charles's own generation of the royal family, the Duke of Gloucester married at twenty-seven, the Duke of Kent at twenty-five, and his sister, Anne, at twenty-three.

The history of his office proved even more formidable. Apart from his immediate predecessor, whose eventual choice of bride led him to renounce the throne, Charles is the only Prince of Wales to have reached thirty unmarried since James Stuart, the Old Pretender, in 1718—and he took a wife the following year. Of those Princes of Wales who became kings of England, only Henry V and Charles II were unmarried at thirty. But each remained so only two more years; and each, already on the throne, had had a singularly busy youth.

Prince Charles had no Agincourt, no exile from a republican government to occupy his twenties. He had time on his hands. Despite his service career, there was leisure enough to be seen escorting the eligible, the well born, the well connected, the merely attractive, even the not so suitable—beauties all, most from the requisite top drawer. There is, moreover, his strong romantic streak. He falls in love easily, and has by his own confession done so "on countless occasions." Throughout his twenties, the attentions of the press cramped his style and alienated the affections of several girls, but at least once he came close to a proposal. Why then did he disappoint matrons and tantalize maidens the world over by delaying?

The reasons are many and varied: personal and public, domestic and constitutional. For no other man in the world, perhaps, is the choice of a bride so complex, so fraught with pitfalls, so hedged with restrictions. Few other men, meanwhile, are so much in need of a paragon among women, prepared to be privately loving and supportive, the sole confidante of a man with many confidences to share, as well as publicly conscientious—prepared, in short, to sacrifice her life entirely to his. When still only twenty, Prince Charles showed himself more than aware of his plight: "It's awfully difficult, because you've got to remember that when you marry, in my position, you're going to marry somebody who perhaps one day is going to become queen. So you've got to choose very carefully. . . . The one advantage about marrying a princess, for instance, or somebody from a royal family, is that they do know what happens. The trouble is that I often feel I would like to marry somebody English. Or Welsh . . . well, British, anyway."

So it is in his choice of bride—if not, before that day, in his quest for one—that Prince Charles's accident of birth perhaps most restricts his life. By the Bill of Rights of 1689 (enshrined in the 1701 Act of Settlement, through which his legal claim to the throne is established) he is forbidden to marry a Catholic—which rules out half the princesses of Europe and, more to his chagrin, many an otherwise suitable English rose. Under the Royal Marriages Act of 1772—introduced, ironically enough, by King George III, the "much maligned monarch" whose reputation he has so struggled to rehabilitate—he is effectively barred from marrying without the consent of his mother or both Houses of Parliament. As he will on accession become head of the Anglican Church, there could be no question of his marrying a divorcée or ever himself being divorced.

Any or all of these choices Prince Charles, the British citizen, could of course make. But marrying a Catholic, a divorcée, or anyone vetoed by the sovereign or Parliament, would force him to renounce his right to the throne. His entire upbringing and all his own personal inclinations and beliefs militate against his becoming a second Duke of Windsor. He will not, like Edward, he has said privately, "become a martyr to the cause."

The prince's own lifetime has seen only one royal relaxation of the rules. In 1955 his aunt, Princess Margaret, was persuaded not to marry the divorced Group Captain Peter Townsend; in 1978, however, she was at length permitted to divorce Lord Snowdon. But Princess Margaret was never heir to the throne, nor ever likely to be after Charles's birth in 1948. The prince saw it as a happy precedent when his sister married a commoner, Captain Mark Phillips, in 1973; but again Princess Anne was always freer to choose, with her three brothers (and any male offspring they may have) between her and the throne.

It is possible that Elizabeth II's lifetime may see the repeal of both the laws restricting royal choice, but scarcely before Prince Charles marries, and scarcely anyway to an heir's advantage. The Queen has it in mind to persuade a prime minister to do away with the Royal Marriages Act, which has long outlived its purpose. George III introduced it in an attempt to curb his sons' erratic sexual behavior, and thus ensured that it affected all those in direct line of succession. In 1978, therefore, the sixteenth in line, Prince Michael of Kent, had to renounce all rights to the throne to wed a Roman Catholic, Baroness Marie-Christine von Reibnitz, whose previous marriage had been annulled. The Pope refused them permission to marry in church, which prompted the Prince of Wales to make a bold public protest about the "needless distress" caused by doctrinal dispute among Christians. But the Act had already been proved unrealistic, in the latter half of the twentieth century, by Princess Margaret's divorce, and the divorce and remarriage of the Queen's cousin, the Earl of Harewood.

The 1689 Bill of Rights is less easily disposed of, outmoded though it is in an age of greater religious tolerance. In 1977, when the nation was briefly convinced that the Prince of Wales was about to marry the Roman Catholic Princess Marie-Astrid of Luxembourg, there was much discussion of dropping the ban on Catholic consorts. But although the Archbishop of Canterbury was meeting the Pope in Rome that very month, there was little sign of the spirit of ecumenism infecting the Church of England's attitude to its monarch and titular head. Plans that such a couple might raise their sons as Protestants and their daughters as Catholics drew sniffs of distaste from the Anglican establishment, and outright condemnation from the Vatican. The debate was reopened late in 1978, when a curiously timed speech from Enoch Powell, the Ulster Unionist MP, declared that such a marriage "would signal the beginning of the end of the British monarchy." The prince, though puzzled by Mr. Powell's motives, was glad of the leading articles he provoked, which again called on the churches to settle their differences on this score at least. But again the indignation of laymen fell on deaf ears; more heat was generated in Mr. Powell's direction for stirring jingoistic anti-Catholic feelings in Ulster for reasons of purely party political advantage.

"If I marry a Catholic, I'm dead," the Prince told a friend. "I've had it." He better than anyone knew the law, but he saw no reason why it should meanwhile inhibit his bachelorhood. As these checks and balances began to assert themselves on his early public romances, another equally striking reason for delay emerged. By the age of thirty this slightly awkward, fundamentally shy figure, still in some ways young for his years, pub-

The cadet: receiving his wings at Cranwell, and
in the passing-out parade at Dartmouth, both 1971

"Bat" in hand: guiding a helicopter aboard HMS *Jupiter*

Butterflies: the first royal in history to make a parachute jump.

Sub-Lieutenant the Prince of Wales shows his mother around HMS *Norfolk*

The bearded commander of HMS *Bronington,* looking uncannily like his great-grandfather, King George V

Last day in the Navy: farewell to *Bronington,* with a lavatory seat slung around his neck

An unhappy visit:
the Nixon White House, 1970

Paired off with Tricia Nixon
at a baseball game in Washington

On safari: Kenya, 1971

Naba Charles Mampasa,
Honorary Ghanaian chieftain

An occupational hazard in Fiji

Children dance for the prince in the Ivory Coast, where
more than a million people turned out to greet him

One day an Indian chieftain, the next a rodeo
cowpoke: with Prince Andrew in Canada, 1977

An exotic samba in Rio, 1978

With Margaret Trudeau at a
state banquet in Canada, 1976

The world's most eligible
bachelor. The bookies' favorite: Lady Jane Wellesley

In his Aston Martin with Davina Sheffield

With Lady Sarah Spencer at the Windsor horse trials

Laura Jo Watkins: a Yankee
at the court of Prince Charles

The meeting that went wrong:
with Princess Caroline of Monaco

The *Daily Express* front page,
June 17, 1977

The Queen with Princess Marie-Astrid
of Luxembourg: matchmaking?

A plug too far: in a promotional T-shirt, with friend

licly noted for his weak chin and jug ears, had developed an extraordinary ex-officio power over women. It took him by surprise, and he began rather to enjoy it.

By his late twenties, the Prince of Wales had become a besieged sex symbol wherever he went. At his approach girls would giggle and scream as if he were a pop star, lunge forth with kisses as if he were a matinee idol, fight to touch him as if he were divine. For once, moreover, their mothers warmly approved. It started during his tour of Wales in the summer of 1969, in the wake of his investiture at Caernarvon; confronted in the flesh by the image etched on their television screens, girls quite literally fainted away. It climaxed eight years later, during his 1977 tour of Australia, the main feature of which was the number of girls daily launching themselves out of a crowd toward the royal cheek, even the royal lips. By this time, he had mustered sufficient self-confidence occasionally to return the compliment.

By the time he left the navy, in November 1976, Prince Charles was of a mind to prolong his independence. It was perfectly possible to separate the public accounts of his love life from the private truth. But his newfound power was not, alas, without responsibility. He must exercise self-denying care in his choice of all friends, but immeasurably more so in his selection of female intimates. Of all the many girls he has dated, only one, Lady Sarah Spencer, has been tempted into talking to a journalist, and that under somewhat harassed conditions. She was careful to insist, after a skiing holiday with the prince in 1978, that their relationship was platonic. Contrary to popular belief, he did not "drop" her immediately after the incident; indeed she was a guest of the Queen at Sandringham, in Prince Charles's company, during January 1979. He was, in fact, more hurt than annoyed by one remark she made: "I am not in love with him . . . and I wouldn't marry anyone I didn't love, whether it was the dustman or the king of England. If he asked me, I would turn him down."

Lady Sarah, however, was very much the exception that proved the rule. She was so excited to be among the prince's known escorts that she preserved every press cutting about their meetings in a scrapbook. Otherwise, his girl friends have thrown a blanket of remarkably loyal discretion over Prince Charles's amorous exploits, doubly remarkable in view of the amount of money any one of them could receive for even a mild indiscretion. His public consorts, however, have all been to the manner, if not the manor, born. Society girls, most with aristocratic backgrounds, they regard the royal family with even more awe than do the rest of its subjects, to the extent of swallowing their feminine pride in Prince Charles's company. They call him "sir," even when alone with him. They will walk a pace or two behind him when protocol requires it. They know, with very few exceptions, that it is he who issues the invitations, he who makes the phone calls. Whatever the feelings in their hearts, they are not allowed to forget the privilege his company bestows on them.

The prince, for his part, is an otherwise chivalrous suitor. He is concerned lest his friends suffer from being seen with him. For some girls, a weekend with the prince has been followed by a week of newspapermen camped on their front doorstep. "It's very hard on them," Prince Charles has said. "I have layers to protect me, but they are not used to it. It tends sometimes to put the really nice ones off." He takes pains to warn them of the strains of appearing in public with him, and urges them to call on his staff for assistance in emergencies. His greatest hidden asset, however, is that they know the slightest word out of place would signal the end of the affair.

Some, who remain close friends after passion has cooled, are prepared to do him even greater favors. They will contentedly be escorted by him to Ascot, to the theater or wherever, to be photographed, gossiped about, and restored to the newspapers' royal marriage stakes, while offstage he woos another unheard of by the waiting world. Prince Charles has become quite expert at raising smokescreens and laying false trails. His male friends will occasionally "lend" him a girl friend with whom to be seen in public, to distract attention from a more discreetly conducted romance. In 1977, for instance, the popular press grew very excited about the prince's friendship with Penelope Eastwood, a twenty-two-year-old graduate of the London School of Economics, the daughter of a wealthy army officer retired to Majorca. She was in fact the girl friend (now the wife) of the prince's old Gordonstoun chum Norton Knatchbull, grandson of Lord Mountbatten. When the deception was discovered, vengeance was extracted—and the rumors prolonged—in the form of stories about the prince "pinching" his friend's girl.

He is also self-confident, even vain enough to enjoy mild public flirtations with the famous and fashionable: pop stars like the Three Degrees, the all-female black soul trio who sang at his thirtieth birthday party, and film stars such as Susan George. They must, of course, be unattached. Given that he should not be photographed in the arms of married women, and given that some of the world's most desired women are intent on being photographed in his arms, the prince has had to develop politely tactful skills. He had to disentangle himself, for instance, from the headlong embrace of Farrah Fawcett-Majors, whom he met in Hollywood in 1977, and who flew hotfoot to London soon after to host a charity show in his presence, confiding her admiration in copious newspaper interviews. Then at the height of her fame as, appropriately enough, one of Charlie's Angels, she was equally well known to be the wife of Lee Majors, television's Six Million Dollar Man. Similarly the revelation in 1979 of Mrs. Margaret Trudeau, estranged wife of the Canadian prime minister, that Charles had once "looked long and hard down my cleavage" was treated with right royal disdain.

The unattached, however, he has been known to telephone, late at night, after a casual meeting at a party or a film premiere. He can entertain in complete privacy, at his own home or that of a friend. His two regular detectives, who have to accompany him even on such private sorties, would scarcely breathe a word of them even to each other; but their occasional reliefs, who take over their duties in holiday periods, have been known to complain of long, boring waits outside private houses in assorted London suburbs. These excursions are kept to a minimum, as the prince is well aware of the risks involved. Besides, his quarters at Buckingham Palace are completely self-contained, and an invitation there from the Prince of Wales is scarcely likely to be refused.

Such invitations can, however, lead to surprises. For at least one girl, an evening alone with the prince meant listening to a catalog of his conquests. Like any other hot-blooded male, he can make the mistake of trying to boast his way into a lady's affections. He can also behave in somewhat cavalier fashion: months can go by without a word, just when our heroine thought she had won a place in her prince's heart. This, of course, is partly of necessity; any escort of the Prince of Wales must prepare herself for the daily shock of seeing someone else in his company in the morning's newspapers. The requirements of rank are a great provider of explanations.

For the most part, it is his tenderness and concern which win hearts, just as they remain the qualities most mentioned by other friends. They are evident in his few public pronouncements on the subject of marriage: "I think an awful lot of people have got the wrong idea of what it is all about. It is rather more than just falling madly in love with somebody and having a love affair for the rest of your married life. Much more than that. It's basically a very strong friendship . . . I think you are very lucky if you find the person attractive in the physical *and* the mental sense. . . . In many cases, you fall madly 'in love' with somebody with whom you are really infatuated. To me marriage, which may be for fifty years, seems to be one of the biggest and most responsible steps to be taken in one's life."

At the age of twenty-seven, he told an interviewer that he thought thirty "about the right age for a chap like me to get married." He regretted the remark, naturally enough, on his thirtieth birthday, when it was flung back in his face with a vengeance. But the popular British press has been marrying off Prince Charles since he was three. Immediately after his mother's accession, the first of countless subsequent lists of eligible brides appeared, casting its net around all the European royal houses as well as the country homes of England. Many in both categories have since become unavailable—a fact of life that Prince Philip, who otherwise brings very little pressure to bear on his son in these matters, has occasionally mentioned in jocular fashion. "You'd better get on with it," he'll say, "or there won't be anyone left."

Bertie, Prince of Wales, was nineteen when Nellie Clifden introduced him to one of his life's lasting pleasures. Prince Charles was just the same age, and also a Cambridge student, when he too embarked upon his first serious romance. The master of Trinity, Lord Butler, was at the time writing his political memoirs, *The Art of the Possible*, and had engaged as his research assistant a young history graduate, the daughter of the then Chilean ambassador to London. At twenty-three, Lucia Santa Cruz was three years older than Charles, and considerably more experienced in the ways of the world. The phrase *in loco parentis* can rarely have had a more resounding ring than it did at that time for Butler, who was aware of all the disadvantages: the girl was a foreigner, a Catholic, and much the more sophisticated of the two. But she was also intelligent, vivacious and, for what it was worth, well connected; and the couple were anyway separated after dark by the Trinity curfew, which locked the gate at night between a student and his girl friend. The master disapproved of the system and was in the process of reforming it. In the meantime, he felt it his duty to help the prince enjoy the dwindling days of as private a life as he would ever know. Lord Butler "slipped" Lucia a key to the Master's Lodge. "The Prince," he remembers, "asked if she might stay in our lodge for privacy, which request we were very glad to accede to."

Charles's feelings for her appear to have been the kind of puppy love most men experience in their teens. Until he met Lucia, his circumstances had prevented the adolescent adventures all too familiar to lesser mortals. Any conversation with any girl had been inflated by the press into romance: a bashful encounter at a Gordonstoun social evening had led one Sunday paper to declare he was being sent to school in Australia "to break up the affair." But Prince Charles, on the threshold of his twenties, was wholly innocent, wholly inexperienced. It was at Cambridge, contemporaries testify, that he "discovered" girls. Lucia Santa Cruz is now married to a Chilean lawyer and living in South America (Prince Charles is godfather to their first child); she remained a good friend to the prince for several years after their Cambridge days; her occasional weekend visits to Balmoral invariably renewed rumors of romance, long after their respective affections had moved on. Whatever she meant to him at the time, since that first friendship with Lucia Prince Charles has never been without at least one steady date in his life.

At Cambridge he soon took up with Sybilla Dorman, daughter of the governor-general of Malta, with whom he spent those two holidays on the island after his investiture in 1969. Both were reading history, and Sybilla shared Charles's enthusiasm for amateur dramatics. He collected her for dinner in a mud-stained Sandringham Land-Rover—"I'd expected the MG, at the very least," she complained—and was popularly supposed to have climbed the walls of her college, Newnham, with other party guests who had outstayed the curfew's welcome. Journalists who pursued the couple to Malta watched quivering as she applied the prince's suntan oil. But it was the first of innumerable false trails. Charles was soon escorting another girl, one of the daughters of Prince Philip's naturalist friend Aubrey Buxton, to a Trinity May Ball. Sybilla is one of Prince Charles's many former girl friends who have since married someone else.

The list of the Prince of Wales's escorts, over the ten years to his thirtieth birthday in 1978, is impressive, not least as a Who Was Who among the debutantes of the 1970s. More than half have since married; some remain good friends, others no more than acquaintances, seen rarely, but seen with pleasure. A few, despite popular rumors to the contrary, were never more than that in the first place.

Some of the first rumors surrounded Rosaleen Bagge, the daughter of a retired major living near Sandringham, who exchanged letters with the prince while he was at school in Australia in 1966. Then came Cambridge, Lucia Santa Cruz, Sybilla Dorman, and the Buxton girls. For the next ten years, the Prince of Wales was quite clearly playing the field. His turnover was high; and there was scarcely one among his many companions without a drop of blue blood.

The roll call, complete with pedigrees, included: Lady Leonora Grosvenor, daughter of the Duke of Westminster (now married to the Earl of Lichfield, better known as Patrick Lichfield the photographer); her sister Lady Jane Grosvenor, now the Duchess of Roxburghe; Lady Victoria Percy, daughter of the Duke of Northumberland, a Roman Catholic, now married to John Cuthbert, a wealthy landowner; her sister Lady Caroline Percy; Bettina Lindsay, daughter of the Conservative politician Lord Balniel, now Mrs. Peter Drummond-Hay; Lady Cecil Kerr, daughter of the Marquess of Lothian, now married to Donald Cameron of Lochiel; Lary Henrietta Fitzroy, daughter of the Duke of Grafton; Lady Charlotte Manners, daughter of the Duke of Rutland; her cousin Elizabeth Manners; Angela Nevill, daughter of Prince Philip's private secretary, Lord Rupert Nevill; Lady Camilla Fane, daughter of the Earl of Westmoreland; Lord Astor's daughter, Louise; Georgiana Russell, daughter of the diplomat Sir John Russell, now Mrs. Brooke Boothby; Rosie Clifton, a colonel's daughter, now married to the prince's polo-playing friend Mark Vestey; Caroline Longman, daughter of the wealthy publisher the late Mark Longman.

Through the interminable catalog of speculation, three girls genuinely did enjoy close and lasting friendships with the prince. A regular companion still, despite her momentary indiscretion, is Lady Sarah Spencer, goddaughter of the Queen Mother and daughter of the Queen's old friend Earl Spencer. Red-haired, vivacious, an ideal public escort, Sarah suffered from *anorexia nervosa* when first she met Prince Charles at Ascot, but his companionship seemed to speed her full recovery, and they were soon indulging their mutual love of outdoor sports. A skiing holiday with the Duke and Duchess of Gloucester in February 1978 led to press innuendo about the number of bedrooms in their Klosters villa, but it was after this that Lady Sarah insisted their friendship was platonic. A year later, she was out shooting with the royal family at Sandringham.

Before Sarah there was Davina Sheffield, the soldier's daughter, blond ex-debutante, his love for whom Prince Charles could not disguise even in public. After their first few meetings she took herself off, somewhat dramatically, to Vietnam, where she worked in an orphans' hostel during the last stages of the war. Forced by the Viet Cong advance to flee, she returned home to more tragedy: the brutal murder of her mother by raiders in their Oxfordshire home. She turned to the prince for solace, and by the end of the year, 1976, was publicly arm in arm with him again. But she was to fall prey to the artificial standards by which he must live. On a discreet surfing expedition to Bantham, a quiet Devon cove frequented by Prince Charles and his friends, she was said to have been discovered naked in the men's changing room. There was scarcely time for the denials to be issued before a greater misfortune befell Davina: her former fiancé chose to let it be known that they had once lived together—enough to preclude her being seen again with the heir to the throne, let alone remaining a candidate for queen. A similar fate befell Fiona Watson, daughter of the Yorkshire landowner Lord Manton, whom the prince had been seeing on occasion until noisy complaints from her boyfriend led to the discovery that she had once revealed her startling 38-23-35 statistics, in full color across eleven pages, to readers of *Penthouse* magazine.

But there was, above all, Lady Jane Wellesley, daughter of the eighth Duke of Wellington, who in a highly competitive field has remained probably the closest and most enduring of Prince

Charles's female friends. They have known each other since childhood—Jane attended some of those sprightly early birthday parties at Buckingham Palace—but did not take more than usual notice of each other until some twenty years later. She was the first of the Prince's true loves who was also an eminently suitable candidate for queen. Daughter of one of England's proudest noble families, she is quite at ease at court; she shared the mischievous nature of his youth, but was prepared to behave with due decorum when necessary. One of the prettiest of all the girls who have passed through Prince Charles's life, she is undoubtedly the brightest and one of the few who enjoys actually earning her own living.

Her father, moreover, owns ancestral estates in southern Spain: thirty thousand acres at Molino del Rey, near Granada, won for the family by the Iron Duke's peninsular campaign. They make an ideal retreat. On one of the first of many sojourns there, during a break from his duties aboard HMS *Minerva* in 1973, the prince became so exercised by the rapaciousness of the press that, for one rare moment, he behaved like his father and swore at them, thus adding strength to their convictions. Lady Jane, they reported home, had been observed pulling the Prince of Wales's hair, and "playfully throwing melons at him." He apologized for his bad language through the sterner of his private detectives, Inspector Paul Officer: "They are just two young people relaxing with friends for a few days. The publicity their friendship has raised has not made it easy for them." But Officer saw the newshounds off with a few words of his own: "I can definitely state that there is no romance. The whole affair has been built up from a molehill to a mountain. It is just not on— the two are just very good chums. The prince will not be a party to deception. That is why he has refused to be photographed with Lady Jane."

Nobody believed a word of it. The more curt and irritated the Duke of Wellington's protests, the more Britain grew convinced its prince had chosen his future queen. Later that year, when Jane attended Sunday morning service at Sandringham as a weekend guest of the royal family, ten thousand people defied both royal denials and a petrol shortage to turn up and watch. Even Davina Sheffield, who was once reduced to tears at Heathrow Airport by the harassment of the press and excited onlookers, had suffered nothing like this. Jane Wellesley braved phalanxes of reporters outside her Fulham home to go to work each morning; after refusing all comment to those who telephoned her at her office, she would leave for home to see newspaper placards announcing MY LOVE FOR CHARLES—JANE TELLS ALL. The irony was that she was a journalist herself, chairman of her union branch, soon to be a member of the national executive.

Friends of Prince Charles are surprised that he did not marry Lady Jane years ago, and they place the blame on him for dithering. It has been suggested that she turned him down, not wishing to make so incomparable a surrender of her freedom. It has also been suggested that insufferable press attention destroyed their friendship. The truth lies elsewhere; Prince Charles had most nearly contemplated marriage at a time when his service career took him away too much for it to be possible, and would continue to do so for several years. By the time he left the navy, he had a taste for seeing more of life before settling down. But Jane Wellesley has remained a better friend than most, despite the prince's penchant for teasing her mercilessly.

Throughout 1973 and 1974 British bookies quoted Jane as firm favorite in the royal marriage stakes. They seemed about to pay up when she accompanied the Queen Mother and Princess Alexandra to the 1974 royal film premiere, a public sign of family approval. Later that year, however, her odds lengthened briefly when a glossy American blonde was among the dignitaries in the Strangers Gallery of the House of Lords to hear the Prince of Wales make his maiden speech. She was Laura Jo Watkins, the daughter of an American rear admiral, whom the prince had met that summer when HMS *Jupiter* called at San Diego, California. Throughout the week she popped up at various smart functions, and newspapers were already waxing lyrical about an unmarried Wallis Simpson when she just as suddenly disappeared again. An unusually large crowd converged on Cowdray Park that Saturday to see the prince's weekly polo game, but they were disappointed. "You don't think I'm such a bloody fool as to bring her here today, do you?" He laughed. And that, it seemed, was that—until four years later, in the summer of 1978, when Guy Wildenstein flew her over to Deauville as a present during Prince Charles's annual polo visit.

By this time he had also had his long awaited, almost obligatory encounter with the glamorous Princess Caroline of Monaco, daughter of Prince Rainier and the former Grace Kelly. It was an undisguised mutual sizing-up operation, and it was not a success. Caroline was forty-five minutes late for their first rendezvous, at which both discovered they had little in common. A second meeting was canceled, and in 1978, pleading pressure of work, Charles regretfully refused his invitation to Caroline's wedding to Philippe Junot, a French businessman.

The number of available European princesses, their names annually trotted out by the women's magazines, was becoming somewhat thin. The Queen, however, is known to hope that her son will marry royalty; such is his duty, she feels, to the blood royal of the House of Windsor. Even the otherwise laissez-faire Prince Philip has said: "People tend to marry within their own circles . . . there is a built-in acceptance of the sort of life you are going to lead." Buckingham Palace has always looked askance at the suggestion, but both Elizabeth II and her husband clearly had a hand in the events of 1977, when what would to the Queen have been an ideal match for her son was finally frustrated. Prince Charles, for his part, appears to have been ready to consider his mother's proposition: that he should marry Princess Marie-Astrid of Luxembourg.

The Queen is an old family friend of the princess's father, Grand Duke Jean, and is said to have returned from her state visit to Luxembourg in November 1976 "enchanted" by the princess, and with hopes of persuading her son to take an interest in her. The following month, on December 8, HMS *Bronington* docked at Ostend, and the Prince drove to Laeken Palace in Brussels for lunch with King Baudouin and Queen Fabiola of the Belgians, and Prince Philip, who was in Brussels for a meeting of the International Equestrian Federation. Princess Marie-Astrid is King Baudouin's niece; she and her sister Margaretha were at the time sharing an apartment in the Belgian Royal Palace, while Marie-Astrid worked at an Antwerp hospital. Few believe Buckingham Palace's denial that she too was at lunch. Also attending was the Belgian primate, Cardinal Joseph Suenens, friend and adviser to both the Pope and Bishop Jean Hengen, head of the Luxembourg Church.

It was the month Charles was due to leave the Navy—an optimum moment for the Prince of Wales to become engaged.

Princess Marie-Astrid was a demure and intelligent, if unexciting, twenty-three-year-old: a qualified nurse, who had attended the prince's investiture in 1969 and visited Britain to learn English in 1974. The problem, of course, was that the Luxembourg royal family is Catholic.

The comings and goings of the next few months, as churchmen met to discuss matters ecumenical, have always been declared wholly insignificant by the royal family's official spokesmen. Prince Charles during this period had separate meetings (both routine, he insists) with the Archbishop of Canterbury and Cardinal Hume of Westminster. The Archbishop, indeed, was to meet the Pope in Rome that June.

Before that meeting could take place, however, any chance of such a marriage was suddenly and spectacularly killed off. News of the palace activity leaked—via a member of the royal family—and on Friday, June 17, the *Daily Express* announced CHARLES TO MARRY ASTRID—OFFICIAL. "Prince Charles is to marry Princess Marie-Astrid of Luxembourg. The formal engagement will be announced from Buckingham Palace on Monday. The couple's difference of religion will be overcome by a novel constitutional arrangement: any sons of the marriage will be brought up according to the Church of England, while daughters will be raised in the Catholic faith."

It was Ascot week, and Prince Charles's friends and relations were assembled in strength at Windsor Castle, where he came down to breakfast to much royal mirth at his expense. Himself far from amused, he had at midnight already for the first and only time in his life issued a formal personal denial—significantly through the Queen's then press secretary, Ronald Allison, rather than his own. It read: "I am authorized by His Royal Highness the Prince of Wales to make the following statement. There is no truth at all in the report that there is to be an announcement of an engagement of the Prince of Wales to Princess Marie-Astrid of Luxembourg."

The wording, Charles's own, was cautious to the point of ambiguity. The *Express*, which had not taken such a flyer without excellent evidence, remained unconvinced; in a cartoon next morning, a royal coronet hung on the editor's hatstand. Other newspapers began to take the statement apart word by word, concluding, not unreasonably, that it did not altogether rule out the engagement, only its imminent announcement. Prince Charles told his own press secretary, John Dauth, to go further, which he did in style: "They are not getting engaged this Monday, next Monday, the Monday after, or any other Monday, Tuesday, Wednesday, or Thursday. They do not know each other, and people who do not know each other do not get engaged. The royal family do not go in for arranged marriages. If the prince and princess have met at all, then it has been briefly at official functions."

This, of course, left the way clear for an engagement on a Friday or Saturday. But it also hedged its bets: "They do not know each other. . . . If the Prince and Princess have met at all . . ." Well, *had* they met? Yes, it transpired, apparently after a rummage through the files. On perhaps two occasions. But the prince, somewhat ungallantly, said he could not remember the first thing about the princess. Thus, with scant ceremony, was she consigned to a footnote of British history.

Princess Marie-Astrid had suffered the same fate as had nearly befallen Prince Philip thirty-six years earlier: premature public certainty precluding a future royal possibility. In 1941, when Princess Elizabeth was fourteen and Prince Philip of Greece and Denmark nineteen, "Chips" Channon wrote in his diary that they were to marry. Philip spelled out the danger to his biographer, Basil Boothroyd: "It had been mentioned, presumably, that 'he is eligible, he's the sort of person she might marry. . . .' Inevitably, I must have been on the list, so to speak. But people only had to say that for people like Chips Channon to go one step further and say it's already decided, you see what I mean?" The implication is startling: had Chips Channon's diaries been published in the 1940s rather than the 1960s, or had Channon indeed worked for the *Daily Express*, Prince Philip might not even have made history's footnotes.

Since Marie-Astrid's dramatic exit from the scene, no new contender for the Prince's hand has emerged publicly, although as he himself puts it: "I've only got to look twice at someone, and next morning I'm engaged to her." Which happens not infrequently, as the prince undoubtedly has a roving eye. The diffident, awkward youth of twenty, a late developer sexually as in other ways, has at thirty all the self-confidence of a man who knows he is the most eligible bachelor in the world. He says he has not yet met the right girl, and might only have added "at the right time." He confesses, "I often look at someone and think 'I wonder if I could marry her?'" but his views on the institution of marriage, uncluttered and chauvinist though they are, severely limit his powers of decision: "Whatever your place in life, when you marry you are forming a partnership which you hope will last for fifty years. So I'd want to marry someone whose interests I could share. A woman not only marries a man; she marries into a way of life—a job. She's got to have some knowledge of it, some sense of it; otherwise she wouldn't have a clue about whether she's going to like it. If I'm deciding on whom I want to live with for fifty years—well, that's the last decision on which I would want my head to be ruled by my heart." Or, even more simply: "Creating a secure family unit in which to bring up children and give them a happy, secure upbringing— that's what marriage is all about. . . . I hope I will be as lucky as my parents, who have been so happy."

Lord Mountbatten, an inveterate matchmaker, will continue to make helpful noises. The Queen will continue to exert a gentle pressure, and the Duke of Edinburgh to treat the whole business with relaxed bonhomie. But Prince Charles will make his own decision, and make it soon.

16

Prince of Wales, Superstar

"I don't feel handicapped by the [royal family's] 'philistine image.' . . . There's no more merit in pretending to be an opera fan than in pretending to dislike polo. . . . I love both."

"**H**IS PRODIGIOUS TALENTS in the arts, in sport, in academic life make him perhaps the most accomplished young man in Britain . . . rich, handsome, intelligent and eligible—the twentieth-century Renaissance man who has done everything, been everywhere, met everyone that matters . . . he is actor, sportsman, pilot, musician, artist, orator, academic, wit, sailor and future King."

British women's magazines tend to get a bit carried away on royal birthdays. Prince Charles at thirty was an accomplished young man, more so than a nation might reasonably expect of one born to his position, but scarcely the prodigy painted by *Woman's Realm*. He could, perhaps, justifiably captain the England polo team (he had already captained Young England). He is a better-than-average amateur skier, fisherman and shot. He has a natural aptitude for flying helicopters. He could probably hold down most of the jobs in which his Oxbridge contemporaries, in their early thirties, are beginning to make their names. But he has long since given up the cello and is unlikely ever to join the National Theatre Company. He is not in line for an Olympic gold medal, an Oscar, or the Nobel Prize. Of all the roles set out for him above, the one for which his accomplishments most fit him is, as it should be, future king.

Curiously enough, his breathless admirer forgot to hail Charles the television star. He is the first Prince of Wales to have grown up in the era of mass communications, and he has taken pains to master its dominant medium. With a growing list of credits behind him, he is quite at ease in front of the cameras, whether conducting the viewer around Canterbury Cathedral or skateboarding with deprived kids in the slums of London. He has made a program with Alistair Cooke about the "much maligned" George III, interviewed anthropologists for a TV series, and broadcast an all-channels fund-raising appeal to the nation at the time of Elizabeth II's Silver Jubilee. From his first TV appearance in 1969, the pre-investiture interview, through his own six-hour spectacular at Caernarvon a week later, to the sequence he himself directed for *Pilot Royal*, he has proved himself a more natural performer than either of his parents. The Queen is still ill at ease in her annual Christmas broadcasts; Prince Charles likes using television to promote his own multifarious activities and enjoys watching himself on the video cassettes he keeps of all his appearances.

Regular TV performers pay tribute to his skills: those characteristic, awkward gestures—the concertina-playing arms, the interlocked, restless fingers—look remarkably cool and professional on-screen. It is through television that he has broadened the popular luster attached to any youthful Prince of Wales, traditionally an icon of postage stamps, medallions, picture postcards, and biscuit tins. Add television and T-shirts, and you have, if not twentieth-century Renaissance man, a twentieth-century superstar.

In an age of short-lived, one-dimensional popular heroes, the Prince of Wales is an enduring, ex-officio superstar. By continuing to expand the realms of his endeavor, he seeks to justify the attention paid to him merely because of his office. He is a born and determined achiever, with more than a streak of machismo, loving any challenge to his masculine powers. "I like to see if I can challenge myself to do something that is potentially hazardous, just to see if mentally I can accept the challenge and carry it out. . . . I'm one of those people who don't like sitting and watching someone else doing something." He does not, for instance, share his mother's enjoyment of race meetings. "I'd rather be riding the horses myself."

It is, of course, royal understatement to say that a way with horses runs in the family. Ben Jonson would have approved. Princes, he wrote, learn no art truly but the art of horsemanship: "The reason is, the brave beast is no flatterer. He will throw a prince as soon as his groom." Prince Charles is a naturally skilled horseman, though not as expert as his sister, who was European Three-Day Event champion in 1971 and a member of the British team at the 1976 Olympic Games in Montreal. After initial indifference, he has grown to enjoy hunting more and more, while well aware of the widespread public hostility to blood sports. A boar-hunting expedition to Liechtenstein in 1978 earned him the accolade of "Hooligan of the Year" from the Royal Society for the Prevention of Cruelty to Animals, and the prince has determined that hunting is the one activity he would give up if ever he felt a majority of popular opinion required it of him. "You can't have everything you want, even if you feel it does no harm. People's susceptibilities count." For the present, his hunting dates are among his most closely guarded secrets; when he joins the Belvoir, the Cotswold, or the Duke of Beaufort's pack, it is usually well after they have moved off, out of public view.

A recent counterpoint to hunting is cross-country riding, which Prince Charles took up early in 1978 after finding its skills and dangers exhilarating. Teams of four race across rugged country terrain punctuated by alarmingly difficult fences. "Good practice for parachuting," he laughed off one afternoon with more than its share of ugly-looking falls. The prince now has two teams of his own, the Duke of Cornwall's chasers and the Earl of Chester's chasers. With its bolder horsemanship and its lack of sacrificial fox, cross-country riding could in time prove a happy alternative to the prince's love of the chase.

But of all his various mounted pursuits, the one with which he is most associated, and which indeed gives him most personal excitement, is of course polo. Whatever else is going on, and wherever he is in the world, Prince Charles will be disappointed if he doesn't fit in one, often two, games a week during the polo season. He started playing under his father's tutelage at the age of sixteen, won his half-blue at Cambridge, and is now one of the country's better players—handicap three. But he is not quite in the international class. His coach, Sinclair Hill, believes that Prince Charles has even more natural ability at the game than

Prince Philip in his heyday—and his handicap was five (the higher the better). But Charles, according to his team mates, does not treat his ponies with sufficient brutality to be world class. Nor does he have enough time to practice, or indeed maintain enough ponies, to make the grade in this extremely expensive pastime. The prince owns a string of six polo ponies, whose up-keep is estimated at some £12,000 a year—neither statistic high enough for those who would like to see him representing, perhaps captaining, his country.

Like most aristocratic pursuits, polo is as obsessive to those who play it as it is tedious to those who spectate. Aficionados among the nobility express outrage that the Prince of Wales's other duties intrude on his single-minded pursuit of polo ex-cellence. His years in the navy slowed his development as a top-class player; in 1977, after he had left the services, he improved so rapidly that a special meeting of polo's governing body, the Hurlingham Association, had to be convened to revise his handi-cap upward. From the nation's point of view, the Prince of Wales's indulgence in the game is quite obsessive enough. Many a lady friend has spent many a cold afternoon at Smith's Lawn, a captive audience to rugged displays of manliness.

Dismounted, the prince is an equally skilled shot and fish-erman. The present royal family's experts at shooting and fish-ing were once, respectively, the Duke of Edinburgh and the Queen Mother. But Prince Charles has bettered them both. Prince Philip, often cited by Sandringham guests as one of the best shots in the country ("which means," they add in hushed tones, "the world"), is now equally lavish in praise of his son. The Queen Mother, who taught her grandson the art of angling from his childhood, was as impressed as the hardy Balmoral fishing guides by his feat in the dry summer of 1976. The River Dee, which winds through the royal estate, was too low to be thought worth fishing, but the Prince scooped out seven salmon in one day. Another challenge more than adequately met.

In the passage outside the dining room at Sandringham, rack after rack of royal shotguns testifies to more than a century of princely slaughter. Since Prince Albert bought the house in 1861, as a country home for the too metropolitan Prince of Wales, the Sandringham game book has recorded some fearsome carnage (the record bag in one day being 3,114 pheasants on November

14, 1896). For each Prince of Wales, it seems, it has become a matter of pride to outdo the feats of his predecessor or parent. "I love shooting more than anything else," the future Edward VIII wrote to his father, George V, in 1912, "& it was very kind of you to allow me to shoot so much here while you were away. I have had some splendid practice, & feel that my shooting has very much improved." In later life, when Duke of Windsor, he could still remember the best days: "A good day's bag was a thousand head, but two thousand was not uncommon on the larger estates."

There were days, however, when even George V said: "Perhaps we went a little too far today, David." On December 18, 1913, at the Beaconsfield estate of Lord Burnham, then owner of the *Daily Telegraph*, all royal records were broken. The Duke of Windsor recalled: "My left arm ached from lifting my gun, my shoulder from the recoil, and I was deaf and stunned from the banging. . . . When in the late afternoon the carnage stopped, almost four thousand pheasants had been killed. The bright, limp carcasses were laid out in rows of one hundred; the whole place was littered with feathers and spent cartridges. My father had shot over one thousand birds; I had even passed the three-hundred mark. He was proud of the way he had shot that day, but I think that the scale of the bag troubled even his conscience. . . ."

The days of such excess—"I always suspected," added the Duke of Windsor, "that in addition to the birds raised on the place, a good many hundred pheasants were brought in and released for the king's benefit"—are happily long gone. Just as well, for there was public outcry when Prince Charles shot his first stag at Balmoral at the age of thirteen, and it has continued ever since. The slaughter of thousands, however, tends to cause revulsion even among sportsmen these days. A good bag by contemporary standards is a few hundred birds, grouse at Balmoral, pheasant and partridge at Sandringham. When the Prince of Wales is holidaying at either, he will be out with his shotgun at least three days a week. Strangely enough, he has never sampled the excellent shooting to be had on his own private estate at Chevening, in Kent, where a private consortium has now subcontracted the rights.

The popular imagination probably most identifies the Prince of Wales with hardy and energetic outdoor pursuits. Apart from his hunting, shooting, fishing, and polo, they have seen him water-skiing, scuba diving, wind surfing, skiing—all rather solitary pursuits, those of the man wishing to pit himself against the elements. But in the best traditions of Juvenal and Kurt Hahn, he does not neglect matters of the mind. Apart from his painting and music—again somewhat solitary, introspective pastimes—he reads as much as he can, and if a particular enthusiasm seizes him he can become positively bookish. Having read history at Cambridge, he has become far the best-informed member of the royal family about his forebears, and is particularly partial to new historical biographies. For a man so written about, with such decisive views on what is said and the way it is put, he is not averse to turning his own hand to the occasional preface, the odd review.

In 1971, at the age of twenty-two, the newly graduated prince first developed his passionate views on history's treatment of King George III, after reading books, pamphlets, and learned correspondence (in the *Times Literary Supplement* and the *British Medical Journal*) on the subject of his "madness." Browsing through the Royal Archives at Windsor one day, he met the historian John Brooke, who had been granted access for a biography of George III he was then writing. They fell into conversation, in which, the prince recalled, "we both agreed that George III had been unfairly maligned by historians and the writers of textbook history." Finding a kindred spirit, intent on portraying the king as a gracious, cultivated and dutiful monarch, Prince Charles agreed to write a foreword to the book. It is worth quoting in some detail.

> If the average schoolchild remembers anything about history after leaving school, then he will remember that George III was mad. If he is American as well, then madness is often given as the reason for the "irrational" behaviour of the King towards the Colonists, making it necessary for them to declare independence. George III's cardinal error was that he "failed" in history—he failed to retain the American

colonies, and in the search to find a scapegoat for this national disaster the King became the obvious target. . . .

Much has been written by learned scholars to the effect that George III was manic depressive, and suffered from sexual frustration, a difficult wife, and hideous family problems—all acting upon an inherently unstable character which finally gave way under the strain. If this was so, why didn't the King "go mad" far earlier than 1788? In that year he celebrated his fiftieth birthday and had apparently solved his longstanding political problems, with Pitt established firmly in the nation's confidence. Not only that. The Prince of Wales' debts had at last been settled and it was three years since the traumatic experience of finding that the Prince, in defiance of Acts of Parliament, had contracted a marriage with Mrs. Fitzherbert—enough to crack any remotely unstable character. George III's illness does not appear to correspond to mania or hypomania. . . .

Brooke's theory was that the king had porphyria. Prince Charles did not entirely agree.

The recurrent toxic and confusional states suffered by the King could have been due to other physical causes such as infectious and metabolic disturbances. The observation of purple urine by itself is not sufficient proof; indeed, medical experience has shown that most cases of modern porphyria are precipitated by barbiturates. . . . There is no evidence that he was schizophrenic, or depressive, or that he suffered from syphilis of the central nervous system which, when untreated, is steadily progressive. Only in the last ten years of his life when between the ages of seventy and eighty, deaf, blind, deserted by his family, surrounded only by "mad doctors" and apothecaries who tied him up in straight waistcoats at the slightest sign of opposition to their will and banished him to the north side of Windsor Castle, did he show signs of mental decay associated with natural senility.

> I think there can now be little doubt that George III suffered from periodic attacks of a metabolic illness . . . there was nothing wrong with his brain *before* the onset of the illness.

The stigma of madness attaching to the king had persisted far too long.

> It is high time that the veil of obscurity stifling the King's true personality, known and loved by his contemporaries, should be lifted. . . . It was, after all, in George III's reign that the office of Prime Minister gradually evolved—thereby reducing the power of the Crown to the role of influential adviser.
>
> He had been, in short, a king "almost over-dedicated to duty" . . . "the father of his people."

The prince did not discuss George's attempts, for a time successful, to control Parliament through bribery, or the merits and demerits of his alliance with Bute against Pitt on the American question. Medical matters and George's neglected reputation as a patron of the arts were Charles's prime concerns; the disastrous conduct of the war with the American colonies and later the king's ill-timed anti-Catholic prejudice (from which Prince Charles himself still suffers under the Royal Marriages Act) became the acts of a well-intentioned idealist. George III became an obsession, and he cropped up whenever the prince had a chance to sound off about him.

In 1976, with Alistair Cooke, he made a TV film entirely devoted to rehabilitating the "much-maligned monarch." He told Cooke: "He was a complete idealist and moralist. Either a thing was right or wrong. I am determined to clear his name. It's very unfortunate if one is misunderstood in history. I personally would hate to be misunderstood."

A clue to his strength of feeling? Does the Prince of Wales already have a weather eye on posterity? Certainly his interest in history has always stemmed from an acute awareness of his own ancestry. His Cambridge supervisors remember his approach as anecdotal, even to the extent of "Oh yes, he was a splendid chap. I remember my mother saying her father had told her . . ."

The vein of continuing royal self-justification can be most clearly seen in the opening of a book review by Prince Charles, in 1976, for *Books and Bookmen* magazine. Although Queen Victoria's sense of humor was the subject for discussion—he was reviewing Alan Hardy's *Queen Victoria Was Amused*—George III again defiantly enters the argument in advance of his imperial great-niece.

> It seems to be one of the curious quirks of human nature that members of our great-grandparents' generation and earlier are invariably regarded as "historical" creatures who displayed few of the normal human characteristics we associate with our contemporaries. Wherever monarchs are concerned this quirk is magnified tenfold and popular impressions of past sovereigns often reach the realms of the ridiculous, remaining firmly imbedded in the minds of successive generations of schoolchildren. The vulgar view of King George III is quite simply that he was mad and, to make matters worse, that he also succeeded in losing the American colonies. The fact that he had wide and civilized interests, was a great patron of the arts and sciences and devoted a vast quantity of time to affairs of state has been conveniently neglected. ". . . the good is oft interred with their bones."
>
> As far as my great-great-great-grandmother is concerned . . .

Two years later, in a foreword to a collection of cartoons of royalty (proceeds to the Queen's Silver Jubilee Appeal), he is still the royal public relations officer par excellence:

> This book comprises an intriguing collection of "royal" cartoons mostly from the past 25 years, and shows the changes which have taken place in that period in both style and approach to the subject. Looking at them I cannot but reflect on how politely we have been treated, compared to the way in which King George III and his family, for instance, were treated by the 18th and 19th century cartoonists, such as Rowlandson . . .

There are, however, subjects which simply won't accommodate the Hanoverians. One was the first novel of the Welsh entertainer Harry Secombe, a friend of the prince (known to him as "Ned of Wales"), a former Goon, made a Commander of the Order of the British Empire in 1963. Prince Charles reviewed the book for *Punch* magazine in 1974, shortly after carving his initial in the celebrated *Punch* table. His first paragraph is a deft, and not uncharacteristic, *de haut en bas* rebuke to the magazine's literary editor, Miles Kington:

> "We would be delighted if you would write a review of Harry Secombe's first novel, *Twice Brightly*," was what the man from *Punch* said. "It doesn't have to be a comic masterpiece" (What does he mean, it doesn't have to be a comic masterpiece? People have wandered feet first into the Tower for less than that . . .) "Nor is it really necessary to cause a literary sensation," the letter continued. What does that leave me with? Presumably a model of memorable mediocrity—but after reading this compendium of Welsh wit and thespianism I humbly beg to submit that mediocrity would be difficult to achieve.

Prince Charles's honorary role as public relations officer for the Goons also produced, at Peter Sellers's suggestion in 1973, a preface to a Christmas volume of *Goon Show* scripts. Declaring himself "one of their most devoted and dotty supporters" (despite such cryptic lèse-majesté as "Eccles for King" in Secombe's contribution), the prince hailed their "mental slapstick and imaginary cartoonery." He went on:

> It has always been one of my profound regrets that I was not born ten years earlier than 1948, since I would then have had the pure, unbounded joy of listening avidly to the Goons each week. I only discovered that the Goon-type humour appealed to me with an hysterical totality just as the shows were drawing to a close.
> Then I discovered the Ying Tong Song in record form and almost at once I knew it by heart—the only song I do know by heart. I plagued everybody with its dulcet tones and "Solo for Raspberry Blower" to such an

extent that when my small brothers heard a recording
of the Goons for the first time, they thought it was their
elder brother.

A love of the absurd, however jejune, is a handy asset in a
man whose job constantly brings him up against it. The rest of
his literary output, however, is rather more sober: forewords or
contributions to books on wildlife preservation, anthropology,
royalty's love of aircraft, underwater diving, and his grandmother, Queen Elizabeth. Only on special occasions does he un-
bend: in 1978 he contributed his favorite recipe—for bread-and-
butter pudding—to a book called *Chevening Cookery*, published
to raise money for the restoration of the parish church near his
country house.

The extracurricular interest which he is most intent on developing, however, is his love of opera. As both patron and
president of the Friends of the Royal Opera House, Covent Garden, he starred in 1979 in a fund-raising film in which he realized every amateur musician's dream: conducting the Covent
Garden orchestra (in the overture to Mozart's *Magic Flute*). But
he is aware that his knowledge is as yet very limited. In an interview in April 1979, to introduce BBC television's Opera Month,
he made some surprising confessions: his favorite opera was *La
Traviata* and his favorite composer Verdi, but he had never
heard *Macbeth*. He liked Bellini, and had seen *Norma*, but he
had never heard any Puccini, Wagner, or Strauss. "I've got a
lot to learn . . . one of the things I really enjoy about being
Patron of the Royal Opera is having the chance to see as many
operas as I can and to find out more about it. . . . I like to
think I can go whenever I want to, at short notice—turning
people out of the Royal Box so I can get a seat."

The Queen Mother has said of her grandson: "If there was
anything left to discover in the world, Charles would have been an
explorer." An earlier verdict, in a *Times* critique of an earlier
biography, was that the prince would have made "an excellent
schoolmaster." In the book under review, *To Be a King* (1968),
Dermot Morrah wrote: "No British prince since the Stuarts has
cared more sincerely for the things of the mind and the spirit."
Several previous Princes of Wales, notably Charles's protégé
George III, might justly feel abused by the claim, especially as it

was made when the prince was barely nineteen years old. But he has developed and maintained a great respect for learning, a genuine love of music, and a deft and generous hand for forewords. A biographer of the last Prince of Wales, rashly predicting a glorious reign, added one caveat: "Unfortunately, among the young people of England Edward does not know the idealists." Prince Charles, by deliberate example, will seek to lead them.

"Royal Action Man," as he has been called, has plenty of time for introspection. It may be the privilege of his position to dive beneath the Arctic ice, explore Caribbean coral reefs, windsurf off Cowes, hunt wild boar in Liechtenstein, play polo on all five continents. It is also his lot, however, to be forced consistently into solitude, read books about his ancestors, write lectures on spiritual values ("a subject on which I have rather strong views"), meditate upon his curious fate. By the time he graduates from the biscuit tins to his coronation plates, this Prince of Wales should have behind him a spread of accomplishment befitting the first Master of Arts to ascend the British throne. The appeal of bachelor youth will have given way to a more sober, cozy domesticity, but the prince will wish to be thought a twentieth-century man for all seasons. Outside his official duties he will remain ever active in a curiously assorted world of parachutes and cave paintings, opera seats and wet suits, polo sticks and paint brushes, beagles and books, guns and Goons.

17

The Ambassador

"The whole idea of these visits is for me to meet as many people as I can, so they can see for themselves that I'm a pretty ordinary sort of person."

IN THE PAST HUNDRED YEARS, Princes of Wales have forged their early reputations as much abroad as at home. In the 1870s and '80s, the mid-period of his long decades of unemployment, the future Edward VII went on protracted, swashbuckling tours of India, Egypt, Europe, and the United States, occasionally traveling incognito, always taking a huge and costly retinue, invariably free to enjoy himself with even more abandon than at home. In like fashion, immediately after the First World War, the future Edward VIII embarked on tours through Canada and the United States, New Zealand and Australia, and later Africa; success after success was reported in the British newspapers, his ability to draw huge crowds anywhere in the world serving only to increase his popular glamour back in England.

The world traveled by the present Prince of Wales has shrunk immeasurably. The age of exotic, prolonged continental tours is gone, and jet travel makes a week to ten days the comfortable length for a crowded schedule halfway across the globe. Apart from which, solo tours on the grand scale still lie ahead of Prince Charles. His busy program in the United Kingdom makes him reluctant to leave it for too long at a time; the six weeks he spent in the Far East, Australia, and Canada early in 1979 were, apart from school and service attachments, the first time in his life he had been away for so long. But he is an ardent collector of new sights and experiences, as acquisitive as most of us about the exotic stamps in his passport.

Heir to the most traveled monarch in British history, he knows the years ahead will provide almost any opportunity he cares to seek, although it was only in his late twenties that he began to venture beyond Europe and the Commonwealth. He is eager to visit the Soviet Union. But the major unknown quantity remains the People's Republic of China, which, like his mother, he would dearly love to see. As Elizabeth II, however, recently told a London orchestral player just back from a tour of China: "I don't think they're too keen on queens out there, are they?"

Sending the Prince of Wales abroad is a complex, protocol-ridden, and costly business. In Commonwealth countries, whether monarchies or republics, he travels as a member of the royal family, and Buckingham Palace bureaucrats must be careful not to tread on the toes of his local hosts. Elsewhere he travels in official pursuit of the British government's foreign policy, and Buckingham Palace must make it clear to his hosts that the usual diplomatic courtesies are the very least he expects. Official visits are penciled into the schedule as much as a year in advance, sometimes more; conditions, political or otherwise, both at home and in the country to be visited often dictate postponements, as of the prince's dearly cherished plans to tour India, put off until 1979 because of the political upheavals of 1975–78. Once the dates are secure, an advance party sallies forth to reconnoiter.

A month or so before the prince's departure, his private secretary, press secretary, and detective travel out to set things up in the minutest detail. They base themselves, wherever possible, at the British Embassy or High Commission, as it is British diplomats abroad who bear a heavy share of the considerable burden. In consultation with host diplomats, they will then inspect every inch of the ground to be traveled by the prince. The detective will discuss security with his local counterpart; the press secretary will ensure that local journalists understand the nature of their prey—no spot questions, no undue familiarity, perhaps a press conference but no political questions—and that the British press traveling with the prince will have ample facilities to transmit the good news home. Above all, the British ambassador and the private secretary will ensure that the program is appropriate.

There must, for example, be official receptions on both sides, hosted respectively by the British ambassador and the head of state or his representative, at which the prince will be guest of honor; there must be a chance for the local British community to meet him; there must be visits to industry, especially any with British connections; there must be visits to the local armed forces (a chance for the prince to don his uniforms); there must be private talks with the president, prime minister, foreign minister, or the local equivalent (mayors, etc., when outside the capital). Tree planting and plaque unveilings are tolerable, but should be kept to a minimum. There must be guards of honor for his inspection on arrival and departure, and at all appropriate points between; the prince's personal flag must fly alongside that of the host country on his car at the head of each motorcade, and so on ad infinitum. Hospitals and specialists are alerted at points along his route; his medical records are sent out in advance. Menus and accommodation are inspected; guest lists are screened; modes of address, seating plans, who enters which room in what order, who wears what decorations when—all requirements are painstakingly spelled out by the prince's representatives.

Even princes are human, and it must be ensured that life's most fundamental facilities are regularly available. The Duke of Windsor once quoted "the two best pieces of advice my father ever gave me: never refuse an invitation to take the weight off your feet, and seize every opportunity you can to relieve yourself." Above all, nothing must be unscheduled. Thus itineraries become inordinately crowded, containing anything from six to twenty engagements a day. Sightseeing, if the hosts wish to cram it in, is optional. The prince is not too keen on it.

On trips of ten days or more, as many as fifty items of baggage travel out under the supervision of the Prince of Wales's baggage master. The author once found himself sharing the hold of an RAF Hercules with the Prince of Wales's luggage, flying up the Amazon in advance of the smaller aircraft carrying the prince and his eight staff members. Half the aircraft's bulk was a wonderworld of pleasantly battered red trunks bearing the prince's name and insignia; old-fashioned hat boxes marked "straw" and "top"; trunk after trunk of military, naval, and air force uniforms, none required by the schedule but all on hand just in case. Leather cases bearing polo sticks protruded through the netting holding it all in place.

Thirty suits and uniforms were being carried, though his valet could not persuade him to venture beyond a choice of six gray suits, which—to the photographers' chagrin—all looked exactly the same. Safari suits were ready, as would be snowsuits in other climates. Prince Charles also takes a full set of mourning clothes wherever he goes, in case of a royal death back home; even black-edged notepaper is on hand to continue, in such an event, the flow of thank-you letters. There are crates of gifts: a few gold cuff links bearing the Prince of Wales's insignia, more signed photographs, graded by the quality of their frame to the rank of the recipient.

He will be escorted on any overseas excursion by his private secretary, his press secretary, his private secretary's secretary, a detective, an air attaché (if traveling by air), his valet, a typist and baggage master and often an equerry. Occasionally there will be a special adviser, such as Sir Fitzroy Maclean on the prince's visit to Yugoslavia in October 1978. The British ambassador will receive him on his arrival and remain with him around the country until his departure. The staff of the British Embassy are at his disposal. The flow of red boxes continues, and each day brings a Central Office of Information digest of the British newspapers. Constant contact is maintained with Buckingham Palace.

If the host country is much more than a thousand miles away, the first-class section of a scheduled aircraft, preferably the British carrier for that route, is reserved for the prince and his staff. Usually a bed will be installed for his use. On long-haul flights across the Atlantic or down to Australia, he will perform the Heathrow handshakes in a suit, and change out of it immediately after takeoff. He will turn down the first-class champagne, but enjoy an in-flight movie, however insipid. (After a scheduled Air Canada flight to Calgary in 1977, the Prince confessed that he had stuck out a "dreadful" film called *Logan's Run* because he was "rather partial" to Miss Jenny Agutter). By the time he reemerges, with a few friendly words for the economy passengers who have gradually grown aware of his presence—the escort of fighter jets is a good clue—he will be back in his suit again, pleasantly rested.

On shorter trips, he will pilot himself in an Andover of the

Queen's Flight—an antiquated but conspicuously safe aircraft which he likes for a number of reasons. Successive Captains of the Queen's Flight have tried for years to update their small fleet, in the last decade hoping for BAC 111s, but have always been frustrated by the fear of public outcry at yet more royal expense. Prince Charles and his father are quietly rather pleased. The Andover, which dates from 1955, travels slowly enough to allow them respite from official duties and to clock up many more flying hours (a matter of some personal pride). They ensure, therefore, that even on far-flung official visits, an Andover travels out for their use around the interior. In South America as in Yugoslavia, both examples from 1978, local dignitaries' first glimpse of the heir to the British throne was through a cockpit window: an aquiline profile obscured only by headphones, at the controls of a quaintly antique, somehow very British aircraft. His personal standard flutters aloft, thrust through a flap in the roof, as he taxies the gleaming red aircraft to the reception area.

Rather to Prince Charles's annoyance, the Andover became something of an issue during his foreign travels in 1978, especially the tour of Brazil and Venezuela in March. His official visits abroad can achieve little but goodwill—a commodity valued highly enough by the British Foreign Office, which pays his way out of a fund set aside for royal tours. But the prince is anxious to extend his role in the only nonpolitical direction he can: toward becoming a trade ambassador for British exports. In Brazil of all countries, therefore, a huge tract constantly criss-crossed by extremely wealthy businessmen, why was he not flying himself around in a British-made executive jet, perhaps the Hawker-Siddeley 128? His acclaimed presence in the country, set off by the even more dashing figure he would have cut in the cockpit, must have ensured a few dozen sales.

He could not himself, of course, answer an essentially political question. But the truth of the matter was made clear, ironically enough, during that same visit to Brazil, when back in London the *Daily Express* announced all over its front page that the Prince of Wales had accepted an offer from a consortium of British businessmen to become a £50,000-a-year roving sales rep. Amid the angry denials telephoned home to the Buckingham Palace press office was an assurance that he could never accept hire and salary from individual British companies. A few days

later, again by chance, he was able to show what he *can* do. By
fortunate timing, his presence in Brazil coincided with the final
approval of a huge investment by British banks in a steel-mill
complex near Rio, expected to yield a profit of some £11 million.
A little delicate blurring at the edges, and the prince could be
said to have clinched the deal. As his ten-day trip had cost the
British taxpayer some £11,000, it showed an equally neat 1,000–1
return on investment.

It was on his first solo official visit abroad, to Japan in April
1970, after touring Australia and New Zealand with his parents,
that Prince Charles genuinely did pull off just such a royal coup.
Visiting Expo '70 in Tokyo, he met the president of the Sony electronics conglomerate and learned of Sony's plans to build a
plant somewhere in Western Europe. "Why not try Wales?"
suggested its prince, less than a year after his investiture at
Caernarvon. Two years later, Prince Charles was able to open
the new Sony plant in Bridgend, Glamorgan, which had created
several thousand jobs in an area of acute unemployment.

In the wake of his investiture and twenty-first birthday, and
thus of his emergence into public life, Charles clocked up his
heaviest year of foreign travel in 1970. After the 1954 visit to
Gibraltar, to greet his parents' return from their coronation tour
of the Commonwealth, he had made only five foreign trips in the
next ten years, all private: to visit his father's family in Germany,
to attend King Constantine's wedding in Athens, to go skiing in
Switzerland and Liechtenstein. The year 1966 saw him at school
in Australia, returning via the Commonwealth Games in Jamaica,
and 1968 took him on his archaeological excursion to France and
Jersey. Between the two, in December 1967, he had joined the
then prime minister, Harold Wilson, and Opposition Leader Edward Heath in setting a modest aviation record: their round trip
to Australia in an RAF VC10, for the funeral of Prime Minister
Harold Holt, was completed in 82 hours 19 minutes, a record for
that class of aircraft.

"Who's representing the family, ma'am?" Wilson had asked
the Queen at his weekly audience. "Well," she replied, "Charles
has expressed some interest." Wilson met the heir apparent, just
turned nineteen, by the elevator. "Fancy a trip to Australia?
All right, go and get your bags packed, then." It was the first
occasion on which the Prince of Wales had officially represented

the Queen. In Perth the prime minister grew concerned about the attempts of various Australian politicians, as they jockeyed for the dead man's shoes, to exploit the prince's presence. They would ask him round for tea and photographs, to show the electorate they had royal endorsement. Charles was too young to cope. Before leaving England, Wilson had asked the Queen's private secretary, Sir Michael Adeane, how he should behave toward the prince. "Treat him like your son," said Adeane— and Wilson took the advice very literally. After the funeral he whisked the Prince of Wales off to Perth to spend the day with forty-three close relatives, the Australian branch of the Wilson family. When prince and ex-prime minister repeated their excursion together eleven years later, for the funeral of Sir Robert Menzies, Charles made a point of greeting them all again, including Wilson's eighty-nine-year-old maiden aunt.

His postinvestiture holiday in Malta in July 1969, as guest of the island's governor, Sir Maurice Dorman, led to a return visit later that year to inaugurate the new campus of the Royal Maltese University. Here he received an early lesson in royal aplomb, remaining impassive during the ceremony as students exploded stink bombs (having earlier stolen a plaque he was due to unveil), and taunted him about his friendship with Sir Maurice's daughter, Sybilla. He proved he had maintained his humor at a banquet that evening, when he reminded his audience of Princess Elizabeth's visits to Lord Mountbatten's villa during the Duke of Edinburgh's naval service in Malta: "I am told many Maltese believe my future appearance was determined whilst my parents were in this island."

Apart from a skiing holiday with Prince (now King) Carl Gustav of Sweden and attending his aunt the Margravine of Baden's funeral in Germany, both also in 1969, that was the sum total of the Prince of Wales's foreign adventuring before his twenty-first birthday. Nineteen seventy was to more than double it. The year began with a trip to Strasbourg with Prince Philip, to attend the Council of Europe's Conservation Conference, and was to end with President de Gaulle's memorial service in Paris. In between, while winning his university degree, Prince Charles circled the globe three times.

In Australia and New Zealand that March, touring with his parents and his sister, the Prince of Wales for the first but by no means the last time occasionally upstaged his mother. The dashing, eligible young prince, his magic aura enhanced by fresh television memories of his investiture, stole Elizabeth II's headlines. In New Zealand a thousand Maoris danced, it was said, for him alone, though he was sharing the platform with the sovereign. It was his visit to a hospital in Dunedin, exchanging operation-scar stories with women patients, which led reports of the day when the Queen visited the University of Otago. In Auckland a square dance by the Prince of Wales was the highlight of the royal family's visit. And so it continued through Australia, where Prince Charles even stole his father's habitual thunder by allowing a few unguarded words to stir controversy. After surfing at dawn on St. Kilda beach, near Melbourne, he declared that it had been "like swimming in undiluted sewage," prompting one local mayor to say he deserved "a good thump under the ear." Three mayors in the Melbourne area were challenged to try the water for themselves, and did so one morning in the photogenic company of a bikini-clad young lady. The mayor of St. Kilda itself, Councillor Jim Duggan, was sufficiently moved to return the abuse. "When that young crank came here," he barnstormed, "he didn't have the brains to tell us he was going to St. Kilda or we would have cleaned the place up. He's the guy who stirred up this idea of pollution and now everyone is running around worrying about it. Pollution has become the in thing, and I'm fed up, sick and tired of the whole business." The prince's aspersion on his beach was "the kind of inane remark you'd expect from an inane person." Councillor Duggan was forced to tract his remarks equally gracefully—"The prince is the son of his father"—after a fellow councillor rose to declare: "Who does this young crank think he is? The future king of England?"

The prince, alas, missed the merriment as he had already left his parents and gone on alone to Japan. Twenty-one Expo '70 pavilions in one morning was a typical item on his agenda, while more unguarded remarks about the comfort of airline seats—"I don't know why I'm the one who gets all these long flights; they should have an asylum waiting for you at the end of them"—earned him a much-publicized back massage from a geisha girl. Japanese girls, quickly warming to a by now intercontinental theme, jumped up and down squealing when he passed by—the characteristic reception they normally reserve for pop stars.

He had been abroad for most of March and half of April, but by July, after taking his Cambridge finals, Prince Charles was traveling again. A two-week trip through Canada was completely upstaged by its *commedia dell'arte* aftermath: three days in Washington with Princess Anne as guests at the Nixon White House. The visit had been announced a year ahead, and America had been anticipating it for months. Memories were revived of the American forays of two other recent Princes of Wales.

In 1860, aged only eighteen, Prince Bertie had chosen the United States, where civil war was already looming, for his first official visit abroad. Under the name of Lord Renfrew, which fooled no one, he traveled from Detroit to Chicago, through St. Louis, Cincinnati, Pittsburgh, and Baltimore to Washington and New York. President James Buchanan, as whose guest he stayed at the White House, personally escorted him to George Washington's grave at Mount Vernon, where George III's great-grandson performed a profound symbolic act by planting a chestnut sapling at America's national shrine (while writing home to his father: "The house is, unfortunately, in very bad repair and rapidly falling into decay"). When he attended the opera in Philadelphia, the audience spontaneously rose to sing "God Save the Queen"; when he attended a ball at the Academy of Music in New York, where his reception had been tumultuous, the dance floor collapsed under the weight of the crowd preparing to greet him.

In 1919 the twenty-five-year-old Prince Edward, traveling as Lord Chester, was the guest of the ailing President Wilson. He visited Mount Vernon in his grandfather's footsteps and received a ticker-tape welcome in New York, where the excitement caused by his arrival could be measured by the twelve columns devoted to it in the *New York Times*. Five years later he returned on a more private visit, a whirlwind round of dances and parties which had his staff wondering each night where he had got to, and the comedian Will Rogers declaring: "The prince is a good kid. Too bad I can't afford to carry a guy like that around with me. I'd have a swell act if I could." Rarely in bed before 5 or 6 A.M., spending his afternoons at polo games and race meetings, he was preceded home by American headlines such as PRINCE GETS IN WITH THE MILKMAN. King George V forbade any of his sons ever to visit America again.

Nearly fifty years later, as the arrival of a new, if less exotic,

Prince of Wales became imminent, America positively quivered. The White House issued a long list of instructions for those whose paths young royalty might cross. "You don't talk to royalty unless they want to talk to you. . . . Prince Charles should be addressed as 'sir' and Princess Anne as 'ma'am,' but a murmured 'How do you do, Your Royal Highness' will suffice. A hand should be shaken only if it is first extended by royalty." Mrs. Nixon's staff director, Connie Stuart, ventured to suggest that the Nixon children "would probably be accorded the privilege of being allowed to call them Charles and Anne." (They weren't.) "And," she went on, "our young people will be quick to respond 'Please call me Tricia, Julie, and David.' " Further White House announcements revealed that a bicycle had been made ready for Prince Charles's use, and that the brass had been polished on his four-poster bed in the Lincoln Room of the White House. *Life* magazine advised its readers not to tire the princess with questions about her hats—"although she will be receptive to chat about tanks and machine guns"—and to discuss drama rather than football with Prince Charles.

The President's press secretary made it clear that although Mr. and Mrs. Nixon would greet the prince and princess on their arrival, their daughters and son-in-law would be the official hosts at all the functions. The Nixons' younger daughter, Julie, was by then already married to David Eisenhower, grandson of the former President; her elder sister, twenty-four-year-old Tricia, was still unattached. American newspapers quickly began to emulate the speculation of their transatlantic cousins. And soon after his arrival by helicopter on the White House lawn, Prince Charles felt a strong sense of unease that the President was trying to pair him off with his daughter. "My wife and I will keep out of the way," said Nixon, "so that you can really feel at home." Seating plans constantly had Charles and Tricia side by side, while the program had them spending all of each day together, even to being left alone in rooms. Tricia was quick to remind Charles that she had represented her father at his investiture the previous year, where —ironically enough, in view of later events—she had sat next to Princess Marie-Astrid of Luxembourg. The Prince, his sense of his position not receiving its accustomed deference, was distinctly annoyed by the episode. So much so that on his next official visit to the United States, after President Nixon's resignation and disgrace, he was to describe Tricia Nixon with uncharacteristic cruelty as "artificial and plastic." Her sister Julie, by contrast, he had found "a bright, warm personality."

Quite as vivid a memory of that trip was his private chat with President Nixon in the Oval Office. Scheduled to last ten minutes —and on tightly planned royal (let alone presidential) schedules that *means* ten minutes—it went on for eighty, longer than most official state visitors had been granted by the President. Nixon gave Charles a broad account of the world as he then saw it, waxing expansive about his own foreign policy. As the conversation moved on to Anglo-American relations and environment, youth, and population problems, the prince began to give as good as he was getting—all of it, he has assumed since the revelations of the Watergate affair, immortalized on tape. Prince Charles had made "a very good impression," said Nixon, somewhat patronizingly, afterward. "We had a very good talk."

In a recent letter to the author, Mr. Nixon recorded his memories of the meeting:

> His visit came during a very busy period, shortly after I had ordered the attacks on Communist sanctuaries in Cambodia. While my staff had allowed only fifteen minutes for what was supposed to be only a courtesy call, I found him so impressive that I extended it to an hour and a half with the result that we arrived late for a dinner in the residence.
>
> From news accounts in the British and American press I expected to meet a rather callow, superficial youth with no particular interest in or understanding of world affairs. His conduct completely dispelled that image.
>
> He was serious without being dull, dignified without being pompous, respectful without being deferential. We discussed the whole range of East-West relations, NATO, the Third World countries, and the attitude of young people toward government in the US and Britain.
>
> His perception and knowledge with regard to developments in the Commonwealth nations was greater than that of many State Department professionals. Without

crossing the line of interfering in British governmental policies, he expressed agreement with my long-held conviction that Britain must continue to play a role on the world stage—particularly in NATO and in those nations in Africa and Asia where the legacy of the British parliamentary system and the common law is so essential if ordered freedom is to survive.

I told Mrs. Nixon after our meeting that the British and American media greatly underestimated him as a student of world affairs and as a man. . . . Should he some day become King, he will assume that responsibility in the very best tradition of the British Royal Family.

For the rest, it was a cookout at Camp David; visits to assorted museums and monuments, including the now ritual homage at Mount Vernon; a tour of the Capitol building, during which the Senate minority leader, Hugh Scott, said of a gilt mirror on his office wall: "That is the mirror Dolley Madison rescued from the White House when your ancestors were burning it up"; a meeting with Neil Armstrong, first man on the moon; a river trip in the presidential yacht, *Sequoia;* a baseball game; and a "young people's dinner dance" at the White House, where the arrangements decreed that the Prince of Wales would lead off the dancing with Miss Tricia Nixon.

Throughout the three days Prince Charles received ecstatic praise in the American press for his "outgoing nature, his dashing charm, his intelligent interest," while Princess Anne was rapped over the knuckles for appearing "sullen, ungracious, and plain bored" throughout the proceedings. The *New York Times* conceded that she was "a young woman of noted independence," but went on: "She made no effort to conceal a mood of incredulity and vague discomfort." Remarked the Washington *Daily News:* "The prince is full of pep, the princess acts pooped."

Matters were not helped by an incident on the last day, when the royal pair were for some reason taken to the Patuxent Wildlife Refuge, near Washington, to witness the dissection of a bald eagle which had died from organic pesticides. When the prince asked why the bald eagle had been chosen as America's national symbol, Princess Anne remarked that it was "rather a bad choice."

That capped it for the American newspapers. "Something about our national bird," mused the Washington *Post*, "and nobody's quite sure what, was bugging our royal visitors from Great Britain." The princess later explained that she had been upset and irritated by the constant attentions of the press, which her brother had long since learned to take in his stride. "Every time I turn round," she said, "twenty million reporters are on my heels, and I can't get used to it." Nor had she been too pleased by the welcome accorded "England's royal siblings" in the New York *Sunday News.* "Good ole Charley Windsor," it enthused, somewhat mysteriously, was "a young feller who's really as common as a new shoe." Princess Anne, meanwhile, was described as an impatient girl. "She has a 35-25-37 figure and likes to display to good advantage the maximum amount of leg."

After an unusually heavy summer of engagements at home, October 1970 saw the Prince of Wales undertake his first extended foreign tour in his own right. He had been disappointed to miss Tonga on his parents' Commonwealth tour that spring; by way of compensation, the Queen had promised him Fiji, to whose independence celebrations he flew via Bahrain, Singapore, and Darwin on October 8–9. A strong draught of the narcotic local brew, *kava*, greeted his late arrival; as other engagements were canceled, he insisted on driving slowly into the capital, Suva, through the huge crowds that had been waiting for him all day. Next morning, he watched the formal hauling down of the Union Jack, the first of many such ceremonies he would attend in the coming years. In the following week, there was much criticism that the visit had been planned by old-style colonialists, despite its purpose; the prince was rarely able to mingle with the people, spending most of his time sandwiched between dignitaries on platforms. His one moment of relaxation, a fishing trip in a flat-bottomed boat, was marred by a sudden storm whipping up the treacherous South Pacific surf. The prince, drenched to the skin and bailing furiously, was offered a ride ashore by anxious British officials aboard an escort launch, and recorded his first fatherlike "Go to hell."

Five more days amid the Pacific islands, stopovers in Fiji and Tahiti, a night in Acapulco, and he was in Bermuda for the 350th anniversary of the island's parliament. Riots had marked his approach, and the ceremony at which he formally opened the new session was boycotted by the opposition Progressive Labour Party. A British frigate, the *Grenville*, hovered in Hamilton Harbour during the three days of festivities, but the promised demonstrations never materialized. Charles had disarmed many with, in the circumstances, a somewhat risqué joke in his speech to parliament: "Bearing in mind I am the first Charles to have anything to do with a parliament for three hundred and fifty years, I might have turned nasty and dissolved you." And there were, as everywhere, the girls, whose Bermudan greeting was to shower him with pink oleanders.

The only tricky moment of the entire tour came, less expectedly, at his next port of call, Barbados, where the twenty-three-year-old president of the university's student union, Victor Alexis, chose to greet the Prince of Wales with a black power salute. The prince, rather revealingly, did not know what it meant. Alexis kept his right fist clenched, stunning the prince into momentary silence, before grabbing Charles's hand, palms across. "Do you always shake hands like that?" asked his visitor. "This is black power," replied Alexis, who then struck his chest with his clenched fist and raised it aloft again. A government statement next day said that Prince Charles had been "deeply concerned" by his meeting with Alexis, who had apparently told him he was studying law so as to defend "all the black people against all the white people." The twenty-one-year-old prince, who otherwise carried off official duties with grave maturity, had for a moment displayed one of his several chinks of innocent naïveté.

Over the next six years, Prince Charles's service career was to take him many times to various parts of the world, including more independence celebrations in the Bahamas and Papua New Guinea. Apart from a trip via India to Nepal in 1975, for King Birendra's coronation, he made no new landfalls until March 1977, when he had his first extended taste of Africa. His Kenyan safari with Princess Anne in 1971, during which a rhinoceros had menaced him as he lay helpless in his sleeping bag, had left him with a taste for another. Before undertaking official tours of Ghana and the Ivory Coast, therefore, he set off once more into the bush, camera in hand, to emerge ten days later apparently aware of reports that he had taken a "mystery blonde" along with him. They were, alas, untrue; but he was sufficiently amused to present the reporter who had started it all with a home-made stuffed bird, complete with blond wig, labeled "mystery bird."

A few days later he was on official duty again, being installed as Naba Charles Mampasa, honorary chief of Bolgatana, capital of Ghana's remotest and most impoverished region. In the steps of his great-uncle fifty-two years before, he had spent several days paying courtesy calls on tribal chieftains around the country. For those accompanying the prince, staff and journalists, the trip was an arduous mixture of extreme heat and administrative chaos. Developing countries tend to be the most punctilious about royal protocol, while not always the most effective at carrying it out. As the prince's Andover came in to land at Bolgatana's remote airstrip, the commander of the 150-man guard of honor chose to order his men to take up position across the runway. The aircraft had to overshoot and circle again. The Prince of Wales, for once, was not at the controls, though in the copilot's seat beside the then deputy Captain of the Queen's Flight, Squadron Leader Derek Lovett. He asked to be allowed to make the second landing, to avoid causing offense to the embarrassed Ghanaians. Feeling that conditions on the ground remained unpredictable, Lovett (though outranked) brusquely took command and ordered the prince out of the cockpit.

Four days in the Ivory Coast gave the prince another chance to wax lyrical about British exports to an emergent nation with a rapidly developing economy. The fact that President Houphouet-Boigny's ruling Democrat Party, the state's only political party, had distributed flags and costumes bearing the prince's face and transported people into the capital from all over the country only added to the prince's astonishment when more than a million people lined his route into Abidjan from the airport. He repaid the compliment by delivering a stylish impromptu address in their native French.

It was the beginning of a very heavy year of travel. That summer saw him installed, again in a tradition set by his great-uncle, as a Red Indian chieftain by the Kainai tribes of Alberta, Canada. His Royal Highness Prince Red Crow, only recently photographed in the striped robes of an African chieftain, was giving his attendant photographers their best year yet: in full Red Indian regalia, complete with headdress blowing in the wind, he donned warpaint and joined enthusiastically in a Kainai war dance, only to reappear next morning in stetson hat and cow-poke gear, astride a nut-brown nonbucking bronco, to open the Calgary Stampede. By October, he was crossing the United States, taking in eleven cities in twelve days, even by his standards the most arduous schedule he has undertaken. Between his civic reception in Chicago and a gala dinner with the stars in Hollywood (at which he sat between two glamorous TV cops, Angie Dickinson and Farrah Fawcett-Majors), he lost fourteen pounds. He braved Irish demonstrators in San Francisco before flying on to another ten-day swing round Australia, marked mainly by the number of kisses he gave and received. Where American matrons had slyly placed their daughters next to him at interminable dinners, Australian girls simply threw themselves at him. One who greeted him at Adelaide airport, and made sure her revealing T-shirt was not obscured from the cameras when she launched her lips at his, turned out to be a blue movie star.

Nineteen seventy-eight brought pastures new. In March he visited Brazil for the first time, and consolidated his reputation as a dancer by joining in a samba with almost hysterical enthusiasm. His party had reached Rio too late for the Mardi Gras carnival, so a minicarnival was specially staged for the prince's benefit in the grounds of the mayor's residence. After watching from a balcony as the exotic throng threaded its way round and round the residence garden, the prince came down to dance in his tuxedo with a young Brazilian female in a few slithers of silver tinsel and little else.

He was able to enjoy some polo with South America's finest players—and a secret night out at São Paulo's top nightclub, the Hippopotamus—before flying on for a rather more staid few days in Venezuela. At his departure point from Brazil, Manaus, he found himself, by complete coincidence, in the same hotel as Lord Snowdon, returning from a photographic assignment for the *Sunday Times* magazine. It was a time of high speculation about Snowdon's marriage to Princess Margaret, which was to end in divorce before the year was out. The two friends had a drink in the prince's suite, but it was not thought appropriate for them to be seen dining together.

The year ended, just before the prince's thirtieth birthday, with his first visit to a Communist country: an easy initiation in nonaligned Yugoslavia, at the invitation of President Tito, a particularly close friend of the British royal family. The tour was remarkably low-key, as Communist states do not announce such visitors in advance. But Prince Charles had a chance to explore the Adriatic coast, visiting those very fleshpots where King Edward VIII had taken his famous cruise on the *Nahlin* with Mrs. Simpson. Over a lavish lunch at the president's Adriatic retreat, Tito gave Charles an elder statesman's rundown on the state of the nation. The prince, according to those present, "gave as good as he got."

With a visit to NATO and SHAPE headquarters in Brussels and long tours of Australia and India in 1979, the Prince of Wales approached the 1980s a seasoned ambassador for his country, more than capable of carrying off the ritual diplomacy required of him. It was not always thus.

Visiting the Wellesley estate in Spain in 1972, he had admired the Moorish Palace of the Alhambra in Granada rather too much. "It's so marvelous," he said, "I can't understand why tourists don't take it away stone by stone," prompting a Spanish politician to remind him: "The prince should remember how his countrymen carried off another Spanish stone, a rather larger one called the Rock of Gibraltar." Before visiting the Arctic in 1975, he said he was "off to rub a few noses," causing predictable offense to his Eskimo hosts. He has since learned that of such asides are diplomatic incidents born, and has grown ever more cautious in the supposedly off-the-record cocktail parties thrown for the journalists accompanying him.

It is another of the frustrations of his position that such vigilance must be exercised. But his last few foreign sorties, into more exotic and controversial lands, have also made him more aware of other limitations to his role. There were fewer opportunities than he had hoped for trade initiatives, even fortuitous, cosmetic ones such as that in Brazil. There was a growing frustration about his political muzzle: in Brazil he could say nothing about human rights, in Yugoslavia he could make no public comment on his first glimpse of life according to Karl Marx. There was also a growing sense of isolation: in Rio he had to view Copacabana beach from his hotel room, in Split he could not join his staff for an early morning swim in the Adriatic. To travel abroad with the Prince of Wales is to see more of the restrictions than the perks of his job. He may not have to worry about air connections and lost baggage, but neither can he drown such worries in a few gin slings beside the hotel pool.

As he grows into middle age, swaps his youthful glamour for domestic stability, adds substance and *gravitas* to his young intelligence, such disadvantages should evaporate. His skill at present is to duck political questions; in time it will be to answer them in broad humanitarian tones. As he learns more of international commerce, of which his current notions are at best sketchy, he will add more than his mere presence to British markets overseas. When he travels abroad as king, it is already clear that he will want more positive duties than looking at things and being looked at. He shows all the promise with which Edward VIII excited his countrymen as Prince of Wales, and all the conscientiousness which Edward turned out to lack. The 1970s, abroad as elsewhere, have been his training ground.

18

The Social Worker

"I believe it best to confine myself to three basic aims at the start: to show concern for people, to display interest in them as individuals, and to encourage them in a whole host of ways."

ON JUNE 15, 1977, at the height of Elizabeth II's Silver Jubilee celebrations, the Prince of Wales paid a visit to the Moonshot youth center in the heart of South London's slumland. It was to be a routine inspection of the kind of place that might receive a grant from the Silver Jubilee appeal, of which the prince was chairman. But twenty-four black youths from the Lewisham area had recently been arrested on mugging charges, and Moonshot members were among a group of antipolice demonstrators who greeted the prince's arrival. As he stepped from the royal Rolls, his eye fell first on one of the noisiest young protesters, who sported a lapel badge declaring "Stuff the Jubilee."

Not for the first time in his life, Prince Charles decided against the soft option of walking straight past. "I must go across and see them," he said, to counterprotests from his staff and police escort. The prince headed straight for the lapel badge, whose owner turned out to be Kim Gordon, secretary of the Committee to Free the Lewisham 24, and a full-time official of Flame, the black section of the Socialist Workers Party. Gordon recounted the group's grievances against the police, and the prince called over Commander Douglas Randall, head of P Division of the Metropolitan Police, whose men had made the original arrests.

A small, somewhat tense conference ensued, which the prince cut short by declaring: "Well, I'm sure there's some truth on both sides. Couldn't you come together and discuss it?"

Next day he was in trouble. The Prince of Wales had intervened in a matter which was *sub judice*. Some police voices told him, in effect, to mind his own business; Kim Gordon blithely accused him of naïveté. But a meeting *was* held, a week later at Buckingham Palace, at which Commander Randall got together with youth and community leaders from the area for a discussion chaired by the prince himself. Those involved testify that a great deal of good emerged. Tension in the Lewisham area was eased and more regular meetings organized. Justice, naturally, proceeded on its due course: in time, nineteen of the youths were brought to trial and all were convicted, seven having pleaded guilty. The Moonshot Club itself, meanwhile, benefited in unexpected ways.

It began to receive a series of cash grants from the Prince's Trust, with which it has improved facilities and been able to attract many more young members in an area notoriously short of such meeting places. The club remains in regular communication with the prince, by way of the reports its members send him about how they have used the money. Before that day in June 1977, few people in Lewisham knew of the existence of the Prince's Trust. To this day many more all over Great Britain still don't. It is one of four charitable organizations to which the prince devotes a great deal of his time, and one of two which he has himself set up. They receive very little publicity: typically, his intervention that morning outside the Moonshot Club was front-page news the following day, while the subsequent follow-up work was never reported. A huge central chunk of his time and interest, which he regards as perhaps his most valuable work as Prince of Wales, has hitherto gone more or less totally unrecorded.

The Moonshot incident was perhaps evidence of a certain naïveté, as the prince had laid himself open to charges of manipulation by a revolutionary political group. He had also, from the police's point of view, publicly helped undermine their authority in an already very difficult operational area. But it was greater evidence of deep-seated good intent. The prince's concern for deprived and disadvantaged youth, especially ethnic minorities, was well-known privately, but in public was evidenced by little more

than rather bland and innocent Lord Bountiful–like pronouncements. In fact, for several years, Prince Charles had already been
organizing practical assistance for many such groups all over the
country—and most of them had never known where the money
was coming from.

One afternoon in December 1972 George Pratt, deputy chief
probation officer for London, was surprised to receive a telephone
call from Buckingham Palace. Pratt had been making a series of
TV and radio appearances to launch a new scheme of community
service for young people in trouble with the law; on the line was
David Checketts, to say that the Prince of Wales had seen one of
his broadcasts and was wondering if there was anything he could
do to help.

Pratt was flattered but dubious. As a professional, he knew
that any new community service schemes tended to complicate
existing ones, and that layer after layer of bureaucracy had to be
consulted, informed, cajoled, and convinced before new projects
could be launched. He would, he said, think it over and come
back with a suggestion. A month later, he had organized a discussion meeting at Buckingham Palace.

Around the table were representatives of the probation service, the church, the social services, welfare organizations, and the
police. From the chair the prince, just twenty-four, made an impassioned speech about Gordonstoun and Kurt Hahn, mountain
and air-sea rescue work; he said how impressed he had been by
young army NCOs taking on responsibilities beyond their years.
Surely there was some role the heir to the throne could play in
helping disadvantaged or delinquent youth?

More study meetings were organized and the group, as Pratt
had feared, grew larger. It was thought prudent to co-opt officials
from the Department of Education, the Home Office, social scientists, representatives of the Welsh and Scottish Offices. Prince
Charles was gently steered away from all notions of traditional
youth work, with which it was thought he should not be seen to
interfere. Nor was an incentive scheme like his father's, the Duke
of Edinburgh's Awards, deemed appropriate. That was designed
to inspire the already motivated to greater heights of accomplishment; Pratt was anxious that any scheme to be launched in the
prince's name should somehow motivate the unmotivated.

But was it to be in the prince's name? The prince thought

not, even when large initial cash donations were made by the Drapers Company and one anonymous individual (who because of the intense secrecy surrounding his or her identity is thought to be someone very close to Prince Charles). The royal involvement was therefore kept under wraps when the first few trial projects got under way.

The police and probation services teamed up to find groups of wayward youngsters who could be persuaded, by small cash grants, to do something useful within their community. A local policeman from Cornwall reported that a group of reprobate kids were plaguing his life: if they formed themselves into a lifesaving team, they were told to their astonishment, the police would pay all the necessary fares and expenses. They did so; and they were made to feel that the initiative had been their own, with the police servicing rather than supervising them.

In London, a group of school dropouts who had been before the juvenile courts expressed a wish to go camping. The request filtered back through the system. They were given £37.50 to cover their rail fares. Buckingham Palace obtained a tent and some pots and pans from the army, and their teacher lent them a camera. A few weeks later an illustrated account of the expedition turned up on Prince Charles's desk, with the news that they were all back at school. He also learned that a young South London gang of bicycle thieves had undergone a miraculous transformation into a bicycle-repair unit.

The prince was in mid-naval career at the time, but every application for a grant was sent to him in the diplomatic bags which pursued him around the world. He would return them all to Pratt, with copious comments scribbled in the margin. As the scheme got going, the reports filed by enthusiastic teenagers were also sent on to him. He personally selected all the original beneficiaries and followed their progress through the system. Few of them knew who it was that had helped them. But after the scheme had been going nearly three years, word had begun to get around. Shoals of letters began arriving at the palace thanking him for what he was doing.

This put him in something of a dilemma when it was decided, in the spring of 1976, to regularize the aid program into a charitable trust. Prince Charles was still against the use of his name, while keen on remaining actively involved. But Pratt's views had changed. Now that the prince had begun meeting groups of youngsters who had received money from the trust, he could see the effect of the royal presence on the enthusiasm with which they went about things. Charles was serving on HMS *Hermes* in mid-Atlantic when a decision had to be made. After a long discussion on the ship-to-shore phone he told Pratt: "Okay, let's call it the Prince's Trust."

The Queen's permission was obtained to use as the Trust's motif his personal insignia—the large letter C which would have been his emblem had he not been Prince of Wales. Regional committees were established in the seven areas where he had titular connections, which gave a satisfying spread around London and England, Wales, Scotland, and Northern Ireland. Bishops, chief constables, youth and social services directors, probation officers and police were co-opted to run them. Three years later, early in 1979, there were fifteen regional committees, and the prince hopes that his Trust will eventually cover the whole of the country. All those who coordinate its work, including the director of the Prince's Trust, George Pratt, are voluntary, unpaid workers.

By 1978, some £35,000 was being distributed each year to about 250 separate projects. At the prince's wish, applicants are not usually given the entire sum they request, but a percentage of the total as an incentive to raise the rest. The Trust smiles with special favor on original or innovative ideas: one group, for instance, has developed a new type of two-seater canoe, in which the ablebodied can take handicapped people for river rides, even shooting rapids. Prince Charles makes a point of including a visit to Trust beneficiaries in every regional tour he makes around Britain. After a fund-raising carol concert in Westminster Cathedral during Christmas 1978, he said his farewells and made his formal departure through the main door, then slipped back in through a side entrance to talk for ninety minutes to young Londoners who had undertaken projects with money from the Trust.

Also in 1978 he was asked to become patron of Operation Drake, a two-year circumnavigation of the globe by 250 young people from all over the world in a British barquentine, *Eye of the Wind*. The prince is patron of many organizations, but does not like to be merely a name on a letterhead. He turns down all such requests unless there is an active role he can play. The only reason, for instance, he made his second parachute jump that same year was that he had just become colonel-in-chief of the Parachute Regiment, and felt he should do something to merit the title. When approached by Operation Drake, he laid down conditions. He would lend his support if the organizers would allot four places to disadvantaged children. Most young people on the voyage were being sponsored, at considerable expense, by their parents, their firms, or other charitable organizations; the costs of maintaining the ship, and flying children around the world to join it for their three months on board, were not likely to attract the underprivileged. As a result of Prince Charles's stand, four young people who had been before the magistrates courts—including a member of the Moonshot Youth Club—were taken onto the strength of Operation Drake.

By stipulating that all applicants must be under twenty-five, that grants would be made only to individuals rather than to organizations, and that those individuals must have no other prospect of assistance, the Prince's Trust established new ground rules in the often muddled world of the social services. Prince Charles himself also tried to see to it—though it could not, of course, be laid down as a condition—that the majority of grants were made to young people who had found themselves brought before juvenile or magistrates courts. For him, as for many who worked with him, it was a new direction, which he attempted to promote publicly in his second speech in the House of Lords. Not a single newspaper noticed what was really rather a good story.

In his maiden speech to the Lords, in June 1974, the prince had made an impassioned plea for more government money to be spent on the nation's leisure time—"to remove the dead hand of boredom and frustration from mankind." He called specifically for the appointment of a Minister of Leisure, to expand the responsibilities of the newly designated Minister of Sport. Because it was his maiden speech, the text was widely quoted; but because it was a familiar theme, royalty harping on about how people should make better use of their off-duty hours, it was quickly forgotten. Two years later he returned to the same theme in the House, and announced in the process that he had been raising money to promote recreational activities for those who might otherwise drift into crime. The formation of the Prince's Trust—a unique event in recent royal history—was specifically mentioned. But few readers of the official text got beyond his first few paragraphs on good intentions and worthy royal works.

Even in Jubilee Year, when Prince Charles expanded these activities as chairman of the Silver Jubilee Appeal, few really grasped what was going on. He launched the Appeal with a television and radio broadcast from Chevening, put out on all channels and watched by the majority of the nation. As usual the words Outward Bound, air-sea rescue, and other such appeals to hairy-chested idealism, showing once again the royal family's great dependence on the precepts of Kurt Hahn, proved a huge turn-off. The prince's speech, even so, had been rewritten; the original version was even more remote from popular values, with lofty sentences about the joys of service and of the great outdoors, and had been gingerly thrown back at him by the Appeal's youth committee. The prince's staff were horrified by such highhandedness, but the prince himself was more than willing to listen. David Checketts attempted to intervene as one hapless committee member, delegated by less courageous colleagues, told the prince what was thought of his draft. "No, it's my bloody speech," he told Checketts, "let them say what they want." They suggested a new version, which he asked them to draft. He inserted his own familiar personal touches, and the compromise version was the one eventually broadcast.

Then came the euphoria of summer 1977, the street parties around the nation, the memories that communities had never felt so united since the Blitz. In May 1978, in the Music Room of Buckingham Palace, the prince was able to announce that more than £16 million had been raised—an astounding sum from a nation of only 56 million people. Almost half a million pounds had been sent to Prince Charles personally at Buckingham Palace, in grubby £1 and £5 notes—much of it from people who could scarcely afford the price of the stamp. The money would go, at the Queen's request, "to help young people help others."

In 1935 Edward, Prince of Wales, had launched a similar scheme to mark the silver jubilee of his father, King George V. "For Youth" was the simple slogan of that campaign, which raised £1 million from a country in the grip of the depression. In 1978 the two funds united, under the joint name of the Royal Jubilee Trusts, with Prince Charles as chairman of the adminis-

trative council. Their joint investment income yields almost
£1 million a year for distribution to youth and community projects—with every application again personally examined by the
Prince of Wales, in the chair at grants meetings four times a year.

The work of the Jubilee Trusts had to be distinguished from
that of the Prince's Trust. With their much larger resources, the
Jubilee Trusts began to make grants to larger-scale, continuing
projects, while the Prince's Trust continued to assist small, one-
shot bursts of individual idealism. Even so, the largest single grant
made by the Jubilee Trusts was of £20,000 to the Trident Trust,
an organization that provides industrial training for young people who might otherwise never have such a chance. Most grants
are much smaller, and at the prince's request go primarily to
help ethnic minorities, to assist those from broken or deprived
homes, to combat urban violence and vandalism, and to improve
life on large, bleak housing estates. Heady ideals indeed, with
which the government's social services departments had been
struggling for years. But the Prince of Wales believes the Trusts,
by concentrating as much as possible on specific, well-argued applications from individuals, provide a valuable support to the
state-financed projects they complement.

Elizabeth II's Silver Jubilee Year has thus had some bizarre
repercussions. Few Londoners realize that the murals painted on
the vast concrete wastes beneath their urban motorways, designed
and executed by teenagers in their spare time, were financed by
the Royal Jubilee Trusts. One group was granted money for a collection of tandems, on which the sighted have been able to take
blind people for bicycle rides. A Derbyshire family received £100
to buy musical instruments, with which they have formed a
cabaret act to tour old people's homes.

"Let's help young blacks," said Prince Charles to the Jubilee
Trusts' director, Harold Haywood, after his Moonshot experience.
"Let's help the young help the old. All that goes without saying.
But do you think there's anything we can do to help in Northern
Ireland?" Haywood went to see. The Prince of Wales, to his cha-
grin, was prevented by the security services from going himself.
But after he had considered a number of ideas, money was pro-
vided for such items as the purchase of a seaside holiday home, to
be shared by Protestant and Catholic children.

When the Trusts had taken over the Jubilee Appeal's work,

still under the chairmanship of the Prince of Wales, there had been criticism that the membership of executive committees was too old and mandarin. The prince thought the criticism justified, and began to make his own appointments. Black faces, at last, began to appear at meetings discussing the problems of black youth. A friend of the prince's from his undergraduate days at Trinity wrote to offer his services; he had now become a social worker and would be happy to do what he could. The prince asked for a discreet check—"You can never," he told George Pratt, "be too careful"—and Anthony Kerwin became a valued committee member of both the Prince's Trust and the Jubilee Trusts, adding a touch more youth to the proceedings. Other younger people, from industry, public relations, the police, and local government, were pleasantly surprised to be asked, after chance meetings with Prince Charles, to join the work of the Jubilee Trusts.

Both enterprises are now launched to last beyond the prince's lifetime, and officials of each expect his contributions to continue as long. Across in Wales the same hopes are held by the staff of the Prince of Wales' Committee, the third of his charitable pre-occupations, and the second he has himself initiated and developed.

In 1968, two years before European Conservation Year, the Prince of Wales agreed to be chairman of the Welsh steering committee. In this role, in Cardiff on December 10, 1968, he took the chair of a meeting for the first time in his life, and made his first public speech. The nation was faced, he told the Countryside in 1970 Conference, with "the horrifying effects of pollution in all its cancerous forms." The cost of many conservation exercises was "fiendish." But the cost of inaction might be even greater. He took the opportunity to announce the Prince of Wales Countryside Award, green and white metal plaques to mark individual enterprise in protecting the environment: "They had great trouble trying to design something which is vandal-proof. I am told that if anyone tries to shoot airgun pellets or .22 bullets at this, they will ricochet back and clobber them."

Throughout 1969, the year of Aberystwyth and his investiture, the prince encouraged conservation work during his progress around Wales. By the end of 1970, the year of internationally coordinated efforts, a great deal had been done, and a great many projects begun which suddenly faced extinction. Prince Charles announced that he was forming a new environmental committee to carry on the good work, to be known as the Prince of Wales' Committee—or, perhaps more appropriately, Pwyllgor Tywysog Cymru. Its chairman would continue to be Ei Uchelder Brenhinol Tywysog Cymru, KG KT PC GCB.

For a decade now, the Prince of Wales' Committee, operating on similar lines to the Prince's and Jubilee Trusts, has raised money, invested it, and awarded grants to conservation schemes around the principality. Many, as again decreed and personally selected by the prince, are small-scale projects dearly cherished by local communities: schoolboys marking out a town trail through the urban wasteland of Splott, in Cardiff; a historic oak tree saved from the encroaching sea by a new sea wall at Picton Ferry, near Haverfordwest; duckboards laid across a marshy footpath by children from Pontypridd comprehensive-school; the conversion of disused railway lines into footpaths and picnic sites; the rescue of the Great Western Railway signal box at Penmaenpool from demolition, and its conversion into an information center and observation post for the Royal Society for the Protection of Birds. A group of secondary-school children researched the history of a Napoleonic War cannon and built a carriage for it, after the prince himself had airlifted it by helicopter from an inaccessible hilltop. In Aberfan, the mining community devastated by a coal-tip collapse in 1966, the Prince of Wales' Committee joined forces with the World Council of Churches to sponsor an international work camp, whose members—of many different nationalities and creeds—landscaped the derelict sites left by the disaster. Prince Charles and the Committee's director, Brian Lymbery, have persuaded the Variety Club of Great Britain to raise £400,000 toward their most ambitious project: the complete restoration of the abandoned Montgomery Canal. The first three miles of one of Wales's most pleasant waterways has already been reopened to small craft and barges. High up Snowdon, meanwhile, volunteers funded by the committee restored unsafe paths and rebuilt a causeway across a mountain lake, shortening the emergency rescue route by more than two miles.

With these three home-based charities steaming ahead on full throttle, the Prince of Wales in 1978 spread his philanthropic wings much farther afield. His great-uncle, Lord Mountbatten, was retiring as president of the United World Colleges, a group of multinational, multiracial sixth form colleges around the world, in whose foundation a major role had been played by the inevitable Kurt Hahn. A non-profit-making, charitable organization, it aspires to develop world understanding by breaking down racial prejudice and national barriers—another time-honored ideal, and a daunting one. But by simply implementing Hahn's thesis, that prejudices evaporate in disciplined communities facing constant challenges and occasional stress, the UWC system aims to raise generations of "multipliers" to spread the gospel through the world.

Students at the three colleges already established in Wales, Singapore, and Canada have been drawn from more than 120 countries. Some 1,750 sixth-formers nominated and financed by their governments are already in the system at any one time—350 at the United World College of the Atlantic, at St. Donat's Castle in South Glamorgan; 200 at the Lester B. Pearson College of the Pacific in Victoria, British Columbia; and 1,200 at the United World College of South East Asia in Singapore. A two-year residential course leads to the International Baccalaureate, an exam pioneered by these three colleges, now used in more than one hundred schools around the world and accepted by four hundred universities including Oxford, Cambridge, the Sorbonne, and the United States "Ivy League." A broad-based diploma, it covers six areas of specialization—from math, languages, and literature to the arts, the experimental sciences, and the study of man.

By contrast, no entrance exam is required. Students are selected by interview, on academic merit and "personal qualities." Family or financial circumstances are irrelevant. No one can buy his way into a United World College, although the members of the international committee are aware of charges that they are out to produce a worldwide elite. They prefer the term "meritocracy," which is their unashamed aspiration. The Prince of Wales—a little disappointed that Gordonstoun has not abandoned the standard state exams for the International Baccalaureate—expressed as he became president "a really deep and personal conviction of the intrinsic merits of the UWC concept."

He now devotes a great deal of his time abroad to promoting it. It is no exaggeration to say that he has specifically convened meetings of former UWC students in every country he has visited since 1977. Plans are now afoot to establish United World Col-

leges in Italy (near Trieste), India, and the Bahamas. Negotia-
tions with the government of Iran were well advanced when the
fall of the shah early in 1979 forced their abandonment. Longer-
term goals include adapting existing schools to the system in
Africa and South America.

When Prince Charles visited Venezuela in March 1978, he
spent some time touring regional farms and agricultural plants,
where the constant complaint—the kind of localized special pleading all too familiar to royal ears—was the lack of training opportunities in a country so dependent on the land. The prince had already had his statutory meeting with the president, Carlos Andres
Perez, but now he asked for another. He spent some time explain-
ing the UWC ideals before offering the president a bargain: You
put up the money for an agricultural college, and we will help
import international experts and a proportion of non-Venezuelan
pupils. Thus Venezuela would not only become agriculturally
streamlined, but house an international center of research and development. Within a year, and despite a change of government in
Venezuela, initial agreements had been signed by agriculture
ministers on both sides.

Before the prince undertakes any foreign visits these days,
the director-general of the United World Colleges, Sir Ian Gourlay, will brief him on UWC connections in the area. If there is no
college to visit or proposal to advance, there will be a network of
ex-pupils with whom a meeting will be arranged. The same is
true of his three British-based trusts. The director of each receives
the prince's monthly schedules and looks for chances to advance
activities in the areas to be visited. Immense sheafs of paper flow
between their offices and the palace: applications for grants or college places, reports on work completed, minutes of meetings, ideas
for fund-raising activities and promotional speeches. The prince
likes to see to this work himself. Each of the four directors is a
regular caller at Buckingham Palace.

But none of these visits appears in the Court Circular. It is
impossible to compute the amount of time Prince Charles devotes
to his "social work," but it must consume something approaching
one-third of his working hours. And yet, he complained consistently in the late 1970s, after leaving the services most of the nation thought he hadn't got a job. Very few, moreover, were aware
of the existence of these charities, or at least of his connection with

them. In February 1979, when the author was in the offices of the Prince's Trust, its director received a telephone call from the Home Office. The Home Secretary had to go to Wales, to present some Prince of Wales' Awards, and "he hadn't a clue what the hell they were." He hadn't even managed to telephone the right place.

Two particular achievements satisfy the Prince of Wales. A Glasgow hoodlum, straightened out by community work financed by the Prince's Trust, has now become a Glasgow policeman; and another young offender, who has been working for the mentally handicapped, hopes soon to join the executive committee of one of the prince's charities. This kind of activity does not always make for exciting reading, which is why it will probably continue to go largely unpublicized, but the Prince of Wales regards it as perhaps his most important work so far. Many a previous heir apparent would have preferred other ways of spending his time.

Prince Charles's ideal accomplishment, while he remains Prince of Wales, would be to rescue a young dropout from the juvenile courts, give him some money to start a youth club, finance him to save a few lives at sea or up mountains, award him a plaque for greening the Welsh landscape, educate him at a United World College, and appoint him to the staff of the Prince's or Jubilee Trust. It may yet happen; but if it does, we'll probably never hear.

19

The Prince and the Press

"It's when nobody wants to write about you or take a photograph of you that you ought to worry in my sort of job. Then there'd be no great point in being around."

I T IS NOVEMBER 14, 1978, the Prince of Wales's thirtieth birthday, and he is cutting a large cake in the unlikely setting of a London clothing store, surrounded by civic dignitaries, shop assistants, journalists, and tailor's dummies. From outside in Regent Street, whose Christmas lights he has just switched on, the cheers of a large, lingering crowd waft gently in through the windows. As he samples his cake, the prince spots a familiar journalist, responsible for one of the weekend's many birthday assignments. "Liked your piece on Sunday," he calls out. "But did you see the *Sunday Telegraph?*" It had said he possessed a squint. "I knew my eyes were close together, but not as close as that."

The Prince of Wales is an avid reader of his own press cuttings. Which is saying something, for he can confidently be declared one of the most consistently publicized men in the world. Prime ministers and presidents come and go, sports and show biz stars have their hour, but a prince is a prince from cradle to throne, when the attentions of the press are scarcely likely to diminish. For once, it is true to say that everything he does makes news. He doesn't in fact, even have to *do* anything; a picture of Prince Charles in the most everyday pose—entering a building, shaking a hand, unveiling a plaque, leaving a building—will normally make the British press. His daily movements are chronicled in the Court Circular. If he has a cold, it rates a front-page paragraph in the *Times* and the *Telegraph*. He sells newspapers.

So it may seem surprising that he has only one press secretary—and a diplomat at that, rather than a professional public relations man. The assistant press secretary to the Queen (at the time of writing, John Dauth, an Australian) handles press liaison for both Prince Charles and Prince Philip, with the support of Buckingham Palace's small but efficient press office. It is a job assigned to a Commonwealth diplomat for two years at a time, and the duties are arduous: organizing press facilities at each of the prince's public appearances, dealing with the conflicting demands of short-tempered reporters and photographers, processing countless requests for interviews, photo sessions, accreditation, and sundry other facilities, handling mountains of paperwork on the prince's behalf, sifting fact from fiction when one newspaper's speculations start all the others ringing up. So constant is newspaper attention that the Buckingham Palace press staff are the only members of the royal household to have been issued with "bleepers," which can find them anywhere in London, day or night.

The quality of these diplomat-press officers has fluctuated wildly in recent years, many devoting their energies much more to the suppression than the release of facts. This may be to the liking of the palace, but it is counterproductive in Fleet Street. It is also the reason why one man can control an apparently enormous and complex operation. There is a strictly limited dossier of biographical nuts and bolts he can make available to any journalist new to "Charles watching," but even as he does so he knows it is less than enough. A great deal of the press acreage devoted to the prince is quite simply fabricated, in the certain knowledge that Buckingham Palace very, very rarely issues formal denials. Disraeli's old adage "Never complain, never explain" has, with very rare exceptions, been the royal family's instruction to its press staff. Such a position can lend a certain dignity to the proceedings, but it also leaves royal reputations at the hands of fantasists.

Elizabeth II's unspoken policy on her press, apart from continuing the hallowed tradition that the monarch is above granting personal interviews to anyone, has been to sit back and let the tide of invention, myth, innuendo, and speculation wash over her

"Do stop snivelling, Emma. Prince Charles will even get around to you—the way he's going!"

MEANWHILE, BACK AT THE DAILY EXPRESS...

"The Palace demands to know the source of this scurrilous farrago of lies!"

and her family. There are times it hurts, of course, and there are times a prince's rage has to be contained by a joint effort of family and staff. (Prince Philip was as annoyed as his son by the suggestion that there might be a squint somewhere in the royal genes.) But more often it amuses. The fantastical inventions of the continental press have long since fallen into this category: QUEEN ELIZABETH TO ABDICATE, ELIZABETH AND PHILIP TO SEPARATE, CHARLES PROUD FATHER OF LOVE-CHILD, ANDREW SECRETLY MARRIED, and so on. One of the few jokes on record from Princess Anne dates from a few months after her wedding, when a distinguished French visitor called at the palace. "Am I," she asked him, "divorced yet?" The only British publication which falls into this category is *Private Eye*, the satirical fortnightly magazine, which nicknames the Queen "Brenda," Prince Charles "Brian," and Princess Margaret "Yvonne." Although naughtily enjoyed by many household and domestic staff, *Private Eye*, they will tell you, rarely finds its way "upstairs."

Palace "spokesmen" frequently on their own account dismiss press reports about the prince, but they have lacked some credibility since 1972, when they denied rumors of romance between Princess Anne and Captain Mark Phillips only months before their engagement was announced. Prince Charles has reason still to be angry that such denials were ever issued.

But the "Asty" affair—in which the *Daily Express* "officially" announced Charles's engagement to Princess Marie-Astrid of Luxembourg—remains the only occasion on which the prince has attached his own name to a statement of refutation. It was a particularly vivid error, as the *Express* added the tag OFFICIAL to its headline CHARLES TO MARRY ASTRID, and confidently stated that a palace announcement would be forthcoming the following Monday. But the incident also signaled a period of disenchantment with the British press's unremitting speculation on his marriage prospects. What had been a source of innocent amusement, which he had been at least partly guilty of encouraging, had suddenly become a tedious, rather unbecoming irritant. At the age of twenty-four, after a long summer of rumor about his friendship with Lady Jane Wellesley, he had felt relaxed enough to joke about it when addressing a luncheon of the Parliamentary Press Gallery: "I have read so many reports recently telling everyone whom I am about to marry that when last year a certain young lady was staying at Sandringham a crowd of about ten thousand appeared when we went to church. Such was the obvious conviction that what they had read was true that I almost felt I had better espouse myself at once so as not to disappoint too many people." Two years and countless other rumors later, he had had enough. King Edward VIII, like Prince Charles an unmarried thirty-year-old Prince of Wales, was never subjected to such a barrage of invention and innuendo. If Prince Charles, indeed, were to form a relationship with an American divorcée, it is difficult to imagine contemporary British newspapers agreeing to a conspiracy of silence on the subject.

For one with so many years' experience of the press, the prince's attitude to it is a strange combination of shrewdness and naïveté. He can "use" it quite as cunningly as the most seasoned politician. In July 1978, for instance, he knew full well what would be the effect of his remark to a Salvation Army congress that doctrinal argument among Christians caused "needless distress": a healthy row among churchmen, and a fortnight of letters to the *Times* (under the gratifying headline THE PRINCE AND THE POPE). Coming after Pope Paul's refusal to allow a church wedding to Prince Michael of Kent and his divorced Roman Catholic bride, Baroness Marie-Christine von Reibnitz, the prince's unspecific remark had an immediately specific context. While appearing to make a vague, humanitarian statement, he had in effect attacked the Pope, provoking an argument as much in his own marital interests as those of his cousin. By the end of the week, with Buckingham Palace still expressing blithe surprise on his behalf, the Vatican was accusing the Prince of "sheer impertinence." He meanwhile had cunningly flown himself off to Norway for King Olav's seventy-fifth birthday party, leaving the controversy behind him on automatic pilot.

At the same time, however, he can display a touching innocence of news values. He chose to play down his thirtieth birthday in 1978, instructing his press officer to turn away all requests for interviews, and asking him to promote instead the tenth anniversary in 1979 of his investiture as Prince of Wales—scarcely a news editor's dream. A giveaway trace of vanity meanwhile crept in: as he turned down the personal interviews sought by virtually every British publication, he gave one (albeit written answers to written questions) to *Time* magazine, so pleased was he to be a *Time* cover story. British complaints were loud and not unjustified.

The decision was also a conscious snub to the British press, an indication of the prince's impatience with its preoccupations. Given unremitting public interest, the most trivial details remain the most sought after. In the handful of formal, on-the-record interviews he has given, Prince Charles has refused to answer only one question: "What, if anything, do you wear in bed?" (This seems to be a perennial poser for Princes of Wales; on his return from the United States in 1924, Prince Edward found his father, George V, muttering "Fancy their saying this about you!" as he fingered an American newspaper cutting head-lined OH! WHO'LL ASK H.R.H. WHAT HE WEARS ASLEEP?)

Popular newspapers have been known to devote an entire front page in recent years to an urgent, lavishly illustrated de-bate on whether the Prince of Wales is losing his hair. His weight and chest and waist measurements are kept up to date in a Buckingham Palace file, though he has balked at revealing his inside leg. On one of his recent foreign tours, a red mark on the prince's nose (in fact caused by the sunglasses he wore while flying his airplane) was the subject of heated argument between journalists and the prince's staff for several days. Had he fallen off a horse? No? Then someone must have thumped him? A girl friend . . . ? Attention was diverted only when a four-year-old English girl, held aloft to greet the prince by her proud parents, bit the royal finger. Front page news.

The prince's sourness was understandable. In his late twen-ties, after leaving the navy, he was occupied on more committee work than ever, notably running the Queen's Silver Jubilee Ap-peal, and he was concerned to be seen performing a constructive role. To news editors, of course, this was worthy but dull stuff, not rating a mention unless something went interestingly wrong. To Prince Charles, it was evident denial of those same news-papers' criticisms that since the end of his service career he had been "out of a job." He had already put his view on press "sensa-tionalism," in more general terms, to the parliamentary press gallery: "The press has a responsibility not to let its compara-tive freedom degenerate into cheap sensationalism. I cannot accept the argument that says 'Oh well, it's a sign of the times' or 'We must keep in touch with present trends of readership demand.' That is nonsense, and simply leads to a vicious circle of unnecessary and sometimes dangerous trivia." He had been talking in broad terms of the state of the nations, but now his own arguments were rebounding on himself.

The problem, from the prince's point of view, is that he has always been the property of the so-called "popular" (i.e., mass circulation) press. The "heavier," "quality" newspapers have rarely taken much interest in anything but the most public and respectable aspects of his life. The daily diet of princely trivia has meanwhile become a full-time occupation for several Fleet Street reporters and a full posse of globe-trotting photographers. They are a colorful crew, in whose company it is a pleasure to travel. But they are not always as beloved of Prince Charles as they would like to think.

He enjoys better relations with the press than any other member of his family, largely through force of circumstance: they surround him wherever he goes, more consistently than they do his sister and brothers, more informally than they do his parents. He knows it is in his interests to be affable. Thus those who dog his footsteps receive many a chummy greeting, which can all too quickly go to their heads. Like anyone with a glancing acquaintanceship with royalty, journalists in their cups will set themselves up as intimate friends. At the same time, they grow unduly familiar. The prince dislikes being hailed by photographers as "Charlie"; he likes even less being embarrassed in front of punctilious hosts.

During his tour of Yugoslavia in 1978, the traveling cameramen, denied their accustomed access to the prince by overzealous state authorities, at one point conspicuously laid down their burden. The Prince of Wales had the unnerving experience of entering a building through an arcade of silent photographers, their cameras lying on the ground at their feet. "What's this?" he asked. "You on strike?"

Yes.

"What, *again?*"

Nervous laughter.

"Are you going home then?"

"No, sir. We ain't got no pictures, and we're staying here till we do."

Leaving his press secretary to smooth things over, the prince registered extreme annoyance and felt obliged to apologize to his Yugoslav hosts.

Later that day, a slow news day, he was surrounded by the same posse of now desperate photographers on a bleak, wind-swept Yugoslav hilltop. The scene of a famous resistance by Second World War partisans, the peak was capped by a bizarre contemporary sculpture, shapeless, ineffable, with whose creator the prince was engaging in polite, if halting, conversation. "Is it," he asked rather desperately, "made of concrete or stone?" As the sculptor's reply wound its way through the interpreter, up piped a photographer: "No, it's made of polystyrene, and it's gonna blow off that cliff in a moment." General hilarity, except on the part of the prince. The sculptor was offended, and Queen Victoria's great-great-great-grandson was not amused.

Such episodes are a measure of the extreme seriousness with which he takes his role as the Queen's representative overseas. They are also a measure of his complete impotence in the face of the handful of men and women who are responsible for his public reputation. They are a motley crew, constantly in dispute about the prince's attitude to each of them, more than usually jealous of any scrap of information any of them turns up. The reporter who has chased Prince Charles more devotedly and more outlandishly than any other is James Whitaker of the London Express group's new newspaper, the *Star*, formerly of Rupert Murdoch's London *Sun*. He also writes for other publications under the name of Jeremy Slazenger; it was Whitaker, for in-stance, who reported the prince's 1978 skiing holiday with Lady Sarah Spencer for the *Sun*, Slazenger who interviewed Lady Sarah for a women's magazine. Since 1974, the majority of Whitaker's life has been spent in royal pursuit, staked out for weeks on end around Sandringham dale or Balmoral glen in the certain knowledge that sooner or later the prince will come his way. Whitaker is a fine distillation of British attitudes to the heir to the throne: he is a passionate monarchist—believing, for in-stance, that the prince was guilty of dereliction of duty for fail-ing to marry by his thirtieth birthday—and at the same time con-siders it his right to make every possible invasion of the prince's privacy. If challenged by a member of the royal staff, he will say his duty to his family comes before his duty to his queen. He is, unsurprisingly, not the prince's favorite journalist (though it should be said he strives heroically for accuracy). One advantage in such a life, which Whitaker is fond of quoting, is that there is no law of trespass in Scotland. This did not help him and his photographer, Arthur Edwards, at Balmoral in the summer of 1978, when they clandestinely watched the prince corner a stag he had been stalking for a week. Up popped Edwards' camera, and off popped the stag. As the royal gillie saw the offenders off the estate, Edwards attempted to make amends. "I think I've got a *picture* of the stag, if that might be of any consolation to His Royal Highness?" The gillie's answer is not on record.

A prince must expect such occupational hazards. Wind-surfing off Cowes the same summer, Prince Charles afforded newspaper readers and television viewers much innocent enjoyment by falling into the gray, cold briny several times. Only those present could know that a launch hired by two photographers from national newspapers had hugged him so closely, criss-crossing his path several times, that their wake was bound to sink him. Whether or not this was deliberate—it certainly made for better pictures—is a matter for the photographers' consciences. The Prince of Wales knows what he thinks. His press secretary refused the request of one of the offenders for accreditation to the prince's next overseas tour; he turned up all the same, under a different name.

Given such harassment, Prince Charles is remarkably long-suffering. He has taken trouble to find out how newspapers work, and has a shrewd understanding of what those familiar faces around him are after. "I look at it from the newspaperman's point of view; he's got a job to do—I've got a job to do. At times they happen to coincide, and compromise must occur, otherwise misery can so easily ensue. I try to put myself in their shoes, and I hope they try to put themselves in mine, although I appreciate that is difficult." He has never, like his father, turned a hose on the press, and only rarely, like his sister, shouted abuse. But he defends her for that: "If you are doing something competitive in public, especially in the top international class, you are inevitably keyed up. To have a lot of people with cameras pursuing you, and possibly frightening the horse, is annoying to say the least; and it is easy to become irritable and to feel that it is only when things go wrong and you fall off that the gentlemen of the press are interested, that it is only when you are upside down or halfway up a tree that photographs appear in the papers or on TV."

The prince's most spirited escapade dates from 1964—between the Cherry Brandy Incident and the Affair of the Missing Exercise Book, a time when his view of newspapers might justifiably have been a trifle jaundiced. The fifteen-year-old prince, during the school holidays from Gordonstoun, was in Athens for the wedding of his cousin King Constantine (to Princess Anne-Marie of Denmark, one of the eligible Europeans the British press had lined up for its own prince). After the ceremony he and Princess Anne, with some of their German cousins and Crown Prince (now King) Carl Gustaf of Sweden, were sunbathing on rafts at the Astor Club in the nearby resort of Vouliagmeni. Greek naval police, patrolling in paddleboats, formed a protective cordon, but three French photographers managed to pick their way through and approach the young royals. What happened next has been analyzed in some detail by previous biographers, as next morning the French newspapers exploded with indignation that their staff had been ducked by "precocious sprigs of British and Swedish royalty." The truth of the matter is that it was one of Prince Charles's cousins who won the race to the enemy raft and helped its already lopsided load—cameras and all—into the water. But the Prince of Wales was not far behind, and still wishes he had got there first.

His early youth was regularly punctuated by such moments of unwelcome attention, at a time when he was least able to cope with it. The Duke of Windsor wrote of his own childhood:

> I recall with wonder and appreciation the ease with which we were able to move about in public places. The thought occurs to me that one of the most inconvenient developments since the days of my boyhood has been the disappearance of privacy. I grew up before the age of the flash camera, when newspapers still employed large staffs of artists to depict the daily events with pen sketches. This artistic form of illustration seldom achieved the harsh or cruel accuracy of the camera lens, nor could it match the volume and mobility of the present-day photographer dogging his unsuspecting victim or waiting in ambush for a candid shot. Because our likenesses seldom appeared in the press, we were not

often recognized on the street; when we were, the salutation would be a friendly wave of the hand or, in the case of a courtier or family friend, a polite lifting of the hat.

Compare that to Prince Charles's own childhood, when his nannies were forced to abandon their walks around St. James's Park because of the attentions of photographers and sightseers. Or to the prince's Bavarian skiing holiday in January 1963, when the *Weekly Tribune* of Geneva wrote: "It was like a snow scene from a Keystone Cops movie, as impatient voices bawled suggestions in English, French, Italian, and German, their cars revving madly, wheels spinning, as they leaped, slithered, and bumped into each other in a frantic race for the best positions behind the speeding sleighs." When finally cornered, the young prince deftly turned his own 35mm camera on the exhausted and disheveled photographers, thus effectively obscuring his own face.

Such scenes are now a commonplace to him, although his detective and his press secretary would these days be likely to insist on some vestige of order and decorum. (Royal reporters have recently taken to preceding Prince Charles on his now annual January visit to Klosters so that they can take some skiing lessons. He skis so fast, indeed so recklessly—in January 1979 he badly bruised his thigh, then declared "We Britons must ski on"— that they reckon they need to approach competition standards to have a hope of keeping up.) Given the competitive nature of journalism, it is from such attempts at keeping order that the worst chaos usually develops. A happy exception was the prince's tour of the Northwest Territories of Canada in 1975, when the ordeal of pursuit through such arduous terrain led the press corps to compose a song for the prince, complaining about the difficulties of keeping up with him "across the ice floes." Next day Prince Charles, his equerry, his private secretary, and his detective performed a ditty he had written himself, appropriately enough to the Welsh hymn tune "Immortal Invisible":

Impossible, unapproachable, God only knows
The light's always dreadful and he won't damn well pose,
Most maddening, most curious, he simply can't fail,
It's always the same with the old Prince of Wales.

Insistent, persistent, the press never end,
One day they will drive me right round the bend,
Recording, rephrasing every word that I say:
It's got to be news at the end of the day.

Disgraceful, most dangerous to share the same plane,
Denies me the chance to scratch and complain.
Oh where may I ask you is the monarchy going
When princes and pressmen are in the same Boeing?

Those journalists who regularly shadow Prince Charles believe he has a moral duty to give them every facility. There is a general feeling that something of the royal presence brushes off on the royal press: it is unseemly to be scrambling and fighting for position, as is always the way, on so smart an assignment. Despite such good-natured episodes as the prince's "witty ditty" (his own name for it), the relationship has grown more tense of late. Especially on tour abroad, where press and prince are often cheek by jowl in the same hotel, if not the same Boeing, he feels a constant need to withdraw; and the accompanying press corps tend to resent this rather than understand it. In Rio de Janeiro, where prince and press alike stayed at the Copacabana Hotel, the first day of the royal tour in 1978 was spent recuperating from mild jet lag, the press in hundred-degree heat beside the hotel pool, the prince cocooned in his top-floor suite. The photographers offered to put away their cameras if he wanted to come down for a swim. "He couldn't do that," said one of his staff. "There'd be a bloody riot."

The prince, for his part, has tired of the trivia that cooperation with the press invariably produces. As he has grown out of his youth, so he has grown more aloof. The boyish enthusiasm, the shared humor of each absurd situation, are on the wane. At the start of each royal tour, a private, strictly off-the-record cocktail party is thrown for all traveling journalists to meet the royal personage—which obviates the need for him or her to speak directly to them again during the trip. Prince Charles's exchanges at these increasingly formal occasions have become much briefer. He is always on his guard. He has had some bad experiences: in Australia his off-the-record remarks about "the creeps and Mafia types" with whom Frank Sinatra surrounded himself were pub-

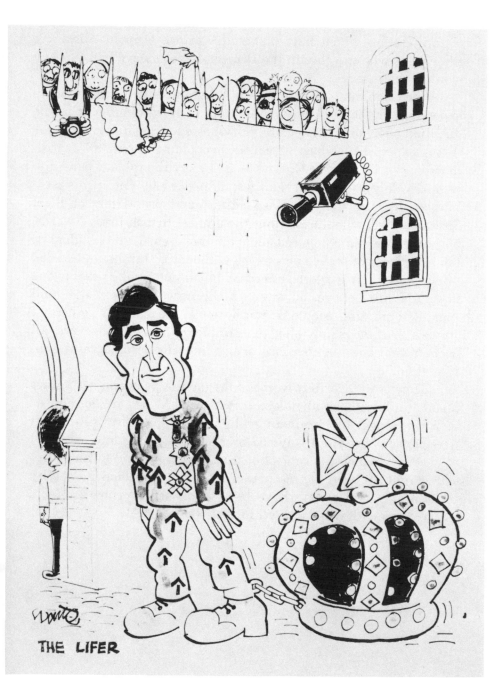

THE LIFER

lished all over the world next day. But it is not only the danger of indiscretion which now makes the prince keep his distance; those press who travel with the Prince of Wales have had to learn to know their place.

The dilemma is that of any public figure: while reluctantly dependent on the press for popular repute, how to nudge it in the direction one wants it to go? Royalty has a head start at home, for it can expect little short of arrant sycophancy from all British newspapers. But Prince Charles is still too vulnerable a person to have developed the imperviousness so needed by one in his position. Addressing the assembled editors and proprietors of Fleet Street in 1978, when presenting the annual British Press Awards, he put in the time-honored plea for more good news: "Regrettably, it does not make news to know that fifty Jumbo jets landed safely at London Airport yesterday, but it does make news if one doesn't. I still believe, however, in the necessity every now and then of reminding people, metaphorically, that vast numbers of Jumbos *do* land safely—for the simple reason that we are all human, and the maintenance of our morale needs careful consideration."

They were heartfelt words. Alas for the prince, news values about Jumbo jets, let alone about Princes of Wales, do not appear to be in danger of imminent realignment. The calm prose of a newspaper page will always be produced from a happy carnival of chaos, in which the subject of that prose is bound to find himself caught up. And the fascination of a constitutional monarchy to its people will always have less to do with a prince's role in society than with what, if anything, he wears in bed.

Part V: *King Charles III*

20

Winning His Spurs

"There is no set-out role for me. It depends entirely what I make of it. . . . I'm really rather an awkward problem."

0925: the executives of Lansing Bagnall Ltd., of Basingstoke, Hampshire, manufacturers of forklift trucks, suppliers of industrial trucks to Her Majesty the Queen, By Appointment, tidy their desks and straighten their ties. They are to be visited today by the Prince of Wales, who is due to arrive at 0930. They hover nervously in the corridor, grown men of the world suddenly become excited schoolchildren. One straightens the portrait of Prince Philip in the boardroom; another tidies the bottles of apple juice, so that their labels all neatly face the front; a third anxiously scans the bleak industrial horizon, hoping front gate has remembered the drill.

At 0950 they are all still waiting. To reassure themselves, they put it down to the weather. They do not know that the prince's day has begun a little later than usual, though with his customary jog around the Windsor estate. The Queen and the Duke of Edinburgh are away, on a three-week tour of the Persian Gulf states; Prince Charles, in their absence, is a councillor of state, empowered to hold Privy Council meetings and sign Acts of Parliament—even to make peace or declare war. In reality, the job is rather less dramatic. Last night, after an eight-hour day touring a metal factory in Wembley, he was kept up late by the chores of royal paperwork, and this morning has left Windsor a little behind schedule. Punctuality may be the politeness of princes, but this one arrives at Lansing Bagnall twenty-five minutes late.

It is the third forklift truck factory he has recently visited, as part of a scheme devised at his request by "Neddy," the National Economic Development Office, to familiarize him with the current state of British industry. He has attended the Neddy working parties on this sector of industry, and is becoming something of an expert on forklift trucks. In Scotland he has seen them being manufactured by an American-owned multi-national, Hyster (Europe) Ltd.; last week he was in the Midlands to see more, at the Coventry Climax plant. As he listens to an extremely dry twenty-minute lecture on the business from Lansing's chairman and governing director, Sir Emmanuel Kaye, the prince knows rather more about the competition than Sir Emmanuel realizes.

The chairman is pushing his luck a little. "And this, sir, is the building we would like you to open."

"Oh, really? I wasn't told anything about that."

"Well, very informally, of course."

"You mean you want me to drive a forklift truck through the wall?"

When he gets there he finds a plaque on the first floor saying it was opened by Mr. Hugh (now Lord) Scanlon, president of the Amalgamated Union of Engineering Workers, last year. The prince's plaque is more conspicuously positioned downstairs, by the front door. "Well," he surmises, as he obligingly pulls the drapes, "presumably you built the upstairs first."

The royal motorcade processes in incongruous splendor, some three hundred yards, along the plant's dowdy byways. Then into an enormous, empty warehouse, for "a demonstration of a broad range of our products." Inside, over the door, against an artificially lit blue sky, a Union Jack is fluttered by an artificial breeze. Canned music strikes up; a sales executive, invisibly microphoned, is spotlit; and the prince and his party, with mounting incredulity, watch a broad range of forklift trucks demonstrate their skills at formation dancing. HRH, unlike the rest of his party, is obliged to keep a straight face.

As the display ends, the press, who had been tidied away after his arrival at the factory gates, suddenly trickle in from the wings. There is a request from the executive microphone—

not on the program, this—that the prince might graciously consent to be photographed aboard a Lansing Bagnall forklift truck
of his choice. Hard to turn down, with the chairman on one side
and the TV cameras on the other. His private secretary looks
anxiously toward him; at the slightest sign, he would demur on
the prince's behalf. But the prince is as anxious for the British
public to see him touring industry as are Lansing Bagnall to have
a picture of him endorsing their product. He climbs aboard. To
general euphoria, he wants to drive the thing. His mastery is
instantaneous; he is quickly bobbing and weaving to the ampli-
fied strains of some martial film music. But he has forgotten the
protruding forks. As he spins round deftly, he comes within an
inch of slicing off the chairman's leg at the ankle.

The royal progress is still twenty minutes behind schedule,
so the severe timings allotted the Lansing Bagnall training
center and apprentice school, the parts and service division,
product engineering, the labs, design department, and testing
facilities are each discreetly trimmed by a few minutes. As he
glides from one to the next, the prince stops to talk to anyone
who looks receptive. "What exactly are you doing?" "Keep you
busy here?" "Pay you enough, do they?" are oft-repeated questions. Each group giggles furiously after he has left it and cannot
remember a word he has said.

Two pleasantly unrehearsed moments occur. In each department, union shop stewards are wheeled forward to shake the royal
hand; in one he asks if they've agreed to settle within the government's pay guidelines. The chairman steps forward anxiously,
but industrial relations at Lansing Bagnall are not a problem:
"No, we haven't," says the senior union official, "but perhaps
we'd better not talk about that now, eh?" In the training center,
a middle-aged woman in an overall is holding a collection box:
an apprentice is getting married. The prince motions to his detective. Prince Charles does not carry money. Chief Inspector
Paul Officer fishes a £1 note out of his wallet and hands it to the
prince, who passes it to the delighted collector. He also, rashly
in the view of his staff, agrees to sign the list of contributors.
Royalty is not supposed to sign anything like that. You never
know what it says on the other side.

Lunch at last. The Board of Directors' men's room is guarded
while under royal occupation; upstairs, the executives wait

nervously, their names attached to their lapels. The prince is motioned to the buffet immediately as he enters, past a portrait of his mother taken some twenty-five years ago. "I'd rather have a drink, if I may." He's just like us, think the executives, and not afraid to show it. He moves from group to group, talking of the problems of British industry. In conversation with the chairman, he had already revealed a few pockets of ignorance; he did not know, for instance, that an unquoted company could not be taken over.

"What, not even by the government?"

"Well, yes, sir, they can take over anyone they like."

Now he asks everyone about the travails of the British motor industry. It may seem incongruous in such an efficient forklift truck factory, he agrees, but his dilemma is that no one will enlighten him. All the factories he has toured, thanks to NEDO, have outstandingly good industrial relations. When he travels abroad as an unofficial British trade ambassador, he comes up against charges that industrial relations in the UK are the worst in the world, that British firms will fail to meet delivery dates, that they have inadequate quality controls, that they are inferior in every way to the Germans, the French, the Japanese. He is unable to answer these charges as no one will let him visit such places as British Leyland. He would have thought that a visit from him would be just the sort of shot in the arm those chaps needed? His voice grows quite animated, and the rest of the room falls silent.

Once again the chairman intervenes. He wishes to mark the prince's visit by making a small presentation: a specially commissioned sculpture in gold, an abstract shape representing perpetual motion, or the finding of solutions to every problem, or remedies to every fault, or something like that. A helter-skelter of gold leaf circles around a central maypole, ending in a sharp, thrusting arrow. "Thank you very much," says the prince. "I'll have to think carefully whose chair to leave it on."

Such is the stuff of royal tours of industry. The insights gained barely rival those of a visiting party of sixth-formers. Prince Charles's attempts to discover more about the current state of British industry are as well intentioned as everything else he does, but they can never—as he himself is the first to admit—

do more than scratch the surface. Yet a week after his day at Lansing Bagnall the prince made a speech geared for the front pages, blaming management for the woeful state of British industrial relations. Communication, he declared, was the problem, then reminisced about his Neddy tour. There was one manager he had met who "breezed in every morning with a pipe clenched firmly between his teeth, never bothering to acknowledge people and giving instructions to everyone. When he had a problem, they all told him to get stuffed."

The manager in question was, of course, easily identified, and thus considerably embarrassed in the following morning's newspapers. Management organizations—the Confederation of British Industry, the Institute of Directors, the Engineering Employers Federation—tactfully expressed the wish that the prince might spend a little more time becoming a little more closely involved with industry before making such sweeping statements. What most surprised those who know the prince well, however, is that in private he is an inveterate and impassioned union-basher. His political views on this, as on most economic and industrial issues, are considerably to the right of center.

In the Commons there were dark hints that the prime minister had put him up to it. Prince Charles had in fact lunched twice with James Callaghan shortly before his speech, at the beginning of an election year (1979) marked by an especially damaging round of strikes. The inactivity of garbage collectors, ambulance and truck drivers, hospital workers, civil servants, and even grave diggers had sent the Conservative Opposition's popularity in the polls to unprecedented heights. Callaghan would certainly not have thought the prince's speech ill-timed.

It is also true that Callaghan was the first prime minister with whom the Prince of Wales had been able to enjoy a mature working relationship. In October 1978, during his official visit to Yugoslavia, the prince had been annoyed by a particular development of economic policy of which he read in the cabinet papers flown to him in Belgrade. He sat down that moment to write a strongly worded note to the prime minister, which his staff—to a man—advised him not to send. But he insisted, and on his return received a note from Callaghan expressing his appreciation and inviting him to lunch. Prince Charles had scarcely altered the course of government policy, but he had injected a dash of his own brand of conservatism into a Labour Government's approach to a long winter of industrial unrest. His helpful speech followed in late February, just a week after he had spent a day at the prime minister's side, observing the workings of Number Ten Downing Street and the peculiar rituals of prime minister's question time in the House of Commons.

Any such collusion would, of course, have been highly unconstitutional. No Prince of Wales has better expressed the limitations on the role, and the frustration they cause, than the Duke of Windsor in his memoirs. A former king uniquely free to express his reservations about the institution of monarchy, he wrote:

> Like the Parliamentary system, the constitutional Monarch who stands aloof from and above politics is a British invention. As a device for preserving the Crown as a symbol of national unity while divesting it from abhorrent forms of absolutism, it is a remarkable example of the British genius for accommodation. But one effect of the system, which is perhaps not so well understood by the public, is the handicap imposed upon a Prince, who, while obliged to live and work within one of the most intensely political societies on earth, is expected to remain not merely above party and faction, but a-political.

Edward when Prince of Wales never took the opportunity to speak in the House of Lords, though he did—as we have seen—later use the privilege of his office to appeal to the consciences of politicians. A hundred years ago, in 1879, Bertie, Prince of Wales, attended debates in the Lords on nineteen occasions. He spoke and even voted in favor of an act in which his family had a special interest (to legalize marriage with a deceased wife's sister) and served on the Royal Commission on the Housing of the Working Classes, for which he toured the slums of London in disguise. Prince Charles has hitherto confined his two speeches in the Lords to the wholly uncontroversial subject of welfare work for the young and has otherwise been an extremely rare attender.

Elsewhere, however, he has felt free to emulate his father by discoursing on the problems of contemporary British society, including those in the economic and industrial fields which are far from apolitical. He is generally saved by the fact that his remarks are wholly innocuous; nevertheless, they are open to a wide range of interpretation by party or faction. In times when party ideologies, if not day-to-day policies, are anyway sufficiently blurred, this is perhaps innocent enough. A more important question, to the prince as to his future subjects, is whether Charles will ever be able to use his unique position to more positive ends.

In pursuance of the heir's apolitical role, Prince Charles has already developed all the skills of a politician to avoid the appearance of being one. He is adept at ducking questions which might tempt him across the sacred divide and a skillful judge of how far he can go in speeches on quasi-political subjects. As Britain saw in the aftermath of the February 1974 election, the monarch still has a political role to play in moments of national crisis. Had Edward Heath chosen to persevere in his attempts to retain power through a coalition with the Liberal Party, and Harold Wilson as leader of the majority party chosen to challenge his right to do so, Elizabeth II would have had the final say between them. It very nearly came to it. Prince Charles, by the time he becomes monarch, will have had more than adequate preparation for what Harold Macmillan has called "the last great prerogative of the crown": to agree to or refuse a prime minister's request for a dissolution of Parliament—"of vital importance," as Macmillan wrote, "at a time of national crisis." But can he meanwhile use his expertise in roles other than that of the effective "viceroy" he will inevitably become?

Much that he is already achieving is admirable: his social work, his visits abroad in pursuit of British foreign policy, his increasing efforts to become guardian of the national morale. But he is faced for the indefinite future with the daunting prospect of continually biting his tongue on subjects about which he is uniquely well informed. His visits to industry, it is true, can never be more than a well-intentioned democratic gesture, and his view of the world from the windows of the royal palaces is scarcely a realistic one. But he sees all cabinet papers and discusses contemporary issues with politicians of every party in complete confidence. Many of his letters are from the disadvantaged or the deprived, whom he can help. But many more seek a lead from him on political or commercial matters in which, however much he may want to get involved, he must stay his hand. He is doomed, it seems, to remain a repository of problems rather than a source of solutions.

Or is he? There is, as was said of the last Prince of Wales, "no doubt of the young man's capacity for goodness." But there is, perhaps, doubt of his capacity for boldness and imagination. On his thirtieth birthday, the otherwise glowing tribute in one of the "quality" Sunday newspapers made an intriguing suggestion. If the prince was so anxious to develop his nonpolitical role, to alleviate unemployment and assist the British export drive, why did he not himself go into industry? What about "HRH Electronics"? It was a time when Britain was dragging its feet in the electronics markets of the world, when British scientists had joined the "brain drain" to the United States and elsewhere to develop the silicon chip and other such innovations likely to revolutionize modern technology, if not society itself. A royally sponsored company could pioneer other exemplary innovations, such as worker participation in management and equal profit-sharing; it would help the monarchy prove its heavy state subsidy cost-effective; above all, it would provide the Prince of Wales with a clearly identified and dynamic role of his own. His two younger brothers could take over some of the ritualistic public duties of royalty for which he would be less free. Was it not time the monarchy dropped its inhibitions and rolled up its sleeves?

The writer of the article received a letter from the Prince of Wales's press secretary, thanking him for his kind words, but passing on the prince's view that the piece as a whole was "tendentious." To be fair, it *had* contained a highly tendentious section suggesting that Prince Charles, footloose and fancy-free at thirty, was about to go the way of the Duke of Windsor. But the notion of HRH Electronics had clearly incurred princely disapproval. There had been no suggestion of any personal profit motive: all profits could be plowed back into the business, or even go to charity. But the twenty-first-century monarchy, it seems, is not about to besmirch its name and ancient dignities by lending them to the commercial market. Still less will the family business, whose assets, investments, and other finances remain a closely guarded secret, ever "go public."

Prince Charles himself has said that he wants "to change the old, remote image of royalty." Yet he seems intent on pre-

serving the gulf between the crown and its people, the illusion
that divinity doth hedge a king. The British royal family has
always been somewhat sniffy about the more democratic gestures of its contemporaries around Europe, seeking to maintain
the prestige of its position at the head of the royal league table.
The Scandinavian monarchs, for instance, are known to them as
"the bicycle kings"; British subjects are never likely to enjoy
the chance of greeting their monarch on a casual stroll through
St. James's Park. But to preserve this mystique, as the maturer
Prince Charles seems intent on doing, could prove a foolish lack
of enlightenment toward the end of a turbulent century.

"In these times," he has said of the monarchy, "this sort of
organization is called into question. It is not taken for granted
as it used to be. In that sense one has to be far more professional
than I think one ever used to be." Britain is in no immediate
danger of a republican upsurge, though the royal family may be
forgiven a certain paranoia on the subject as it watches the gradual disappearance of other monarchies, most recently that of
Iran, around the world. But it should not, perhaps, be forgiven
for thinking more "professionalism" the answer to a less class-
ridden society. If anything has underlined the irrational nature
of a constitutional monarchy in recent years, and posed any
threat to its survival, it has been the improvement in the conditions of the working classes and the rapid rise in the political
power of the trade unions. The royal family's traditional professionalism, however twentieth century the current brand, has
meanwhile served rather to preserve, even strengthen class distinctions. These are the countervailing forces with which the
twenty-first-century King Charles III will have to contend. At
present, however, he appears to aspire to a reign more of en-
trenchment than innovation.

The latest evidence can be found in his recent appointments.
The keynote has been caution. In Edward Adeane he has found
himself a private secretary young enough to have hopes of one
day becoming private secretary to the king, and thus the most
powerful single figure beside the monarch himself in royal
policymaking. Adeane is not a radical thinker. His expertise is
legal, and his instinct deeply conservative. It was his great-
grandfather, Lord Stamfordham, who suggested the name "Windsor" to King George V in 1917 (when everything from York,

Lancaster, and England to Fitzroy and D'Este were under consideration). It was his father, Sir Michael (now Lord) Adeane whom Lord Altrincham described in 1957 as the leader of "an unimaginative, second-rate lot, simply lacking in gumption." The latest Adeane to serve the royal family has not yet had time to win a more generous judgment; but in certain private matters he has already steered the prince along the safest, most traditional paths.

In 1978 Lord Altrincham, now plain John Grigg but still a staunch monarchist, saw no reason to alter his judgments of 1957: "Unfortunately, much of what I wrote about the royal household twenty-one years ago still seems to apply. The royal family's 'official' family is still nothing like socially or racially representative of the community. Still less is it representative of the Commonwealth, of which the British monarch is head."

There is, for instance, still not one black face anywhere in the royal entourage, for all the Prince of Wales's frequently voiced and palpably sincere concern for greater racial understanding. It is the kind of public example, however specious, for which the royal family exists, and which a younger and popular Prince of Wales is ideally placed to make. His many public panegyrics of the Commonwealth make it an even more extraordinary omission.

In these as in other matters, such as his own marital prospects, he has shown an understandable wish not to be hurried. He is still, to a large extent, feeling his way. But this Prince of Wales will have in time to make some radical gestures to win his spurs. He will have to take the crown into new, more pragmatic roles. He will have to integrate it more fully into the economic working life of its people, if at the expense of some of that cherished mystique. He has so far shown few signs of being willing to do so.

Charles's parents have shown themselves sound, if cautious, royal innovators, not least in the decisions behind his own upbringing. But it will fall to him to see the monarchy into a new millennium, which will call for new directions as momentous as the times. Conscientiousness and deep-seated good intentions may not, for once, be enough. He will be required, as will those in whose advice he places his trust, to demonstrate radicalism of a kind they now conspicuously shun. The prognosis, for the present, does not sparkle.

In the years ahead much will depend on how far he can liberate himself from the influence of his parents, who still place stern restraints on his public behavior. After his "anti-Vatican" speech in 1978 a member of his staff was sent to London Airport ostensibly to greet his return from Norway; in fact he had been delegated to ensure that the prince talked to no one, least of all the press, before arriving home to a carpeting. Unless Charles can win himself more freedom to take such stands, he may, like his great-great-grandfather, simply grow bored and resentful. "I don't mind praying to the eternal father," Bertie, approaching sixty, told the archbishop who conducted Queen Victoria's diamond jubilee service, "but I must be the only man in the country afflicted with an eternal mother."

21

Vivat Regina

There once was a man who said: "Damn.
It is borne upon me that I am
An engine that moves
In predestinate grooves:
I'm not even a bus. I'm a tram."
MICHAEL E. HARE

O N APRIL 18, 1977, the Prince of Wales dined privately at Chequers with the prime minister and half a dozen members of the Labour cabinet. The evening was long and convivial, and the exchanges increasingly frank. Prince Charles, by one account, grew somewhat morose as he listened to a discussion of political power by those, unlike him, in a position to wield it. At length he told them the story of the Qantas air hostess who not long before had summoned the chutzpah to say to him: "What a rotten, boring job you've got!" The cabinet laughed politely. "But you don't understand," complained the prince. "She was right!" At which one of the most senior politicians present at the end of a long evening is said to have tweaked the heir apparent gently on the cheek, and remarked: "Well, you shouldn't have taken the job, then, should you?"

The joke, for once, was on Charles. But the monotony of his life, coupled with its frustrations, could in time prove ever harder for him to handle. Walter Bagehot, discussing the prospects of Bertie, Prince of Wales, in the 1867 edition of *The English Constitution*, declared that the ideal monarch would be one who is "willing to labour, superior to pleasure and . . . begins early to reign." Prince Charles's early introduction to affairs of state, as Elizabeth II's logical antidote to what she herself called the "Edward VII situation," could over the years quicken his impatience to occupy center stage. And the longevity of recent royal females suggests that he *will* be at least as old as Edward VII when he inherits the throne; his own children, as yet figments even more of the public imagination than of his own, will probably themselves be parents before King Charles III is crowned. The Queen Mother, as Prince Charles entered his thirties, was as old as the century and still going strong; George V's widow, Queen Mary, lived to be eighty-five and Edward VII's widow, Queen Alexandra, to be eighty. Queen Victoria died at eighty-one.

The present Queen is a shrewd and sympathetic mother, who understands only too well the grim prospect facing her son. The need to provide him with a more positive and specific role—at first a governor-generalship, later perhaps that of an executive "vice-president" to an aging and less active monarch—will become more and more pressing. There will be ever more frequent discussion of the pros and cons of Elizabeth II's abdication.

In 1978, when the Queen was only fifty-two, an Opinion Research Centre poll for *Woman* magazine showed as many as a third of young people in Britain in favor of a handover to Prince Charles "before too long." The figure dropped to a quarter among the over-sixty-fives, typical among whom was an elderly woman who said: "We want the Queen and I'd hate to see her go!" A younger voice added: "Let her decide for herself when she's had enough."

Abdication will remain a perennially vexed question around Britain, but the answer will grow increasingly simple. The Queen recognizes the logic of handing over the central role to her son before his time, before he is past the height of his powers. As a private woman, she would be only too happy to retire to the country homes, the family life, and the animals which occupy her most natural affections. But of late the question has been less frequently raised in royal circles. There was a time she would discuss it quite freely. As long ago as 1965, at the dinner party to plan Prince Charles's higher education, the Queen herself tried to start a debate among the select group of family, political, and ecclesiastical intimates at her table.

"It might be wise," she said, "to abdicate at a time when Charles could do better."

"You may be right," said her husband lightheartedly, "the doctors will keep you alive so long!"

But the subject was not on the agenda, and Prince Philip's joke deflected further serious discussion. In the intervening years, Elizabeth II has changed. In Silver Jubilee Year, 1977, she was not averse to boasting that she had already been served by seven prime ministers. Gladstone once said of Queen Victoria: "Parliaments and ministers pass, but she abides in lifelong duty and she is to them as the oak in the forest is to annual harvest in the field." In 1977, those close to Elizabeth II suddenly perceived her vision of advancing to Victorian venerability. The older and more experienced a monarch she becomes, the greater the affection and respect she will command among her people. However much she may wish as a woman to quit the public scene, she will grow stronger in her determination as a constitutional monarch that it can never be done.

Since 1936 the very word abdication has sent a collective shudder through Buckingham Palace, and still does. Though the circumstances would be very different, a handover of the office would be thought to devalue it, to reduce the British monarchy to the ranks of its junior European counterparts, who believe—as two British royal ladies sneered of two Dutch after Queen Wilhelmina's abdication in 1948, that the crown is a pensionable job like any other, to be tossed lightly aside at the age of sixty-five.

Abdication would also, as has happened in Holland, create an irresistible precedent. Prince Philip was once tempted by a newspaper proprietor's advice that he should hold regular press conferences, but eventually abandoned the idea for fear of committing his heirs to continuing the tradition. Prince Charles himself—he will be forty-two, an ideal age for accession, when the Queen reaches sixty-five—would be the first to defend this principle: that an abdication, however honorable its intentions, would be a mortal blow at the monarchy's foundations, the beginning of the end of its survival in its present form. He has said on several occasions, and is the only member of the royal family to have put it publicly on record, that the Queen will not abdicate in his favor. He would not wish her to.

Those who advocate abdication fail to understand the nature of the British monarchy's popular appeal. Its majesty lies in its antiquity; its prestige, its dignity, its preeminence as the fount of all wisdom are based on continuity and tradition, on apparently infinite experience. A prince is hailed as king in the very minute of his parent's death; the chain of succession, renewed rather than broken by mortality, is a lingering contemporary echo of the divine right of kings.

Irrational, of course, but so is the monarchy's sustained hold over its people. Britons revere it as a symbol of Christian qualities of which they have long since made light in their own personal lives. In his book *Crown and People*, based on the reports of all manner and class of British subject to the social studies group Mass Observation, Philip Ziegler made the same point about the success of Elizabeth II's Silver Jubilee: "It was striking in 1977 how many tributes were paid to her conscientiousness and dignity, to the way in which she embodied qualities such as decency, respectability, family loyalty, which were often represented as being out of fashion. . . ."

In this context, both the Queen and Prince Charles recognize the importance of his establishing a family life of his own, both to provide the nation with more royal infants to coo over, and to continue the tradition of domestic virtue which is the contemporary monarchy's mainstay. Elizabeth II would, of course, remain matriarch of the royal family, but the nation will grow restless unless Prince Charles's junior circle is soon built around her grandchildren and heirs. In all the furor over Edward VIII's abdication, both in 1936 and thereafter, the one central issue was neatly pinned at the time by J. H. Thomas, the trade union leader and Socialist politician, who told George V's biographer, Harold Nicolson: "And now 'ere we 'ave this obstinate little man with 'is Mrs. Simpson. Hit won't do, 'Arold, I tell you that straight. I know the people of this country. I *know* them. They 'ate 'aving no family life at Court."

Philip Ziegler went on to suggest that "the British people like their monarchs either old, wise and paternal or young and hopeful." A sixty-year-old King Charles III would be neither. The logical conclusion, he said, was for the Queen to hand on the crown to a grandson of twenty or so years old. "The Golden Jubilee of 2002 might be a suitable occasion."

Ziegler was gracious enough to acknowledge that this might constitute something of a waste of the present Prince of Wales, requiring as it would his "premature disappearance . . . the need for which he might reasonably consider inadequately proven." But it is an eerie coincidence that the first sons of monarchs have fared less than happily this century. Both George V and George VI were second sons, the one promoted by a death, the other by default. (The Duke of York's unsuitability for kingship led in 1936 to serious consideration within the royal family as to whether the throne should pass instead over the then Duke of Gloucester to his younger brother, the then Duke of Kent, who was better equipped for the role and already had a male heir. Had the plan gone ahead, the Duke of Kent would presumably have been kept back from active service in the Second World War, which saw his death in an air crash in 1942; the present Duke of Kent would now have been either Prince of Wales or king, and Prince Charles would at best be duke of somewhere considerably less profitable than Cornwall.)

Hence, perhaps the continuing anxiety about Prince Charles's penchant for risking his neck to prove himself a royal he-man. Both George V and two of his prime ministers, Stanley Baldwin and Ramsay MacDonald, attempted for the same reason to talk the future Edward VIII out of his love of reckless steeplechasing, which more than once involved him in dangerous falls.

Prince Andrew, moreover, has yet to prove himself a worthy next-in-line. There has been ill-disguised concern in the royal family recently about the abandon with which he has embarked upon the princely life, and his early reputation as a ladies' man. When her sons were young, Elizabeth II decreed that members of the royal household should call them by their Christian names until they reached the age of eighteen, when they were to be more correctly addressed as "sir"; significantly, on Prince Andrew's eighteenth birthday in 1978, the Queen instructed her staff that the rule need not yet be observed.

The way ahead may seem to hold no dangers for Prince Charles. Polls consistently acclaim him the royal family's most popular member apart from the Queen herself; the most recent, the ORC survey for *Woman* in 1978, awarded him 61 popularity points out of 100 to the Queen's 73, with Prince Philip third at 56, the Queen Mother—surprisingly—fourth with 52, and Princess Anne and Princess Margaret bringing up the rear with a mere 30 and 29 respectively.

But closer analysis shows that the prince's popular appeal is strongest with age groups older or younger than his own, and that this has remained a constant throughout his adolescence, youth, and early manhood. Both his adherence to the values of his parents' generation rather than his own and his outspoken rejection of many of his contemporaries' values have grown more marked in recent years. They are in danger of losing him the sympathy, even the interest, of many Britons his own age.

Though it is too early to pass fuller judgment on his younger brothers, he will always compare favorably with his sister, Princess Anne, whose constant public surliness serves only to underline Prince Charles's self-denying devotion to duty. In 1976 she moaned to the British Airways in-flight magazine *High Life:* "We've never had a holiday. A week or two at Balmoral or ten days at Sandringham is the nearest we get." Going out and about, moreover, was "purgatory . . . either too many people or too many press." The first sentiment was palpably untrue, the second scarcely regal. It was left to Prince Charles, a few months later, to mend his sister's fences in another interview with the same magazine. "Britain has indulged in far more self-indignation than is good for her. There are millions of people who work incredibly hard and achieve magnificent things without any recognition whatsoever."

Charles is becoming a master of such populist rhetoric—British Airways' motto, Fly the Flag, could be ripe for princely adoption—but his future will need to be made of sterner stuff. Whatever role is found for him, he will need to prove himself of more substance in those areas which still occasionally expose his naïveté. He will need to prove himself more in touch with the progressive thinking and relaxed life-style of a large proportion of his own age group, who approach the seats of power quite as remorselessly as he approaches the throne. It is the greatest irony of the many innovations of his upbringing, and the many royal "firsts" he has himself achieved, that they have combined to produce the most conventional young Prince of Wales of modern times.

When the future King Edward VIII was but a few days old, the Scottish radical and Socialist leader Keir Hardie rose in the Commons to make a dire prediction: "From his childhood this boy will be surrounded by sycophants and flatterers by the score, and will be taught to believe himself as of a superior creation. A line will be drawn between him and the people he might be called to rule over. In due course, following the precedent which has already been set, he will be sent on a tour round the world, and probably rumors of a morganatic marriage will follow, and the end of it will be that the country will be called upon to pay the bill."

Remarkably prophetic words in that instance, they will always hold true of any Prince of Wales. Prince Charles knows he would have to do something utterly drastic to lose his ex-officio popular glamour. He is by definition a jet-setter, even if he prefers a more stately progress by turboprop. He has already established his own racy permutation of the annual royal routine: skiing at Klosters in January, polo at Deauville and fishing in Iceland in August, amid the familiar Sandringham winters, Balmoral summers, and Windsor weekends. Around his traveling circus, in time, as his mother grows into an elderly, revered, perhaps more retiring monarch, a glittering junior court will gather. A place at his table will be the most sought after in the land.

The magic attending his presence in a room will not diminish; tides of humanity will continue to ebb and flow around him; enthusiastic crowds will always wait hours for the merest glimpse. Yet it is a very twentieth-century irony that probably the most publicized Prince of Wales of all time is perhaps the most misunderstood. Whatever the efforts made on his behalf, his people will always regard him as a swashbuckling, hard-living extrovert prince rather than the kindly, hesitant, very vulnerable man he really is. The popular imagination will always picture him astride a polo pony, where he in fact spends very little of his time, rather than toiling at his desk, where he spends a great deal.

In the summer of 1978, the director of one of the prince's charitable trusts arrived at Buckingham Palace for a routine meeting. He was due to have a few words with the prince before escorting him into committee, but HRH was nowhere to be found. Eventually a footman said he had last seen Prince Charles in the garden, sitting under a tree, writing a speech. The director waited patiently as the prince was summoned, then heard a door close at the far end of the vast palace corridor. As he watched the

distant, solitary figure advance toward him, head hung in preoccupation, he wondered: "What sort of a life is this? What are
we doing to this young man?"

The young man himself, in his darker moments, shares such
qualms. Yet in public he has a dogged ability to put the bravest
possible face on things. He may feel boredom, patience, even dis-
gust, but he is perhaps unique among the royals in managing to
conceal it. He has a series of standard get-out lines to smooth over
such moments, the best being one that he has used on several of
those occasions when royalty is required to perform gastronomic
feats from which its subjects would shrink. After eating raw fish
with Eskimos, snakemeat in Australia, a mysterious gruel in dark-
est Africa: "The things I do for England!"

Prince Charles has more natural intelligence than most previous heirs apparent, and a more conscientious spirit than a nation has any right to expect of one born to such a fate. Britain, in
this respect, has been lucky. Or, in the words of the prince's
great-uncle, Lord Mountbatten, closest personal friend of three
British monarchs in this century: "It's not luck at all. It's a
bloody miracle."

Yet these, Charles knows, are the public bones he must make
flesh. It will not be easy. The monarchy is not the most adaptable
of institutions, but ahead lie times with which it must change.
As Prince of Wales, and one day as King Charles III, he will have
to see to it that he subtly alters both offices, rather than they him.

It says a good deal for Charles's record so far that his future
subjects wish this idealistic young prince well in the unenviable
years ahead. His enthusiasm for making the most of his birthright, more than many of those who have gone before him, is one
of his greatest assets. An even greater one is his modesty in knowing that he is not yet fully equipped for the task, that there is
still much to learn.

During his coast-to-coast tour of the United States in 1977,
the most arduous itinerary he has yet undertaken abroad or at
home, an awe-struck American journalist remarked: "My God!
That guy works so hard you'd think he was running for office."

In a way, he is.

APPENDICES

BIBLIOGRAPHY

INDEX

Appendix A: A Royal Entry in Who's Who

MEMBERS OF THE royal family are above individual listings in Who's Who; they have their own dignified, cursory mention at the front. If the Prince of Wales did have his own individual entry, it would read something like this:

WALES, 21st Prince of, *cr.* 1301; His Royal Highness the Prince Charles Philip Arthur George (Mountbatten-Windsor), KG 1958; KT 1977; GCB 1975 (Great Master of the Order); PC 1977; Prince of Wales and Earl of Chester, Duke of Cornwall and Rothesay, Earl of Carrick and Baron of Renfrew, Lord of the Isles and Great Steward of Scotland; heir to the throne of the United Kingdom; b. Buckingham Palace, London, 14 November 1948; *e. s.* of Her Most Excellent Majesty Elizabeth II of The United Kingdom of Great Britain and Northern Ireland and of Her Other Realms and Territories, Queen, Head of the Commonwealth, *e. d.* of His late Majesty King George VI and Queen Elizabeth The Queen Mother; and His Royal Highness the Prince Philip (Mountbatten), Duke of Edinburgh, Earl of Merioneth and Baron Greenwich, only *s.* of HRH the late Prince Andrew of Greece and Denmark and HRH the late Princess (Victoria) Alice Elizabeth Julia Marie of Battenberg.

Educ.: Hill House School, London; Cheam School, Hampshire; Gordonstoun School, Morayshire; Geelong Grammar School, Melbourne; Trinity College, Cambridge (MA); University College of Wales, Aberystwyth. Served in Royal Air Force 1971, and Royal Navy 1971–76. Flight Lieutenant, RAF Cranwell, 1971; Wing Commander RAF, 1976. Royal Naval College, Dartmouth, 1971; Sub Lieutenant RN, 1971; Lieutenant, 1973; Commander, 1976. Served aboard HMS *Norfolk*, 1971–72; HMS *Glasserton*, 1972; HMS *Minerva*, 1973; HMS *Fox*, 1973; HMS *Jupiter*, 1974; HMS *Hermes* (with 845 Squadron, the "Red Dragons"), 1975; Commander, HMS *Bronington*, Jan–Dec 1976.

Personal ADC to Queen Elizabeth II, 1973–. Prince Charles of Edinburgh, 1948–52; Duke of Cornwall, 1952; *cr.* Prince of Wales, 1958. Invested Prince of Wales at Caernarvon Castle, 1969. Took seat in House of Lords, 1970. Chairman: Elizabeth II's Silver Jubilee Appeal, 1977.

Colonel-in-Chief, The Cheshire Regiment (1977), The Gordon Highlanders (1977), Lord Strathcona's Horse (Royal Canadians) (1977), The Parachute Regiment (1977), Royal Australian Armoured Corps (1977), Royal Regiment of Canada (1977), Royal Regiment of Wales (1969), 2nd King Edward VII's Own Gurkha Rifles (The Sirmoor Rifles) (1977), Royal Winnipeg Rifles (1977). Colonel, Welsh Guards (1975); Hon. Air Commodore, RAF Brawdy (1977); Air Commodore in Chief, Royal New Zealand Air Force (1977); Colonel-in-Chief, Air Reserve Group of Air Command in Canada (1977).

Grand Cross, Order of the Dannebrog, Denmark (1974); Grand Cross, Order of the White Rose, Finland (1969); Grand Cordon, Supreme Order of the Chrysanthemum, Japan (1971); Grand Cross, Order of the Oak Crown, Luxembourg (1972); Grand Cross, Order of Ojasvi Rajanya, Nepal (1975); Grand Cross, Order of the House of Orange, Netherlands (1972); Order of the Seraphim, Sweden (1975); Hon. Member, the Order of the Wapiti, USA (1969). Queen Elizabeth II Coronation Medal, 1953; The Queen's Silver Jubilee Medal, 1977.

President: Bach Choir (1976), British Sub Aqua Club (1974), Cambridge University Polo Club (1975–79); Commonwealth Youth Exchange Council (1977–80), Council for National Academic Awards (1977–), Devon County Agricultural Association (1979), Friends of Covent Garden (1977–), Highland Society of London (1978), The Lord's Taverners (1975–76), The National Rifle Association (1977–82), Peterborough Royal Foxhound Show (1978), Prince of Wales' Company Club (Welsh Guards) (1975–), Printers Charitable Corporation (1977), Royal Aero Club (1975–80), Royal Agricultural Society of England (1978), Royal Bath and West Show (1977), Underwater Conservation Year (1977), Wells Cathedral Appeal Trust Fund (1976–), Welsh Committee, European Architectural Heritage Year (1972–75), Welsh Environment Foundation (1971), Youth and Music (1977–80), *Vice-President:* Society of the Friends of St. George's and the Descendants of the Knights of the Garter (1968–). *Chairman:* Canterbury Cathedral Appeal Fund (1974–79), King George's Fund for Sailors (1977–), King George's Jubilee Trust (1974–78), Prince of Wales' Committee for Wales (1970–), Queen Elizabeth II's Silver Jubilee Appeal (1977), Steering Committee for Wales "Countryside in 1970" Conference (1968–70), The Royal Jubilee Trusts (1978–).

Patron: Abbeyfield Society (1978–), Bath Preservation Trust (1973–78), British Deer Society (1978–83), British Flight Team (1977–79), British Transglobe Expedition (1979–), British North Pole Expedition (1977), British Surfing Association (1978), City Arts Festival (1978), Council for British Archaeology (1978–83), Elgar Foundation (1975–80), English Chamber Orchestra and Music Society (1977–82), Friends of Brecon Cathedral (1974–), Game Fair (1975–80), Joint Services Expedition to the Elephant Island Group (1970–71),

Joint Services Expedition to the Chagos Archipelago (1978), League
of Venturers (1974–), Men of Trees Society (1978–), National Ski
Federation of Great Britain (1978–), Old Cranwellian Association
(1978–), Operation Drake (1977–78), Royal Anthropological Institute
of Great Britain (1972–78), Royal Asiatic Society (1972–), Royal
Opera House, Covent Garden (1975–80), Royal Cornwall Yacht Club
(1977–), Royal Regiment of Wales Officers' Dining Club (1969–),
Royal Regiment of Wales Regimental Association (1969–), Royal
Tournament (1978), Society for the Promotion of Nature Reserves
(1977–), Society of Friends of Royal Naval Museum, Portsmouth
(1977–), Somerset County Federation of Young Farmers Clubs (1973–
76), Thames Angling Preservation (1974–81), United Nations Organization 25th Anniversary, 1970, National Co-Ordinating Committee
(1969–75), Wales in Bloom Campaign (1970–75), Welsh Association
of Male Voice Choirs (1977–), Wiltons Music Hall Trust (1971), York
Archaeological Trust (1977–80), Transglobe Expedition (1979–).

Member: Air Squadron, Armed Forces Benefit & Aid Association
(USA), Army and Navy Club, Association of Royal Naval Officers,
Aston Martin Owners Club, Athenaeum, Automobile Association, Blue
Seal Club (Household Divisional Dining Club), Boodles, British Auto-
mobile Racing Club, British Deer Society, British Horse Society, Buck's
Club, Cambrian Archaeological Association, Cambridge Open Regatta,
Cambridge Union Society, Cavalry and Guards Club, Cercle de Deau-
ville, Cheam School Association, Circolo Della Caccia, Confrérie des
Chevaliers du Sacavin, Cornish Club, Country Gentlemen's Association,
Cowes Corinthian Yacht Club, Faculty of Advocates, Fleet Air Arm
Officers Association, Fly Dressers Guild, Friends of St. Michael the
Archangel Church (Mere), Game Conservancy, Glide Royale St.
Sebastian, Gordonstoun Association, Ham Polo Club, Hawaii Polo Club,
Helicopter Club of Great Britain, Highland Brigade Club, High Peak
Hunt, Honourable Artillery Company, Imperial Service Club (Syd-
ney), Institution of Electronic Radio Engineers, International Variety
Club, Island Sailing Club, Leander Club, Les Ambassadeurs Club, Lin-
colnshire Constabulary, Lloyd's Register of Shipping, Lord's Tavern-
ers, Magic Circle, Marylebone Cricket Club, Melbourne Cricket Club,
Mounted Infantry Club, National Equestrian Centre (Stoneleigh),
Naval Club, Naval and Military Club (Melbourne), New Club (Edin-
burgh), Norfolk Club, Order of the Road, Other Club, Oxford and Cam-
bridge Rifle Association, The Parlour, Punch Table, Royal Air Force
Club, Royal Air Forces Association, Royal Automobile Club, Royal
Brighton Yacht Club (Melbourne), Royal British Legion, Royal Dart
Yacht Club, Royal Forestry Society, Royal Fowey Yacht Club, Royal
Institution of Chartered Surveyors, Royal Institution of Navigation,
Royal London Yacht Club, Royal Naval Bird Watching Society, Royal
Naval Club, Royal Motor Yacht Club, Royal Naval Saddle Club, RNVR

Club (Scotland), Royal Ocean Racing Club, Royal Thames Yacht Club (Commodore), Royal Yacht Squadron, St. David's Society of New York, Singapore Polo Club, Ski Club of Great Britain, Society of Merchant Venturers, Students Union Society (University College, Cardiff), Surrey County Cricket Club, Taupo International Fisherman's Club, Tiger Club, Traveller's Club, Trinity House (Elder Brother), Turf Club, United Oxford and Cambridge University Club, United Service and Royal Aero Club, Variety Club of Australia, Variety Club International, Zoological Society of London.

Freeman: Worshipful Company of Drapers, Worshipful Company of Fishmongers, Worshipful Company of Shipwrights. *Member:* Honourable Artillery Company, Honourable Company of Master Mariners.

Hon. Fellow: Institute of Water Pollution Control; Institution of Mechanical Engineers; Royal College of Physicians; Royal College of Physicians (Edinburgh); Royal fellow of Royal College of Surgeons of England; Society of Antiquaries of London; Master of the Bench, Society of Gray's Inn.

Hon. LL. D.: The Citadel, The Military College of South Carolina (1977), Cleveland State University (1977), University of London (1974). *Hon. D. Litt.:* University of Wales (1972), Council for National Academic Awards (1976). Chancellor, University of Wales, 1976–. *Hon. D. Eng.:* Stevens Institute of Technology (1977).

A Freeman of the Cities of Cardiff, Chester, London, Montgomery, Portsmouth, Windsor. *High Steward:* Royal Borough of Windsor and Maidenhead. Honorary Citizen of Chicago and the State of Oklahoma. Companion Rat in the Grand Order of Water Rats.

Publications: Contributions or forewords to numerous books, including *King George III* (1972), *Captains and Kings* (1972), *The Living World of Animals* (1970), *The Puffin Annual No. 1* (1974), *More Goon Show Scripts* (1973), *The World Underwater Book* (1973), *The Country Life Book of Queen Elizabeth, the Queen Mother* (1978); occasional journalism (*Punch, Books and Bookmen, Gordonstoun Record, Varsity, Triton*, etc.).

Recreations: Hunting, shooting, fishing, polo, skiing, flying, painting, reading, listening to music, jogging.

Addresses: Buckingham Palace, London SWI; Windsor Castle, Berkshire; Balmoral Castle, Aberdeenshire; Sandringham House, Norfolk; Palace of Holyroodhouse, Edinburgh; Chevening, Sevenoaks, Kent; Tamarisk, St. Mary's, Isles of Scilly.

Appendix B: Chronology of Principal Events in Prince Charles's Life, 1948-79, Including Foreign Visits

1948

November 14: Born at Buckingham Palace

December 15: Christened at Buckingham Palace

1950

August 15: Birth of Princess Anne

1952

February 6: Becomes heir apparent and Duke of Cornwall on death of his grandfather, King George VI, and accession of his mother as Queen Elizabeth II

1954

April 22–May 11: Visits Malta, Libya (Tobruk) and Gibraltar to greet his parents home from coronation tour of Commonwealth

1957

January 28: Joins Hill House School as day boy

September 23: Joins Cheam preparatory school as boarder

1958

July 26: Created Prince of Wales and Knight of the Garter

1960

February 19: Birth of Prince Andrew

1962

April 1: Leaves Cheam School

April 11–14: Visits relatives in Germany with Prince Philip

May 1: Joins Gordonstoun School

1963

January 9–19: Skiing holiday in Switzerland (guest of Prince Ludwig of Hesse)

1964

March 10: Birth of Prince Edward

July: Passes five GCE O levels

September 14–15: Private visit to Germany (Langen) en route for

September 15–20: Athens, for wedding of King Constantine

December 29:   Visits Paris with Prince Philip and Princess Anne en route for
December 30–January 8, 1965:   Skiing holiday in Liechtenstein
1965
November 26:   Plays Macbeth in Gordonstoun school play
December 20:   Wins Duke of Edinburgh's Silver Award
December 28–January 9, 1966:   Skiing holiday in Liechtenstein
1966
February 2:   Joins Timbertop, country annex of Geelong Church of England Grammar School, Melbourne, Australia, for two terms
May 12–31:   Visits Papua, New Guinea and travels in Australia during school holidays
August 1–3:   Visits Mexico en route from Australia to
August 3–16:   Commonwealth Games in Jamaica
November 14:   Eighteenth birthday. Made councillor of state. Now eligible to succeed to throne in own right
1967
January: Made head boy at Gordonstoun
April 20–21:   Private visit to France (Nice)
July: Passes two GCE A levels
October: Joins Trinity College, Cambridge, to read archaeology and anthropology, later history
October 31:   Attends first state opening of Parliament
December 20:   Visits Melbourne for funeral of prime minister, Harold Holt
1968
March 8:   Contributes article to *Varsity* magazine
March 25–April 1:   Archaeological expedition to France and Jersey
June 9:   Wins half-blue for representing Cambridge at polo
June 14:   Wins II-1 in first part of Cambridge exams
June 17:   Invested as Knight of the Garter at Windsor
July 2–10:   Holiday in Malta as guest of governor, Sir Maurice Dorman
July 11:   Attends first Buckingham Palace garden party
July 30:   First flight (familiarization)
December 10:   Chairs first meeting (Steering Committee for Wales, The Countryside in 1970 Conference, Cardiff). Also occasion of first public speech
1969
January 14:   First solo flight
February 25–March 3:   Takes part in Cambridge revue, *Revulution*
March 2:   First sound radio broadcast: interview with Jack de Manio (1315 hrs, BBC Radio 4)
March 21–30:   Skiing holiday in Sweden (guest of Crown Prince Carl Gustav)

April 20:   Arrives for one term at University College of Wales, Aberystwyth

June 11:   Inauguration ceremony for Royal Regiment of Wales, of which is colonel-in-chief. Receives freedom of City of Cardiff

June 26:   First television appearance. Interview with Brian Connell and Cliff Michelmore

July 1:   Investiture as Prince of Wales at Caernarvon Castle

July 2–5:   Tour of Wales

July 7–14:   Holiday in Malta (guest of Sir Maurice Dorman)

October 23:   Germany: funeral of Margravine of Baden

November 21–25:   Malta: inaugurates new campus at Royal University

1970

February 8–9:   Strasbourg: Council of Europe's European Conservation Conference

February 11:   Takes seat in House of Lords

March: Obtains Grade A private pilot's license

March 12–30:   Tours Australia and New Zealand with Queen and Prince Philip

March 31–April 8:   Continues tour with Prince Philip

April 9–14:   Tours Japan (Expo '70)

June: Graduates BA (Honors) from Cambridge

July 2–15:   Visits Ottawa, then joined by Queen and Prince Philip for tour of Canada

July 16–18:   With Princess Anne, guest of President Nixon in Washington

October 1–4:   France: private visit (Paris-Amiens)

October 9–15:   Fiji: independence celebrations

October 15–19:   Gilbert and Ellice Islands

October 20–22:   Bermuda; 350th anniversary of parliament

October 22–25:   Barbados

November 11–12:   Paris: funeral of President de Gaulle

November 29–December 4:   Germany (private visit)

1971

February 6–20:   Kenya: safari with Princess Anne

February 25–27:   Germany: visits Royal Regiment of Wales at Osnabruck

March–August: Flight lieutenant in RAF. Trained at RAF College, Cranwell

September–October: Acting sublieutenant in Royal Navy. Six-week course at Royal Naval College, Dartmouth

November 5:   Gibraltar: to join HMS *Norfolk*. Promoted sublieutenant

1972

–July: Serves aboard HMS *Norfolk*

May 17–18:   Joins Queen and Duke of Edinburgh on state visit to France

July: Shore courses at HMS *Dryad*, Portsmouth. Familiarization flying with RN and Queen's Flight

October 29–31:   Berlin: military and civic engagements

October 31–November 3:   Spain: private visit as guest of Duke of Wellington

November 22–24:   Holland (private)

November: Serves with HMS *Glasserton*, coastal minesweeper

1973

January 25–26:   Visits Royal Regiment of Wales in Germany

February 12:   Leaves Portsmouth aboard HMS *Minerva*, on which he serves until September. (Gains bridge watchkeeping and ocean navigation certificates; promoted lieutenant)

June 1:   St. Kitts: opens newly restored Prince of Wales' bastion

July 6–11:   The Bahamas: independence celebrations

October: Completes shore courses for divisional officer

November 4–5:   Luxembourg: guest of Grand Duke

November 14:   Wedding of Princess Anne to Captain Mark Phillips

November 20–25:   Spain: guest of Duke of Wellington

1974

January–August: Serves aboard HMS *Jupiter* as communications officer

January 2:   Flies to join *Jupiter* at Singapore

January 29–February 6:   New Zealand: joins Queen and Duke of Edinburgh for Commonwealth Games

September–December: Royal Naval Air Station, Yeovilton, for helicopter conversion course

September 4:   New Zealand: funeral of Prime Minister Kirk

October 8–12:   Fiji: represents Queen at independence celebrations

October 12–30:   Australia: inaugurates Anglo-Australian telescope; visits Tasmania

1975

January: Returns to Yeovilton for advance flying training

February 20:   Visits Delhi en route for

February 22–26:   Nepal: coronation of King Birendra

March–June: Serves aboard HMS *Hermes*, commando ship, with 845 Squadron ("Red Dragons"). Visits Caribbean

April 11–20:   Bahamas: guest of Brabournes at Eleuthera

April 20–30:   Canada: tours Northwest Territories

August 3–9:   Iceland: fishing holiday as guest of Tryons

September–December: Lieutenant's course at Royal Naval College, Greenwich

September 14–19:   Papua New Guinea: represents Queen at independence celebrations

September 19–21: Indonesia (private visit to Bali)

November 9–11: Germany: visits Royal Regiment of Wales in Berlin

December 21–22: Netherlands: private visit as guest of Prince Bernhard

1976

February–December: Commands HMS *Bronington*, minehunter, based at Rosyth

July 23–25: Canada: private visit to Olympic Games in Montreal

August 2–8: Iceland: fishing holiday as guest of Tryons

December: Promoted commander in RN and wing commander in RAF on leaving services

1977

March 6–16: Kenya: safari holiday

March 17–25: Ghana: official visit

March 25–28: Ivory Coast: official visit

April 1–10: Bahamas: private holiday

April 26–28: France: skiing holiday (Isolo)

April 28–29: Monaco

May 9: France (Bordeaux)

July 5–9: Canada (Alberta): official visit. Made Red Indian chieftain; opens Calgary Stampede

August 3–16: Iceland (fishing holiday with Tryons)

August 20–22: Deauville: polo

October 18–30: USA: official visit

November 1–11: Australia: official visit

November 17–18: Germany: visiting 1st Battalion, Welsh Guards

1978

March: Brazil, Venezuela: official visit

May 18–19: Australia: funeral of Sir Robert Menzies

July 1–2: Norway: King Olav's 75th birthday party

August 31: Kenya: funeral of Jomo Kenyatta

August: Fishing in Iceland with Tryons and polo at Deauville

October 22–27: Yugoslavia: official visit

November 14: Thirtieth birthday

November 30–31: Brussels: official visit to NATO and SHAPE headquarters

December 1–4: Spain: private visit as guest of Duke of Wellington

1979

March–April: Visits Hong Kong, Singapore, Australia, and Canada

November: Visits Nepal and India

Appendix C: Prince Charles's Descent

IN AUGUST 1977, at the age of ninety-two, Mr. Gerald Paget of Welwyn Garden City, Hertfordshire, published his first book: in two volumes costing £60, containing nearly 1,000 pages and weighing thirteen pounds, it is entitled *The Lineage and Ancestry of HRH The Prince Charles, Prince of Wales*. Mr. Paget's introduction opens with the rare and enviable sentence, "This book had its origin about 75 years ago . . ."

It was in Queen Victoria's diamond jubilee year, 1897, that the schoolboy Paget first became interested in genealogy. G. W. Watson's work on the ancestry of King Edward VII, published in *The Genealogist* some ten years later, gave him the idea of tracing the pedigrees of various European monarchs. With the birth of Princess Elizabeth in 1926 he decided to trace her ancestry, hopefully as far as William the Conqueror; but he was still immersed in his project twenty-two years later, when Princess Elizabeth gave birth to Prince Charles. So Paget, then sixty-three, decided to start afresh and pursue the new prince's ancestry, though the introduction of Prince Philip's lineage of course doubled his workload. Had he stuck to his original intent, to trace Prince Charles back to William the Conqueror, the theoretical number of ancestors would have risen to the astonishing figure of 1,073,741,-824. So he decided to call a halt in the fourteenth and fifteenth centuries at the eighteenth generation. Even so, his monumental publication leaves only some forty thousand ancestors untraced out of a total of 262,142.

These two paragraphs are by way of tribute to Mr. Paget's life work, without which this appendix could scarcely have been written. I must also acknowledge a debt to an excellent two-part review of his work, in *Books and Bookmen* (Vol. 23, Nos. 7–8), by the genealogist Sir Iain Moncreiffe of that Ilk, Albany Herald. Sir Iain's voluminous knowledge of his subject was able to detect a few minor errors, and add some intriguing new dimensions; he has also had a large hand in the compilation of this appendix. As he himself says, "HRH's breeding is the most important in the world . . . he is heir to the world's greatest position that is determined solely by heredity."

Through cousin marriages many of the ancestors traced by Paget, more than a quarter of a million of them, are of course the same people. The total number of individuals is thus greatly reduced, which is as it should be. The blood royal is proportionately the purer.

In Prince Charles's veins runs the blood of emperors and kings, Russian boyars, Spanish grandees, noblemen of every European nation, bishops and judges, knights and squires, and tradesmen right down to a butcher, a toymaker, and an innkeeper. Readers curious for more detail than this appendix can provide should turn to Mr. Paget's work. His discoveries include the fact that Prince Charles is a cousin or nephew, in varying degrees, of all six wives of Henry VIII; that he has many descents from the royal houses of Scotland, France, Germany, Austria, Denmark, Sweden, Norway, Spain, Portugal, Russia, and the Netherlands. Many of his ancestors died bloodily, in battle or by the ax, especially in the Wars of the Roses and the reigns of the Tudor sovereigns.

The most significant of Prince Charles's forebears fall into three categories. First there are those who were historic figures in the British Isles, the immediate realm. Secondly, there are similar figures, especially royalty, in the rest of Europe from which emigrants have gone out in such numbers to the Old Commonwealth. And thirdly, there is leaven of solid British stock of all classes: just enough to keep HRH down to earth, but not enough to dilute his royal blood unduly, or to give him too many inconvenient near-relations among his family's subjects.

In England, he descends over and over again from the Anglo-Saxon, Norman, Plantagenet, and Tudor kings, indeed from every English king who has left descendants (even including Henry IV) except Charles I and his sons. He descends from the nonroyal Protectors of England, Edward Seymour, Duke of Somerset, and John Dudley, Duke of Northumberland (but not from Cromwell; curiously enough, HRH does not take sides genealogically in the Civil War). Other famous characters abound in his ancestry: Alfred the Great; Hereward the Outlaw (better known, incorrectly, as the Wake), hero of the Anglo-Saxon epic, together with the King Harold slain at Hastings and their foe William the Conqueror; Simon de Montfort, Earl of Leicester, the first Parliamentarian; Harry "Hotspur," Lord Percy, hero of the Ballad of Chevy Chase; Warwick the Kingmaker; and the great Elizabethans, Essex—the queen's favorite—Sir Frances Walsingham, and William Cecil, Lord Burghley.

Thanks to the lineage of Queen Elizabeth the Queen Mother (born Lady Elizabeth Bowes-Lyon, daughter of the fourteenth Earl of Strathmore), the blood of some of England's noblest houses runs in the Prince of Wales's veins: including de Vere, Earl of Oxford; Courtenay, Earl of Devon; Percy, Earl of Northumberland; Talbot, Earl of

Shrewsbury; Stanley, Earl of Derby; Clifford, Earl of Cumberland; Cecil, Earl of Salisbury; Howard, Duke of Norfolk; Russell, Duke of Bedford, and Cavendish, Duke of Devonshire. Queen Anne's chief minister Robert Harley and the prime minister Portland were direct ancestors; Sir Philip Sydney and the "Iron Duke" of Wellington, his ancestral uncles; Charles Darwin, and—through the relationship of the Hastings, earls of Huntingdon to the Ardens—probably Shakespeare were the prince's ancestral fifth cousins.

In Wales, the present Prince of Wales descends from such renowned characters as Davy Gam and such historic families as Morgan of Tredegar, but above all from the great Owen Glendower (Owain Glyndwr), proclaimed "Prince of Wales by the Grace of God" during the last Welsh rising. Moreover, he descends many times over from Llewelyn the Great, Prince of Wales, and all Welsh kings and princes by way of Hywel Dda back to Cunedda and Old King Coel himself, who reigned in the fifth century, soon after the Romans left Britain.

In Scotland, the prince derives his title of Great Steward of Scotland from his ancestors the Stewart kings. Through George VI and Prince Philip he descends *twenty-two times over* from Mary Queen of Scots, and he has more than two hundred direct lines of descent from King Robert Bruce and thus from the ancient Celtic kings of the Picts and Scots. Through the Lyons of Glamis, most of the historic Scottish houses contributed to his lineage: the "Black Douglas" earls of Douglas and the "Red Douglas" earls of Angus; the "lightsome" Lindsay earls of Crawford; the "handsome" Hay earls of Erroll; the "gey" (which means ferocious, not gay in any sense) Gordon earls of Huntly; the "proud" Graham earls of Montrose. A rather surprising ancestor was Cardinal Beaton, the murdered archbishop of St. Andrews.

On the Borders his forebears included the Homes of Wedderburn, the "bold" Scotts of Buccleuch and their foes in many a ballad, the Kerrs of Fernihurst. In the far north, through the first Sinclair earl of Caithness, he comes from the old Norse jarls of Orkney. In central Scotland, the prince springs from the Lords Drummond and the Murrays of Tullibardine, the Moncreiffes of that Ilk and Stirlings of Keir, and the Stewart earls of Atholl. Elsewhere in the Highlands, through his descent from the Grants of Grant and the tenth Chief of Mackintosh, the prince has Hebridean blood of the mighty Clanranald—and in the west, too, he descends not only from the MacDougall chiefs of Dunollie and the Campbell earls of Argyll, but above all (as befits the present Lord of the Isles) at least two dozen times over from the paramount Macdonald chiefs who were the original Lords of the Isles.

In Ireland, Queen Elizabeth the Queen Mother has brought Prince Charles the most distinguished Irish ancestry, the blood of the Dal Cais and Eoganacht dynasties of Munster and that of the Ui Neill high kings. Among his ancestors were the O'Brien earls and kings of

Thomond (including the high kings Brian "Boru" and Toirdhelbhach); the McCarthy Reagh chieftains of the line of King Cormac, who built the famous chapel at Cashel; the O'Donnells of Tyrconnell; the Mac-Donnells of Antrim (including "Sorley Boy"); the wild Burkes of Clanricarde; the FitzGerald earls of Kildare and Desmond, and the Knights of Glin; the Butler earls of Ormonde; and, above all, Red Hugh O'Neill, Earl of Tyrone, the last native king of Ulster, who died in exile in Rome in 1618.

To turn to the continent of Europe: Prince Charles, through his father, is Danish, in the direct male line of the Royal House of Denmark, which still also reigns in Norway. He descends father-to-son through Christian IX, King of Denmark (1863–1906) from Christian I, King of Denmark, Norway, and Sweden (1448–1481). Among his celebrated Viking ancestors were King Sven Forkbeard of Denmark and King Harold Haardrade of Norway, but he also springs from the ancient "Peace Kings," whose vast grave mounds can still be seen at Uppsala in Sweden. King Canute was his ancestral uncle. So too were Gustavus Adolphus and Charles XII of Sweden, for his Scandinavian ancestry is octopoid, taking in the Royal House of Vasa as well as such locally historic names as Oxenstierna and Sture, Sparre and Gyllenstierna, Baner and Konigsmark, Bonde and Bielke.

In Russia, he is descended through Czar Nicholas I from both Catherine the Great and Peter the Great. He also has innumerable descents from the Grand Princes of the House of Rurik, who originally founded "all the Russias," among them St. Vladimir of Kiev, who Christianized the Russians; Yuri Dolgoruky, celebrated as the founder of Moscow; and St. Michael of Chernigov, executed by the Tartars for refusing to kneel to a statue of Genghis Khan. In Poland, he descends from the original Piast dynasty and from the Jagiellons up to King Zygmunt I (d. 1548). His Lithuanian ancestry goes back to Gedimin, last pagan sovereign of Lithuania (1316–41). His Byzantine imperial blood flows from the Angeloi and Comnenoi emperors of the East, and through the House of Savoy from the later Emperors Michael VIII and Andronicus Palaeologue.

In Bohemia, the prince descends from all the kings who have left descendants, from the original Czech house of Premsyl (the family of Good St. Wenceslas) down through the House of Luxembourg to Anne of Bohemia, wife of the Emperor Ferdinand I. So his ancestors include the "Blind King" slain at Crecy, the Emperor Charles IV, who founded the University of Prague, and above all the popular Hussite elected King George of Podiebrad. Other historic Czech names in the prince's ancestry are Lobkowicz and Sternberg, and Ulric, "the lame lord" of Rosenberg. In Hungary, he similarly descends from all the kings (who left issue) of the original royal House of Arpad; moreover, the famous King John Szapolyai was his ancestral uncle. Also, through his great-grandmother Queen Mary, the blood of many Magyar noble families, including several of the Bathory voivodes of Transylvania, flows in his veins. In Romania, by way of Queen Mary's ancestry, he descends from Vlad Dracul, Voivode of Wallachia (father of the original Dracula), and thus from the Bassarab dynasty who were very possibly derived from Genghis Khan himself.

In what was the Holy Roman Empire, he descends over and over again from Charlemagne and Frederick Barbarossa and all the great dynasties, Habsburg and Hohenstaufen, Guelph and Hohenzollern, Bavaria and Saxony, Hesse and Baden, Mecklenberg and Würrttemberg, Brunswick and Anhalt, the Electors Palatine and other Wittelsbachs, plus many of the historic houses such as Hohenlohe and Galen, Moltke and Sickingen, Schwarzenberg and Trauttmansdorff. Otto the Great and Phillip of Hesse were his direct forefathers. Frederick the Great and the Emperor Charles V were his ancestral uncles.

In Portugal, the prince descends from the marriage of the son of King John I of Aviz, Alfonso, Duke of Braganza, to Beatrix, daughter of the Blessed Nuno Alvarez Pereira, the "Holy Constable." The equally celebrated infante Henry the Navigator was an ancestral uncle.

In Italy, his forefathers include the Dukes of Savoy and the Emperor Frederick II, "Stupor Mundi," and the medieval kings of Sicily, as also the Orsini of Rome (Pope Nicholas III was his ancestral uncle), the Visconti of Milan, della Scala of Verona, Doria of Genoa, and Gonzaga of Mantua (besides the great *condottieri* Colleoni and Hawkwood); in Spain, they include Ferdinand and Isabella (who financed Columbus' discovery of America) and thus El Cid himself. In France: the Carolingian, Capetian, and Valois kings up to Charles VII (the Dauphin of Joan of Arc fame), among them St. Louis many times over, and such historic names as Montmorency and Rohan, Polignac and La Rochefoucauld and La Tour d'Auvergne. In the Netherlands: through his wife Charlotte of Bourbon, none other than William the Silent, Prince of Orange and founder of the Dutch Republic. In the Low Countries, too, Prince Charles bears a remarkable likeness to portraits of Charles the Bold, Duke of Burgundy, who was his direct forefather.

HRH's immemorial roots of course go back far, far beyond the generations covered by Mr. Paget's monumental work. The prince's Anglo-Saxon and Danish royal forefathers sprang from Dark Age kings who incarnated the storm-spirit Woden (after whom Wednesday is named), and among his pagan Celtic royal forefathers were King Niall of the Nine Hostages and the dynamic Iron Age sacral kings of Tara, the great sanctuary of ancient Ireland. Through the Lusignan crusader kings of Cyprus, titular kings of Jerusalem, Prince Charles descends a millennium farther back from King Tiridates the Great, the first Christian monarch of all (under whom Armenia was converted in AD 314, before even Rome itself), and thus from the divine Parthian imperial House of Arsaces (247 BC), which reigned over Persia and Babylonia and was in its time the mightiest dynasty in the ancient world.

Finally, down to earth. In 1779 Mr. George Carpenter, of Redbourn in Hertfordshire (writes Sir Anthony Wagner, Garter King of Arms, in his *English Genealogy*) "had the plumber down from London to repair the roof of his house. With the plumber came his daughter, and both remained at Redbourn some time. Mary Elizabeth Walsh, the daughter, was then eighteen years of age, and Mr. Carpenter upwards of sixty, yet notwithstanding the disparity of their ages and positions, he married her. Their daughter married the eleventh Earl of Strathmore"—the Queen Mother's great-great-grandfather. The Prince of Wales is thus eighth in descent from that plumber, John Walsh. There are many other plain English names in his ancestry; but it is through the plainest of them all, John Smith, that Prince Charles is one of the nearest living relations of George Washington, first President of the United States.

Appendix D: Prince Charles's Surname

HISTORY DECREES that princes do not have surnames. In modern times, however, when even those of such exalted rank occasionally have to fill in forms which require one, it has become the fashion for royalty to lay claim to a "hidden" surname from somewhere in their family history. When Prince Philip became a naturalized British subject in 1947, dropping his Greek and Danish titles, he had to borrow a surname from his mother's side of the family: Mountbatten, the anglicized version of Battenberg. Through the Prince of Wales that name has now, in the wake of complex legal argument, become enshrined in past and future British history.

For the first few years of his life, Prince Charles made do without a surname. On his mother's accession to the throne in 1952, however, the brows of genealogists clouded over. English law dictates that a child born in wedlock takes the name of his father. But this child was the eldest son of the Queen, the only woman in the land to outrank her husband. It would not do for Prince Charles to make use of his father's name. The law would have to be changed. Thus—on the insistent suggestion of her prime minister, Winston Churchill—the Queen issued an Order in Council on April 9, 1952, barely two months after her accession:

> It is my Will and Pleasure that I and my children shall be styled and known as the House and Family of Windsor and that my descendants, other than female descendants who marry and their descendants, shall bear the name of Windsor.

In the ensuing years, however, the Queen looked back on her decree with mixed feelings. On February 22, 1957, in recognition of his ten years of public service to the country, she gave her husband the style and dignity of Prince of the United Kingdom (which most of the nation thought he already bore). The 1957 Order, she felt, unfairly ignored his contribution to the country's future. She changed her mind, and on February 8, 1960, issued another Order in Council:

> It is my Will and Pleasure that, while I and my children shall continue to be styled and known as the House and

Family of Windsor, my descendants other than descendants
enjoying the style, title or attribute of Royal Highness and
the titular dignity of Prince or Princess and female descendants who marry and their descendants, shall bear the name
of Mountbatten-Windsor.

It didn't help much. The Queen's aspiration was that her son,
who had been born Charles Mountbatten and had in 1952 become
Charles Windsor, should now be known as Charles Mountbatten-
Windsor. But the clause excluding princes and those of the rank of
royal highness had everyone, including the genealogists, confused.
It was a gesture to history, reasserting the constitutional view that
princes are too grand to bear surnames. If ever he *was* to use a surname, she was trying to say, I want it to be Mountbatten-Windsor.

But whoever drafted the Order for the Queen had made matters
worse. She was compelled to issue an explanatory statement: "The
Queen has always wanted, without changing the name of the royal
house established by her grandfather, to associate the name of her
husband with her own and his descendants."

Even that didn't really help much, either. Writing in the *Daily
Express* the then editor of Debrett's, Cyril Hankinson, tried to explain.
"It is most unlikely that there will ever be a Mountbatten-Windsor
dynasty. But this is how it could come about. If the Queen's third
baby were a prince [it was: Prince Andrew, born on February 19,
1960, less than a fortnight after the Order in Council] . . . If that
prince married and had a son who was created a duke and the son
then had two sons . . . The elder son would then take one of his
father's secondary titles and would not then need a surname, but the
younger son would be a Mountbatten-Windsor. . . . If the line of
the Prince of Wales became extinct . . . If the Mountbatten-Windsor's
elder brother died without issue . . . then the Mountbatten-Windsor
would succeed to the throne. It is as remote as that."

Even the editor of Debrett's had got it wrong. The House of Windsor would remain the House of Windsor, even if the Queen's third
son's second son became king—though as king, of course, he would be
entitled to change the dynasty's name to whatever he liked. The point
was that the Queen wanted her children to acknowledge their father's
name as well as hers, despite her precedence. A constitutional lawyer,
the late Edward Iwi, attempted to put matters straight in the March
18, 1960 issue of the *Law Journal:*

Reading the words of the Declaration and message together, as we are entitled to, and bearing in mind that they
were given out on the same day and only eleven days before
the birth of the infant Prince (Andrew), we may well feel
that the Queen intended the name Mountbatten-Windsor to

be in the lineage of her children, not merely to be given to her great-grandchildren and their descendants. To give the Royal children the name of Mountbatten-Windsor—even if they never use it—is in keeping with the idea that it is the birthright of every legitimate child in a Christian country to be identified with its father. . . .

Reading the Queen's Declaration in conjunction with the contemporaneous message and in the light of the surrounding circumstances, the writer feels that the conclusion is patently clear. While sympathizing with the difficulties of cautious presentation felt by the draughtsman, working perhaps at speed, it is yet natural to interpret the Declaration simply as intimating that Her Majesty's real intention was to confer on each of her children what has been, so the writer, believes, properly described as a "hidden" surname. . . .

The common man using his common sense will arrive at the same conclusion as most lawyers. They will understand the 1960 Declaration to be that the Queen's House and Family is named Windsor; that of her children if they ever use a family name after their Christian names would be Mountbatten-Windsor, and it is that name which they will pass on to their descendants and which will be used by those descendants when the use of a surname becomes necessary.

Iwi had judged the Queen's intention correctly, but it was still far from clear whether her Declaration had achieved the legal and constitutional effects she desired. She consulted successive Lord Chancellors, who discerned the simple heart of the matter: whatever the monarch says goes. Thus it was that Princess Anne, when she married Mark Phillips on November 14, 1973, signed the Westminster Abbey register as Anne Mountbatten-Windsor. Prince Charles, said a statement from Buckingham Palace, would sign as Charles Mountbatten-Windsor "at such time as he needs to use a surname."

For now, he sticks simply to Charles, not even using the suffix of P (for *princeps*) to which he is entitled. Perhaps he always will. When he becomes King Charles III, his mother's declarations ensure that the dynasty will still be known as the House of Windsor—unless King Charles III chooses to start issuing more declarations of his own.

With which in mind, it is worth pointing out that he is under no obligation to call himself King Charles III. He likes the name, despite its inauspicious historical associations, so he probably will. But he is equally entitled to call himself King Philip, King Arthur II, King George VII, or indeed any other name he cares to choose. His first constitutional act on becoming king will be to announce the name by which he wishes to be known.

Appendix E: Previous Princes of Wales

WELSH PRINCES, AD 844–1282

RHODRI THE GREAT	844–878
ANARAWD, SON OF RHODRI	878–916
HYWEL DDA, THE GOOD	916–950
IAGO AB IDWAL (OR IEUAF)	950–979
HYWEL AB IEUAF, THE BAD	979–985
CADWALLON, BROTHER OF HYWEL	985–986
MAREDUDD AB OWAIN AP HYWEL DDA	986–999
CYNAN AP HYWEL AB IEUAF	999–1008
LLEWELYN AP SITSYHLT	1018–1023
IAGO AB IDWAL AP MEURIG	1023–1039
GRUFFYDD AP LLEWELYN AP SEISYLL	1039–1063
BLEDDYN AP CYNFYN	1063–1075
TRAHAERN AP CARADOG	1075–1081
GRUFFYDD AP CYNAN AB IAGO	1081–1137
OWAIN GWYNEDD	1137–1170
DAFYDD AB OWAIN GWYNEDD	1170–1194
LLYWELYN FAWR, THE GREAT	1194–1240
DAFYDD AP LLEWELYN	1240–1246
LLEWELYN AP GRUFFYDD AP LLEWELYN	1246–1282

ENGLISH PRINCES OF WALES, since AD 1301

		DATE CREATED
EDWARD OF CAERNARVON (EDWARD II), SON OF EDWARD I	1284–1327	1301
EDWARD, THE BLACK PRINCE, ELDEST SON OF EDWARD III	1330–1376	1343
RICHARD (RICHARD II), YOUNGER SON OF THE BLACK PRINCE	1367–1400	1377
HENRY OF MONMOUTH (HENRY V), ELDEST SON OF HENRY IV	1387–1422	1399
EDWARD OF WESTMINSTER, ONLY SON OF HENRY VI	1453–1471	1454

|---|---|
| EDWARD OF YORK (EDWARD V),
 ELDEST SON OF EDWARD IV | 1470–1483   1472 |

		DATE CREATED

EDWARD OF YORK (EDWARD V),   1470–1483   1472
ELDEST SON OF EDWARD IV

EDWARD OF MIDDLEHAM,   1473–1484   1483
SON OF RICHARD III

ARTHUR OF WINCHESTER,   1486–1502   1489
ELDEST SON OF HENRY VII

HENRY OF GREENWICH (HENRY VIII),   1491–1546   1503
SECOND SON OF HENRY VII

HENRY FREDERICK,   1594–1612   1610
ELDEST SON OF JAMES I AND VI

CHARLES (CHARLES I),   1600–1649   1616
SECOND SON OF JAMES I AND VI

CHARLES (CHARLES II),   1630–1685   1630
SECOND SON OF CHARLES I

JAMES, THE OLD PRETENDER,   1688–1766   1688
SON OF JAMES II

GEORGE AUGUSTUS (GEORGE II),   1683–1760   1714
SON OF GEORGE I

FREDERICK LOUIS,   1707–1751   1727
ELDEST SON OF GEORGE II

GEORGE WILLIAM FREDERICK (GEORGE III),   1738–1820   1751
SON OF FREDERICK LOUIS

GEORGE AUGUSTUS FREDERICK (GEORGE IV),   1762–1830   1762
SON OF GEORGE III

ALBERT EDWARD (EDWARD VII),   1841–1910   1841
ELDEST SON OF QUEEN VICTORIA

GEORGE (GEORGE V),   1865–1936   1901
SECOND SON OF EDWARD VII

EDWARD (EDWARD VIII, LATER DUKE OF   1896–1972   1910
WINDSOR), ELDEST SON OF GEORGE V

CHARLES PHILIP ARTHUR GEORGE,   1948–   1958
ELDEST SON OF ELIZABETH II

Edward I
|
(1) Edward of Caernarvon (Edward II) (1301)
|
Edward III

Edward The Black Prince (1343) — John of Gaunt Duke of Lancaster — Edmund of Langley Duke of York

(3) Richard (Richard II) (1377)

Richard, Earl of Cambridge

(First marriage) — Third marriage with Katherine Swinford

Richard, 3rd Earl of York

Henry IV — John Beaufort Marquess of Dorset — Edward IV — Richard III

(4) Henry of Monmouth (Henry V) (1399) — John Duke of Somerset — (6) Edward of York or of the Sanctuary (Edward V) (1472) — (7) Edward of Middleham (1483)

Henry VI — Margaret = Edmund Tudor 1st Earl of Richmond

(5) Edward of Westminster (1454) — Henry Tudor 2nd Earl of Richmond (Henry VII)

(8) Arthur of Winchester (1489) — (9) Henry of Greenwich (Henry VIII) (1503) — Margaret = James IV of Scotland

James V of Scotland

Mary, Queen of Scots

James VI of Scotland and I of England

(10) Henry Frederick (1610) — (11) Charles (Charles I) (1616) — Elizabeth Stuart = Frederick V Elector Palatine of the Rhine

(12) Charles (Charles II) (1630) — James II — Sophia = Ernest Augustus Duke of Brunswick Luneburg, Elector of Hanover

(13) James Francis Edward (The Old Pretender) (1688)

George I

Charles Edward (The Young Pretender)

(14) George Augustus (George II) (1714)

(15) Frederick Louis (1727)

(16) George William Frederick (George III) (1751)

(17) George Augustus Frederick (George IV) (1762) — Edward Augustus Duke of Kent

Victoria

(18) Albert Edward (Edward VII) (1841)

(19) George (George V) (1901)

(20) Edward (Edward VIII) (1911) — George VI

Elizabeth II

(21) Charles Prince of Wales (created 1958, investiture ceremony 1969)

THE TWENTY-ONE
ENGLISH
PRINCES OF WALES

The year of investiture is shown in brackets

Appendix F: The Prince of Wales's Flying Hours

Collated by the Queen's Flight

SUMMARY FOR THE YEAR ENDING DECEMBER 31, 1978 IN HOURS AND MINUTES

ANDOVER	95.15
WESSEX	28.05
HAWK	1.15

TOTAL SUMMARY BY TYPE UP TO DECEMBER 31, 1978 IN HOURS AND MINUTES

CHIPMUNK	80.25
BASSET	92.50
SPITFIRE	.35
VULCAN	3.00
NIMROD	7.05
PHANTOM	2.00
GANNET	1.05
JET PROVOST	123.35
HUNTER	1.05
WESSEX	338.15
ANDOVER	248.30
HARRIER T4	2.05
BUCCANEER	1.45
HAWK	1.15
	903.30

SUMMARY OF GROUPS

SINGLE ENGINE	209.00
MULTIENGINE	356.15
HELICOPTER	338.15
	903.30

Bibliography

ANY BIOGRAPHER of the present Prince of Wales will always owe a considerable debt to the late Dermot Morrah's book, *To Be a King*, an account of the prince's early life and education made possible by the express approval and cooperation of the Queen. This biographer is no exception. Other books consulted, or which would provide the reader with more detail in specialist areas, include:

Arnold-Brown, Adam. *Unfolding Character: The Impact of Gordonstoun*. London: Routledge & Kegan Paul, 1962.

Bagehot, Walter. *The English Constitution*. London: Chapman & Hall, 1867; London: Longmans, Green, 1915.

Beaton, Cecil Walter Hardy. *Photobiography*. London: Odhams Press, 1951; Garden City, N. Y.: Doubleday, 1951.

Beaverbrook, William Maxwell Aitken. *The Abdication of King Edward VIII*, edited by A. J. P. Taylor. London: H. Hamilton, 1966; New York: Atheneum, 1966.

Birch, Neville Hamilton, and Alan Bramson. *Captains & Kings*. London: Pitman, 1972.

Boothroyd, John Basil. *Philip: An Informal Biography*. London: Longman, 1971.

————. *Prince Philip: An Informal Biography*. New York: McCall Pub. Co., 1971.

Brereton, Henry Lloyd. *Gordonstoun: Ancient Estate and Modern School*. Edinburgh, London: W. & R. Chambers, 1968.

Brooke, John. *King George III*, with a foreword by HRH the Prince of Wales. London: Constable, 1972; New York: McGraw-Hill, 1972.

Cathcart, Helen. *Prince Charles: The Biography*. London: W. H. Allen, 1976.

Channon, Sir Henry. *"Chips": The Diaries of Sir Henry Channon*, edited by Robert Rhodes James. London: Weidenfeld & Nicolson, 1967.

Charles, Prince of Wales. "Legend and Reality," a review of *Queen Victoria Was Amused* by Alan Hardy. *Books and Bookmen*, November 1976.

Charles, Prince of Wales. Review (unheadlined) of *Twice Brightly*, a novel by Harry Secombe. *Punch*, November 6, 1974.

Coolican, Don, and Serge Lemoine. *Charles: Royal Adventurer*. London: Pelham Books, 1978; Edison, N. J.: Two Continents, 1978.

Counihan, Daniel. *Royal Progress*. London: Cassell, 1977.

Crawford, Marion. *The Little Princesses*. London: Cassell, 1950; New York: Harcourt Brace, 1950.

Donaldson, Frances Lonsdale, Lady. *Edward VIII*. London: Weidenfeld & Nicolson, 1974; Philadelphia: Lippincott, 1975.

Doran, John. *The Book of the Princes of Wales. Heirs to the Crown of England*. London: R. Bentley, 1860; Boston: F. A. Niccolls, n.d.

Duncan, Andrew. *The Reality of Monarchy*. London: Heinemann, 1970. Garden City, N. Y.: Doubleday, 1970.

Edgar, Donald. *The Queen's Children*. London: A. Barker, 1978.

Edward VIII, King of Great Britain. *A Family Album* by the Duke of Windsor. London: Cassell, 1960.

Edward VIII, King of Great Britain. *A King's Story; The Memoirs of H. R. H. the Duke of Windsor*. London: Cassell, 1951; New York: Putnam, 1951.

Fisher, Graham and Heather. *Charles: The Man and the Prince*. London: Hale, 1977.

Gore, John. *King George V. A Personal Memoir*. London: J. Murray, 1941; New York: Scribner's, 1941.

Inglis, Brian. *Abdication*. London: Hodder & Stoughton, 1966; New York: Macmillan, 1966.

Iwi, Edward. "Mountbatten-Windsor." *The Law Journal*, March 18, 1960.

Lacey, Robert. *Majesty: Elizabeth II and the House of Windsor*. London: Hutchinson, 1977; New York: Harcourt Brace Jovanovich, 1977.

Laird, Dorothy. *How the Queen Reigns: An Authentic Study of the Queen's Personality and Life Work*. London: Hodder & Stoughton, 1959; Cleveland: World Pub. Co., 1959.

Lane, Peter. *Our Future King*. London: A. Barker, 1978.

Liversidge, Douglas. *Prince Charles: Monarch in the Making*. London: A. Barker, 1975.

The Living World of Animals. London: Published by the Reader's Digest Association in conjunction with the World Wildlife Fund, 1970.

Magnus, Sir Philip Montefiore, Bart. *King Edward the Seventh*. London: J. Murray, 1964; New York: E. P. Dutton, 1964.

Marples, Morris. *Princes in the Making; A Study of Royal Education*. London: Faber and Faber, 1965.

Martin, Kingsley. *The Crown and the Establishment*. London: Hutchinson, 1962.

Masters, Brian. *Dreams about H. M. the Queen and Other Members of the Royal Family*, illustrated by Michael Ffolkes. London: Blond and Briggs, 1972.

Milligan, Terence Alan. *More Goon Show Scripts*, written and selected by Spike Milligan; with drawings by Peter Sellers, Harry Secombe, Spike Milligan. London: Woburn Press, 1973; New York: St. Martin's Press, 1974.

Morrah, Dermot. *To Be a King*. London: Hutchinson, 1968.

Nicolson, Hon. Harold George. *King George the Fifth: His Life and Reign*. London: Constable, 1952; Garden City, N. Y.: Doubleday, 1953.

Paget, Gerald. *The Lineage and Ancestry of H. R. H. Prince Charles, Prince of Wales*. 2 vols. Edinburgh: Skilton, 1977.

Peacock, Lady Irene Cynthia. *The Queen and Her Children: An Authoritative Account*. London: Hutchinson, 1961.

Peel, Edward. *Cheam School from 1645*. Gloucester: Thornhill Press, 1974.

Pine, Leslie Gilbert. *Princes of Wales*. London: H. Jenkins, 1959.

Pope-Hennessy, James. *Queen Mary, 1867–1953*. London: G. Allen and Unwin, 1959; New York: Knopf, 1960.

Röhrs, Hermann. *Kurt Hahn*; from the German edition. English ed., with additional material, edited by H. Röhrs and H. Tunstall-Behrens; preface by the Duke of Edinburgh. London: Routledge & Kegan Paul, 1970.

St. John-Stevas, Norman. *Walter Bagehot*. London: Published for the British Council and the National Book League by Longmans, Green, 1963.

Sidney, Thomas. *Heirs Apparent*. London: A. Wingate, 1957.

Skidelsky, Robert Jacob Alexander. *Hahn of Gordonstoun*. Harmondsworth: Penguin, 1969.

Stewart, William Alexander Campbell. *The Thirties and Gordonstoun*. London: Macmillan, 1968.

Talbot, Godfrey. *The Country Life Book of Queen Elizabeth the Queen Mother*. Feltham, Middlesex: Country Life Books, 1978.

Wakeford, Geoffrey. *The Heir Apparent: An Authentic Study of the Life and Training of H. R. H. Charles Prince of Wales*. London: Hale, 1967; South Brunswick, N. J.: A. S. Barnes Co., 1968.

Warren, Allen. *Nobs and Nosh*. London: Leslie Frewin, 1974.

Whitaker, James. *Prince Charles*. London: City Magazines Ltd., 1978.

Ziegler, Philip. *Crown and People*. London: Collins, 1978; New York: Knopf, 1978.

Index

Anthony Holden

Born in Lancashire, England in 1947—just one year before Prince Charles—Anthony Holden won the Pfizer Young Journalist of the Year Award in 1972, was commended in the British Press Awards of 1976, and in 1977 was named Columnist of the Year for his work as the diarist Atticus in the London *Sunday Times*. This last award was presented by Prince Charles, who said: "He thoroughly deserves it. . . . His style is most enjoyable—witty, amusing, slightly sardonic. . . . His English is a pleasure to read."

Mr. Holden lived in Washington, D.C., as chief U.S. correspondent for the London *Observer* from 1979 to 1981, when he returned to London to become assistant editor of the London *Times*. Having written a second "royal" book, *Their Royal Highnesses*, to mark the wedding of Prince Charles and Princess Diana, he is now a free-lance journalist and writer.